aLover of
Unreason
the Life and Tragic Death of Assia Wevill

a Lover of
Unreason

the Life and Tragic Death of Assia Wevill

Yehuda Koren and Eilat Negev

ROBSON
BOOKS

First published in the United Kingdom in 2006 by
Robson Books
151 Freston Road
London
W10 6TH

An imprint of Anova Books Company Ltd

ISBN 1 86105 974 4

A CIP catalogue record fo ͏ ͏ e British Library.

10 9 8 7 6 5 4 3 2 1

Typeset by SX Composing DTP, Rayleigh, Essex
Reproduction by Anorax Imaging Ltd, Leeds
Printed and bound by Creative Print & Design, Ebbw Vale, Wales

This book can be ordered direct from the publisher.
Contact the marketing department, but try your bookshop first.

www.anovabooks.com

Contents

Preface	vi
Acknowledgements	ix
Prologue	xvii
One: Childhood	1
Two: A New Life	10
Three: A Tabeetha Girl	18
Four: A Teenager in Love	25
Five: First Marriage	36
Six: A Second Husband	49
Seven: Falling in Love	60
Eight: Third Marriage	73
Nine: A Fateful Meeting	84
Ten: An Illicit Affair	95
Eleven: Leaving Plath	106
Twelve: The Shadow of Suicide	115
Thirteen: Domesticity	123
Fourteen: Torn Between Two Lovers	132
Fifteen: Birth	145
Sixteen: Bliss	154
Seventeen: Banished	165
Eighteen: Love Me Back or Let Me Go	172
Nineteen: Despair	184
Twenty: The Die Is Cast	194
Twenty-one: Agony	206
Twenty-two: Aftermath	219
Notes	228
Select Bibliography	260
Index	269

Preface

Twenty years ago we were leafing through a book by the Israeli poet Yehuda Amichai, when we chanced upon a poem entitled 'The Death of Assia G'. 'I can't understand your death in London,' Amichai wrote, and we were curious to know who this woman was and what she was to him that he vowed 'to publicise' her death.

We called him the next day.

Amichai's answer was laconic and mystifying: Assia was the beloved of his best friend Ted Hughes and an ex-Israeli who died tragically in 1969. The G stood for her maiden name, Gutmann. This set us on our quest.

Ever since, we have been tracing the many facets of Assia Wevill's story, and have published a number of features about her in major British, German and Israeli newspapers. In October 1996, we had a world-exclusive interview with Ted Hughes – the only personal one he ever granted. For once, he spoke about Assia.

Like Sylvia Plath, Assia shared her life with Hughes for six years, and she, too, bore him a daughter. Still, she has been effectively written out of his story. Any influence she may have exerted on him or his work has been diminished or dismissed. The story of the ultimately tragic failure of his marriage to Sylvia Plath has been related in numerous books and articles from one of two conflicting points of view: his or hers. Either way, Assia was reduced to the role of a she-devil, enchantress, Lilith, Jezebel, the woman alleged to have severed the union of twentieth-century poetry's most celebrated couple.

Assia Wevill was a complex person, born to dichotomies. Her remarkable life evinces both the limitations and the possibilities of a gifted, independent-spirited, ambitious woman in the mid-twentieth century. To gain a variety of perspectives on her character and to amass as much detail and as many dimensions as possible we have interviewed seventy people, including her sister and brother-in-law. Her schoolfriends in Tel Aviv and the British soldiers who dated her there have contributed substantially to our sense of the beautiful, rebellious teenage Assia. Her three husbands have provided insights into the captivating woman she was. Intimate friends of Assia and her colleagues from advertising, as well as friends of Hughes and Plath, have shared with us their memories of Assia in London in the sixties.

Our intensive search for new primary source material has not gone unrewarded and in its course we have uncovered a wealth of documents and private papers, many of which were not known to exist. We worked in numerous archives around the world, and gathered new findings from the Hughes and Plath archives and from those of prominent poets who corresponded with them. Some of the material was censored until recently.

The examination of this material in conjunction with Assia's diaries, letters and poems is of great importance in the understanding of the writing of the protagonists of the book and of the events that surrounded the two suicides. It reveals the inter-relationship of their work and is all the more important for the fact that some of Assia and Plath's writing was destroyed.

A Lover of Unreason charts the emergence of a singular twentieth-century woman. Exotic, cosmopolitan, cultured, she mesmerised men and women alike. Yet she was also a divorcee (thrice), a career woman, the other woman, and a single mother: she openly defied the conventions of a censorious pre-feminist society.

Assia was on a quest to moor herself emotionally and express herself creatively. Yet security would continually elude her, for all her apparent self-assurance, charm and sophistication. At the same time as she strove to free her creative spirit and declare her independence, so she defined herself by, and bound herself to, the men in her life, ultimately to catastrophic effect. In her increasingly obsessional relationship with Hughes, doubt, fear, distrust and humiliation would dog her, and dislodge her. She and Hughes would not marry, they would not find the house that they would make their own. Instead, Assia – unmoored, again the nomad, always the mistress or muse – would end the journey.

The exquisitely beautiful Assia inspired, or provoked, many epithets in the pursuit of a destiny that took her, via several continents, from dark pre-war Berlin via Tel Aviv, Vancouver and Mandalay, to London in the swinging sixties. In the end, none would prove to be more fitting than the epithet (and epitaph) she chose for herself in her last will and testament: 'Here lies a lover of unreason and an exile'.

Jerusalem, May 2006

Acknowledgements

We gratefully acknowledge the following sources from which we have drawn and quoted: our interviews with Celia Chaikin, Assia Wevill's sister, telephone interview, January 1999, email exchange, January 1999–May 2002, interviews in Canada, May–June 2002, and subsequent emails, letters and telephone calls, July 2002–April 2006; Arnold Chaikin, Assia's brother-in-law, interviews in Canada, May–June 2002: the Chaikins kindly provided us with photographs from their family album, as well as with correspondence and documents pertaining to Assia and the Gutmann family; John H Steele, Assia's first husband, letter exchange and excerpts from his diary, July 2002–January 2004; Richard (Dick) Lipsey, her second husband, interview in Canada, June 2002, and email exchange, July 2002–June 2003; his sister, Thirell (Lipsey) Weiss, email exchange, August–December 2002; David Wevill, Assia's third husband, interview in Texas, November 2003, and email exchange, September 2002–December 2005; Ted Hughes, interview in London on 8 October 1996; Olwyn Hughes, letter exchange, August 2002–June 2003; about Assia's life in the 1940s, we interviewed Leila Andreas and Wedad Andreas, in Israel, November 2001; Hannah Weinberg-Shalitt, interview in Israel, January 1999; Mira Hamermesh, interview in London, October 2001; Keith and Pam Gems, interview in London, December 2003, and letter exchange, August 2002–February 2004, as well as correspondence and photos from the 1940s and 1950s that they have kindly provided us with; John Bosher, telephone interview and email exchange, July–August 2002, as well as excerpts from his diary; Esther Birney, telephone interview, December 2001, and a letter from January 2002; about Assia's life in England and Burma in the 1950s, we interviewed Liliana Archibald, in London, March 2003; Alton Becker, email exchange, March–July 2002; Marilyn Corry, email exchange, September 2002; Martin Graham, interview in London, October 2001; Philip Hobsbaum, email exchange, October 2001–May 2003; Edward Lucie-Smith, interview in London, October 2001, and email exchange, December 2001–August 2003; Patricia Mendelson, interview in London, September 2001, as well as correspondence and photos of Assia and Shura; Don Michel, email, September 2002; Ian Montagnes, email exchange, September–October 2002; Roger Philips, email exchange, November 2001; Peter Porter, interview in London, September 2001, and letters, October–December 2001; Jo (Reed) Price, email exchange, September–October 2002; Kenneth Reed, a letter from November 2002; about Assia's life in England and Ireland in the 1960s: Al Alvarez, interview in London, September 2001; Anne (Adams) Alvarez, interview in London, October 2001; Martin Baker, interview in Oxfordshire, October 2001, and email exchange, November 2001–January 2004, as well as footage of Assia's film and photographs that he took of her and Shura; Kathleen Becker, interview in London, September 2001, as well as a memoir written by her late husband, Gerry Becker; Tom Boyd, telephone interview, September 2004; Anna (Owen) Bramble, interview in London, October 2001; Sue Byrne, email exchange, November 2001; John Chambers, interview in London, September 2001; Douglas Chowns, email exchange, November 2001–June 2003; Barrie Cooke, telephone interviews in November 2002 and in March 2004; Janos Csokits, interview in Budapest, March 2006, and letter exchange, December 2003–September 2005; Jane Donaldson, email and letter exchange, November 2003–February 2004, as well as photographs of Assia; Dan Ellerington, telephone interview, January 2002; Ruth Fainlight, email exchange, January–February 2004; Jonny Gathorne-Hardy, interview in London, October 2001; Michael Hamburger, letters June–July 2002; Brenda Hedden, interviews in England, September–October 2001; Guy Jenkin, interview in London, October 2001; Ann Henning Jocelyn, interview in Ireland, March 2005; Robert Jocelyn, Earl of Roden, interview in Ireland, March 2005; Angela Landels, interview in London, October 2001; Richard Larschan, interview in Massachusetts, USA, June 2004, and email exchange, September 2001–December 2005; Fay Maschler, interview in London, October 2001; Julia Matcham, interview in London, September 2001, and letters and email exchange, September 2001–December 2002; Horatio Morpurgo, email exchange, April 2003; Lucas Myers, email exchange, November 2001–December 2003; Hugh Musgrave, interview in Ireland, March 2005; Keith Ravenscroft, email exchange, October 2001; Clarissa Roche, interview in England, September 2001, as well as a copy of the

Acknowledgements

unpublished memoir written by the late Trevor Thomas; Teresa Reilly, telephone interview, April 2005; Philip Resnick, email exchange, April 2004; Chris Roos, interview in London, October 2001; David Ross, interview in London, March 2003; Ann Semple, telephone interview, January 2002; Elizabeth (Compton) Sigmund, interview in England, August 2001, and subsequent email exchange, September–December 2001, as well as Assia's tapestry letter to Sylvia Plath, and Hughes's letters to the Comptons; Ben Sonnenberg, email exchange, August 2002; Royston Taylor, email exchange, November 2001–February 2002; John Wainwright, interview in London, October 2001; Daniel Weissbort, interview in London, May 2002, and letter exchange, April 2002–September 2005; Fay Weldon, interview in London, September 2001; Chris Wilkins, email exchange, October 2001.

We have drawn and quoted from the works of: Amichai, Yehuda. *Poems*. New York, Harper & Row, 1968; *Selected Poems*. Penguin, 1971; *Selected Poems*. Introduction, Ted Hughes, Faber and Faber, 2000. The quotations from Amichai's poems and papers in his archive at Yale are reproduced by kind permission of Hannah Amichai; Hughes, Ted. *Collected Poems*. Keegan, Paul ed., Faber and Faber, 2003; Plath, Sylvia. *Ariel, The Restored Text*. Faber and Faber, 2005; *Journals of Sylvia Plath, 1950–1962*. Kukil, Karen V. ed., Faber and Faber, 2000; *Letters Home: Correspondence*. Faber and Faber, 1999; Tarn, Nathaniel, 'A Requiem for Two Daughters of Israel', in *Selected Poems 1950–2000*. USA, Wesleyan University Press, 2000. Reproduced by kind permission of Nathanial Tarn and his publishers; Wevill, David. *Birth of a Shark*. Toronto, Macmillan, 1964; *Casual Ties. Prose Sketches*. Curbstone Press, 1986; *A Christ of the Ice-Floes*. Macmillan, 1966; *Departures, Selected Poems*. Shearsman Books, 2003; *Firebreaks*. Macmillan, 1971; *Solo with Grazing Deer*. Toronto, Exile Editions, 2001. All quotes from David Wevill's poetry and prose are reproduced by his kind permission; Alexander, Paul ed., *Ariel Ascending: Writing about Sylvia Plath*. New York, Harper & Row, 1985, and *Rough Magic*, 2nd ed. New York, Da Capo, 1999; Alvarez, A. *The Savage God: A Study in Suicide*. Weidenfeld & Nicolson, 1971, and *Where Did It All Go Right?* Richard Cohen Books, 1999, and 'Sylvia Plath: A Memoir', in Alexander, Paul ed., *Ariel Ascending*; Bennett, Bruce. *Spirit in Exile: Peter Porter and his Poetry*. Melbourne, Oxford University Press, 1991; Blumenthal, Susan J ed., *Suicide Over the Life Cycle*. American Psychiatric Publishing Inc., 1990; Butscher, Edward. *Sylvia Plath: Method and Madness*. New York, Simon & Schuster, 1976, and *Sylvia Plath: The Woman and the Work* ed., New York, Dodd, Mead, 1977; Cameron, Elspeth. *Earle Birney – a Life*. New York, Viking, 1994; della Casa, Giovanni, *Galateo, or, The Book of Manners*. Penguin, 1958; Efron, John. *Medicine and the German Jews*. New Haven, Yale University Press, 2001; Farberow, Norman L and Shneidman Edwin ed., *The Cry for Help*, New York, McGraw-Hill, 1965; Feinstein, Elaine. *Ted Hughes: The Life of a Poet*. Weidenfeld & Nicholson, 2001; Fromm, Erich. *The Art of Loving*. Harper World Perspective Series, 1960; Gammage, Nick ed., *The Epic Poise, A Celebration of Ted Hughes*. Faber and Faber, 1999; Gelber, Yoav. *A New Homeland – the Immigration from Central Europe and its Absorption in Eretz Israel 1933–1948*. Jerusalem, Leo Baeck Institute and Yad Izhak Ben-Zvi 1990 (in Hebrew); Goodwin, Isobel. *May You Live to Be 120! The Story of Tabeetha School, Jaffa, 1863–1983*. Saint Andrew Press, 2000; *The Hagana Book. Maarachot, 1955–1972* (in Hebrew); Hamermesh, Mira, *The River of Angry Dogs – a Memoir*. Pluto Press, 2004; Hayman, Ronald. *The Death and Life of Sylvia Plath*. Sutton Publishing, 2003; Kater, Michael, *Doctors Under Hitler*. USA, University of North Carolina Press, 1989; Kroll, Judith. *Chapters in a Mythology: The Poetry of Sylvia Plath*. New York, Harper Colophon, 1976; Lucie-Smith, Edward. *The Burnt Child: An Autobiography*. Victor Gollancz, 1975, and *A Group Anthology* ed., Oxford University Press, 1963; Middlebrook, Diane Wood. *Her Husband: Hughes and Plath – A Marriage*. New York, Viking, 2003; Morgan, H G. *Death Wishes?* John Wiley, 1979; Morgan, Robin. *Upstairs in the Garden: Poems Selected and New*. New York, W W Norton, 1990; Bere, Carol. 'Complicated with Old Ghosts: The Assia Poems', in Moulin, Joanny ed., *Alternative Horizons*. Routledge, 2004; Murphy, Richard. *The Kick, A Memoir*. Granta Books, 2002 and 'Lullaby', which is reproduced by kind permission of the author and The Gallery Press, Loughcrew, Oldcastle, Co. Meath, Ireland, from *Collected Poems*, 2000; Musil, Robert. *The Man Without Qualities*. Secker & Warburg, 1953; Myers, Lucas. *Crow Steered, Bergs Appeared*. Tennessee, Proctor's Hall Press, 2001; Newman, Charles ed., *The Art of Sylvia Plath – A Symposium*. Bloomington, Indiana University Press, 1970; Ogilvy, David. *Confessions of an Advertising Man*. New York, Atheneum 1976; Orr, Peter ed., *The Poet Speaks*. Routledge & Kegan Paul, 1966; Rayfield, Tom. *Fifty in 40*. Rayfield Writers, 1966; Sagar, Keith. *The Laughter of Foxes*. Liverpool University Press, 2000; Segev, Tom. *The Seventh Million*. New York, Henry Holt, 2000; Skea, Ann. *Ted Hughes: The Poetic Quest*. Australia, University of New England Press, 1994;

Acknowledgements

Stevenson, Anne, *Bitter Fame: A Life of Sylvia Plath*. Penguin, 1990; Tennant, Emma. *Burnt Diaries*. Canongate Books, 1999; Trevor, William. *Excursions in the Real World*. Hutchinson, 1993. Permission granted by PFD Agency on behalf of William Trevor; Wagner, Erica. *Ariel's Gift*. Faber and Faber, 2000; Wagner-Martin, Linda. *Sylvia Plath: A Biography*. New York, Simon & Schuster, 1987, and *Plath: a Literary Life*, 2nd ed. revised and extended, New York, Palgrave Macmillan, 2003; Weldon, Fay. *Auto da Fay*. Flamingo, 2002; Williams, Mark. *A Cry of Pain*, Penguin Books, 1997.

We have drawn and quoted from the following articles; Barber, Jill. 'Ted Hughes, My Secret Lover'. *The Mail on Sunday*, 13 and 20 May 2001; Barraclough, Brian and Harris, E Clare. 'Suicide preceded by murder: the epidemiology of homicide-suicide in England and Wales, 1988–1992'. *Psychological Medicine*, 2002, 32, 577–584, Cambridge University Press; Becker, Gerry. *'Plath – Hughes: One of Us Had to Die'*. Unpublished memoir, courtesy of Kathleen Becker; Bowland, Eavan. 'Ted Hughes Recollections'. *PN Review*. Manchester, 25: 5 May 1999; Brown, Mick. 'Poetic Justice' (interview with Frieda Hughes). *Telegraph Magazine*, 16 June 2001; Cornwell, John. 'Bard of Prey'. *Sunday Times*, 3 October 1999; Fainlight, Ruth. 'Sylvia and Jane', *Times Literary Supplement*, 12 December 2003. Feay, Suzi. 'The Ghost Winter' (interview with Emma Tennant). *Independent on Sunday*, 20 May 2001. Heinz, Drue. 'Ted Hughes: The Art of Poetry, LXXI' (Interview with Ted Hughes). *Paris Review* 134, spring 1995; Helle, Anita. 'Family Matters': An Afterword on the Biography of Sylvia Plath.' *Northwest Review*, 26, no. 2, 1988; Hobsbaum, Philip. 'Ted Hughes at Cambridge'. *The Dark Horse: The Scottish-American Poetry Magazine*, 8 autumn 1999, and 'In Conversation with Nicolas Tredell'. *PN Review* 119, January–February 1998; Horder, John. 'Desk Poet'. *Guardian*, 23 March, 1965; Hughes, Frieda. 'A Matter of Life and Death'. *The Times Magazine*, 30 September 2000, and 'Daddy, I hardly read you'. *The Times*, 4 October 2003; Marzuk, P M, Tardiff K, Hirsch C S. 'The epidemiology of murder-suicide', *Journal of the American Medical Association*, 1992; 267:3179-3183; Mercy, James et al. 'Is suicide contagious?' *American Journal of Epidemiology*, 15 July 2001, vol. 154, no. 2:120–127; Meyer, Beate: 'The Mixed Marriage: a Guarantee of Survival, or a Reflection of German Society during the Nazi Regime', in, Bankier, David. *Probing the Depth of German Antisemitism, German Society and the Persecution of the Jews, 1933–1941*, New York, Berghahn Books, 2000; Morpurgo, Horatio.

'The Table Talk of Ted Hughes'. *Arete*, issue 6, autumn 2001; Niederlander, Doron. 'The Influence of Immigrant Physicians from Germany on the Development of Medicine in Palestine, 1933–1948'. Jerusalem, Hebrew University, 1982 (MA thesis in Hebrew); Nikunen, Minna. 'Media, Myth and Mother-child Murder-suicide'. Department of Women's Studies, University of Tampere, Finland; Pero, Thomas. 'So Quickly It's Over', an interview with Ted Hughes. *Wild Steelhead & Salmon*, winter issue, 1999; Porter, Peter. 'Ted Hughes and Sylvia Plath: a Bystander's Recollections'. *Australian Book Review*, August 2001, and 'Some People: Slogans for the Sixties', *Guardian*, 20 December 1988; Reich, Daniella. National Mission and Social Ostracism: the Liaisons between Jewish Women and British Servicemen, 1940–1948, Haifa University, 2003 (MA thesis in Hebrew); Resnick, Philip J. 'Child murder by parents: a psychiatric review of filicide'. *American Journal of Psychiatry*, 1969; 126:325–334; Robson, Jeremy, 'Copy for Mr Feinstein', *London Magazine*, July–July 1971; Sewards, Lisa. 'In the Name of My Father', interview with Frieda Hughes. *Daily Mail*, 3 November 2001; Sigmund, Elizabeth. 'Sylvia 1962, a Memoir'. *The New Review*, vol. 3, no. 26, May 1976; Sonnenberg, Ben. 'Ted's Spell'. *Raritan* 21, no. 4, spring 2002; Stanton, A and Simpson, J. 'Maternal Filicide'. *Criminal Behaviour and Mental Health*, 2000. 10, 136–147; Thomas, Trevor. *Sylvia Plath: Last Encounters*. Unpublished memoir, 1989, courtesy of Clarissa Roche; Tyrer, Nicola. 'Secret Life of Sylvia Plath'. *Daily Mail*, 5 February 2004; Walker, Iain, 'Poetic Justice? The Trials of Ted Hughes', Australia, *The Advertiser*, 7 May 1987; Zoritte-Megged, Eda. 'Intersections'. *Mosnayim*, no. 9, September/October 1984 (in Hebrew).

We have drawn from the following archives: correspondence of Ted Hughes, Keith Sagar and Assia Wevill in the Department of Manuscripts, the British Library, London; correspondence of Ted Hughes with Leonard Baskin, Janos Csokits, Frieda Hughes, Gerald Hughes, Olwyn Hughes, Bill and Dido Merwin, Lucas Myers, Aurelia Plath, Jane Prouty-Smith, Peter Redgrove; a postcard from Ruth Fainlight to Assia Wevill, 7 July 1967; a letter to Janet Malcolm, 2 March 1992; a letter to Mr Price-Turner, 5 April 1962; a letter to Leonard Scigaj, 28 July 1989; Ted Hughes's preface about Susan Alliston, and his notes from August 1968 and April 1969, all in Ted Hughes Papers, Manuscript, Archives and Rare Book Library, Emory University, Atlanta, Georgia, USA; letters of Sylvia Plath to her mother Aurelia and her brother Warren Plath and to Olive Prouty, correspondence between Aurelia Plath and

Acknowledgements

Ted Hughes, Elizabeth Compton, Hilda Farrar, Winifred Davies, Dr John Horder, Jillian Becker, all in the Sylvia Plath Collection, the Lilly Library, Indiana University, Bloomington, Indiana, USA; Sylvia Plath's calendar and Dr Ruth Beuscher's letters to Sylvia Plath 17 and 26 September 1962 in Sylvia Plath Collection, Mortimer Rare Book Room, Smith College, Northampton, Massachusetts, USA; Nathaniel Tarn's notes and correspondence with Assia and David Wevill, in the Nathaniel Tarn Papers, Department of Special Collections, Stanford University Libraries, Stanford, California, USA; letters from Assia and David Wevill to Earle Birney, in the Earle Birney Papers, Thomas Fisher Rare Book Library, University of Toronto, Canada; correspondence of Richard Murphy with Ted Hughes, in Richard Murphy Letters, McFarlin Library, Department of Special Collections, University of Tulsa, Oklahoma, USA; correspondence of Yehuda Amichai with Assia Wevill and Ted Hughes, in the Yehuda Amichai Papers, Beinecke Rare Book and Manuscript Library, Yale University, New Haven, USA; files of the Tel Aviv Hospitality Committee and of the Religious Council, 1940–1947, Tel Aviv Municipality Archives, Israel.

Our deep thanks to Stephen Enniss, Curator of Literary Collection at Manuscript, Archieves and Rare Book Library, Emory University, Atlanta, Georgia; and his assistants Elizabeth K Shoemaker, David Faulds, and additional thanks to Melissa H Maday for research assistance; Breon Mitchell, Director of the Lilly Library, Erika Dowell, Public Services Librarian, and a special thanks to Kathleen D Connor for research assistance at the Lilly Library, Indiana University, Bloomington, Indiana; Christopher Fletcher, Curator of Literary Manuscripts, the British Library; Karen V Kukil, Associate Curator of Rare books, Smith College; Roberto G Trujillo, Head, Department of Special Collections, the Stanford University Libraries, and his assistants Bill O'Hanlon and Polly Armstrong; Lori N Curtis, Head of Special Collections and Archives, and her assistant Milissa Burkart at McFarlin Library, University of Tulsa; Carl Spadoni, Research Collections Librarian, McMaster University Library, Ontario; Ellen R Cordes, Head of Technical Services, Anne Marie Menta, Public Service Assistant, and Ayehlet Cooper, for research assistance at the Beinecke Rare Book and Manuscript Library, Yale University, New Haven; John Wells, Department of Manuscripts and Cambridge University Archives, and Raphael Sylvester, for research assistance at the Cambridge University Library; Chris Hives, student registration at University of British

Columbia; Edna Haynal, librarian at the Thomas Fisher Rare Books Library, University of Toronto; Brenda Weeden, Archivist, University of Westminster; and John Barber, historian, Hertfordshire.

We are grateful to the following scholars and biographers, for their good and generous advice: Tracy Brain, Lynda K Bundtzen, Elaine Feinstein, Ronald Hayman, Judith Kroll, Diane Wood Middlebrook, Kate Moses, Anne Skea and Keith Sagar.

Most of the pictures in this book are from private collections. We are deeply grateful to the following for their ready help and generosity in providing photographs, letters, illustrations and other material: Celia Chaikin, John H Steele, Richard Lipsey, David Wevill, Patricia Mendelson, Martin Baker, Jane Donaldson, Jeremy Robson (for the photographs from the Israel poetry tour), Alton Becker, Elizabeth (Compton) Sigmund and Steve Enniss.

We are greatly indebted to the personal contribution of Tamara Chaikin, Eddie Levenston, Peter Skutches, our diligent agent Scott Mendel, David Hooper for his invaluable legal guidance, our supportive publisher Jeremy Robson, and our meticulous editor Anthea Matthison, who enabled us to make this book what it is.

Prologue

At noon on Sunday, 23 March 1969, Assia Wevill telephoned Ted Hughes at his home, Court Green. They had spent the past five days house-hunting in Yorkshire. On Saturday Assia had returned to her young daughter in London, and he to his children in Devon. For six years they had been trying to set up a home together but every failed attempt drove another wedge between them. They had a vicious quarrel over the phone that culminated with Assia insisting that they should separate for good: the relationship between them was no more than hobbling on and she simply did not believe any longer that he really wanted to be with her. Still, Assia did not slam the door on their future together completely. She remarked that she had spotted an ad for a house to rent in Devon, in the old market town of Barnstaple. Ted asked for the address and promised that he would take a look at it. Assia was not pacified, however, and they resumed arguing until, finally, she told him that her bags were packed and she was going to visit some friends in Dorset for a week. He was not to phone her back, she said, and without waiting for his response, she put down the phone.

Ten minutes later, Ted did phone back, and they continued their squabble. The two of them had endured scores of similar dead-end arguments over the past years and he felt that Assia was reciting her old grievances towards him. In apathy and exhaustion he had repeated his worn-out reassurances. After hanging up, Assia returned to the lounge, but Else Ludwig, her German au pair, sensed nothing unusual.

It was a cloudy, dry, cold day, just four degrees Celsius and they all three – Assia, her daughter Shura, and Else – stayed indoors. Else had asked for permission to visit her friend Olga, who lived a short walking distance away and, at 7.30 p.m., before leaving, she went into the four-year-old Shura's room, 'and saw that she was in her bed, and asleep. Mr Wevill was in her bedroom. She was still dressed.'

Assia then acted quickly. She made sure that the sash-type window in the kitchen was fully shut and pushed the small dining table and chairs over to the wall. From her bedroom she fetched some sheets, pillows and an eiderdown, and laid them on the kitchen floor, next to the gas oven. She poured herself a tot of whisky that she kept for occasional guests – she had abstained from alcohol throughout her life – and gulped it down. With another tot she then swallowed some sleeping pills. Seven times she gulped the whisky and swallowed the pills. Wobbling, she went into Shura's bedroom and lifted the sleeping child tenderly in her arms. In the dimly lit corridor she carefully negotiated the two steps that led back down into the kitchen. She laid Shura on the makeshift bed, closed the kitchen door tightly, turned all the gas taps fully on and opened the door of the Mayflower gas cooker. She switched off the kitchen light. Then she lay down quietly beside her daughter, so as not to wake her up. Their heads were lying close to the gas cooker. Assia's feet almost touched the door.

One

Childhood

Russia, 1896–Germany, 1933

Times were changing and Ephraim Gutmann turned a blind eye when his son found all sorts of excuses not to accompany him to the synagogue on Friday evenings. Lonya had stopped wearing his yarmulke, smoked on the Shabbat and ignored the dietary laws of Kashruth but Gutmann trusted patriarchal authority – and his son's financial dependence – to prevent him from breaking the ultimate taboo.

Nevertheless, when Lonya announced his marriage plans, his father's world fell apart. Ephraim Gutmann could barely tolerate the age gap – the prospective bride was already 37 years of age, seven years older than his son – and the discrepancy in status – his favourite son was a doctor from a well-to-do bourgeois family, while his lover was a farmer's daughter, who earned her living as a nurse. But he could never consent to the difference in faith: since they reached adolescence, Gutmann had constantly warned his three sons that, come what may, they were not to marry outside the Jewish religion. Elizabetha Bertha Margarete Gaedeke was a Lutheran and Ephraim Gutmann threatened to disinherit his son. The Gaedekes were much more tolerant, eager to see their daughter saved at long last from becoming an old maid. The groom's Jewishness proved no obstacle and, being proud German nationals, they only had to overcome the embarrassment of their daughter marrying a non-German, a man from Latvia. When the marriage did take place, obviously without Gutmann's blessing or presence, he announced that the newly weds were never to set foot in his home.

The roots of the Gutmann clan were in the Ukraine and Ephraim, son of Nachman Gutmann, was born in 1866 in Kagarlyk, a village southeast of Kiev. At a young age he took the 250-mile journey northwards, settled in the city of Lutsk and married Menja Lipowa Pintchuk. Lew (Lonya), born on 9

1

December 1896, was their third son. Ephraim Gutmann made his fortune by supplying rubber boots and uniforms to the tsar's army, at the peak of his success employing 200 workers in his factory. With a view to expanding his business activities, Gutmann sent his sons to London with a stock of caviar. Lonya and Vanya, bedazzled by the temptations of the city, gave away or ate most of the samples, squandered the money and returned home shamefully empty-handed.

Gutmann's wealth allowed him to send his eldest son Vanya to law school and to finance Lonya's medical course in far-away Moscow. Russian law limited the quota of Jewish students in universities (one Jew for every nine students). Gutmann was obliged to pay a heavy fee to lift the *numerus clausus* and subsidise several non-Jewish students, for his own sons to be enrolled. Before departing for Moscow, Lonya was given a silver cigarette box with an engraving of a Teutonic warrior: a puzzling gift for a pious Jewish father.

In his fantasies, Lonya Gutmann saw himself not in the operating theatre with a surgeon's mask and gown, but in a tuxedo. Basking in the limelight of the concert hall, his fingers would dance on the black and ivory keys of the grand piano and he would take his bow to a cheering audience. Arriving in Moscow, he defied his father and enrolled in the music conservatory. But despite the distance, hundreds of miles away, his father soon discovered the deceit and forced Lonya to attend the medical school of the First Moscow State University as planned. It was the oldest university in Russia and boasted of having Anton Chekhov among its medical students.

Lonya Gutmann's surviving report card shows him to have been a mediocre student. 'Father never wanted to be a doctor,' explains his younger daughter Celia Chaikin. 'He enjoyed the student parties and took part in vodka-drinking competitions. He was a practical joker and had a great sense of humour. One day, at the opera, some Greek Orthodox priests were sitting in front of him, their long hair tied at the back of their heads. Father caressed it, his friends choking with laughter, the priests unaware of the reason for the commotion.' The American writer Lucas Myers, who met Dr Gutmann decades later in his daughter Assia's flat in London, remembers his 'marvellous tales of dancing and drinking in the gypsy camps on the outskirts of Moscow, when he was a medical student.' A born storyteller, Lonya Gutmann often mixed fact with fiction to amaze his audience and create an aura of intrigue around himself. He thus told Myers that he 'had once been physician to the Bolshoi Ballet'.

Hearing this same story, her future lover, Ted Hughes, incorporated it into his poem about Assia, 'Dreamers': 'Her father/Doctor to the Bolshoi Ballet'. No documents were found to prove that Gutmann ever worked for the Bolshoi, and his daughter Celia never knew whether it was true or not. There were more tales, impossible to verify or disprove: that Tolstoy used to visit the Gutmanns' home and that they were neighbours of the violinist, Yasha Hefetz: Lonya remembered Yasha's mother, urging her son to stop playing outside and to practise the violin.

While Lonya was frolicking in Moscow, his parents back in Lutsk were caught in the turmoil of the First World War. Their town fell first into the hands of the Austrians and then was recaptured by the Russians, passing back and forth between the sides, until finally, in June 1916, it was Russian again. Instability increased with the Bolshevik Revolution of February 1917. Having lost much of their property, Lonya's mother Menja was compelled to sell her jewellery and they migrated to Riga. Ephraim Gutmann soon regained his wealth, enjoying a spacious house, four servants and a coachman.

In 1921 Lonya Gutmann returned home after graduation, choosing not to specialise in any specific medical field. This hedonistic pampered young man, who indulged in the luxuries of life, had a taste for choice cuisine, flowing conversation, a good laugh and being a tourist. A man of culture, who loved music, frequented concerts and was an avid reader, he was delighted when his father sent him to Germany to attend to the family business and estates. Just before leaving, he fell in love with the German nurse Elizabetha (Lisa) Gaedeke. The tall, stately and striking Lisa specialised in nutrition and was accompanying a private patient to a convalescent home in Riga. Her parents were devout churchgoers, farmers from Kladen, halfway between Hamburg and Berlin.

Lisa followed Dr Gutmann to Berlin and they lived in the affluent quarter of Charlottenburg. For five years they conducted a passionate affair that he kept secret from his father. They married on 5 May 1926, and for some reason, the marriage certificate gives Lonya Gutmann's profession as 'merchant', though he made his livelihood from the then popular physiotherapy and electrotherapy; treating rheumatic pains was less demanding than other medical professions. Assia Esther was born on 15 May 1927. The birth of his first grandchild softened Ephraim Gutmann's heart and he broke the year-long ostracism. When Assia was six months old she was taken to Riga, and the

Gutmanns showed some goodwill towards their daughter-in-law, presenting her with a silver goblet with the initials EG (Elizabetha Gutmann) engraved on it. However, Lisa was never accepted into the family and was a thorn in the flesh of her mother-in-law.

A photograph in the Gutmann family album portrays the unsmiling, reserved two-year-old Assia, standing tall in a studio setting. Her straight dark hair is cut short and stiff like a helmet, her small hands folded obediently on her chest. She is flanked by a king-size picture book portraying two kittens, and by a large doll sitting on the floor, raising her hands in vain for the child to pick her up. It would be tempting, in hindsight, to interpret this as Assia's innate detachment and flawed maternal instinct; but the doll could well have been a fragile prop in the photographer's studio, which the well-behaved little girl was forbidden to touch. On 22 September 1929, her sister Celia was born.

Accustomed to princely life since childhood, Lonya Gutmann now enjoyed the bourgeois pleasures of Berlin: concerts, cafés, strolling along Kurfurstendamm in his elegant clothes. The three daily meals were not complete without a gorgeous white, embroidered damask tablecloth, stiffly ironed napkins folded in silver rings and silver cutlery. But Berlin did not dull his longings for his native land and temperamentally he remained a buoyant Russian. Lonya and Lisa had polar personalities to accommodate – he was jubilant and buoyant, she was stiff and controlled; he was an extrovert, she a brooding introvert; he was an atheist and she, a devout Christian. But the core of discord was over their daughters' education, and especially Assia's. Lonya doted on his elder daughter, the apple of his eye. He never criticised her and defended her from the wrath of her mother. She was his little princess and was treated like one. He adored Assia's every witty remark, every childlike observation and made her believe that, like him, she was born for grandeur.

'Don't sing in the morning, or you're bound to cry at night,' was a constant motto of Lisa Gutmann's. Her character strict, her methods of education and punishment harsh, she had firm ideas about Good and Evil. Short-tempered, she blew up quickly at any of her daughters' misbehaviour. 'Mutti was very Germanic. She often hit me with Assia's violin bow, which was very painful,' Celia still nurses the insult. 'Once she picked up Assia's favourite china doll, broke it and hurled it out of the window. Vati made no secret of his disapproval of Mutti's methods, and she accused him of being too indulgent with Assia.' Lisa Gutmann read to her daughters from *Grimm's Fairy Tales*, but her favourite and often-repeated story was Heinrich Hoffman's *Struwwelpeter,* about Slovenly Peter, who never combed his hair and whose filthy nails grew so long that his mother had to cut them off with a saw. 'We were brought up like any German girl, without a trace of Jewishness. The house rules and manners were German, but the backbone was Russian,' Celia Chaikin recounts.

When Hitler was appointed chancellor on 30 January 1933, 525,000 Jews were living in Germany, less than one per cent of a total population of 67 million. The largest Jewish centre was Berlin, with 160,000, four per cent of the city's population. The celebrations that followed Hitler's appointment immediately turned into violent rallies: the first victims were the Ostjuden, Jews who had emigrated from Russia and Poland. They were beaten in the streets, their beards were set on fire and locks, which had been grown and groomed since childhood and were an integral part of Jewish orthodoxy, were brutally twisted and cut off.

On Saturday, 1 April 1933, at 10 a.m., the Gutmanns shut themselves in when vigils of uniformed Nazis blocked the entrance to every Jewish-owned shop, lawyer's office and physician's clinic, preventing customers, clients and patients from entering. Windows and office plates were painted over with the word *Jude* and those Germans who dared to enter were photographed and were made notorious the following day in the local press. Vehicles carrying loudspeakers roamed the streets, broadcasting slogans that condemned those who did business with Jews. Windows were smashed and the shops looted in the Jewish quarters of Berlin. The organised boycott by the Nazi Party was the first countrywide initiative to ignite anti-Jewish activities and sanctions. At the end of that week, on 7 April the first law to curtail the right of Jewish citizens was enforced. The Law for the Restoration of the Professional Civil Service was aimed at excluding Jews not only from the Civil Service but also from other organisations in order to segregate them from Aryan society. The medical profession hastened to implement the law with extra rigidity.

Already, in the First World War, the entire German medical profession had rallied to the call of national duty. The horrors of that military experience brutalised many doctors to a crude Darwinian view of life and a subsequent affiliation with right-wing political causes, writes John Efron in *Medicine and the German Jews*. Nazi ideology described the Jews in metaphors of disease: as a bacillus, a parasite, or a malignant tumour in the body of the nation. Hitler was thus perceived as the Good Doctor who would remove the Jewish malignancy and cure the German patient. It was the task of the medical profession to join the effort, restore 'hygiene' to the German nation and cleanse it of Jews. Removing Jewish doctors from practice was perceived as a necessary step towards saving the Germans from the Jewish plague. But it was not ideology alone that motivated these moves: the profession suffered from overcrowding and a decline in earnings. In 1933, the 8,000 Jewish doctors in Germany constituted sixteen per cent of the profession and in Berlin and other major cities they even comprised fifty per cent. It is no wonder that, with deep recession and economic competition, German medicine became 'the most easily and eagerly Nazified of any professional group', in the words of author John Efron. Around fifty per cent of all German doctors became members of the Nazi Party.

Following the Aryanisation of the public health services, more than half of the Jewish doctors lost their jobs. As many as 3,500 Jewish physicians in Berlin alone were made redundant, more than half of them reduced to the brink of starvation. 'In Berlin, graffiti outside physician's offices such as "Jewish Swine" proliferated. Here, also, several Jewish doctors were temporarily rounded up, taken to the exhibition grounds near Lehrter Bahnhof, and shot in their legs during a roll call improvised by Nazi colleagues,' writes Professor Michael Kater, in *Doctors Under Hitler*. Many were sent to concentration camps, one of them near Berlin, and never returned. Only Jewish doctors who had begun practising before 1 August 1914, or who had fought in the First World War, or had lost a father or a son in that war, or were exposed to lethal epidemics in quarantine camps, were exempted at this stage. Dr Lonya Gutmann did not qualify for any of these exemptions. Many Jewish doctors, proud of their German nationality, tried to hang on even at the price of not practising medicine, but by doing odd jobs, hoping that soon their nation would sober up and return to sanity. Dr Gutmann, who retained his Latvian citizenship, was not ready to undergo such a sacrifice for a country that he did not call home. He felt vulnerable on four counts: as a Jew, a foreigner, a doctor, and as married to an Aryan.

In pre-Hitler times, inter-marriage offered Jews the opportunity to integrate into German society. In 1933, there were 35,000 mixed couples in Germany, most of them, like Lonya Gutmann, Jewish men married to Christian wives. A survey, published in 1940, found that Jewish men in mixed marriages came as a rule from the upper or upper middle class and generally married beneath them. With the Nazis in power, those who had married a *Deutschblutige* (German blooded), became 'even more undesirable than other Jews, as they posed a direct threat to the *Deutschen Blutsverband*' (German blood union) wrote Dr Beate Meyer in her article, 'The Mixed Marriage: A Guarantee of Survival, or a Reflection of German Society during the Nazi Regime.'

For most of his life, Dr Gutmann had distanced himself from his ancestral faith and Judaism seemed to him a meaningless biographical detail that he did not feel responsible for and which bore no reflection on his lifestyle; nevertheless, Nazi ideology classified him as a member of the Inferior Race. From feeling a Russian in a Teutonic milieu, he was now forced to reassert his Jewish identity. In general, German wives were no shield against persecution and when the men lost their jobs and livelihood, the mixed families crumbled as they failed to maintain their standard of living. 'The Jewish husbands found it difficult to come to terms with the loss of their position and reputation in society; the wives had to provide them with the emotional support they needed, especially when they were plagued by depression and thought of suicide,' wrote Dr Beate Meyer. Discord rocked the mixed families and the German in-laws exercised pressure on their daughters to divorce their Jewish husbands and save themselves and their children. Many did. One doctor, Dr Arthur Bear, took his own life in order to set his Christian wife free from the pressures. He was one of several hundred doctors who could not withstand the strain and chose death. Lisa Gutmann, though, stood by her husband, and they decided that their only hope was to leave Germany.

Spring 1933 was Assia Gutmann's last term in kindergarten and she was looking forward to starting school in the autumn. Her parents managed to hide their anxiety and plans from their young daughters and, on 15 May 1933, Assia celebrated her sixth birthday in grand style in their Berlin home. This was a time when bonfires were burning throughout Germany, consuming Jewish 'degenerate literature'. Soon after, the Gutmanns took the train to Italy, via Switzerland, getting off at Pisa, which became a haven for refugees. The Gutmanns rented a flat in 21 Via Mazzini. They were in the first wave of Jews who left Germany: 25,000 in just three months.

In later years, Assia's tales of the flight from Germany portrayed an ordeal. Lucas Myers recounts her stories, of how the whole family narrowly escaped internment. 'Assia described hiding in a railway compartment and listening to the tramp of Nazi guards coming down the corridor.' The poet Philip Hobsbaum, like several of Assia's friends, remembers that she had been shunted about in various displaced persons' camps and suffered semi-starvation and dirt, 'But I'm inclined to think she embroidered or even fantasised it,' he has said. Assia indeed had a taste for drama but post-war knowledge of the hideous fate of Jews in the Holocaust, which confused the memory of many of her friends, may have painted her relatively smooth exodus in darker colours than it actually merited. Relating to Assia in his poems, Ted Hughes incorporated words like 'death-camp', 'ex-Nazi Youth Sabra', 'Hitler's mutilations' and 'swastika', all of which hardly touched on Assia's actual experiences. In 'Dreamers', he addressed Plath's fascination with Assia's Germanic background: in Assia, Plath saw 'hanged women choke'.

When he left Germany, Lonya's diplomas and certificates were confiscated, and he spent weeks corresponding with Berlin until he received the authorised copies in Pisa. He was pondering his options. It was all but impossible to get a visa to the USA. England, Italy and France demanded that every foreign doctor would have to repeat years of study and undergo extensive examinations. Switzerland set even stricter immigration laws and allowed only few doctors to enter, let alone practise there. Belgium, Holland and the Scandinavian countries offered some asylum, but immigrants were not allowed to practise medicine. Canada and Australia had tight immigration quotas and forbade German-Jewish physicians from practising there, allegedly on account of the low standards of German medicine. At 37 years of age, the last thing on earth that Lonya Gutmann wanted was to start medical school all over again.

Shanghai, Brazil and South Africa were the exceptional places that welcomed Jewish doctors and allowed them to practise; but Dr Gutmann, who estimated that Germany was passing through only a temporary bad spell, was reluctant to sail to the other side of the world. There was a fourth option: Palestine. He was no Zionist but, at this crucial moment in his life, he felt that he would be better off among his peers and relatively close to Europe. Since he left his childhood home, Lonya had never lived among Jews, and it did not cross his mind that living with a non-Jewish wife in Tel Aviv, the only all-Jewish city in the world, might be a problem. But running for his life, there was no time to check or inquire about the population, the standards of living, or how developed and Westernised the country was; at that stage, he consoled himself that he would not be required to repeat his medical studies and, with his savings, would be able to set up a private clinic. In the new country, which was being built by people hitherto unaccustomed to physical labour, a physiotherapist like Dr Gutmann could expect queues of patients seeking a cure for their back pains and aching muscles.

Towards the end of 1933, word reached the Jewish refugees stranded in Italy: General Sir Arthur Wauchope, the British High Commissioner of Palestine, declared that although there was a surplus of doctors in Palestine, he was not yet thinking of cutting back the number of work permits for medical staff. Dr Gutmann was rather alarmed by the implications of this declaration and decided to hasten his departure to Palestine. Meanwhile, Assia was attending the first grade in the Padre Augustino Catholic School and, having an ear for languages, soon chattered in Italian. But after six months, she had to bid farewell to her newly acquired schoolfriends. The Italian experience left fond memories with her and, almost thirty years later, when she spent a holiday in Elba with her third husband David Wevill, she took him to Pisa, to look for the family home and old school.

The porters of the *Italia* loaded crates with Dr Gutmann's medical equipment and a choice of furniture from their Berlin home: a heavy mahogany dining table with six chairs, a glass cabinet, Persian carpets. On the occasion of her marriage, Lisa Gutmann's dowry from her parents was packed in a beautifully carved wooden crate, bearing the year 1751, and the initials JM–AR, from the betrothal of some ancestral mother. Into this crate, which had been handed down in her family for generations, Lisa folded her cherished bedlinen and tablecloths, and added some kitchen utensils and the carefully wrapped silver cutlery and china plates.

Two

A New Life

Tel Aviv, 1934–1938

Not yet seven years of age, Assia Gutmann was tackling her fourth new language. She spoke German with her mother, loved conversing in Russian with her father and continued to chat in Italian to everyone's delight. She glided easily between the languages but Hebrew proved a trickier obstacle: it was written from right to left, with unfamiliar letters, pronounced harshly and stressed on the gutturals. The revival of the Hebrew language in the old-new Jewish homeland meant that at school she was Esther, the name she was given at birth but had never used before. At home, she continued to be Assia. From the depths of his past, Dr Gutmann's Jewish roots caught up with him too and he had to recognise his long-forgotten name Aryeh, the Hebrew for Leo. Celia became Tseeley and only their German mother retained her name, Elizabetha.

When the Gutmanns arrived in the British-mandated territory of Palestine at the beginning of 1934, there were only 190,000 Jews in the entire land. They comprised fifteen per cent of the population, the majority being Arabs. Forty-five thousand Jews emigrated to Palestine that year, twelve thousand of them from Germany. Seeking refuge from Nazi persecution, the Jewish population more than doubled to 475,000 by 1940. The small community had no means to assist the flow of newcomers in such a short time and the immigrants were left to fend for themselves in finding work and housing.

Palestine was not an appropriate breeding place for German Jews and only a few thousand of them emigrated there before Hitler came to power. Most of the first settlers were East European Jews, who established a small, homogenous community of pioneers and socialists. Inspired by Russian culture and the Communist Revolution, they were eager to create a new Jew, who was to be a manual labourer, a farmer rather than a scholar or a merchant.

Until the 1930s, most arrivals in Palestine were young and single, ready for hard work and harsh conditions. The flow of sixty thousand German Jews brought, for the first time, entire families from middle and upper class backgrounds, with property and university degrees, liberal and assimilated, pampered by high standards of living. Most East European pioneers left their homelands out of choice and were keen to take part in building the Holy Land, but the Gutmanns, like many of their fellow expatriates, felt like refugees; they would never have left home if their lives had not been in danger. A year earlier, Dr Gutmann considered himself a Russian exiled in Germany and his world was shattered when he was classified by the Nazis as neither a Russian nor a German, but a Jew. Now, in the Jewish community of Palestine, he was considered German, on account of the country he had left.

Many suffered from culture shock and a sense of regression. Tel Aviv was not a bustling metropolis of millions, but a city without a history named after a novel: *Altneuland*, by the founder of the Zionist movement Theodore Herzl. It was a new town that in 1909 had sprung from the sands of the Mediterranean under the blazing sun. It now had only a hundred thousand inhabitants and could obviously not supply a fraction of the delights of the German capital. Moreover, the social ethos of the pioneers was one of asceticism and austerity, khaki shorts and sandals, and of denouncing the bourgeoisie with their tailored suits and bow ties.

Dr Gutmann wanted no change; just to maintain the standard of living he enjoyed in Berlin. In their humble habitation, crammed with furniture and household utensils from Berlin, the Gutmanns built a haven, with their damask tablecloths and three meals a day eaten with silver cutlery. Forbidden to raise their voices at home, Assia and Celia had to ring a Tyrolean shepherd's bell to attract their mother's attention and call her to their room whenever one of them was ill and wanted a drink. Lisa continued to attend church in the nearby Arab town of Jaffa. On Christmas Eve, she sneaked with her daughters to join the congregation for mass. Oblivious of their Jewish neighbours, they decorated their flat and behind closed curtains celebrated with the traditional Christmas meal, German biscuits and cakes and singing carols. 'As we grew up, Assia and I made fun of the carols, to annoy Mutti,' Celia recalls. 'If we wanted to taste any Jewish tradition, our neighbours and friends always invited us to light candles at Hanukah.'

Immigrants were expected to integrate quickly in their host country and praise its culture and achievements but most German newcomers felt superior. They stuck to their own customs, reluctant to learn Hebrew, feeling that in speaking the ancient tongue they were becoming more Jewish than they cared to be. The sound of the language irritated Dr Gutmann and, frustrated that he, a man of culture, felt lost for words, he preferred to speak German and Russian with his patients. His wife spoke hardly any Hebrew at all and was furious when people insisted that she address them in the language of the land. Assia and Celia spoke Hebrew between themselves, turning the language into a secret code to exclude their parents. They wished the earth would swallow them up when, walking in the street and entering a shop or sitting in a café, their parents conversed with them in German. The language barrier kept the Gutmanns from being involved in their daughters' education and they could not assist Assia and Tseeley with their homework. In their miniature Berlin in the heart of Tel Aviv, ready to pack and leave at any moment, the parents remained nomads. Assia inherited her parents' sense of alienation and found it difficult to put down roots in the historical Fatherland.

After years of just mothering her daughters, Lisa Gutmann had to share the burden of supporting her family. She used her talent for embroidery to make dresses for other doctors' wives. At lunchtime, she would place four tables in the living room and, being a talented cook, served lunches to regular clients. At a later period she counted herself lucky to find a job at the Hadassah Hospital to don the white nurse's uniform again. The family was hard up, and Professor Richard Lipsey, Assia's second husband, recalls Assia's many stories of deprivation, 'one of which was how her parents made her go to the butcher's, to get the meat at a reduced price, and in return, she allowed him to hold her hand and fondle her rather innocently, but repulsively to her.'

With the money they brought from Germany, the Gutmanns rented a three-room flat on the first floor of 9 Balfour Street, with a balcony closed by shutters to add some extra living space. It was one of the first streets to be built in Tel Aviv and named in honour of Lord Balfour. This British foreign minister was renowned for his declaration of 1917, stating that His Majesty's Government viewed with favour the establishment of a National Home for the Jewish People in Palestine. Balfour was a central street, just a short walk from the bustling Carmel Market. Number 12 Balfour Street housed an elementary school and, even more appealing, number 30 was the Ohel Shem Concert Hall, home of the Palestine Philharmonic, recently established thanks to the arrival in Palestine of German-born musicians. The municipal public clinics were in 14 Balfour Street and the Hadassah Hospital was just around the corner but Dr Gutmann did not find work in either institution. In the mornings, Lisa Gutmann would fold their double bed into a sofa, turning their bedroom into a makeshift clinic. The living room served as a waiting room. Having no telephone, just a small plaque on the building outside, the few patients just dropped in.

In 1932, there were 476 Jewish doctors in Palestine. By 1934, the year that Dr Gutmann arrived, the number increased to 1,282, all recent immigrants like himself. Five years later, there were nearly two thousand doctors. There were not enough patients for so many doctors, especially as most of the population were twenty-something, young, healthy and penniless. In a situation of unemployment and low pay, few could afford a massage or treatment with an ultraviolet lamp to ease their muscle pains. Electrotherapy, Dr Gutmann's specialty, was not included in the essential services that were provided by the General Sick Fund, the medical insurance co-operative that most citizens were members of. He was now paying the price of his reluctance to make a greater effort to acquire a more prestigious and indispensable specialisation. Competition among private doctors was so tough that sixty per cent of them earned less than the minimum income needed to support a family. Many changed careers and became farmers, builders or taxi drivers. There is a story about a pregnant woman, who went into labour while commuting on a Tel Aviv bus. A passenger cried out, 'Is there a doctor on board?' Six men, all immigrants from Germany, jumped to their feet and rushed to help the woman. The driver pulled the vehicle to the side, stood up and said, 'Clear the way, on my bus I'm delivering the babies': he was an obstetrician.

Having shied away from hard work throughout his life, Dr Gutmann would not consider manual labour. In his frustration he reverted to his Russian self, immersing himself in Chekhov and Pushkin. 'Vati liked the easy life, and wasted his time by playing chess with and in between patients. He loved entertaining guests and, on the summer nights, they played gin rummy on the balcony,' says his daughter Celia. 'He was a weak, selfish man, and he preferred being supported by a woman to working.' As financially hard up as they were, Lisa insisted on eurhythmic classes to improve her daughters' posture. 'Mutti made us walk straight, one foot behind the other, like young ladies, and kept us on a strict diet, so that we should be thin and attractive,' recalls Celia. 'However, she frowned when people said how pretty we were, afraid that it would go to our heads.' The Gutmann girls stood out in their appearance and, with the little money they had, their mother took extra care to adorn them with dresses meticulously sewn out of identical patterned cloth and decorated with lace collars. 'Mutti made a point of maintaining the façade and, in our appearance and behaviour, we had to pretend that we were actually an affluent doctor's family.'

All shared alienation and hardship, but being a Lutheran in a totally Jewish environment, Lisa Gutmann was doubly affected. She tried to disregard the whispers of *goya* (Gentile) behind her back. A gloomy side to her nature, which had always been there, surfaced. 'She was a fine person but didn't know how to be a mother. She tried to make us better people, but at times she lost control completely, venting all her frustration on us. She would tie Assia and me to the window for minor wrongdoings, like not washing the dishes,' Celia recalls. In later years, when Celia accused her mother of cruelty, Lisa Gutmann would answer that it was nothing compared to what she herself had been through as a child. Lisa's manic-depressive traits and fits of rage got worse because she could not bear the family's insecurity and lack of means. 'Once, after a bitter confrontation with father, Mutti ran out of the house,' Celia remembers. 'That week, a curfew was imposed on Tel Aviv following clashes between the Jewish underground and British soldiers and Mother was hoping that the soldiers would shoot her for breaking the curfew.' Little Celia chased her mother, pulling at her and begging her to return home. Assia, too, had similar fits of rage, and would fling herself on the floor when she could not get her own way. With the lack of adequate psychiatric services, the only way Dr Gutmann could calm his daughter down was by giving her shots of tranquillisers.

The persecution of Jews in the Third Reich was intensifying and yet there were normal relations between Palestine and Nazi Germany: ships carried imports and exports, and there was traffic in tourists from both sides. In the summer of 1935, Lisa Gutmann and her daughters wished to cheer themselves up by travelling to Germany at the invitation of her parents, her passport, issued by the British authorities in Palestine, serving as a political shield. The girls' most vivid memory of that visit was Granny's frightening bedtime stories, and a trip to the heart of the forest, when she ordered them to sit

down: 'Don't dare to move, or else the Evil Witch will come and grab you!'
Decades later, Assia was still troubled by those memories, and in 1963, while
living with Ted Hughes and his children in Sylvia Plath's death flat, she wrote
in her diary:

> Last night, in the half dark, as he laid naked – and his thick hair on his
> chest and stomach formed a diffused, moving monster's face – like a
> tattooed snake – I came into a panic fear, like the kind I had when I was
> 4. Was that the black, manic negress-eater – the killer, who was quite
> formally showing himself like a harmless photograph, for the first time.

Lisa Gutmann was horrified to see the brown Hitlerjugend uniforms of her
nephews, Fritz and Hans; from then on she severed her relationship with her
sister. She and her daughters set out for Tel Aviv just as the Nuremberg Race
Laws were enforced and Lisa was spared the humiliation of being pressured to
leave her Jewish husband: sexual relations between Aryans and Jews was
forbidden. Those same laws also forbade Jews from keeping a dog and the girls
counted themselves lucky that in Palestine they could enjoy the company of
Befy, their beloved brown cocker spaniel. It was the last time Assia and Celia
ever saw their German grandparents. In subsequent years, it would be too
dangerous, and later, impossible, to venture into Germany.

That autumn their paternal grandparents came from Riga to check out the
possibility of settling down in Tel Aviv and they all crowded together in the
three-room flat. The girls were impressed by their grandmother's fur coat and
crocodile handbag, which stood out in its extravagance. In February 1936, just
five months after his arrival, Grandfather Ephraim Gutmann suffered a heart
attack and died in the Hadassah Hospital. For some reason or other, whether
through financial hardship or blatant atheism, Dr Lonya Gutmann failed to
erect a tombstone on his father's grave and it was left to the Hevrah Kaddisha,
the burial society, to erect a standard cement slab, reserved for the city's
paupers. Not wishing to linger on, Grandmother Gutmann packed her
suitcases and sailed for Latvia.

In May 1936 Palestine was catapulted into three years of bloodshed. The
Great Arab Revolt brought chaos to the country and victims fell on all sides:
Jews, Arabs, British policemen and soldiers. Dr Gutmann was in despair; the
shelter he had been seeking was not only economically precarious and

culturally inferior, but now had also become life threatening. The girls were seemingly unaware of all this: a serene studio photograph from that time shows Assia and Celia in identical checked pastel-coloured dresses and frilly white collars, lovingly coiled in the arms of their smiling mother. Assia seems the tallest of the three, against her mother's shadow on the wall behind her.

A classmate from Balfour Elementary School remembers Assia as weird and beautiful, a bright girl who excelled in painting and wrote poems and bitter-sweet love stories. She appeared to daydream and even her walk seemed to hover above the ground and float on a cloud. All in all, she gave the impression of a fluttering, lost butterfly, afraid to touch the earth. There was something bewildered and uneasy about her; her personality traits and the shadow of her Gentile mother pushing her to the margins of school social life. Her well-mannered behaviour was under attack from the ruggedness of the Sabras, the native-born Israelis.

The school was overcrowded, with more than fifty pupils in each class; there was a permanent shortage of books and equipment and only one map for geography for the entire school. The result was substandard education and filth that the caretaker could not cope with. There was a never-ending influx of new pupils, some of them in torn and dirty clothes, their hair sticky and unkempt. A separate class had to be set up for them, so that they would not contaminate the rest of the school with lice and contagious diseases. 'We ceased being an educational institution, and became an asylum to hundreds of forlorn children,' complained the principal, Judith Harari, in a letter to the Tel Aviv municipality, appealing for emergency assistance.

Dr Gutmann did not relinquish his dreams of grandeur and infused his elder daughter with them. Assia was to embody everything that he wanted to be but couldn't manage, and she willingly sat on the throne he set up for her. 'Throughout my childhood, I believed that I was not my parents' daughter; Assia told me that the gypsies left me on their doorstep,' recalls Celia. 'She would say that she was a princess born in a palace, and was kidnapped from her real mother, while I was a gypsy child. It had a lasting effect on both of us.' One day Assia took their mother's precious bottle of perfume, poured it over a cloth and wiped the floor with it. She escaped her mother's wrath through her father's indulgence, which also helped her evade the tough household duties. Celia was the one sent to the market to buy a block of ice for the icebox, dragging the heavy bulk along the ground. Though meticulously dressed when going outdoors, Assia's clothes were always scattered around the room, and she left it to others to tidy up after her. 'Assia thought that she deserved everything, and that everyone around her would serve her and do what she wanted,' her sister remembers. 'But Father was the only one that she placed under her spell.'

Three

A Tabeetha Girl

Tel Aviv, 1939–42

When the Second World War broke out, anything German in Palestine became automatically suspect – to both the Jewish community and the British authorities. Expatriates like Lonya and Lisa did everything possible to downplay their 'German' backgrounds, both out of shame at the atrocities committed in their former homeland, and to protect themselves from accusations of guilt by association. Even trivial public arguments over service in a shop or office could result in a Palestinian Jew or British soldier saying, 'If you don't like it here, go back to Hitler.' But the Gutmanns knew that the way back was blocked for ever. In the dead of night, Assia and Celia listened to the troubled whispers that came from their parents' bedroom. The irony of the family's situation was painfully obvious to all of them. Six years earlier, in Berlin, Dr Gutmann had been in peril of being separated from his Aryan wife and deported to a concentration camp. And the Nazi racial laws would not have spared his daughters from sharing his fate. Now, in Palestine, the Gutmanns feared the opposite scenario: that Lisa, though she hated Hitler and was married to a Jew, might be detained in Tel Aviv as a possible enemy sympathiser. Assia and Celia were too horrified to discuss the matter and their parents either would not or could not speak openly to them about it. But Lisa Gutmann had packed a small suitcase containing some essentials and waited for the knock on the door. She worried that her daughters might not be spared deportation along with her.

In May 1941, the pendulum was swinging again when the Afrika Korps, under the command of Field Marshal Rommel, reached the borders of Egypt. A year later, they were so far advanced that their Panzer tanks were just a week's drive away from Tel Aviv. The small Jewish community in Palestine feared that in case of an invasion, the Germans would retaliate on those who managed to escape Europe. The threat was so imminent that the Jewish Agency, the representative body of the Jews in Palestine, made plans to fortify Mount Carmel, and to cram the entire Jewish population up there. They were following their forefathers who, in AD 73 were entrenched in the fortress of Massada by the Dead Sea. Massada remained the only pocket of resistance against the Romans, who crushed the Jewish kingdom. Facing a final defeat after a blockade that lasted two years, the 960 Jewish men, women and children besieged on Massada committed mass suicide, preferring death to deportation, slavery and abuse. A possible Nazi occupation of Palestine was less of a threat for Lisa, being a German national, but it would mean death to her Jewish husband and daughters.

When news of Nazi atrocities in Europe reached the Jewish community in Palestine, the German Templars who were living in their own colonies throughout the country, feared for their life and property and the revenge of their Jewish neighbours. As the war proceeded, the British administration deported the Templars to Australia and Lisa Gutmann dreaded that she would be associated with them and exiled too. Her daughters would whatever happened, since they were regarded as the enemy by both sides. They were on two sides of the barricade: perpetrators on their mother's side, victims on their father's. The memory of being trapped in the middle lingered on with Assia; in 1968, she would visit Germany with Ted Hughes and their three-year-old daughter Shura, as guests of the West German Federal Republic. Her postcard to their friend, the Israeli poet Yehuda Amichai, concluded with a sentence in Hebrew: 'Me, half-German? No, no, no. Suddenly Germany disgusts me.'

As far as her daughters' education was concerned, the Balfour Elementary School in Tel Aviv was not up to Lisa Gutmann's standards, and she was not going to send Assia to a high school that was part of the Hebrew education system. The curriculum seemed to her too Zionist, alien and constricting, detached from the richness of European culture. She inquired at Emmanuel Church and was advised to enrol her daughter at Tabeetha High in Jaffa. It seemed an odd choice for a Jewish girl from Tel Aviv. None of Assia's friends, and no child of her parents' acquaintances, had ever studied there. Located in an Arab neighbourhood, it charged a high tuition fee and required a long journey by bus. The main drawback for Tel Aviv students was that it was run by a Christian organisation. But this was no obstacle to the atheist Dr

Gutmann. Appreciative of good education, he was willing to face the heavy burden of tuition and extra expenses.

The school had been established by 29-year-old Jane Walker-Arnott, who had left Glasgow in 1863 for the Holy Land to escape the tyranny of her mother. It was named after Tabeetha, the good woman of Jaffa, who died tragically and was resurrected by Peter the Apostle. Originally, it had catered for deprived Arab girls of poor families, who were trained by Miss Walker-Arnott to be good, efficient maids and governesses. In 1914, some years after her death, the Church of Scotland took the school over and changed its approach, turning it into the best in Jaffa. In September 1941, when Assia Gutmann started her education at Tabeetha, only distinguished, wealthy Arab families could afford to send their daughters there. A column of smart chauffeured cars would stop each morning at the school's gates on the main street of Jaffa, dropping off the Arab girls in their school uniforms of pink dresses with blue sweaters. At lunchtime, maids would hurry with cooked lunches on a dinner tray. Assia commuted by bus all the way from Tel Aviv and at the lunch break had to make do with her mother's cold sandwiches.

Contrary to the prevailing attitude of both Jews and Arabs in Palestine, who wanted to see the British ousted, Tabeetha was loyal to the Empire and everything British; a recurrent conversation piece and role model among Tabeetha girls was the Royal Family, and more so because they were of the same age as Princess Elizabeth and Princess Margaret. A haven of Little Britain in the Middle East, the school had a British syllabus and the language of tuition was English. History lessons, as well as geography, literature and natural sciences, were all British oriented. 'We learned nothing about our own surroundings,' remembers former student Wedad Andreas, an Arab Christian. 'Even in maths, the exercises were given in pounds and shillings, and not in the monetary system we were using in the shops of Jaffa; likewise, we weighed ourselves in stones and not in kilos, which was the standard measure of Palestine. After all, we were being geared towards matriculation exams which were sent from London.'

Most girls attended Tabeetha from nursery school, getting accustomed to the English language and manners from a young age. Assia, who only joined at the ninth grade, was doubly deficient; not only did she have a background of just three years of English – three hours per week at Balfour Elementary – but her community frowned upon the tongue and customs of the foreign ruler.

Still, she mastered the language in no time and in later years impressed all with her rich vocabulary and impeccable accent, which gave no hint of her mixed background. Richard Lipsey, her second husband, remembers that Assia gave the credit to her English teacher at Tabeetha, a graduate of Cheltenham Ladies College. 'Assia emulated her adored teacher's manners and accent, and always quoted the teacher as expecting her to be one of the "crème de la crème".'

It was a Protestant school, so there were no nuns among the staff, but each morning began with a prayer, a hymn, and a reading from the New or Old Testament. In addition to the usual British syllabus and daily Scriptures lessons, the girls played tennis and netball, and danced to Scottish Highland music played on the school gramophone. They were taught some French, polished their English in decorous conversation, and were given piano lessons so that they would be able to entertain guests in their future salons. In drawing classes, much attention was paid to decorating Easter eggs and, in domestic science, they did embroidery and tapestry. There were no cookery classes, because the girls were certain to have a cook in their husbands' homes, and they only learned to bake cakes and delicate biscuits. The pupils sold their pastry and needlework at the annual bazaar and, at the end of each year, would stage a British classic, to an audience of parents, diplomats and dignitaries: in 1944, it was *A Midsummer Night's Dream*. There is no record of what role, if any, Assia Gutmann had in the play.

The graduates were not expected to continue to university but, rather, to be accomplished in graceful living, in everything that would serve them in their future social lives and their roles of perfect hostesses. 'Our goal was to find a good husband and raise a family, and already in the last year of school, many of us got engaged,' recalls former pupil Leila Andreas, Wedad's sister. 'The matriculation certificate was meant to enable us help our children in their homework.' Only a handful graduated and became career women, and those who did became nurses, teachers or secretaries; the Andreas sisters went on to university and became teachers at Tabeetha.

Assia stuck out at Tabeetha not only on account of her beauty, and as the only Jewish student at that time, but also because she was the most unruly of her classmates. The school prided itself that it 'habituates to discipline', and her teachers found it difficult to tame her. So did Dr Gutmann, who was himself drifting and not professionally focused; he did not guide Assia into any specific career or into acquiring any marketable skill. Her Tabeetha education fell into line with his vision of her as a grande dame, a society lady running a literary salon. Already at fifteen, Assia was destined to build her father's castles in the air and be her mother's knight in shining armour.

Tabeetha was to provide Assia Gutmann's basic education, equipping her with some solid fuel to last her throughout her short life. Ted Hughes had the impression that in order to become an Anglophile, she let go of her Russian, German and Israeli heritage. Britain was for the rootless and restless Assia a shining beacon, lighting the way in all her future wanderings. With the legacy of Tabeetha, Assia would write poetry and excel as a London copywriter, comfortably moving around in literary circles. The drawing classes developed her artistic taste, made manifest in her style of dressing and knack for home decorating. But as much as it shaped her, Tabeetha was also her drawback, since it nourished her fantasies, bedazzled her and filled her with illusions.

'All of a sudden, she began to speak English with a haughty, hot-potato accent. We laughed at it, mimicked her, and she looked at us con-temptuously,' her sister recalls. Assia's different curriculum and interests cut her off from her Jewish friends too, and she no longer felt part of their world and leisure activities. Their idea of fun was to volunteer to pick fruit on a kibbutz in the summer holidays, while Assia's was to sunbathe on the Tel Aviv beach.

She developed into a stunning young woman, for ever staring at her reflection in shop windows, sitting behind the bus driver to peek at his mirror and admire herself, savouring the looks coveting her beauty. Mira Hamermesh, the film-maker who later became a good friend, never forgot the sight of a stunning girl who stepped on a Tel Aviv bus, wrapped in a halo of crisp, fresh-smelling soap. The girl was wearing an off-the-shoulder, crisp, white cotton blouse, edged with black velvet, with a silver choker around her long neck, her brown hair hovering above her shoulders. A flowered velvet skirt with a tight belt hugged her waist, and Roman sandals encircled her ankles. She was carrying a leather shoulder bag in the shape of a bucket and was holding *Vogue* under her other arm. Like other Israeli teenagers at the time, Mira usually wore shorts, and was overwhelmed by this mysterious girl, who seemed to her the most beautiful and graceful creature she had seen outside a film. 'She was a cooked teenager, while I was raw, and when I came home, I told my sister that I had fallen in love with a girl, a total stranger, and I would do everything to see her again, and if not, at least to dress like her.' With a limited budget, Mira made a shirt of cheesecloth and sewed together some scarves to make a skirt. She drew the shape of the satchel from memory and sent her brother to look for one, but she could not find a choker.

During the Second World War, Palestine became an important strategic centre for over a hundred thousand British troops who were stationed in the Middle East. The seas, full of German mines and submarines, prevented them from travelling home on leave during the five years of the war, and Tel Aviv became their oasis. On their first long leave after a year, airman John Steele and his close friend, Keith Gems, made the 24-hour train journey from Cairo across the Sinai Desert to Tel Aviv. From there they planned to hitchhike up the coastal road to the snowy hilltops of Lebanon. The son of a banker at the Yorkshire Penny Bank, John Steele had left his home in Bromley to serve with the RAF. In April 1942 he was stationed in Port Taufik, in Egypt, servicing and refuelling flying boats in the marine craft section and picking up ditched flyers.

While Europe was in flames and Jews in the millions were being herded into ghettos and concentration camps, hundreds of thousands having already been shot dead over open pits in the woods near their towns and villages, Jews in Palestine enjoyed prosperity brought about by this same war. The number of cafés and restaurants in Tel Aviv soared to four hundred. 'Palestine seemed like paradise after the dirt and flies of Egypt,' remembers John Steele. 'It was all so cultured, so civilised. It is there that I discovered for the first time Wienerschnitzel and Apfelkuchen and, in the coffee shops facing the sea, you could sit for hours, leafing through British journals and newspapers, playing chess, while music was all around you. To this very day, every time I hear Mendelsohn's violin concerto, the memory of Café Nussbaum makes me mellow.' The two friends registered at the Forces Hostel near the beach, and for the first time in so many months, savoured a Pimms No.1. Fortified, they set off to see what the local Jewish hospitality committee had in store.

For two decades, the Jews in Palestine had clashed with His Majesty's Government over issues of sovereignty and the right of free immigration. Having Nazi Germany as their joint adversary changed the mood and policy from thorns to roses. 'Give a warm welcome to the army,' the Tel Aviv municipality appealed to the Tel Avivians in a huge Public Announcement Number 6 on 2 April 1940, which was plastered on barrel-shaped billboards all over town. 'We should make their stay among us as pleasant as possible. When they dine in our restaurants, we should serve them the best cuisine and beverages.' In the shops, the soldiers were to get extra-attentive service and the citizens were reminded that any misbehaviour would disgrace the entire town. 'Safeguard the honour and interests of our city, and help make it a magnet for visitors and tourists,' pleaded the mayor, Mr Israel Rokach.

The hospitality committee organised grand, lavish balls that attracted over a thousand officers and soldiers and the high society of Tel Aviv. The Ark, a Service Club Entertainment Centre on the sea front at 91 Hayarkon Street, had a restaurant, milk bar and a well-stocked library, and tickets were offered at reduced prices for concerts, opera and theatre. The soldiers could take a shower and have their clothes washed and ironed, while they were playing ping-pong, billiards, bridge, skittles, chess and darts. There were rackets and balls free of charge for tennis players and boats on the Yarkon River waited for those who preferred to row. Ladies volunteered to guide groups of soldiers on shopping sprees. In an attempt to round up support for the Zionist idea, there were organised trips across the country. Army doctors and nurses were shown around hospitals, engineers were put in touch with local Jewish colleagues, and soldiers, who had been teachers in their civil past, were taken to visit schools.

The Tel Aviv Hospitality Committee had a list of several hundred girls who volunteered for the tea dances every Wednesday at the San Remo Hotel. The admission fee of one shilling covered tea, cakes, cabaret and a dance band, which played from 5 to 7.15 p.m. But the most sought-after service was home-hospitality. Some 250 Jewish families opened their homes for tea and a chat, giving the soldiers a touch of family warmth in the midst of the rigours of war. Being shy, John Steele was reluctant to go, but Keith Gems insisted and, on one free afternoon, they registered. They were given a note with the address of the Gutmanns.

It was Lisa's idea, to have a fresh breeze from abroad to relieve her suffocation. She was not just seeking a chess rival for her husband and a chat partner for herself: welcoming soldiers could also be an insurance policy for rainy days of hostility towards German nationals. Moreover, she was devising ways to get her family out of Palestine. Assia was to be the spearhead. Her upper-crust education should enable her to pick up a uniformed groom, plant roots in England, and serve as the lever to bring her family over.

Four

A Teenager in Love

Tel Aviv, 1943–46

Not entirely confidently, John Steele and Keith Gems walked down Balfour Street towards the Gutmann home. The evening was still. Windows were open and sounds of live music seemed to pour from every house.

The two airmen were a little nervous about meeting Assia and Celia's parents but their apprehension quickly dissolved in the presence of their hosts. Lonya Gutmann regaled them with tales of adventure that conjured up fragrances of distant places. Indeed, all the Gutmanns' memories of life in Riga, Moscow, Berlin and Pisa held the two young men, who had never left England before the war, riveted. 'Dr Gutmann looked like Sigmund Freud,' recalls Keith Gems. 'He was caged in his own iron discipline, his Russian soul hidden somewhere, I suppose. Mrs Gutmann was tall, strong, full but not fat. She was bound by her Germanic discipline, obeyed her husband without question, kept an immaculate house, and cooked copiously. I remember her German cakes – very plain to look at, with different colours of layered mixtures. They were delicious.'

They had all been chatting in the living room while they waited for Assia to put on her final touches and make her grand entrance. The two airmen were spared any duel over her, however, since Gems found Assia 'cold, calculating, and ill at ease'. He preferred the fourteen-year-old Celia, who seemed to him 'warm, energetic in her blue denim shorts'. On his bed back at the Forces Hostel, the enamoured 21-year-old Sergeant John Steele wrote in his marbled blue diary: 'Assia was but 16, but coupled with a schoolgirl innocence, she had a well-developed figure, and an exceedingly pretty face. I was definitely struck, and on finding she liked music, quickly monopolised her the whole time.' For Assia, Steele embodied her image of the ideal Englishman: middle-class, public-school, tall and, on top of that, he resembled her favourite film star, George Sanders.

The Gutmann girls enchanted Steele and Gems enough for them to cancel the trip to Lebanon. Instead, they spent their entire leave in Tel Aviv. Before returning to their base in Port Taufik, the soldiers received an open invitation to visit the Gutmanns in Tel Aviv as often as they wished.

The following week, a smitten John Steele squeezed in an extra leave – no matter the tedious 24-hour journey from Egypt to Tel Aviv – so that he could again see Assia. He picked her up at the Gutmanns' flat and they then strolled along the shore until they found a secluded spot. They spoke very little. Girls made Steele feel awkward and he was ill at ease in Assia's company: 'My parents had no friends with daughters my age, and I would have been expelled if found with a girl at school,' he recalls. 'After my schooling as a boarder in an English public school from age 13 to 18, and almost immediately transferred to the military and overseas posting, one can imagine how inexperienced I was in this my first encounter with the female sex.'

Steele did gain a bit more experience that afternoon on the beach, when Assia removed her dress and, clad in a bathing costume, lay basking in the sun. Later that night John Steele jotted down the events of their day together: '"May I kiss you, Assia?" There was a long, pregnant silence. Then she took my hand and pressed it tearfully to her face. We lay there. The only sound was the gentle lapping of the surf on shore. "I think I want to cry . . . nobody has wanted to kiss me before . . . I'm only sixteen." These, and other broken sentences, she whispered to me as we lay there. Time seemed to stand still.' Although she was five years his junior, it was the more dominant Assia who took the lead.

As evening set in, Assia donned her clothes and the two of them climbed to the top of a precarious cliff, where they watched the sun go down. On their way back to town they kept off the main streets, as Assia's fear of scandal was acute. They turned into a tree-lined boulevard and sat on a bench. Steele felt as if he was playing the leading man in a romantic movie. '"You may kiss me, John . . . May I whisper something? . . . I love you," she said.'

Assia was no exception in dating a British soldier; many Jewish girls were attracted to the men in uniforms. Tel Aviv was bustling with activity, wartime having made it a vital, international city. In the course of a short stroll on the promenade, a girl could meet robust Australians, sun-tanned Greeks, blond and blue-eyed Poles and, most of all, tall English servicemen. 'They all behaved like perfect gentlemen,' remembers Hannah Weinberg-Shalitt, a friend whom she had met at the Ark. 'They asked permission for a goodnight kiss and were good at courting, something that the rough, arrogant Israeli men were lacking. They were good dancers, and had the money to spend on a drink, a cinema ticket, a meal and a small gift; all the indulgences that our boys couldn't afford. The girls were caught in the middle; the British were cross that they were losing their fine men to us, and our people were furious that the most beautiful girls preferred soldiers.'

Assia's father was very cold towards his favourite daughter's suitor. 'But the Mrs was all over me,' recalls Steele. For he had already sensed that Lisa Gutmann had formulated a plan by which she would use his infatuation with her daughter to get the family out of Palestine. He, though, was not so sure that he was ready to commit himself. As for Assia, while she clearly enjoyed casting herself as the heroine of her own romantic novel or film, she was far from being head over heels in love with John.

The film soon became a war movie. After Italy dropped out of the war, Steele was assigned to a pinnace carrying a platoon of soldiers to the Greek island of Kastellorizon, which the British planned to occupy. The Germans promptly reacted and the bombarded British retreated. In the fray Steele's boat was damaged by the dive-bombing and machine-gun fire. For two months Assia knew nothing of his whereabouts. 'I have imagined the worst, so nothing would surprise me, but it is still harder and most unpleasant to stay in doubt, and not be sure of anything,' a worried Assia wrote to Keith Gems on 18 November 1943. The tone of the letter, essentially an inquiry into the reason for John's silence, does not suggest alarm over the destiny of one's beloved but rather concern for an acquaintance. The letter may also have been an attempt by Assia to secure Gems as her other English option, should Steele have been lost. In any case, Gems passed the message on to Steele, who resumed his correspondence with Assia.

Lisa Gutmann did not place her hopes on Steele alone. Casting her net wider, she regularly invited Allied soldiers over for cakes and tea. There was a constant parade of British, Canadian, Australian and South African servicemen to the small flat. She pressed her daughters to perfect their English-language skills and further familiarise themselves with English culture. Assia complained to Gems, who by now had become her intimate confidante, that her mother had urged her to finish reading *The History of England* by Andre Maurois: 'Instead, I read *The Adventures of Tom Sawyer* and *The Life of Huckleberry Finn*. Great fun, great fun. It makes one regret having been born a girl.' She took a special preparation course for the London Matriculation exams. ('I am very doubtful about Maths, though. The language and literature were all cakes.')

Assia's parents also tried to impose the morals and etiquette of Old Europe upon her. They questioned her every move and demanded to know the purpose of her every visit to the shops or even to the library. 'They remember exactly how young ladies behaved 40 years ago. The war doesn't seem to have changed their ideas,' she fretted to Gems. It had changed Assia's. Once she'd finished her exams, she could finally attend to having some fun and she turned the service club into her second home. She bore no real loyalty to Steele. There was little passion in their relationship and, whatever its spark, it was not strong enough to survive their geographical distance, the disrupted postal services and his rare leaves.

Nearly every evening Assia went out partying. She did not drink and was not fond of dancing – in fact, she moved rather ungracefully – but invariably she was surrounded by men who enjoyed engaging her in animated conversation. When she wished to spend a whole night out, she would tell her parents that she was staying with her friend Hannah Weinberg-Shalitt. 'We were living in a very conservative society, but Assia, with a dare-devil laugh, defied rules and exploited opportunities. I was very naïve, and I admired her for her courage, and could not refuse to cover up for her. She knew how to manipulate people, without making them feel exploited.'

Dating was unthinkable for a Tabeetha girl. It was considered to be totally improper, punishable by the parents and reprimanded by the teachers. Among Tabeetha graduates of the 1940s, the story still circulates about the alarmed Jewish parents who begged the headmistress to help them find their daughter: the girl had failed to return home from a date with a soldier. For the first time in her life, the headmistress found herself, despite profound aversion, visiting the bars and clubs of Tel Aviv in her search for the prodigal daughter. The stray sheep was never named, but all her schoolmates agree – it could only have been Assia. Concerned about their daughter's reputation, the Gutmanns were especially wary of her friendship with another girl accustomed to hanging around with the Tel Aviv smart set. 'My parents don't want me to take part in it,' Assia wrote to Gems on 30 January 1944. 'I will, though. It's fun. And the people I meet are more broadminded, and are intellectuals. Still, I'm going to get my freedom through evolution.' Nonetheless, Assia was not frivolous, and if behaviour on the racy party scene descended towards the dissolute, she would sneak quietly to the cloakroom, collect her bag and go home. 'I began to wonder whether these are first signs (of their kind) of deterioration of mankind,' she concluded.

Assia's letters to Gems, written in perfect English, convey a confident, optimistic, witty girl, a girl full of laughter as well as self-irony, whose observations reflect an insight beyond her years. She appreciated and enjoyed the way words work and, as she would come upon a clever pun or some hilarious mistranslation, she would write it down in her copybook. She was especially amused by a ludicrous notice declaring the freshness of the products at a butcher's shop. The translation in English read: 'Butcher, kills himself every morning.' Wishing to enlarge her linguistic repertoire, she asked Keith to send her a dictionary of RAF jargon. She was disappointed with the booklet, which was neither precise nor comprehensive enough to meet her expectations.

In spring 1944 John Steele was transferred to Palestine and stationed in the Ein Shemer camp, just an hour's drive from Tel Aviv. As a meteorologist, he was able to work a number of nightshifts in a row so that he could get a few days off to spend with Assia: 'lots of walks and snuggles on benches'. And Café Nussbaum became a regular haunt. They applauded the Palestine Philharmonic Orchestra playing Dvorak's *New World Symphony*. At the cinema they were moved to tears by *For Whom the Bell Tolls* and *Un Grand Amour de Beethoven,* a 1936 French film about Assia's favourite composer. Lena Horne, though, was her idol; Assia was captivated by her dark, beautiful face and seductively husky voice.

Steele realised that his renewed presence at the Gutmanns' home had meanwhile become a red rag to a bull. 'Dr Gutmann got very tired of this uniformed Man Who Came to Dinner, with designs on his daughter. He made all sort of dirty cracks, and I'm sure, wished me far away.' Adding to Steele's discomfiture and bewilderment, was the fact, according to Assia, that her mother was in love with him. So as not to annoy the host, Steele decided to stop going to the Gutmanns' for lunch. It was a decision Lisa could not entirely accept. Her solution was to make a sumptuous picnic lunch for Assia and John to eat under the trees in the back yard. She confessed to John that her husband was jealous because she had 'robbed him so completely of his wife and daughter's affection', Steele recalls.

Rarely did Assia and John let politics come between them but, on one occasion, Assia indignantly compared the British activities in Palestine to those of the Nazi Gestapo. At first Steele was shocked. 'But I was bound to admit that the whole Palestine affair is rather a black page in English history.' Assia's words, though, continued to affect him. On one of his trips to Tel Aviv Steele hitched a ride on a bomber from a nearby RAF base. As he sat in the nose of the aircraft and gazed at the world beneath, he saw the brown, monotonous wilderness, lifeless and forbidding, suddenly change into a fertile green. 'The Jewish homeland! I think at that moment I became something of a Zionist, it was all so crystal clear that the land should belong to those who would work it. And while since then I may have lost some of my youthful naïveté, I see it as a life-long inoculation against anti-Semitism.'

The affair between Assia and Steele often went sour. They had squabbles; accusing each other of not loving enough and often he'd vowed to break it all off. Independent of John, Assia's social life was blossoming, and he knew that she was dating others. He knew that she was being courted by a variety of glamorous officers who, unlike a sergeant in the RAF, could open the doors to many of the places in town that Assia wanted to go. And Assia was absolutely delighted when one of them – an Australian officer, John Lefebure, who served with Steele at the Ein Shemer base – took her up in a plane. Lefebure captured Assia's heart and they would date regularly when Steele was on duty. In her photo album, under the photo of the tall, handsome Lefebure, Assia wrote the words 'Amour Blue'. Nor did she spare Steele the details. 'It irritates me to hear the catalogues of the times they had together, the things they do that I so desperately want to do, like going on moonlit bathes, visiting dances and fairs, that always come off when I'm on duty,' Steele complained to his diary. As would all of Assia's future lovers, Steele swallowed his injured pride while he strove to tolerate, and even justify, the presence of other men in her life. 'I never did blame her for seeking more privileged company, although she probably got spoiled by all the attention.'

Christmas in Tel Aviv was a defiantly ordinary working day, with no festive atmosphere. The stores were open, people went to work, and passengers filled the buses. But the Gutmanns celebrated the holiday to the hilt and Lisa cooked an English turkey with all the trimmings. She and Celia presented Steele with a hardcover edition of Dostoevsky's *Crime and Punishment*; Assia gave him Tolstoy's *War and Peace*. That Dr Gutmann chose to ignore him in the gift giving irritated Steele a bit. The two hardcover Russian novels survived Steele's kit bag and the war; both now stand like honoured veterans on the bookshelf in Steele's home. The front pages of *War and Peace* did suffer one injury, but not in the war: years later Steele's second wife tore out the front page, which bore Assia's inscription.

'The 1940s in Palestine and in England were prudish times, scarcely believable today,' Steele recalls. 'The kind of "shacking up" without benefit of clergy was almost unknown in my recollection. Sex between Assia and me was surreptitious, hole-in-the-corner, fumbling gropes.' Even the most innocent associations between British soldiers and Israeli girls were discouraged, however. Before the end of 1944, more than three hundred girls had already 'left their nation and country, some of them even their religion', as one Hebrew newspaper indignantly reported. While one arm of the Tel Aviv municipality was embracing the foreigners in uniform, the other was pushing them away. Fearful that Jewish girls would marry out of their faith, the Committee for the Defence of the Honour of Daughters of Israel, which was sponsored by the Religious Council of the Tel Aviv municipality, published leaflets denouncing girls who dated British soldiers and policemen. Armed with details of the girls' misconduct, emissaries of the committee pressured them to break off their relationships with the foreigners. If that failed to alter the girls' behaviour, the committee visited the parents with the threat of having their daughter's name displayed on billboards throughout the city.

The threats and pressure were not only verbal. A fanatical, secret fringe organisation named B'nei Pinhas (Sons of Pinhas) followed the teachings of the biblical High Priest Pinhas Ben Elazar, who famously advocated the eradication of sexual promiscuity by violent means. His twentieth-century counterparts would ambush and kidnap an allegedly wayward girl, then tie her to a tree and either shave off her hair or smear her with tar. The activities of these zealots, in turn, prompted common hoodlums to hound couples in the streets and on the beach. They routinely beat up soldiers and drove their tearful girlfriends away. Soldiers on leave were frequently harassed and often wounded in fistfights as they left pubs and dance halls. Shocked by the conduct of the hoodlums and the B'nei Pinhas, the distinguished novelist Yehuda Burla publicly denounced it in an article in the *Hazman (The Times)* newspaper: 'While Britain is engaged in a war against the most savage enemy of the Jewish people, these unsightly acts of violence might portend disastrous results for our reputation, our country and our future. Instead of nourishing some friendship and sympathy for us among the Allies, we cause exactly the opposite.'

Soon after V-Day, in May 1945, Steele was unexpectedly posted to the Libyan Desert, without a chance even to bid Assia farewell. There were no tears and, since they had not discussed a joint future, Steele never expected to see her again. In January 1946 he was discharged and returned to England. Assia tried to keep up their correspondence, but her letters to him went unanswered.

With the Second World War over, the Jewish underground factions renewed their anti-British activities, especially their protests against His Majesty's Government policy to keep out and expel Holocaust survivors who wished to settle in Palestine. At night the Municipal Public Health Centre, which was only a few doors away from the Gutmanns' home, became a training centre for the Haganah, the military wing of the Jewish Agency. Like many of her generation, Assia took the courses in small arms, field training, first aid, radio communications and self-defence. Lisa Gutmann disapproved; she did not wish her daughter to get involved in any illegal and dangerous activities. Ever since they had settled in Tel Aviv, the Gutmanns had been trying to stand aside and not get involved in local politics, a feat that was becoming impossible under the current circumstances. On one occasion, they were startled by a banging on their door and, when a wounded British soldier burst in, they were nonplussed. 'You must hide me, or else they'll kill me,' the soldier whispered. Apparently, he was running away from the squad of a Jewish underground organisation. Dr Gutmann was horrified. 'As a physician, and a man of conscience, he had to rescue a man from death. On the other hand, he didn't want to be counted a traitor,' recalls Celia Chaikin. 'So Vati took the middle road, kept the soldier for half an hour, and then asked him to leave. Fortunately it was long enough to save the soldier's life.'

Since her graduation Assia had been supporting herself with odd secretarial jobs and was taking evening drawing classes at the studio of a prominent Israeli artist. She was doing 'a lot of drawings, still-life, portraits of impossibly plain girls, in whom we are supposed to find beauty, Yemenite charwomen, and squalid and bearded old men.' She had also begun to feel less and less patriotic as the Jewish underground organisations had intensified their campaign to drive out the British by attacking their bases, offices, and personnel: 'We feel like frightful heroes, and think the world is a wretched place.'

Mixed couples, too, were now being more actively targeted by the underground zealots. Being seen with a soldier 'is sheer suicide . . . People here think it is high time for me to change my ways. How dare I, in those days of great National rebirth, associate with non Jewish people, and thus "expose" myself to an ever increasing danger of complete assimilation,' Assia wrote to Gems. Any girl who was 'sleeping with the enemy' was deemed to be a collaborator, a potential traitor who might pass on secrets to her foreign friends. In some cases, the girls were court-martialled for fraternisation, forced to sign a confession and executed. Assia, though, was fearless. Defiantly she threw away the hate mail and threatening notes that strangers handed her in the streets. Yet life in Tel Aviv was becoming close to being totally unbearable for her: most of her soldier friends had left for England, as had some of her girlfriends. 'It is all so disgusting, and so much like Fascism, that I want to cry. You will be surprised to find Tel Aviv so literally changed, the pleasant, sunny, fairly hospitable little town has completely vanished,' she wrote to Gems on 21 May 1946.

The Hebrew press launched a campaign to deter Jewish girls from following their demobilised boyfriends back to England. Moshe Medzini, the *Ha'aretz* correspondent in London, reported that twenty Jewish women, who had married soldiers, had already appealed to the Jewish Agency in London for assistance to return to Palestine. The actual number was estimated to be much higher. In one case, the Hebrew press reported, British in-laws forbade their son's young wife from using the living room and they introduced her to relatives and friends as the maid. The newspapers were filled with similarly horrific stories, like that of 27-year-old Maria Atkins, who was stranded in London with her baby son when her husband left her for another woman. Cleaning houses but still unable to support herself and the child, Maria gassed them both. The nine-month-old baby died. The bereaved mother survived and was put on trial for manslaughter.

The Gutmann mother and daughter paid no heed to these horror stories, however. 'For God sake, tell me why you never write? Even if you wanted to stop, why didn't you let me know?' an exasperated Assia wrote to Steele. But it was neither friendship nor romance that Assia was looking for with Steele. What she wanted was his help in finding a place for her in one of the London art schools. 'Friendless, miserable and lonely, this is the only thing I'm looking forward to,' she wrote to him and assured him that he need not worry – she was not trying to impose herself upon him: 'If your feelings have changed – I shall always try and understand.' If she came to England in September as she hoped and planned, she promised, 'I shall never call on you or ring you up, unless you want me to.' Lisa Gutmann was no less offended than her daughter by Steele's withdrawal and, without Assia's knowledge, sent a letter to him via Keith Gems. 'I can't understand what happened with you. You get Asja [*sic*] absolute down. That girl is waiting and waiting for a letter from you, and every day this is disappointment,' she wrote in her Germanic English. 'I didn't think you would forget us so quick.'

In June, on her own merits and with no help from Steele, Assia was admitted to the Regent Street Polytechnic School of Art and began preparing for her trip. She planned to study art and interior decorating, 'so that I shall end up with painting lampshades and china,' she noted ironically. Her parents agreed to finance her trip to London, but not because they were committed to or even interested in her artistic promise. They were sending her to London expressly to find, and to marry, Steele, thereby acquiring the British passport by which she could in turn bring her family to England. It was the only way, given the immigration restrictions, that the Gutmanns could get there from Palestine.

On Monday, 22 July 1946, Assia took a day off and travelled to Jerusalem to apply for a passport. There, she chanced upon a friend who invited her to a café next to the luxurious King David Hotel. The southern wing of the hotel had been requisitioned to house the offices of the Secretariat of the Palestine Government and the British Army Headquarters. At about eleven o'clock, six members of the Jewish underground organisation IZL, disguised as Arab porters, carried seven churns of milk, each containing fifty kilograms of explosives, into the basement of the hotel. They placed the churns in the food storeroom and then slipped away. Twenty-five minutes later, in the middle of Assia's coffee date, a shattering explosion was heard. Assia saw all seven floors of the deluxe hotel's southern wing tumble down into clouds of dust. The death toll was enormous: 92 dead, 58 injured. The disaster only strengthened Dr Gutmann's conviction that there would never be peace in the Holy Land and that his family must get out of Palestine as soon as possible.

Twelve years in Palestine had failed to create a Jewish identity for Assia and throughout her life she had no strong feelings about her Jewish heritage one way or the other. In September 1946, with her faith in the future, Assia took the train to Port Said, where she boarded the ship to England. She never again set foot in Tel Aviv.

Five

First Marriage

London, 1946–Vancouver, 1952

The SS *Andes* was launched in 1939 as the flagship of the Royal Mail Line, but this splendid passenger ship made no more than a few cruises before the war effort had it converted into a troop carrier. Six years later, with the war over, it carried British servicemen to their families back home. Decorated with the royal crest, the SS *Andes* seemed to Assia a step towards glory. Emerging from her stifling cabin on the lower deck, she adopted the airs of a lady accustomed to a floating grand hotel, a kind she had only seen in films. Promenading on the upper deck, she looked fresh and well groomed, while most of the passengers were wind-blown or seasick. Men were falling for her, showering her with tokens of attentiveness. 'She was like a goddess, the belle of the ball, and her attractiveness had less to do with her striking good looks, than with her personality,' observed Mira Hamermesh, as she recognised the beautiful stranger from the Tel Aviv bus. 'She gave the impression of a girl with everything in store for her.' They sunbathed together in shorts on the upper deck and discussed their plans in a mixture of English and Hebrew. Apparently, both of them were heading for art schools in London: Mira to the Slade, Assia to the Polytechnic. John Steele's name and existence were not mentioned.

On a foggy autumn morning they docked in Liverpool, and Assia and Mira took the train to London. Mira's cousin was waiting for her but there was no welcome party for Assia, since she had not notified Steele. In the weeks that followed, Mira found it difficult to fit into her friend's busy schedule. There was one brief tête-à-tête they had during which Assia fancied a choker that Mira was wearing and talked her into lending it to her for a grand party she had been invited to. The following day Assia vanished and Mira never saw her favourite piece of jewellery again. 'She was like a mythical creature, emerging from nowhere and dissolving into thin air once you tried to touch it.' Although a full-time art student, Assia preferred the shops and the pavements of Oxford Street to the confined classrooms of the nearby Polytechnic. She wandered about London in a daze; she had always dreamt of such magnificence and her visions were suffused with her father's tales of the marble palaces of Moscow and her own memories of the glittering avenues of Berlin. Tabeetha had groomed her perfectly for that kind of life and the sites seemed as familiar as if she had been born there.

From her daughter's letters home, Lisa Gutmann realised that Assia had not established contact with John Steele. She was exasperated and grumbled to Celia that she had not sent Assia to England in order to spend the little money they had on treats and pleasures. She ordered Assia to either marry Steele, or return home immediately. But going back to Palestine was out of the question for Assia; she would never return to a place she considered a dungeon. Once out, she would not lock herself in again. Celebrating her independence from the bonds of her mother's tyranny, Assia played for time and when the ultimatum was not lifted she pleaded for mercy; she could not be coerced into a union that held no affection, no passion, no compatibility and no future.

A year and a half had passed since Assia and John last saw each other and it had been quite some time since their correspondence had come to an end. Steele was living at his parents' home in Shortlands, Kent, and was working in London as a government-sponsored trainee under a resettlement plan for veterans. He passed daily over London Bridge, in the great jostling black-clad throng of workers, on the way to his office at Alexander Young Ltd, a subsidiary of the conglomerate Mitchell Cotts. In the bleak old building, surrounded by rubble and bombsites and never properly heated, Steele was bored to death writing letters about shipments of lavatories to Bombay.

In spite of the deep selfish streak in Assia, she could not harden her heart against her family and eventually she wrote to Steele. She later confided to Keith Gems that she did it only because her parents had appealed to her to save them: 'In a family ruled by iron discipline, she had no option, and had to sacrifice herself.' Steele was surprised, and although he was dating other girls, he was won over in a flash. 'She has decided she loves me again, and as time does nothing to alter my feelings, we have the basis of happiness anyway. I think we shall cope all right,' he broke the news to Gems. Within days they got engaged. 'Assia and I want to get hitched fairly soon. I think we have waited quite long enough,' he wrote to Gems. He thought that Assia was not mature enough for marriage, 'but I gamble that she would change as she grows up.' Steele was so perplexed and so unsure of Assia's place in his life that he made a curious slip, describing Assia to Gems as 'that fiancée of yours'. He crossed out 'yours', replaced it with 'mine', and then, in brackets, scoffed at himself with the word 'Freud!!!' as if he could not believe he was really heading towards marrying her. Gems thought that John and Assia were an unlikely pair. 'But I was glad for him,' he recalls, 'because he was never any good with girls, and here he was, in love and infatuated. He wasn't much of a Romeo, so I thought: bully for him!'

With the propriety of marriage in view, Assia and John went to bed for the first time. The occasion was laden with anxiety and Steele urged Gems to send him an 'anti-Chico mixture [some abortion-inducing liquid] and also any other abortive measures you know or can find out about.' In the following month Assia's period failed to arrive, she had morning sickness, and John foresaw a disaster: 'I saw myself losing all my money over an abortion, and then, impoverished, marrying a cripple.' After three nerve-racking weeks they breathed a huge sigh of relief. Evidently, it was a false alarm and they decided to quit sex until the wedding, when they would get 'all possible help from the clinic'.

Assia remained carefree and independent and John was annoyed that she was too friendly to all and sundry, and so eager to cultivate as many friends as possible: 'Any man has only to see Assia, with or without me, to try to get off with her . . . I go through all sorts of private hells at the thought of losing her.' On the evenings he was unable to take her out, Assia nevertheless went off on her own. John had an urge to keep her confined and locked up 'in a gilded cage', but admitted she was playing fair with him, stopping short of romantic dates. He decided to subdue his jealousy and trust her, especially since her manner of 'friendly affection' towards him was not affected. It did not escape John Steele that Assia had been driven into marriage in order to get her family into England but he could not harden his heart to her parents' predicament, nor could he send Assia back to a life she loathed in a country she hated: 'Yet, I cannot wait, for Assia's money is running out, and I have to marry her as surely as if she was holding an unborn offspring at my head like a pistol.' There were moments when he wished Assia would vanish from his life altogether, when he regretted that he had ever got to know her. But just a day or two without her and he would 'moan like a schoolboy'; he couldn't cope and felt that if he didn't marry her life would be 'a far worse hell'.

They set the date to be married in May and Steele asked Keith Gems to be the best man to a 'clueless groom', who was marrying 'a dizzy bride'. Steele's parents and two sisters found Assia a strange, exotic plant. His father, a quiet, witty man, was so glad to see his only son emerge unharmed from the war, that he accepted the bride and supported him in his 'folly' with little comment. Deep down Assia hoped for a miracle that would save her from marriage but the money she got from her parents was running out and she could not find a job, so she resigned herself to her fate. Like a child holding a bunch of colourful balloons, she saw her fantasies vanish one by one: the expensive car, the service flat in Kensington and a life of leisure and luxury. Steele was aware of her dreams and was pleased that she was relinquishing them: 'God bless her,' he wrote to Keith Gems, 'she's actually facing up to it – and we'll, my dearest friend, go forward together arm in arm and cheek to cheek.' All this while, Assia had no idea that her future husband had already decided – indeed, he had told all his friends – that he was determined 'to get out of this wretched isle' as soon as he possibly could, and settle in South Africa for good. Had she known that he intended to emigrate, it might have provided her with the excuse to cancel the wedding.

They decided to spend the last weekend of their bachelorhood apart and travelled in opposite directions: John Steele to Bournemouth and Assia Gutmann to Oxford. Five days before the wedding, Steele confessed to Keith Gems that neither he nor Assia had any colossal light of happiness in their eyes. 'Assia is a bit peculiar lately, she wants to marry me but she seems to be thinking herself into a peculiar state of indecision, she says she can never leave me, but she doesn't really like the thought of being married as an absolute state.' Nevertheless, Steele tried to convince himself: 'It'll all work out . . . we'll both be happy.'

The marriage was solemnised at the register office in Hampstead, at noon on Saturday, 17 May 1947, two days after Assia's twentieth birthday. In the register office, Assia stated her occupation as an art student, living at 6a Primrose Hill Road, NW5. Her small room overlooked the lush green park of Primrose Hill, with a breathtaking view of London. She would return to her adored area and live there in the 1960s, the most turbulent years of her life. In a time of austerity, a white wedding was an excessive luxury, so the bride wore a severe black suit, very tailored and chic, with a calf-length skirt, and a white, off-the-face hat, which gave a halo effect. She had no relatives in London, so with Steele's family and friends they had a wedding lunch at the smart restaurant of the Berkeley Hotel, where they spent the wedding night as well. Reluctantly, they relinquished their former idea of an expensive honeymoon in Switzerland and instead settled for Lake Windermere. On a postcard, Assia wrote to Keith, 'if this is paradise, I'll see no more', though she was probably referring to the beautiful scenery.

The young couple moved to a self-contained flat in Purley, south of London, where they shared the household chores. 'We are being surprisingly temperate in bed, but I'm still tired out,' Steele reported to Keith Gems a month after the wedding. 'I find now, I've always had a frustrated longing to chat, argue and hold forth in bed, and we do so until too bloody late every night.' Assia cut short her art studies and the boredom and loneliness of suburban life, with John away in his office, took their toll. What was left of her fantasies of a sophisticated literary salon and a life of indulgence and luxury was replaced by a mundane, boring existence with her clerk of a husband who was exhausted from commuting daily to the City. She had dreamt of splendour but was stuck with shabbiness.

With Assia away in London, the Gutmanns in Tel Aviv managed somewhat to ease their financial straits by letting her room to a nurse, who also paid for the meals that Lisa cooked for her. Winds of war between the Jews and the Arabs were blowing at full strength again and Dr Gutmann felt the earth shaking beneath his feet. Too impatient to wait for the longed-for visa to Britain that Assia was supposed to get for her family, he hit the road in the autumn of 1947. In his wallet, he put Celia's radiant photograph, inscribed on the back: 'To my darling father, who left his girl behind, all the best of luck, and keep smiling.' South Africa was a popular destination, since its prime minister, General Jan Smuts, was very welcoming towards Jewish refugees. It was supposed to serve as Dr Gutmann's temporary shelter until he had made enough money to move his family to London. But a few months after Gutmann's arrival, Smuts lost the premiership, and the National Party with its blatantly anti-Jewish policy came to power. Gutmann, who was wary of historical upheavals and always prepared for the worst, hastily packed his few belongings again and moved to the neighbouring Lourenço Marques, the Portuguese colony in Mozambique which had a large immigrant Jewish community.

First Marriage

When her husband left for South Africa, the rent for their three-room flat became too much for just Lisa and Celia and another refugee doctor took it over. Fourteen years previously, the Gutmanns had left Germany very much against their will and had reluctantly dismantled their home in order to replant it in a barren new land; now they were glad to go. Disillusioned, with a bitter sense of failure, Lisa Gutmann wished to be relieved of the burden of the past. With the high cost of shipment in mind, she sold their precious, heavy furniture and most of the household utensils that they had so lovingly brought with them from Berlin. She could not join her husband in Mozambique and aired her distress in her correspondence with British army veterans, who had been frequent guests at her home. One of them suggested that she be his family's housekeeper, thus qualifying her for an entry visa. In retrospect, Assia's marriage to Steele was unnecessary; her parents extracted themselves from Palestine without her assistance.

The young Steeles were in financial straits: Assia was not working, and John, at 25, was restless and fed up with the plumbing business. To top it all, 'Assia was being difficult. There was considerable evidence of making up to men, of deceit, lies and strange absences,' Steele recalls. His hope that marriage would put an end to Assia's behaviour was shattered. Assia complained to Pam Gems, Keith's newly wedded wife that John was 'cold, unkind and repulsive' and she could not bear him, finding it difficult even to sleep in the same bed with him. 'I told her she must leave him, but she had no money, and nobody else in England,' Pam remembers. Returning from a visit to an old schoolfriend who had emigrated to Vancouver and been very successful, Steele's father encouraged his son to move there as well and offered to cover the travel expenses. Without consulting Assia, John bought two tickets to Canada, hoping that a change of scene would also help the marriage. It was during a holiday on the Isle of Wight, as guests of Keith's parents, that Assia heard for the first time that she was soon to leave England. Shocked and outraged, she swallowed fifty aspirins. A good pumping at the hospital left her with deafness that passed after only a few days. 'She was a woman with intellectual aspirations, immersed in books. Leaving Europe, with all its delightful decadence, and settling in Canada, which meant intellectual death for her, was something Assia could not bear,' explains Keith Gems.

In April 1948, John and Assia Steele left England for New York on the Holland–America liner *Veendam*, then continued by train to Toronto, and across the grand sweep of Canada to Vancouver. A short while after Assia's departure, her mother arrived in England and started a job as housekeeper in Ramsgate. Seeing her own future in the newly established state of Israel, the eighteen-year-old Celia insisted on doing her military duty. With her mother gone, Celia became virtually homeless and became an unhappy lodger in rented rooms during her leaves from the army. In the spring of 1948, therefore, the Gutmann family was scattered across four continents: Dr Gutmann a doctor in Mozambique, Lisa Gutmann a housekeeper in England, Celia a soldier in the Israeli army and Assia a manual worker in Canada. Two years would pass before they would all be reunited.

Assia and John lived in a series of tiny apartments and old houses, disappointed that in spite of their monumental upheaval, the only job John could find was that of a low-paid bank clerk. An acquaintance talked him into selling books and magazines from door to door. Assia was reduced to being a chambermaid, and later a hat-check girl in The Cave nightclub. It was hardly a reassuring prospect for an increasingly jealous husband, who was working late most evenings. She moved on to modelling furs, then, as she wrote to Gems, to working as a 'secretary for a local radio producer and a mad actress, with whom [she] became very pally, and from whom [she] got hardly any salary at all.' She showed a remarkable talent for fitting in and meeting people, and used to drag Steele with her on outings with local celebrities she happened to meet. Riding on a bus, she struck up an acquaintance with an elderly gentleman, who turned out to be a reporter for the *Vancouver Sun*. It resulted in an interview with John Steele about the difficulties of post-war immigration to Canada.

But the change of place did not restore their marriage and John was exasperated, admitting that Assia's voltage was much too high for him; helplessly, he watched her restless dependence on the overtures she received from other men. 'How much was entirely sexual – I don't know. My experience was that she was frigid in bed, but how much this was due to my own youthful ineptness – I don't know,' he says. In January 1949, the Steeles once again tried to escape their financial and matrimonial problems by moving to the town of Victoria, on Vancouver Island. John continued his door-to-door book selling, this time with considerable financial success. His job involved much travelling and absences and he installed Assia at the Cherry Bank Hotel, at off-season rates. Assia made herself known to Sarah Spencer, a grande dame of Victoria society, a department store heiress with a penchant for the arts. Assia impressed her so much that soon she became the receptionist and sole employee of the newly established Art Gallery of Greater Victoria. In that small front-of-shop undertaking, Assia met the cream of Victoria society. The experience would later prove useful for the girl from Tel Aviv in getting involved in literary London.

Assia's move to British Columbia determined her family's fate for the worse. Dr Gutmann would have enjoyed England much better and would have benefited professionally and culturally but, once his beloved daughter was no longer in London, he had no option but to follow her. One by one the family arrived in Canada. Dr Gutmann landed in Vancouver, his trunks full of typical African souvenirs: hippopotamus skin canes and small black wooden statues. His wife soon followed from England. Celia wanted to stay in Israel but her parents put their foot down and forbade her to live on her own in what they perceived as a war zone. The enforced move to Canada caused constant friction between the sisters.

In the summer of 1949, John Steele decided to change career and become a teacher. He and Assia moved back to Vancouver and lived on the top floor of an old converted house in Cambie Street, near to the Gutmanns in the centre of town. The flats were so close together that they rigged a means of communication between them. Steele took a one-year course, in a special post-war emergency programme, designed to remedy the shortage of teachers. He enjoyed his studies and 'found some consolation among the horde of young women students for the neglect and evasions of Assia.' Then, one day they had 'a bit of a fight', and he moved out. The agreement to separate was mutual and civilised.

The only possible grounds for divorce in British Columbia at that time was adultery, which created a boom for lawyers and professional co-respondents. Steele, who agreed to play the guilty party, was instructed to go to a hotel, book a room and wait in the lobby for a lady that his lawyers would supply. They nodded to each other and went up to the room; he took off his jacket, she her dress, and they lay down on the bed. 'We never touched or exchanged names. Then in came a pair of investigators: "What's all this then!" Maybe they took a photo, and the theatrical scene came to an end. Never saw the lady again.' It was an uncontested divorce and, since neither owned property nor had capital, no financial support was asked for or given. Assia was the one who faced the judge, who seemed sick to death of the adultery charade as he signed the decree. Steele was waiting in the lobby of a hotel across the street. When Assia came towards him to announce that the deed was done, she added tenderly, 'You know, John, you and I grew up together.' Steele felt it was an accurate description of the nature of their relationship. Her words still 'stick like a burr' in his mind and eased the pain of what he knew to be her infidelity and duplicity.

Mrs Gutmann was the only one who lamented the break-up, and Steele's parents rushed from England to support their son and help with the financial difficulties of student life. Two years later John married a fellow teacher, they had a son and a daughter, and he held a variety of posts as teacher and then principal. During a few years' time off school, he established a wax museum in Victoria with his old army friend Keith Gems, who had inherited a wax business. They were very successful and opened or franchised more wax museums. Still he was not content and, missing teaching, he went to university and with his degree became a high school teacher of English literature until his retirement in 1983. Fifty years after the divorce from Assia, and having divorced again, Steele's most enduring memory of Assia is of her tripping along beside him, rather splay-footed, leaning forward as they hurried down Allenby Street towards the seashore in Tel Aviv.

In later years, Assia painted her marriage to Steele as a melodrama, telling her friends that when she was fourteen, her mother fell for an Englishman. Unable to admit the infatuation, the mother transferred her emotions to her daughter, forcing her to marry the man as soon as she was legally of marriageable age. The story goes that Assia refused to consummate the marriage with a husband who was twice her age. It was only through her father's intervention that, a few months after the wedding, she ran away from her husband and the marriage was annulled, causing her mother a nervous breakdown. Steele was actually just five years older than Assia, but apparently, she couldn't settle for an everyday story of marriage and divorce – as it really was – and needed to portray her early life as sensationally as possible.

She could not support herself and, reluctant as she was, the 23-year-old divorcee returned to her parents' home. For the first time in four years, the Gutmanns were now all living under the same roof again. Since Dr Gutmann's medical licence was not recognised in British Columbia, he had to sit more examinations, and even then he was only allowed to work as a physiotherapist.

His clinic was empty most of the day, his wife having to practically knock on doctors' doors, to implore them to refer their patients to him. Celia got up every morning at 5 a.m. to walk to a whisky distillery, where she was standing up all day long, sticking labels on bottles. As backbreaking as this job was, her mother asked to join her. The company rule was that no two members of the same family could work in the same plant, so Celia lied to the foreman that Lisa was a divorcee, so that he might feel sorry for her and take her on. Assia was the only one who contributed nothing to the family income.

She enrolled at the University of British Columbia, her studies a pretext for spending most of her time away on the campus, stretched out on the lawn in front of the library with friends. She studied art and took an active role in campus life, participating in drama groups and literary clubs. Fellow-student John Bosher, later a distinguished professor of history, got the impression that Assia was neither academically inclined nor had any clear or steady notion of what she wanted to do. Like many undergraduates, she was carried away with intellectual excitement. 'We all thought that ordinary life was contemptible, and the poets we read – Eliot, Auden – influenced us all.'

In the university records, Assia was registered as Pamela A. E. Steele; the 'A. E.' stood for 'Assia Esther', but it was after her divorce that she started calling herself Pamela, like her husband's younger sister. It infuriated the Steele family, since the little Pamela had died tragically in infancy and they accused Assia of wilfully and callously stealing the dead baby's persona. Assia was driven to changing her name following the ribbing she got at university, when the derogatory term 'ass' was applied to her broad buttocks. Her singular exotic Russian name becoming a hindrance, she found refuge in a nondescript English one, erasing her foreign identity. 'With anti-Semitism in Vancouver, she wouldn't go back to her maiden name Gutmann either,' says her sister Celia. 'Refusing to feel Jewish, she wanted nothing to set her apart from becoming a true Canadian.'

Her jaw, heavy in her teens, now became more refined, her cheekbones high and her mouth well shaped. She had a big bosom, a flat bottom and thick ankles, and turned the heads of students and instructors alike, radiating magnificence rather than sex appeal. She looked self-conscious, always aware of herself, but was very touchy when people referred to her looks. Her wardrobe was too scanty for her vast social needs and she helped herself to her sister's clothes – much to Celia's dismay. On other occasions she did not hesitate to forge her sister's signature and charge her shopping account; she also shoplifted small items like nylon stockings or cosmetics. With her haughtily cultivated English voice, John Bosher thought that Assia came from an upper-class British boarding school; still, she was not a snob, and made friends on every side: 'She made an immediate impression by her beauty, exotic intensity and lively conversation, but was an anxious and troubled young woman in search of a way out of her circumstances. She was frightened of becoming a steady, sensible, hard-working adult with ordinary limited horizons, and was ready for any wild adventure, eager to have a busy social and intellectual life.' Richard Lipsey was Bosher's best friend and a fourth-year undergraduate student of economics at the university, when he first met her: 'She and John Bosher had a passionate affair. She was everything that we were not; we were naïve undergraduates who had never been outside Vancouver and here she was, an exotic creature who experienced the world.'

Only in the summer vacations did Assia do her share of supporting herself. It was her beauty, no doubt, that got her the much-desired job of chambermaid at the fashionable Harrison Hot-Springs Resort and Spa Hotel. That summer of 1950, actress Joan Fontaine went on a fishing trip in British Columbia, paying a surprise visit to her father, Walter de Havilland, who had retired to live in Canada. Assia was thrilled to hear that the Hollywood star was staying at the hotel and could not take her eyes off her. She coaxed one of the other chambermaids to sneak with her into the actress's suite in her absence. Opening the wardrobe, they took out Joan Fontaine's dresses and Assia tried them on one by one, slipping easily into the alluring evening gowns of the 33-year-old star of *Rebecca* and *Jane Eyre*. Suddenly the door burst open; the flabbergasted Fontaine could not contain her rage. Assia's charming excuses and pleas tipped the scales and saved her job. She turned her mischief into a gag and for years made her friends roar with laughter as she mimicked the star's hysteria and acted out the hotel scene.

Her next summer jobs, however, were much less glamorous; in August 1952 John Steele and his new wife were sailing from Vancouver to their teaching posts at Prince Rupert, on Kaien Island. The boat called at Namu, a small island and the site of a fish cannery. Steele used the stopover to stretch his legs and stroll around by himself. As he glanced idly through the cannery window, a bunch of women were gutting salmon; there, in an apron and head covering, brandishing a long knife, he saw Assia. 'Our eyes met, we smiled.

We couldn't converse, and my ship was about to sail. I turned away. I never saw, nor heard from her again.' Assia bit her lips and battled on in the cannery, urging her sister to send her a pair of rubber gloves, a copy of *Vogue* magazine and a bottle of perfume. This experience as well was added to her repertoire of tales and she enjoyed shocking future audiences with vivid descriptions of blood and guts. Ted Hughes incorporated it into his poem 'Descent', as he described 'the cannery, with its erotic motif/Of porcupine quills, that pierced you.'

Assia frequently quarrelled with her parents, who criticised her idle existence and urged her to settle down with a husband and children. Lisa Gutmann looked at John Bosher with blazing anger. 'I was only a boy, two years younger than her daughter, and hardly a decisive figure in the situation,' he says. 'Assia was not willing to pursue fixed objectives, or to be what people might call "sensible" or faithful. She wanted to open as many doors as she could for intellectual experiments and excitements.' Assia was grander and worldlier than anyone he had ever met, filled with the prospects befitting a person with such qualities, a wild, romantic woman, 'who might also be seen in the context of poems by Byron or Shelley, and tragic, too, in that sense'. And yet she always surprised him by her willingness to spend time with him in his 'simple life'. On one occasion, having spent his summer working as a lumberjack and forest surveyor's assistant, he took her for a walk in the thick woods beyond the university. 'We lit a fire, and spent the night eating food toasted at my fire, and talking, talking, talking.'

Bosher was aware that Assia was not exclusively his; she had a series of men friends whom, he thought, she became involved with out of unhappiness and a search for some kind of relief or shelter: 'But when anyone offered support and affection, she continued looking for the next step in some undefined direction.' In a diary note from Saturday, 20 January 1951, John Bosher made the following entry: 'Pam Steele phoned this afternoon, and wanted me to go to see her. She's not well. I went, of course, to see her at her parents' place on Cambie Street, opposite the City Hall, and found her as attractive as ever, but in trouble as ever. It seems she conceived a child by a man she was in love with (until last night) and had an abortion.' Her parents knew nothing of this, but she divulged all to her younger sister Celia, who, then and on another occasion, helped her find a clandestine abortion clinic. In those pre-pill days, abortion was the prevailing, though illegal and aggressive, method of birth control. In later years Assia never hid her past abortions and Ted Hughes gave her the derogatory title of 'Lilith of abortions'.

Her relationship with John Bosher was plagued by his lack of time and money, as well as by his immaturity. She continued to look for a stronger, much older, more mature, man with a creative spark. She found it in Professor Earle Birney, the energetic, charismatic 'crucible of Canadian literature', as he was described by his biographer, Elspeth Cameron. Birney, an avid mountaineer, was a giant of a man, but thin and built like a whiplash; red-haired, blue-eyed and with a sandy-grey beard. He established the first department of creative writing in a Canadian university, which Assia attended. His wife, Esther Bull, a fellow Marxist and the mother of his son, was aware that her macho husband was an insatiable womaniser and that 'he needed women to feel significant and worthwhile'. He pursued women of all ages and marital status and did not stop at his own students. In her photo album, Assia glued a newspaper cutting from a class at the university; she was photographed sitting in the front row, glaring at her 48-year-old professor, who ensnared the students with accounts of his arrest in Germany for failing to salute a Nazi parade. Some years later, Birney confided in poet and art critic Edward Lucie-Smith, telling him about his relationship with Assia. 'He just wanted a fling, and when he discovered that Assia wanted his identity as a poet, he withdrew from the affair.'

Six

A Second Husband

Toronto, 1952–London, 1956

In his childhood, the distinguished economist Richard (Dick) Lipsey had resolved to become a cosmologist. 'I often regret that I got seduced by this crazy subject, economics, that purported to have universal laws about the behaviour of people rather than stars.' A native of Victoria on Vancouver Island, Lipsey graduated from the University of British Columbia with first class honours in economics. He was doing his MA at Toronto University, and in the summer vacation of 1952 returned to Vancouver to work at the Bureau of Economics and Statistics in the provincial government of British Columbia.

One night in August, after a long day's work at City Hall, he was on his way home. In the rear of the bus he spotted the young woman he knew as Pam Steele. It was two years since they had seen each other on campus and the last he had heard was that she was the mistress of a married friend of his. 'Before I knew it, we were on a romantic whirl.' She pulled him off the bus, to cruise the nightclubs. She led him to the dance floor, and he was completely won over when she sang to him hits from the musical *Oklahoma!* After a week of intense courtship, Lipsey invited her to come to Victoria, and paid for her hotel room. 'I'm your kept woman,' she teased him. He recalls that the idea seemed romantic to her, 'and probably to me too, that I was the keeper of a kept woman. It was really just a post-adolescent game.'

After this dizzy escapade lasting all of one week, Dick proposed to her. It was an act of revolt – he had never rebelled during his adolescence – and now, by getting involved with a wild, exotic woman, he was protesting against the middle-class morality he had grown up with. 'I was rather impressed with the romanticism of marrying a Russian-Jewish divorcée, and a woman of the world, while I was still inexperienced in worldly matters. But I wasn't so rebellious as to forgo the notion I grew up with, that if you want to sleep with a woman, you must marry her.'

Assia agreed instantly. At 25, living with her parents, her future bleak, a sudden marriage proposal fitted her romantic fantasies. She clearly enjoyed the company of the 24-year-old Lipsey, who came from a well-to-do family and may have hoped that his parents would support the young couple in a grand style. 'She liked to do things impetuously, and I think she married me for a lark – much as I did her, though I was deeply in love with her.' They did not disclose their plans to their parents and, at the end of the summer, Dick returned to Toronto for the second year of his MA. Assia found an excuse to travel there a few weeks later and booked into the YWCA. One night she spirited Dick into her room and they slept together for the first time. He crept out at dawn. 'I'm very law-abiding, and it worried me all the time I was there. But it was the sort of mildly anti-authoritarian thing that she liked.'

Assia was once again dreaming of a white wedding but they could not find a minister who would agree to perform the ceremony when the bride was a divorcee. They had to settle for a rude man smoking a cigar in Toronto's register office. On 21 October 1952, they signed the papers and went to celebrate in a friend's house. Assia compensated with a glorious white evening gown, one shoulder totally bare and with a deep cleavage, a white garland embracing the nape of her neck. Neither pair of parents attended the wedding – they lived on the other side of Canada and were told only at the last moment – and were surprised and dazed by the hasty nuptials. That same week John Bosher, Assia's former lover and Dick's best friend, got married as well, and the four of them spent much of their time together.

With a taste for intrigue, Assia charmed Dick into keeping the marriage a secret. In the Canada of the early 1950s, cohabitation seemed improper, and the young Lipseys boasted of their supposedly illicit relationship and glowed under the halo of being an unconventional, daring couple. (Just four years later, Sylvia Plath would talk Ted Hughes into concealing their marriage, but for a different reason: so as not to jeopardise the rest of her Fulbright scholarship at Cambridge.)

Dick and Assia rented a basement bedsitter in Toronto, the telephone an extension from the main line in the landlord's flat upstairs; in less than a month they were ordered to leave, because Assia slammed down the phone if the call was not for her, and the landlord lost many important business calls. They moved to a larger bedsitter with a cupboard-sized kitchen and a bath shared with other tenants on the same floor. The nosy landlady inspected their room whenever they were absent; soon she was expressing worries that they would pollute the entire house with bugs if they continued to keep their room so filthy. It was Dick who had to add housekeeping chores to his overloaded schedule of studies for the final year of his master's degree.

With an incomplete university degree and no marketable skills, Assia once again had to settle for monotonous, mundane, subservient jobs. She was a copy typist in an advertising agency and, in the pre-computer, even pre-Xerox days, spent hours typing and retyping the same memos and letters. Dick Lipsey sympathised with her distress. 'It was demeaning, but she had only herself to blame for it.' Already only six months into the marriage, he realised that he had made a terrible mistake: 'In today's terms, when I met her I would have said, come live with me, and we would have had six months of a crazy, intense wonderful affair, and then we would have split up. Assia was a wonderful person to have an affair with, but we just weren't compatible as husband and wife. Our tastes were different, our values contradictory.'

They returned to British Columbia in the late spring of 1953, settling into the splendid Lipsey family home on Vancouver Island. Dick put enormous pressure on Assia to take the summer course at the university but she stuck it for just a few weeks and then dropped out. A social animal to her core, she hobnobbed in the intellectual celebrity circles with the architect Arthur Erikson and his like. Dick studiously avoided Assia's friends, and took no part in her social life. His parents could not comprehend their daughter-in-law: she was so far beyond anything they had experienced, they did not understand her frame of mind and she made them feel uncomfortable. His mother complained that Assia was not looking after her son's clothes and even neglected her own. Assia's messiness was so monumental, chronic and ugly, that Mrs Lipsey urged her son to tidy up their 'pigsty' before allowing the maid to clean their room. 'I believe that Assia's mother took care of the many petty details of her daughter's life, whereas, in our family, each child was responsible for their own laundry, tidying their room and making their own breakfast,' observed Dick's younger sister Thirell Lipsey, now Weiss.

Assia annoyed the Lipseys by frequently sleeping late, then storming into the kitchen to make some tasty dishes just for herself. She performed household tasks only when asked and even then grudgingly and with the air of someone put upon. Nevertheless, Thirell Lipsey was delighted with her sister-in-law and found her gorgeous, sophisticated and stylish. Assia drew Thirell into the drama of her life, always with a captivating tale about the effect of some event or person on her psyche: 'She would listen to my own "stories" quite attentively, but the subject always miraculously returned to her life and trials. I loved her as the person she could have been, and I tried to accept and understand her strict devotion to her own needs, and no one else's. She seemed aware only of her own desires and pursued them with single minded diligence.' While Assia found it difficult to fit into the Lipsey ambience, Dick was enchanted by her father: 'A solid, impressive, and sentimental man, a Hollywood type of Russian'. Dick admired Dr Gutmann's ability to spout Chekhov at length, and they spent many hours over the chessboard. When losing to his son-in-law, Lonya did not hide his irritation and did not let go until he eventually won.

Lipsey was undecided whether he should do his Ph.D. in Chicago or at the London School of Economics. The advantage of the latter was that French was no longer a requirement. More than that, it was Assia's preference to go back to England and she talked him into it. The most momentous decision of Lipsey's career, then, was taken 'for the wrong reasons, though in retrospect it turned out to be the right decision', he recalled. In September 1953, they travelled to Montreal and boarded an Empress Liner to Liverpool.

Assia was so happy to return to London after five years of absence that she hurried to Primrose Hill, her favourite part of town. She showed Dick around and proudly led him to her local pub. She was disappointed that no one recognised her. Looking up the ex-servicemen that she had known from Tel Aviv, she was glad to renew her friendship with Keith Gems and his wife. Gems, who was the best friend of her first husband, now became a lifelong friend of Dick Lipsey. Assia was still using the name 'Pam', sometimes signing 'P. A. E. Lipsey': Pamela Assia Esther. Only after meeting the Gems did Dick learn that Pamela was not his wife's given name. It took him six more months to switch to Assia.

The Lipseys rented a basement room in Mayfair, near Hyde Park Corner — a shabby dwelling, which Assia picked on account of its posh address. All they had to live on was Dick's small and inadequate student's grant of £500 a year and his savings from summer jobs, with no financial support from either pair of parents; the Gutmanns were struggling to earn a living, and the Lipseys, believing in the character-building nature of being self-supporting, left their children to fend for themselves. Assia enrolled at an employment agency as a temporary copy typist. She counted herself lucky when assigned to work, in different offices all over town, filling in for sickness or holidays. Since her pay depended upon typing speed and hers was only twenty words per minute, she was always at the bottom of the ladder, getting the minimum wage of about five pounds a week. In between the odd secretarial jobs, she worked as a stewardess at a car show at Earl's Court and was a door-to-door market researcher for soap products. She blossomed in street interviews, introducing products to passers-by, turning them into street performances.

Ten years after the end of the Second World War, England, still immersed in austerity, was a visually dull place. During the war, colourful clothes were hardly to be seen; everything was drab, often copying navy and air-force blue and army khaki. But Assia wore reds and purples, hats with veils and, with her wonderful flair, could transform otherwise shabby or unfashionable outfits with a scarf or cheap jewellery, and end up looking chic and unique. By English standards she was definitely exotic, stunning without being theatrical, and had an eye for fashion, always knowing what would be *dernier cri*. Women turned to look at her and men were overwhelmed. 'To be with Assia was like being admitted into the presence of Aphrodite. We were stopped in the streets – one man clutched at her sleeve, and stared and stared before apologising,' recalls Pam Gems.

In the spring of 1954, the Lipseys moved into a basement flat in Bayswater, 72 Palace Court, a red-brick block showing the signs of years of wear and neglect. The five bedrooms all opened on to a large L-shaped central hall, for the use of the eight tenants, members of a commune, who shared expenses, chores, food and friends. Assia's friends in the commune were irritated by her concept of sharing: she took the best and the most of what was offered or available. Jo (later Price) and Ken Reed suspected that in their absence, she browsed in their room, 'borrowing' things. When caught, she would look scared and try to elicit pity. Thirell Lipsey, who joined the commune, soon became wary of spending time with her sister-in-law. Assia was a heavy smoker and used to wheedle cigarettes all the time: 'Or she would say, oh, can you pay this time, for lunch, or bus, or museum, and it was very often my turn, and seldom hers, to pay,' Thirell remembers.

Architect Ken Reed recalls that Pam – as she was still calling herself – hardly participated in the workload: 'She was rather slothful, and was content to lounge around. However, she entertained us all with her tall tales and fine performances, which included Near-Eastern dancing and singing.' With an entire repertoire of body language to accompany her words, Assia would hold the floor, imitating people, putting on foreign accents, fabricating adventures from her flight from Germany and her travails on a kibbutz. 'She was never boring, and above all, she was funny. Women were not funny then,' remarks Pam Gems. From time to time Assia would take her diary, and read aloud scenes from her past. If the Lipsey door was ever open wide enough to permit a look inside, flatmate Don Michel recalls, a pile of dirty bedding blocked the view. But if going out for the evening was on the cards, Assia metamorphosed into a rare beauty, her face immaculate. Dressed and made up to kill and astound the world, she was a force to be reckoned with.

Her friend Pam Gems saw more to Assia than her outgoing persona: a crippling self-consciousness and shyness. Before entering a room full of people, Assia would panic at the door, unsure what impression she would make and what people would say about her. Then, suddenly the adrenalin would flood her, and she would burst in. However, when at times she dropped out of the conversation and withdrew into herself, it was unnerving for everybody. 'When someone looks as sensational as Assia, and keeps silent, people become stressed, and then they blame her for being a snob,' says Gems. Before returning to the United States, Jo and Ken Reed left their promising business of ceramic jewellery to Assia. She grabbed the opportunity, only to discover that the effort of moulding, baking and painting each item by hand, and then keeping up with orders, was just too much for her to handle. She backed out. Later, she planned to buy crocodile bags, modify and upgrade them to be sold for a higher price. Nothing came of that either. 'We all did things for her often, not because she expected or demanded it, but because she messed up,' recalls Pam Gems. 'There was in her something fragile and brittle about her, in need of protection, though I used to accuse her of exploitation. She did not seem so much lost, as for ever in the wrong place, in the wrong country, with the wrong man.'

As hard up as they were, the Lipseys still scraped up enough money to go skiing at the fashionable Swiss resort of Zermatt at Christmas. While Dick enrolled in the beginners' class, Assia, boasting of being a skilled skier, joined the advanced class. Her failure was too obvious and, four days later, she sneaked out, but was too proud to go down to the beginners' class. She spent the rest of the holiday by the fireplace in the hotel lounge. 'It was typical of her: first showing off; then, if encountering crisis, seeking a way out,' Dick Lipsey comments. Despite Assia's ineptitude on the slopes, she insisted on ski vacations abroad each Christmas. Magnificently dressed in her ski outfit, she posed radiantly for the camera, three of her photos making it into a Norwegian newspaper.

In the summer of 1954, Assia was both nervous and excited when she visited Germany after twenty years' absence. The Gutmann family had not been spared; the Nazis murdered Vanya, Lonya's brother, together with his wife and small daughter. Lisa had severed her connections with her sister, whose two sons had been soldiers in the Wehrmacht and they had become prisoners of war. The sense of belonging that Assia experienced in the first few hours of her visit was soon laced with fear; she sensed that it was still dangerous to be a Jew in Germany. The perfect Prussian accent that accompanied her act made things more complicated, since she was constantly asked why she, a German citizen, had left the homeland.

She and Dick travelled to Dachau concentration camp, but Assia only reached the gate and could not make herself go in. It was a hitchhiking trip; with Assia's striking looks, cars always stopped for her waving hand. Dick would squeeze in the back seat, while she sat in the front and stretched her body, impressing the drivers with her bubbling chat and upper-crust language. Wishing to prolong the encounter, the mesmerised drivers would treat the young couple to free meals. Once they were mortified when a driver proudly declared that he had been a senior SS officer and insisted that they have coffee and *kuchen* at his home. Once there, he rushed in to the next room, returning with a large framed photograph of Hitler decorating him with the Iron Cross. In obsessive and fervent Hitler-style staccato, the ex-SS officer praised the wonderful and great leader, as Assia and Dick shrunk back on the sofa. As they were about to leave, the host took out a flat object from a drawer, slid it into Assia's palm and dramatically closed her fingers into a fist. He drove them to the train station and, before bidding farewell, he hugged Assia, saying, 'Thank you for a most wonderful day.' Only when the train pulled out of the station and they had lost sight of the man, did Assia dare open her hand. Her face drained of its colour; it was the Iron Cross on a red velvet background. 'The monster became enamoured of this gorgeous creature and gave his dearest possession to a Jewish Madonna,' Lipsey interprets. As if bitten by an adder, Assia sprung up and opened the carriage window, hurling the medal out with all her might. The trip, which Assia hoped would help her find her roots, only intensified her sense of dispossession. Unable to bond with Germany and turning her back on Israel and Canada, she threw herself on Britain. It was doomed from the start – Lipsey thinks – because only by birth could one find a place within the British class system. Assia aspired to something she could never get.

Dick and Assia moved from one grim flat to another, one of which was a fourth-floor garret in Goodge Street that they rented for next to nothing from the Gems. It was one room with the lavatory three floors below, which they shared with the employees of the ground-floor shops. They had no refrigerator, and could afford meat only once a week, their main staples being potatoes, cabbage, tomatoes and sausages. 'My diet this week has again consisted of sardines and unbuttered bread for lunch, tomatoes and home-fried potatoes for dinner. Oranges are a mere window decoration in greengrocer's shops,' Assia complained in a letter to her sister Celia.

A frequent visitor was Jacques Parizeau, Dick's fellow Ph.D. student at LSE, who subsequently acquired fame as the Prime Minister of Quebec. 'Jacques was quietly in love with Assia, but it never came to anything,' remembers Lipsey. They always welcomed Parizeau's visits, enjoying his company and the bottles of beer that he invariably brought. They would return the empty bottles to the pub for the deposit and spend it on potatoes and small scraps of bacon left after all possible slices had been taken off the bone. 'We loved hiding away from reality and the tough world outside, pretending to be children, calling each other pet names, a romance I've never played with any other woman before or since,' Lipsey recalls.

Assia quenched her champagne taste by embarking on shopping sprees in the most expensive shops, masquerading as a rich woman. She would open charge accounts, spend hours bossing the shop assistants around and almost tearing the shop apart and, at the last moment, find an excuse to leave the shop empty-handed. In bookshops, she would ask – and get – two for the price of one. She would finish one book overnight and the following day return it to the shop, saying she had received the same book as a present, and swap it for another. She and Pam Gems shared the frustration of being married to men with little concern for arts, while they read avidly and adored the theatre, opera and ballet. 'The trouble was money, paying for admittance. People often thought she was an actress, and she would wangle tickets,' says Pam Gems. 'Assia was very critical and got straight to the heart of the matter. She made a very good critic, summing up in one word everything that was wrong with the play, and spoiling the whole experience for me.'

'The things here are absolutely exquisite, there are no more elegant children's clothing in the world, than those in the children's department of Fortnum and Mason,' Assia exclaimed in a letter to her sister in Canada. She aired her dilemma as to whether to buy Ronnie, Celia's firstborn, a white tailored doeskin coat with a hat to match, or a navy-blue coat with gold buttons, a white linen collar and beautiful tiny white gloves. Both unbought presents were equally impractical for Celia's son and, in any case, way beyond Assia's means. But playing rich only increased her distress. Wealth had always eluded Assia, and ending up living in near-poverty, the kind that she and her parents had tried to escape, exasperated her. She felt cheated, thinking she was entitled to a better life. So deep was her despair, that she tried to kill herself twice – in her husband's presence – by swallowing a handful of aspirins. Lipsey perceived his wife's act as 'a clear cry for help, and not a deliberate attempt to end her life'.

It was the beginning of his career and, being assiduous and self-motivated, Lipsey spent days on end in the library or with his colleagues, staying at work till midnight. 'My work took up most of my sexual and other energies,' he admits. Assia felt locked out. Bored in the company of Dick's economist friends, she poisoned his relationship with some of them, causing break-ups. He was aware that men were falling in love with his wife and that she savoured their attention. His sister Thirell felt: 'Assia was compelled to try and conquer every man in the room, and she was usually successful, but I think she never followed it up with physical seduction. I felt humiliated for the poor silly man who allowed himself to become intoxicated by her intense manner and apparent complete absorption in him. My woman friends recognised Assia's exotic and sexy appearance (none of us could compete) and seemed to enjoy Assia even though she might make a fool of their boyfriends.' A herd of besotted admirers was much more thrilling to Assia than a relationship with a specific man. Lipsey was flattered that it was his woman that everyone was after. 'She was not driven by sex, and was not looking to have affairs. With her fatal attraction, men met her and melted. I got pleasure from her beauty as well, sensing other men's envy that Assia was mine.' Once, when Lipsey was away for the weekend to attend the Oxford–Cambridge–London Joint Economics Seminar, Assia flew to Berlin with a wealthy businessman who dealt in ball-bearings. Lipsey never had any inkling of the escapade.

Beauty, rather than sensuality, was her calling card, but she felt resentful and misunderstood when people found it unnecessary to look further and undervalued her intelligence. 'She drew rather well, occasionally wrote poetry, but lacked self-discipline and focus, and never pursued either with the dedication that is needed to excel,' thinks Pam Gems, who later became a playwright. The letters that Assia left behind bear traces of her observant, critical eye and flowing pen:

> The English are inequipped [sic] to deal with heat – they are gorgeously stupefied by the sun they are used to see [sic] in the cinema and on travel posters . . . what other culture devotes so much of its lyric poetry to heat, sun and Summer as do the English? Even love finds an inaccessible competitor in Summer – '. . . shall I compare thee to a Summer's day?' Go, catch me a Parisian poet saying that.

She confided in Pam that she wished to marry a blond, tousle-haired English poet: Rupert Brooke would have answered her requirements. But not content with the role of a poet's wife, she wanted to be part of a milieu of poets. 'In the past, someone like Assia – with an artistic temperament but no specific talent to express it – could become a muse as a way of self-fulfilment. I used to tell her she was born in the wrong century. She would have managed better in the nineteenth century, with Shelley and Browning and Keats. But now, women have to be existential like men.'

In August 1955, the 27-year-old Dick Lipsey was appointed assistant lecturer at LSE and was also teaching statistics in an American army camp near London. 'The very worst of times are over,' Assia broke the good news to her sister, 'which brings his salary up to a point where it will no longer be necessary for me to work.' They planned to stay in London for two more years, and then Lipsey would have the prospect of 'returning to North America, calling his own tune, or rather his own salary, and a professorship at the age of 29.'

Four years into their marriage, with their financial future so promising and

A Second Husband

Assia's biological clock ticking 29, they could think of raising a family. But the very idea repulsed her. Her married women friends sometimes had fun recounting their childbirth experiences, laying it on thick as soon as they saw Assia's obvious horror. She was not in the least interested in other people's babies, never cuddled or attended to them. It was never clear whether it was the pregnancy, labour, delivery or motherhood that Assia abhorred so much. Despite Lipsey's craving for children, he went along with his wife's fears and the subject was not brought up.

In the summer of 1956, Lipsey got a teaching job at the summer school of the University of British Columbia. They stayed with the Gutmanns in central Vancouver and sailed at weekends to the Lipsey family mansion on the island. Assia did not use the opportunity to try to complete her university degree and, instead, lay about, occasionally painting, reluctant to show her work. 'She had a charming self-deprecating way of showing us her various artistic fragments, as though afraid of our reaction,' remembers her sister-in-law Thirell. When one of Lipsey's professors asked Assia about her future plans, she said that she wanted to be a satirist. When he asked what she wished to satirise, she had no answer.

In September, Dick and Assia joined Thirell and her boyfriend and the four of them drove together to Montreal. To cut expenses, they slept under the stars in sleeping bags, washing in restaurant toilets. They lived off cakes and biscuits that Mrs Gutmann had lavishly provided, passing the time singing and telling stories. Dick remembered it as 'one of the most wonderful and romantic times' of his life and he thought it was similar for Assia.

Seven

Falling in Love

London, 1956–59

The head waiter led Dick and Assia to their seats in the dining room, telling them that he had found the most perfect table, with 'some other middle aged persons'. At the sound of these words, Assia threw a fit: are there no young people aboard? She demanded an immediate replacement and it took the bewildered head waiter some minutes to examine the floor plan before leading them to another table. 'Fate took a hand, and we were seated with David Wevill,' Dick Lipsey comments. Tall, willowy, pensive, with a sculptured face and a shock of blond hair falling over his forehead, Wevill had the 'look of the young Gary Cooper and sounding like him too, a whispering Canadian drawl,' as the writer William Trevor later described him.

A few hours earlier, the 21-year-old Wevill had been sitting by the purser's office, waiting to present his passport. He was using the time to write a letter to his French-Canadian girlfriend, apologising for terminating their relationship. Wevill lifted his eyes and was stunned by the profile and posture of a dark-haired woman who was standing in the queue. Occasionally, he stole a look, but no word was spoken. Wevill was returning from a summer holiday with his parents in Ottawa for his final year at Caius College, Cambridge, where he was reading History and English. A budding poet, Wevill played the accordion and never went anywhere without his sketchbook, tenderly drawing faces and landscapes on his travels.

At dinner, David and Assia were thunderstruck by each other's presence. She was instantly and totally drawn into a tête-à-tête, which left her husband trailing behind. After almost giving up on her lifelong fantasy of rubbing shoulders with men of letters, she was captivated when Wevill spoke with passion about Wordsworth; it was then that she fell in love with him. David was intrigued by Assia's personality: 'I have not met anyone like her. She was a good conversationalist, an engaging person, witty and animated, who also possessed depth and silence.' He found her grey-green hazel eyes and very dark brown hair strikingly beautiful, 'but she was no houri, no nymph of paradise. She had a deep beauty, not a woman of glamour in a stage or screen sense.' He was touched by her tales of a grievous past, with her family of landless, tragic refugees, and admired her struggle to reconstruct herself almost from scratch. 'We felt an immediate kinship, since both of us were first-born children, nomads, who came naked to Canada,' Wevill remembers. He had been born in 1935 in Yokohama, Japan, moved to Canada as a child, then moved constantly, until his parents finally settled down in Ottawa. 'I find I have a certain restlessness, an inability to stay very long in one place,' he said in a radio interview.

In his poem 'Apples and Apples', published in 2001, Wevill wrote: 'Seven years between us. / Seven planets, seven stones smeared with blood.' But the age difference, his timidity and her worldliness, did not create a rift: 'It was more two lives than two ages, I think, that Assia and I had to bring into focus,' he explains. 'I had always been drawn to people unlike myself, who were in some way different from those I saw every day.' Assia and David spent most of the six-day voyage in each other's company. He gave her books to read and they discussed Nietzsche's *Birth of Tragedy*. Only for meals did they join Dick, who clearly sensed that his wife's feelings for their travel companion were passionate and deep, involving body and soul. It was different this time from her customary behaviour, but he was not alarmed enough by the shipboard romance to try to stop it; he immersed himself further in his economics books. A day before docking at Liverpool, Assia declared her love to David.

Before leaving for their summer holiday in Canada, Assia and Dick had vacated their London flat and planned that, upon returning, they would stay with friends until they found a new place. Arriving at London, they went their separate ways – Dick, to one of his LSE colleagues, and Assia, presumably, to one of her girlfriends. He did not know that instead she booked into a hotel in Kensington with David. A few days later, David returned to Cambridge. The clandestine affair became easier to manage a month later, when Assia was offered a job away from London. On 29 October 1956, Britain, France and Israel launched a military campaign to stop Egypt from nationalising the Suez Canal. Reuters monitoring station in Dane End in Hertfordshire was desperately looking for people fluent in English, Hebrew and Arabic to monitor and translate broadcasts from the Middle East. It had been ten years since Assia had left Tel Aviv but her Hebrew was impeccable and she was assigned outright to the highly paid job. Living in the village of Dane End, she worked shifts around the clock, and Dick stayed in London at the Worsely Court Residential Hotel, which also provided meals.

The war was over in six days and, in November, things were already quieter in the Suez Canal. Assia, though, was as busy as ever. On cloud nine, she scribbled her infatuation on her 1936 edition of Pushkin's poems, prose and plays. She had bought the book in 1950 in Vancouver, and autographed it 'Assia Steele'. Now, she added the inscription 'Assia and David W', as if toying with new matrimony.

Just before Christmas, she informed Dick that she was grounded by Reuters and would not be home for the holiday. He celebrated with mutual friends but just before sitting for dinner, phoned to wish Assia a merry Christmas. He was taken aback when the operator told him that she had gone away. Inquiring further, he was told that Assia had gone off with a man, and it hit him that he might be the young man from the ship. Days later she returned to London and Dick confronted her with his suspicions. Assia admitted outright that she had spent Christmas in a hotel with David. Her initial discretion in matters of the heart enabled her husbands to turn a blind eye but, when exposed and her secret was out, she became mercilessly blunt. She spared no details, laying the problem at the feet of the miserable cuckold himself, enlisting his devotion to make him a tolerant ally.

In March 1957, after receiving international guarantees that the Suez Canal would remain open, Israel withdrew its troops from the Sinai. As the crisis ended Assia was laid off, and she joined Dick at the Worsely Court Residential Hotel. But the affair went on and she could not wait to introduce David to her woman friends. Liliana Archibald, the wife of Lipsey's colleague from LSE, often gave Assia a ride to Cambridge to be with David. He was not allowed to have female guests in his lodging, so Assia waited in the Blue Boar Inn, or in other inns in the neighbouring villages. 'It was an exceptional time, the sexual mores were like those of the Bloomsbury Circle,' says Liliana Archibald, now Professor Emerita of Russian History and living in London. 'Assia was not considered promiscuous, and her behaviour was not unusual, at least among poets and economists.'

Falling in Love

It was obvious to the Lipseys that they were having a major marital crisis, but the possibility of divorce was not even raised. 'Assia said, let's get the hell out of London, and live in the country for a change – it might do our marriage some good,' Lipsey remembers. His good friend and colleague Kurt Klapholz warned him that changes of venue would solve nothing and they would only take their problems with them, but Lipsey would not listen. They probed the To Let columns until they found a cottage in Great Hormead, Hertfordshire. The district was familiar to Assia from her recent job at Reuters and her romantic escapades with David. It was a charming, affordable house in a hamlet, a convenient twenty miles from London – Dick's place of work at LSE – and the same distance from Cambridge, where David was studying. Without a car, and at the beginning, not being able to afford even a bicycle, it was a three-mile walk from Great Hormead to the railway station.

In the spring of 1957 Assia got a job at Notley's advertising agency, as a secretary in Philip Mellor's TV department. At that time David Wevill had completed his studies at Cambridge and moved to London, supporting himself as a copywriter. Now the ménage à trois operated in the following way: Assia travelled to London on Sunday evenings, joining David in his Hampstead bedsitter in Chesterfield Gardens. Dick left Great Hormead only on Tuesday mornings, and stayed in Fitzjohn's Avenue with Chris and Liliana Archibald, his London friends. He did not know that Assia and David were actually living just a few streets away; somehow they never bumped into each other. Assia conducted the affair quite openly, taking David to her favourite jazz clubs, and introducing him to the films of Ingmar Bergman, Antonioni and Fellini. She met Dick only at weekends; often they made the journey back to the village together. Dick paid the rent and the household expenses in Great Hormead and Assia was keeping her salary to herself. Poet Peter Porter, who was grateful to Assia for getting him a job as a copywriter at Notley's, came for a weekend in Great Hormead, and sensed that she and Dick were living in 'uncomfortable tolerance of each other'.

Dick Lipsey was aware that he was sharing Assia with her lover but did not insist that she stop seeing him. Although he was younger than Assia by a few months, he perceived himself as a forgiving father of an unruly daughter. Playing the father figure loaded him with responsibility and anguish but rewarded him with a sense of purpose and significance: 'I don't think she ever grew up fully, she was still attracted to undergraduate things and undergraduate behaviour. She was damaged emotionally, my parents called her "the wounded angel".' In Lipsey's eyes, Assia's weekend homecomings from London were like those of a daughter coming home from university, unloading all her problems before recharging her batteries, and he found great strength in responding to her needs. 'I was someone she could kick around, abuse in any way she pleased, abandon and then come back to for love and security. My place in life is to shoulder and support people,' he said. Keith Gems, his close friend for many years, interpreted it more bluntly: 'Dick has a masochistic streak. She treated him like a dog sometimes.'

Lipsey was rather content to have Assia just for the weekend: he was overloaded with his studies and hardly had time for her anyway. He was never the jealous, possessive type and believed in matrimony 'for better or for worse'. So he did not give up on the marriage and did not view their status as any form of separation. They continued taking their winter holidays together, going skiing in Austria. Summer photos show Assia painting in the yard, wearing only a swimsuit, and Dick Lipsey dozing in a deckchair.

Wevill believed that Assia was virtually separated from her husband, though not without affection, and that she was all his. Neither man made a decisive move nor forced her to choose between them and she had no intention and apparently no need to do so. 'She often spoke about loving two men,' explains David Wevill. 'If she was seeing two people, it was not out of fickleness, but because she loved them both, they answered two sides of her personality. She was open to life, and when encountering a new experience, she could not stay away. It may sound strange, but she was a very loyal person. She was loyal to me, and she was loyal to Dick.' At times Assia felt that the burden was too heavy, and she tried to leave David, only to come back.

One weekend, after returning from a week with David, Assia teased Dick, did he still love her? He paused and finally said, 'You've been kicking me around for a long time now, and I am not sure.' Assia threw the window open, leaned out and had an enormous fit of rage, screaming loudly so the entire village would hear her. Immensely jealous by nature, she made public scenes whenever she sensed some attraction around her husband. A year earlier, at a party at his parents' home in Canada, she goaded him to kiss a girl. Dick initially refused but finally complied. Assia threw a fit and the party was called off, Dick having to walk her around the grounds for a few hours until she calmed down: 'She liked to create scenes and then have a histrionic reaction to them.'

Falling in Love

With David at her side, Assia now had a partner for everything that excited her: both art lovers, they drew a fair amount together and sketched each other. 'She would pose for me, and I drew her, reading a book.' At Easter, they travelled to the Lake District with sketching materials, leaving Lipsey in Great Hormead. Assia took evening classes with artist Derek Greaves, and one of her major inspirations was the English mystical landscape painter Samuel Palmer. She had an intense interest in life and all its forms: plants, flowers, trees, creatures and the like. Of her numerous paintings, some of them decorating her flats, only four have survived: an elaborate blue fruit dish with an array of apples, peaches, plums, cherries and a bunch of dark grapes lying on top. The fruit seem unappealing, their colours lifeless and sterile, the impression of repugnance enhanced by a bee and a cockroach that flank the dish. Another drawing bears the title 'Bird from Nubia' and is more exotic and aesthetic and, instead of insects, features a colourful bird. Another one, an incomplete watercolour sketch, shows a black woman at domestic work, her three children playing beside her. The fourth is an ink drawing of David Wevill, reclining and relaxed, gazing pensively.

Assia blossomed. They wrote poems to each other, and shared books – Dostoevsky, Tolstoy, Lorca and Hart Crane – each of them underlining their favourite passages in turn. They read to one another and, with her gift for languages, Assia introduced David to Pushkin, Akhmatova, Pasternak, Günther Grass, Enzensberger, Rilke and Nietzsche. She translated poems for him from German and Russian and he gave her his old and cherished Robert Browning's *A Blot in the 'Scutcheon,* dedicating it 'To my sweetest Assia. D'. 'Those years, when Assia and I were passionately together were a strange time in England. Rich but poor. Threatening but promising,' Wevill recalls. 'There was a spirit in the air, both malevolent and promising. And we were not English, but were of England.'

Notley's advertising agency was famous for employing poets: Peter Redgrove, William Trevor and Edward Lucie-Smith were all working there at the time. Assia joined them for a drink at the pub, with David and other copywriter-poets who worked in the nearby agencies. It was Lucie-Smith who told Assia about the Group, and she was delighted: her old dream, and her father's, of a literary salon, seemed to be within her reach. She asked if she and David could attend their weekly meetings.

The Group was established at Cambridge in 1954 by the undergraduates

Philip Hobsbaum and Peter Redgrove. A year later, when Hobsbaum and his wife Hannah moved to London, the Group was reconvened at their flat and moved with them when they changed addresses. 'The thing that bound us together was our belief that poetry could be discussed,' recalls Philip Hobsbaum. The Group's policy was to welcome anyone, not necessarily writers, but also lovers of poetry. They met every Friday evening around seven, each session devoted to the work of one writer, whose texts were cyclostyled and distributed by post a week earlier. 'The discussion group would be a complete democracy. The moderator would undertake a purely technical function – keeping the discussion going on reasonably coherent lines,' recalled Edward Lucie-Smith. He describes Philip Hobsbaum as 'impatient and inclined to hector and browbeat, and the disputes would often go noisy and acrimonious.' Several of the Group members were born outside Britain: Julian Cooper in South America, his wife Catherine in the United States, Peter Porter in Australia, Pat Hartz in South Africa, Lucie-Smith in Jamaica, Hannah Hobsbaum in India, Zulfikhar Ghose in Pakistan – no wonder David and Assia, with their foreign backgrounds, felt at home.

When Philip Hobsbaum first saw the slim, fair David, partnered by the dark, voluptuous Assia entering his basement flat in Stockwell, it struck him that she was 'one of the most beautiful, if not the most beautiful woman' he had ever seen, and David was about the only poet he'd ever met, 'who actually looked like one'. Assia was wearing cream or white, which set off her dark good looks, and Peter Redgrove leaned across to Hobsbaum and whispered, 'I know who she is. She has killed two men already, and will be the death of David.' Hobsbaum believed that it might have been Redgrove's way of calling her a femme fatale: 'Like me, he was fond of David, and probably felt protective towards him.' Assia did not speak much in the discussions but was especially lively socialising before and after. She stood out with her 'sharp boss-class sort of accent', and impressed Hobsbaum in being not only witty but a fabulous linguist: 'and some might have resented her tendency to pounce argumentatively on points they had made.'

The London Group was modelled on university seminars and was certainly not a fashionable bourgeois or bohemian salon like those in Germany at the turn of the nineteenth century. Literature was then the first point for German Jews to melt into the intellectual milieu of their native country, and artistically minded Jewish women ran the most prominent salons, with grand style and opulence financed by their husbands' wealth. The most well known were Henriette Harz (nicknamed 'the beautiful Jewess'), Dorothea Schlegel and her sister Henriette, and Rachel Varnhagen, whose salon was favoured by Heinrich Heine and Alexander von Hamboldt. The social integration of these ladies was so complete that before long they all converted to Christianity.

No food and alcohol were allowed at the London Group meetings and, if badly needing a drink, members rushed to the nearby pub afterwards, or slipped out during the interval, which came halfway. Outsiders mocked this rule; the Group was characterised 'as a band of severely puritan teetotallers' and compared with the monthly open-house literary soirées that the critic George Fraser ran in his Chelsea flat, and which Assia and David sometimes took part in – a bottle party in an overflowing, smoke-filled salon. 'Poets came with manuscripts, and read, drank, stubbed out their cigarettes on George's first editions of Yeats, Eliot, Pound, etc., vomited on the Fraser carpets, quarrelled on the stairs, sometimes bashed one another with fists or bottles,' remembered Peter Porter. In 1959, when Hobsbaum left for Sheffield, the meetings were convened in Edward Lucie-Smith's two-bedroom flat in Sidney Street in the more fashionable Chelsea.

Though never a formal member of the Group, Ted Hughes attended several meetings. 'Ted once scandalised my Rhodesian landlady by using her frying pan to fry a black pudding, which was his supper for the night,' recalls Philip Hobsbaum. Hughes outraged the landlady even more by singing ballads in his fine *Heldentenor*, at two in the morning. Anyone who came to the Group was warned that the discussion was conducted on the basis of frankness. 'Some writers, when it came to the point, have found us a trifle too frank for their taste,' recalled Lucie-Smith. Hughes handed Hobsbaum four meticulously typed manuscripts of Sylvia Plath's poems, which he realised 'must have been some kind of audition for the Group'. Hobsbaum was not impressed and regarded it as 'college girl stuff', a verdict that resulted in coolness on Hughes's part. Plath never came to the Group. 'She could not accept criticism, especially public criticism,' explains Edward Lucie-Smith.

David and Assia never met Ted Hughes at the Group's meetings but, nevertheless, Hughes must have known of David Wevill through the magazine *Delta*, to which they both contributed. In 1958 all three poets, Hughes, Plath and Wevill, were published in Christopher Levenson's anthology, *Poetry from Cambridge*. Though they never exchanged a word, David remembered Plath from Cambridge, walking in Trinity Lane, standing out in her spring dress among students in their rumpled clothes. Hughes kept in touch with the Group during the two years he spent in the United States by sending some of his poems, which they read aloud. His poems acquired totemic status there and they all saw him as a scene-setter, a magical, mythical figure.

Being an ardent reader, sharing her life with a poet and being exposed to the critical, but supportive, atmosphere of the Group had an effect on Assia's creativity:

> . . . And I do praise the force that falls
> With loosened stones and plunging force
> Of clear ghost-rivers in dried beds.
> And besides this watchful course
> Of hours and currents, watersheds
> Of welcome, do I praise the eye
> That finds me welcome,
>   needing no reply.

This poem, 'Magnificat', was a love hymn for David and for nature. It is one of Assia's two surviving poems, set in the same typing style of the Group. The other poem, 'Winter End, Hertfordshire', records the impact of seeing a tombstone of a pauper and his wife and child.

> . . . To see again and no more
> The black northern pond,
> Its autumn spent,
> Its eye burning with crippled cedar wings
> And four black feet deep with
> Summer's rotting rooks,
> Like Thomas Head's and my time's
> Unlamented, spring less, passed.

David and Assia walked a great deal in Hertfordshire, drawn to the poignancy and mystery of cemeteries. David recalls that they saw the name Thomas Head on a headstone and a conversation ensued. Thomas Head was buried in the grounds of St Nicholas Church in Great Hormead, just a few yards from Assia's window. Apparently, the place where she lived with her husband was not off-limits to David Wevill: 'The poem records something coming to an end, the season, a phase of life too. The tone is grave and elegiac. I don't find any poetic influence of mine there; the mood is almost like Thomas Hardy. Her marriage was soon to end, and her life to change, and though we were much in love, the future was not clear.' Wevill sensed sadness beneath Assia's humour and vivacity but did not think that she was prone to depression. Though optimistic by nature, she had a sense of catastrophe, but it did not stop her from moving into new experiences. Philip Hobsbaum finds in some of Assia's lines, 'a community of vision linking Hughes, Plath and Wevill'. Although she signed the poems with her married name Lipsey, Assia never showed them to her husband. Too intimidated and self-critical, she also did not use the opportunity to show her poems to the Group. 'There was a poetic spirit in Assia, but she was not intentionally a poet or writing poems with a view to publishing them,' recalls David Wevill.

During the summer of 1958, Dick Lipsey lived like a hermit in Great Hormead, working on his doctoral thesis on the theory of customs unions. He often rode eight to ten hours at a stretch on an old bicycle that Liliana Archibald lent him. Pedalling along, he composed chapters of his thesis in his head, and committed them to paper upon returning home. He christened those solitary months 'my summer of discontent'. Assia extended her stay in London and returned for the odd weekend. At the end of summer, she and Dick had to vacate the cottage but decided to stay on in the village, moving further up the hill. They occupied one wing at the Great Hormead Bury, a large manor house that was shared by several tenants. Cold and damp, in a poor state of repair, the roof leaked and it was almost uninhabitable, but Dick, who had meanwhile resumed his work in London, remembers tender moments there, arriving on Friday evenings with Assia and lighting the coal fire. By bedtime, the place would have warmed enough to allow them to take off their coats. 'We just enjoyed ourselves, the country was beautiful, and we walked around in it. Both of us needed the peacefulness before going back to the battle: I was fighting the intellectual battle, she was fighting whatever battles she had, and together we found a retreat.'

David Wevill was undecided about his career: whether to continue his English studies and aim for academia or to follow his childhood yearning for Japan and specialise in its language and culture. He applied for a teaching position with the British Council and settled for a two-year contract to teach history and British and American literature at the University of Mandalay. It was to begin in autumn 1958 and he hoped that Burma would also break the deadlock: 'We thought that if I went east she would get a divorce and would follow.'

Assia made no steps towards a divorce and neither was Lipsey in any hurry. With David away in the East, Assia and Dick were left to themselves for the first time in two years. Although they enjoyed some intimate moments, Dick had no illusions about their future: 'It was very clear that I was still a secondary figure, and her heart was out there, with David.' Assia and David corresponded intensely, but her husband respected her privacy and did not pry into her mail. 'My love, I'm so lonely – what have I done, I've gone thousands of miles away and could cry because I miss you,' she read in one of David's lovelorn letters. He tried to lift their spirits and eliminate time and distance by sending snapshots of the Burmese home awaiting her, describing the exciting future lying ahead of them. Her absence dominated his poems and they were all dedicated to her:

> Wherever we walked together, there was
> This assertion of melting. As if
> Underneath, the cells spoke and begged.

The first dramatic move towards a resolution had been made but all three protagonists were too paralysed to proceed. Assia discussed the dramatic crossroads of her life with anyone who cared to listen: Peter Porter spent an entire evening with her, wandering around Bayswater pondering her dilemma, whether or not to leave her husband and follow her lover to Mandalay. She was insensitive enough not to spare even her sister-in-law, Thirell Lipsey. 'All of a sudden, she confided in me that she was in love with a Canadian poet: "Oh, dear Thirell, what should I do, I really don't know what to do".' Thirell thought the marriage was harmful for her brother and Assia dragged him down but, although tempted to grasp the opportunity to set her brother free, she refused to get involved.

If Assia was waiting for her husband to cut the umbilical cord, Lipsey was equally too inert to declare their marriage over: 'It still didn't get to the stage that called for a divorce, and anyway, I grew up in a world where people didn't divorce. In retrospect it was hell. I was nuts, and should have broken it off and got on with living my life.' And, for his part, David Wevill was too gentle to prod Assia into getting a divorce. In the midst of the turmoil, Assia discovered that she was pregnant. It was clear both to her and to Dick that she must abort the child, and he took her to a clinic in Harley Street. David Wevill was not consulted, or even informed of, either the pregnancy or its termination.

In the early spring of 1959, Lisa Gutmann was diagnosed with cancer. Lipsey borrowed money to cover the heavy cost of Assia's trip home. To boast that she crossed the Atlantic on one of the majestic boats, Assia was willing to suffer great inconvenience, and travelled third class on the *Queen Mary* in a ghastly cramped cabin, though she would have obtained much better conditions for the same price on one of the less illustrious Canadian Pacific ships. She spent a month with her family in Vancouver and visited the Lipseys in Victoria, giving no hint to either set of parents that the marriage was on the rocks.

During Assia's absence, Lipsey had a heart-to-heart conversation with his close friend Professor Kurt Klapholz. They recalled an incident in Cambridge with several American professors and their wives. Assia had stormed in late and announced loudly that they should all have some fun and go out to raise hell. Lipsey had been both humiliated and sorry for Assia for making such a fool of herself. The memory of that episode led to Klapholz's firm advice. 'Even after years of the ménage à trois with David, I was so steeped in the old ways, that it came as a shock that I might get divorced.' After much soul searching, realising that his intense student days were behind him and he was on the verge of a major career move, Dick decided to end the marriage. On Assia's return, picking her up from the port at Southampton, he told her of his decision. She agreed outright. Assia knew that Lipsey was close to a professorship with all the perks involved but, materialistic though she was, she opted for David, who had no career and no financial prospects, his future, vague. She was 32 but for love she was ready to start all over again from scratch.

Dick and Assia contacted their lawyer friend, Martin Graham, with whom they had spent holidays at the ski resort of Zermatt. Graham was invited for a weekend in Great Hormead and was not surprised at what he saw. 'The marriage was an empty shell, with no intellectual or physical or any other sort of mutual interest, they were both rather disenchanted with each other. There was no violence and no arguments, just a drifting apart, though out of

convenience they shared the same dwelling.' But incompatibility and estrangement were not grounds for divorce at that time in Britain, and the court
demanded indisputable proof of a matrimonial offence: namely, cruelty,
desertion or adultery. Assia agreed to write down a detailed account of her
affair with David Wevill, giving places and dates in Cambridge and London
where the misconduct had taken place. Since David was already in Burma, the
court would have to do without a private detective's report, and photographs
of the guilty couple engaged in adulterous sexual activity.

Assia waited for Martin Graham to submit the application to the High Court
of Justice and only then was she ready to leave. In June 1959, Dick drove her
with all her luggage to London, and they spent the last night with the
Archibalds. In the morning, on her way to the port, they bid each other
farewell at the train station.

Eight

Third Marriage

Mandalay, 1959–London, 1961

Burma suited Assia like a glove. The ancient kingdom conquered by the British in the mid-nineteenth century had become a young, aspiring, independent republic, retaining remnants of its colonial past. Joining David at his house on the edge of the University of Mandalay campus, Assia faced strong competition: a brown, orphaned female monkey, which David got from one of his students to nurture and keep him company. 'Monkeys are monogamous, and the little female monkey considered me her man. When Assia arrived, she jumped on her and tore her dress. Sadly, the monkey had to go.'

Other changes soon followed; Assia did not get along with David's household staff, and she fired the cook and hired Francine, an Indian Christian woman, whose one-legged husband served as gardener. David's two-room house was far from majestic, but still, for the first time in her life, Assia tasted the pleasures of comfort. She was exempt from the tedium of humdrum employment; the maid did all the housework and served the meals. Assia had ample time to paint and read and she brushed up her father's native tongue with *Hugo's Russian in Three Months*. Curious and enthusiastic, she developed a modest expertise in Eastern art, and began to take an interest in netsuke – miniature Japanese sculptures made of wood, ivory or bone – which later developed into a passion. She practised Burmese dancing and often wore a sarong, which she made into a sleeveless dress tied above her breasts or around her waist as a long skirt. She spent her time leafing through magazines and doodling designs, sewing her own clothes and dressing up for afternoon garden parties. Her photographs of the time show her in starched flowery dresses with a low décolletage, several strands of white pearls hugging her swan-like neck. Her crisp elegance contrasted with the other Western women, who wore Bermuda shorts and sandals, which were much more practical for the heat and humidity. 'Assia stuck out in her long white gloves, which were too extravagant for the rest of us,' remembers her friend Patricia Mendelson. 'She presented herself as very glamorous, and was quick to adopt the colonial etiquette, wearing wide-rimmed hats, puffing on her cigarette, doing everything very stylishly and classy.'

At weekends, wicker chairs were set up on the lawn, around a table laden with muffins and marmalade and multi-layered chocolate cakes, and tea poured into delicate china cups. One of the party highlights was a game devised by a fellow teacher, anthropologist Alton Becker. Each of the guests impersonated a celebrity or a historical figure and, through Becker's questions, they had to unveil the identity. David Wevill masqueraded as the poet Stephen Spender, who became a Communist in 1936 and reported the hunt for the Russian battleship *Comsomol*. Assia's choice was especially perplexing. 'I was interviewing her, and it went on and on, and none of us could guess who she pretended to be, until she said in a heavy German accent, "my husband, Adolf Hitler",' remembers Professor Alton Becker. Assia's impersonation of Eva Braun, Hitler's long-standing young mistress, whom he married just a day before their joint suicide in his bunker in Berlin, astounded all and left them too upset to continue the game.

At those garden parties, men always buzzed around Assia and David usually sat a bit further away. Many foreign academics used the weekends and holidays for picnics and sightseeing and Assia was always energetic and keen to join in, David more reluctant, resigned to staying at home. He had three seminar-size classes and regarded teaching English literature as both fascinating and baffling. Most of his students were older than him, and 'their "Sir" falls a bit heavy,' he wrote to Earle Birney, with whom Assia had once had an affair. He found it difficult to delve into English poetry and explain the merits of Gerard Manley Hopkins, while monsoon rain was swamping the ground outside his class. A common practice among students was to write a note detailing their life circumstances, the family income, their devotion to their loving mother and tyrannical father and to their country and, finally to the exam-subject they were worried about, and ask the examiner for mercy in advance. Wevill felt that he could not deafen his ears to their pleas, especially when he was 'a visitor among them', and had 'no right (even in the interest of good English), to make their future even less certain than it was.'

It was a prolific time for Wevill and he wrote a great deal, publishing his poems in major British and American weeklies and magazines. He and Assia kept in touch with the Group, Lucie-Smith updating Assia on the recent gossip from Notley's, and planning an entire session in absentia for Wevill's new poems. The only cloud in their sky was the intolerable delay in the divorce proceedings in London. Assia had been assured, when leaving for Burma, that her letter of confession would make it a straightforward case and that her marriage would be dissolved in a few months. But justice took its course and Burma proved a problematic waiting room. There were whispers and frowns behind their backs; the illicit liaison of one of Her Majesty's employees, living with a married woman, was unacceptable to Wevill's employers. Alton Becker recalled that Assia and David were very upset when the British ambassador gave them an ultimatum. Assia tried desperately to prod Lipsey into action but her letters had no effect.

Wevill pondered his next move: if Assia's divorce came through quickly enough, he could hope to be sent by the British Council to Japan or to extend his work in Burma for another year. If that failed, he thought of going to Vancouver to continue for a Ph.D. in English. In January 1960, Richard Lipsey finally informed Assia that the decree had been granted and that their marriage would be dissolved within three months. But it was too late: by then, the British Council had turned down Wevill's application for Japan and refused to extend his contract in Burma. Disappointed at having to part from the East, they bought ivory carvings in the market, and Assia filled her crates with yards of colourful silk cloth and Burmese artefacts, including a number of Buddhas and a Burmese knife with a wooden handle.

On 16 May 1960, a day after Assia's thirty-third birthday, she married David in Rangoon. It was her third marriage, once again without a white bridal dress and with her family absent. On the marriage certificate, Assia deducted three years from her age and, to balance David, who wrote down his profession as 'lecturer', she promoted herself to a 'teacher'. The Burmese judge, in traditional headdress, handed her a book-shaped package. She thought it was his gift for the wedding and thanked him for it. 'The judge said, no, don't thank me, it's the Holy Bible and you must swear on it,' David recalls. Two days later the newly weds boarded the ship for the month's journey through Ceylon and the Suez Canal to England. London was supposed to be a stopover before continuing to Vancouver in September.

Upon arrival in England, Assia again found herself pregnant. She welcomed the forthcoming child and for the first time in her life made no plans to abort it. Lonya and Lisa Gutmann were clearly overjoyed. 'It's high time,' her mother wrote and urged the young couple to change their plans and settle in Montreal, where the Gutmanns were now living. Assia's sister, who was expecting her third child in September, offered her own velvet maternity outfit, slacks and a few tops. 'So, my children, save your money and hold on to every penny, we'll help you a bit as well,' Mrs Gutmann concluded.

A short while after Assia's departure for the East, Richard Lipsey had renewed his friendship with John Bosher, which had been derailed because of Assia. Bosher and his wife were sharing a large Georgian manor with six other couples, and Lipsey joined the commune. Apparently, the tumultuous seven years with Assia had shaken his strict morality and soon enough he began an affair with a fellow tenant, Diana Daniels, who was married with a child. In the winter of 1960, Diana left her husband, and moved with Dick into a large house in Marylebone. Like Assia, they were waiting impatiently for the divorce papers, since Diana too was pregnant. But in September, when Dick and Diana embraced their first son, Assia suffered a miscarriage and sadly lost hers.

By that time, David and Assia had decided to stay on in London and rented a garden flat in Holland Park. Wevill divided his time between writing poetry, polishing his Japanese at the School of Oriental and African Studies and grudgingly earning his living. He was a porter at Harrods furniture department, before finding a copywriting job at Ogilvy, Benson and Mather. 'We never made plans for the future, and were living from one day to the next, working to make a living, with no sense of a career,' Wevill summed things up. He preferred the pub counter at The Coach and Horses to his office desk and the novelist Fay Weldon, who was his copy group head, recalled that David 'was upset at having to make his living, if only temporarily and perforce, writing copy'. Weldon kept him going and covered for him by adding his name to submissions he never made, since she regarded him as a good poet: 'It was our duty to do what we could in the name of art.'

Assia and David were not allowed to work together since the policy in most advertising agencies was not to employ couples 'because they breed politics', as David Ogilvy, the head of the company, declared. She was welcomed back at Notley's and promoted to copywriter, her salary as a trainee a mere £500 a year. The agency inhabited two Georgian houses – one of them a former brothel – at 15 and 17 Hill Street, Mayfair, 'in discomfort and smartish squalor', remembered her colleague Peter Porter. Douglas Chowns, an art director at Notley's, remembers the agency as a mixture of leisure and work: 'It was a wonderfully mad place with Beaujolais after lunchtime in the studio with members of the corps de ballet from Sadlers Wells, while a couple practised their fencing technique in the centre of the floor.' The world of advertising depressed the introverted David Wevill, but Assia felt far from exploited, and blossomed in this blend of materialism and creativity. In a profession that requires charm and seduction in the selling of dreams and fantasies, the alluring, sometimes hedonistic Assia found herself in her element.

In June 1961, Notley's published an ad to promote the agency with a charity ball programme. The slogan 'We really *live* our work at Notley's' ran with a photograph of two sophisticated-looking couples in a dinghy on the Serpentine. Trevor Cox — later known as novelist William Trevor — was seen hammering away at a portable typewriter resting on his knee, and copywriter Sean Gallagher, wearing a bow tie, was holding a bottle of champagne. It was a sunny day, and a chic-looking Assia was elegantly holding a glass of champagne in her left hand, sucking a pencil, half-listening to her colleague Marisa Martelli. The text read, 'No, we don't have a champagne account at Notley's; we just happen to like product testing. We came out here because things were "not conducive to creative thought" back at the office. And you can bet your elastic-sided boots that *something* will come out of this session.' Though a novice at the agency and not yet an accomplished copywriter, Assia was a perfect publicity choice, wearing a white straw hat, a sleeveless top and a three-piece summer ensemble, with her jacket off.

Assia doted on shopping sprees and was always quick to offer unsolicited advice to her friends, derived from her own experience in fashion and make-up. 'Her figure was rather dumpy, heavy legs and thick ankles, and being a perfectionist, she was very conscious of these defects,' remembers Edward Lucie-Smith. 'Curiously she was unaware of the beauty which made one overlook these flaws. If you paid her a compliment on her beauty, she was rather put out. I remember that once Marisa and I reduced her to tears by telling her the whole morning how beautiful she was.' Once installed in advertising, Assia found it easier to move on, and found a job at Colman, Prentice and Varley in Grosvenor Street, doubling her salary. CPV held the long-time record for being the advertising agency for the War Office. In the 1959 elections, when Labour looked almost certain to topple the Conservative government, Harold Macmillan resorted, for the first time, to the services of an advertising agency. CPV conducted the campaign under the slogan, 'Life's better with the Conservatives – don't let Labour ruin it,' winning a victory of 107 seats and gaining the party account. Assia was working at CPV when they earned their place in the history of advertising with their campaign for Yardley, entitled 'A Woman's Ammunition': influenced by the James Bond films, the ad showed a delicate, feminine bandolier with lipsticks for bullets.

The copywriters were a closed shop, with their own pubs and restaurants: 'and seldom met anyone who wasn't in the trade, who might look at us askance and mock our enthusiasm,' recalled Fay Weldon, who often lunched with Assia. 'Advertising was still an innocent toddler, as was television: they had not yet created the consumer society.' The copywriters got together again in the evenings, this time wearing their literary hats. Drifting along with no agenda, the mere thought of career and ambition was loathsome; the main thought was to get through the day and wait for the great literary break-through. Once Peter Redgrove complained that he was broke, and someone suggested an easy way to make money. '"Oh," said Peter in a tone of absolute outrage, "but that would be 'work'!" "Work" in that sense was the enemy of poetry and the poetic state,' recalls Edward Lucie-Smith.

Handling the publicity accounts of Assia's favourite department stores – Fortnum & Mason and Dickins & Jones – CPV matched her aspirations and coveted lifestyle. Art director Julia Matcham remembers Assia's strong, slightly swarthy face graced by an amused, rather ironic and wondering smile. Matcham admired Assia's chic, a scarf thrown with splendid artistry over her shoulder, her glossy hair held back with a round tortoiseshell clasp. 'She was a pirate on the sea of life, and life could not possibly ignore this rather beautiful and rather animal woman. She was charming, but she did not exploit her power. Like a satisfied lioness, she waited,' Matcham recalls. Assia was bursting with ideas; she would entertain her colleagues by outlining a complicated plot for a novel, indifferent to the fact that somebody might pick it up and turn it into a book. 'What she related never sounded quite like fiction, more a sleight of hand involving real people and the real world,' was William Trevor's observation. She electrified them with her plan to purchase an old bread van, install a refrigerator, drive it to Hampstead Heath on warm Saturday afternoons and, dressed in white, sell homemade ice cream, prepared from an Italian recipe book. Although she was sure that they would make a

Assia childhood and family photographs courtesy of Celia Chaikin.

Lisa Gutmann

Dr Lonya Gutmann

Assia, Berlin 1929

Assia and Celia, Berlin 1931

Lisa Gutmann and daughters – Tel Aviv, mid-1930s

Assia, aged 16, Tel Aviv, the photo she gave
John Steele (courtesy of John Steele)

Dr Gutmann with Assia and Celia, Tel Aviv, early 1940s
(courtesy of Celia Chaikin)

Assia, date unknown
(courtesy of Richard Lipsey)

Tel Aviv, early 1940s
(courtesy of Richard Lipsey)

Assia and Keith Gems in Tel Aviv, early
1940s (courtesy of Richard Lipsey)

Assia bathing in Tel Aviv, 1946
(courtesy of Richard Lipsey)

Assia and John Steele, England 1947
(courtesy of Celia Chaikin)

Assia and John Steele on their
wedding day, London, May 1947
(courtesy of Richard Lipsey)

PROOF PRINT

Assia and her parents in Vancouver, Canada, 1950 (courtesy of Celia Chaikin)

Assia, a secretary in Victoria, Canada, 1950 (courtesy of Richard Lipsey)

Assia (right) and Celia, Vancouver 1951
(courtesy of Celia Chaikin)

Assia on her wedding day to
Richard Lipsey, October 1952
(courtesy of Celia Chaikin)

Assia Lipsey, Montreal, 1952
(courtesy of Celia Chaikin)

Assia and Richard Lipsey at his parents' home,
Vancouver Island, 1956
(courtesy of Celia Chaikin)

Assia and Richard Lipsey, 1957
(courtesy of Celia Chaikin)

WINTER-END, HERTFORDSHIRE.

At this time's end
Lulled by the end alone
I look through all the windows
Of this time's passing

To look again and no more
At the triple death of
Thomas Head and no identity
Like his child and bitter wife
Stalled in their moss eroded cattle
       grave
In a pauper's winter.

Unhollied, unmarked, spring less
Thomas, tamer of yew partridge
Master of none but the brewer's weeds
Procurer of rat tails and winter lover
of Mrs. Head's, has eaten his fifty
Year old death and had no time,
No sun, no annotation.

To see again and no more
The black northern pond,
Its autumn ~~was~~ spent
Its eye burning with crippled cedar wings
And four black feet deep with
Summer's rotting rooks,
Like Thomas Head's and my time's
Unlamented, springless, passed.

       A. Lipsey

A poem by Assia, Great Hormead, 1957 (courtesy of Celia Chaikin) fortune, it was not the money she was after: but 'being loved for herself alone was what she hoped for when she tried to sell ice cream,' recalled William Trevor. The scheme never went beyond passionate pub talk.

Assia's free spirit and ability to imply elegance even in the most ordinary ads impressed Angela Landels, who was Assia's group head. 'She was very innovative, everything she wrote had charm, and she brought a touch of poetry to mundane subjects like bread.' But Assia was also difficult to work with, brazenly lying to excuse her regular lateness or complete absences. Landels found her unpredictable, untrustworthy, manipulative, devious, argumentative and petty, but still was charmed by her unconventional, often wild and stimulating ideas, a priceless advantage in the profession. To her fellow workers, Assia's bubbling vitality seemed feverish; her radiant glare was at times menacing, slightly insane: 'all that beauty could turn ugly in an instant.' Assia seemed self-assured and above criticism and Angela Landels did not dare risk her wild temper. She often had to defend Assia against the management: 'and it always puzzled me why she was in advertising, when she could have been a diva; our world was too limited for her.'

Assia continued to feel that the score with her ex-husband remained unsettled: she blamed him for deliberately holding up their divorce in order to jeopardise her relationship with David. One day she phoned and demanded to see Dick at once; they met at the entrance to the South Kensington underground station and had a stormy row. 'She suddenly pulled a long Burmese ceremonial dagger and tried to stab me. I grabbed her arm and we fell in the gutter. The bystanders – how typical of the English – walked by while we struggled, no one trying to separate us,' he says. After a tussle in the gutter, Lipsey managed to overpower Assia, and wrenched the dagger away from her. 'Be careful, I have a gun,' she screamed at his receding back.

Did Assia attempt to harm her ex-husband? Lipsey was not scared enough to go to the police station which was just around the corner. Instead, he travelled to another part of town, laying the dagger on his solicitor's table. 'The world was Machiavellian to Assia, and she saw everything in terms of pacts. If something had gone wrong with the divorce, she couldn't accept that it was simple bureaucratic negligence, but rather, evil intention, meaning that I must have been at fault,' says Lipsey. But still maintaining his role of the protective father, he persuaded himself that Assia was incapable of doing any serious damage and did not press charges.

But Assia would not let go. Dick and Diana's sleep was disturbed constantly by late-night phone calls, the mysterious caller hanging up as soon as they picked up the phone. It became such a nuisance that they had to have their phone number changed. They never found out the intruder's identity but were quite sure that it was Assia. One evening, when the Lipseys were out, there was a knock on the door. The au pair, watching over Diana's child and the newly born Matthew, opened the door to Assia, who introduced herself as a friend of Dick's and asked to see the children. 'Christine caved in at Assia's persistence, and followed her warily into the nursery. Assia just stood there and stared at my son with a frightening look, and then turned and left,' Lipsey recalls. He was distraught at the incursion – he remembered that Assia claimed to have a gun – but still, did not turn her in, nor did he reproach her.

Assia's possessiveness and vanity would not let her get over her husband's quick recovery from their divorce. 'How dare he! He's mine!' she exclaimed to Edward Lucie-Smith. In her wounded pride she initiated more acts of revenge, canny and sophisticated. 'Assia had an original entertaining mind, with crazy ideas highly coloured by an exaggerated romanticism,' thought her colleague Julia Matcham. 'In its rather tenuous relationship to reality, it allowed her free reign to be quite ruthless in the pursuit of anything that she wanted, without the burden of a bad conscience.' Matcham was lost for words when Assia told her and Angela Landels of her little revenge *en passant*. No sooner said than done, Assia went out at lunchtime with colleague William Trevor, and led him to top florist Moyses Stevens near their office in Berkeley Square. She went as far as introducing herself 'as somebody's secretary – which she was not – and ordering flowers in his name'.

She set her mind on four dozen roses but, glancing over the vast array of flowers, she scaled it down to a dozen and a half long-stemmed red roses, to be dispatched immediately to her so-called employer's wife. She told William Trevor that the flowers were for a pregnant woman, whose husband was a cold fish, incapable of such romantic gestures: 'in error, I married him once,' she added. The grand bouquet arrived at the Lipsey residence with no note attached and Dick and Diana could not fathom the sender's identity. A month later they were aghast to get a bill, close to a week's salary. The indignant Lipsey phoned the shop to complain and was told that his secretary had ordered the flowers. 'I couldn't think of anyone but Assia whose mind would work in such a convoluted way,' he recounts. 'But if she wanted to make me insanely jealous over my wife's unknown lover, which is what I guess she would have wanted, she failed.' Once again, Lipsey decided not to confront Assia, but, gnashing his teeth, paid the bill.

The Wevills renewed their ties with the Group, spending many Friday evenings at Edward Lucie-Smith's in Chelsea. In the summer of 1961 they took a holiday in Italy and upon their return decided to move, since the flat in Holland Park was a bit expensive. They searched the property section of the *London Evening Standard* for flats in Hampstead or its vicinity.

It was at this time that Ted Hughes and his wife, Sylvia Plath, having also returned from holiday, decided to sublet their flat at 3 Chalcot Square, at the foot of Primrose Hill. They had taken the unfurnished flat on the top floor in January 1960 on a three-year lease that allowed them to sublet it for the remaining period. Now, with baby Frieda and another baby due, it became too cramped. A move to their own house in the village of North Tawton sounded a great improvement: less expensive, healthier for the children, the marriage and the creative careers of two poets.

When Assia dialled PRI 9132 to inquire about the flat, the name Hughes sounded familiar, though she did not ask whether the prospective landlords were the two poets. 'I think we realised it was them, putting two and two together, and since I liked Ted's and Sylvia's poetry, it seemed serendipitous,' says David Wevill. Getting the address, Assia was quick to draw a map on the back of 'One-eyed Monster', a poem by Peter Redgrove that they had discussed in one of the recent Group meetings. She marked in arrows the shortest way to the flat from the 74 bus stop, opposite the Zoo gate at Regent's Park. This page has survived all the turbulent decades that followed.

Assia knew the area well, since she had lived around the corner when she arrived at England in 1946. She and David were thrilled to reside close to the place where they first lived together as illicit lovers in 1957. Chalcot Square was in a run-down neighbourhood but Hughes and Plath raised the rent to cover the expenses incurred by painting and decorating, and putting in shelves and linoleum on the kitchen floor. The flat was tiny – one living room and a bedroom that could hold only a double bed – but the Wevills fell for it instantly. They seemed to Plath 'too slow and polite to speak up', and as they were looking around, another customer, a 'chill, busybody man' arrived. He was so eager to have the flat that he immediately sat down to write a cheque and stormed out. His brashness put Sylvia and Ted off, especially since they took a liking to the couple, 'the boy, a young Canadian poet, the girl, a German-Russian, whom we identified with', as Plath wrote to her mother. Sylvia was 29, 'the boy' David was 26, and 'the girl' Assia, 34. Apparently, Plath regarded the Wevills as a recent couple, although they had been a couple for nearly five years, only slightly less than she and Hughes. But there was something fresh and intimate in the well-dressed childless pair, which may have reminded Sylvia of her own early conjugality with Ted. She found an excuse to cancel the busybody's transaction and by her affirmative action the Wevills got the flat.

'We got on with them like a house on fire,' recalls Wevill. He and Assia were invited to Chalcot Square for supper and a few days later Ted and Sylvia went with baby Frieda for dinner at the Wevills'. In the next three weeks they met about half a dozen times. Once – as Hughes told Professor Judith Kroll – Assia gave Sylvia a painted wooden handcrafted snake, from the collection of artefacts that she had brought back with her from Burma. It is tempting to interpret the gift symbolically but 'Assia was indifferent to the occult, and for her, it was just a decorative object, with no subtle reasons behind it,' David Wevill believes. Plath, on the other hand, must have been aware of the totemic significance of the seducing snake but, although she tended to be jealous of any woman who came near her husband, she did not regard Assia as a threat or a rival in her own Garden of Eden. She had only compliments for Assia, finding her 'very attractive, intelligent'. Did Assia's charm numb Sylvia's suspiciousness, or was Sylvia so excited about her prospective new life in Devon that she could think of nothing else?

Hughes collected a round dining table belonging to the Wevills to take to North Tawton and, on Thursday, 31 August his own last remaining items – the double bed, the cot and the cooker – were loaded on the small van.

In the following months the couples corresponded and exchanged a few phone calls. When a Mr Price Turner from the *Yorkshire Post* wrote to Plath and Hughes and inquired whether they had any poems to publish, they apologised that they were too busy settling at their small farm, and recommended David Wevill, who took over their London flat, and had already published some very good poems.

Despite Hughes's occasional visits to the BBC in London, he did not visit the Wevills. Apparently, he was not yet overwhelmed by what he later described, as Assia's 'many blooded beauty', 'With tiger painted nails' and 'erotic mystery'. The seed of lust was not yet sown. For several months there were opportunities but apparently no interest in adultery on either side.

Nine

A Fateful Meeting

Devon, May 1962

London in the swinging sixties: the pill, the Beatles, acid trips, the sense that the times were changing and 'anything goes' – but none of it was blowing Assia's mind. She had neither the figure nor the taste for a miniskirt; she easily resisted beehived hair. The psychedelic revolution in no way altered her classic elegance, and Harrod's, not Carnaby Street, was her Mecca.

Indifferent to popular culture, Assia did not swap Antonioni, Bergman and Fellini for fourteen hours of *Technicolor Dream* at Alexandra Palace, and Beethoven remained her favourite composer. Permissiveness did not change her bed manners; she was as reserved as ever about casual sex, marriage being her preferred lifestyle. Many of her friends were in analysis but not Assia. For all the rebellion against propriety in speech and language, Assia clung to her upper-class accent and Standard English. Her pre-war European cultural roots as well as her maturity vitiated any enticement of the druggie-hippie culture. LSD was definitely not her poison; in fact, Assia abstained even from alcohol. Not that Assia was unfamiliar with the latest trends; she worked, after all, in advertising and, as her husband David Wevill observed, 'she was tolerant of the superficial, as long as she wasn't asked to take it seriously.' Demonstrations against the war in Vietnam were regularly held near Assia's office, in front of the American Embassy in Grosvenor Square; if she acknowledged them, she also passed them by.

Youth had become the new Moloch, and mature women were the ravenous god's burnt offerings. To this trend, the 34-year-old Assia was not immune. Terrified of ageing, she would talk about having a facelift in virtually the same breath as she did about dying. She told her boss, Angela Landels, that she wanted to die young, 'because growing old, with one's skin wrinkled and hanging down, losing one's feminine potency, was ghastly'. Since she looked absolutely ravishing, Landels did not interpret Assia's sentiments as a death wish but rather as another instance of her dramatic posturing.

Assia had never wanted for dramatic flair and she and David together made a striking pair. Their colleague and friend Fay Weldon, in her autobiography, *Auto da Fay,* savours David's grandeur and Assia's brooding, sultry beauty: 'a glorious poetic pair that for a time rivalled the Ted Hughes and Sylvia Plath conjunction. When either pair entered rooms, heads turned and a kind of glow came in with them.' William Trevor found Assia's features to be 'reminiscent of Sophia Lauren in a tranquil moment'. Together they were like 'Scott Fitzgerald people, sixties-style, their innocence brushed over with sophistication, their devotion to one another taken for granted'. Some of the Wevills' friends felt that Assia was overly protective of David, in a proud, big-sisterly way.

Philip Hobsbaum recalls an incident he witnessed at a party celebrating the publication of Peter Redgrove's first book, *The Collector.* Among the guests at Redgrove's house in Chiswick was the critic G S Fraser, who, Assia complained to the hostess, was making passes at her husband. 'I didn't know David was queer,' Barbara Redgrove replied coolly. 'But he's not!' Assia protested, and Mrs Redgrove said sweetly, 'Well, I don't see why you are worried then.'

The Wevills exulted in the good fortune that had brought them together. Says David Wevill:

> We were equals, sharing most things. We were partners, lovers, friends, companions. Assia taught me a great deal. She was more sophisticated and experienced socially, without being false. I don't know what or how much I taught her; we exchanged ways of looking at things, at the world, at life. She was less shy than I, more willing to engage with others.

They encouraged each other, and he found Assia to be a good and precise critic of his poems, neither too harsh nor too gentle. 'We were very much a couple, a pair, for the while that things went well for us.'

The sixth year of the marriage between Plath and Hughes, meanwhile, became increasingly stressful with the birth of their second child, Nicholas, in January 1962. Sylvia was steeped in the motherhood smells of milk and urine, and Ted was discontent. Poet and critic A Alvarez observes that Ted was confined in Sylvia's world, held fast in a union of 'intolerable similarities', and Lucas Myers asserts that Hughes was depressed, a prisoner, though a willing one, in his own marriage. Already in March 1960, in a pub near Chalcot Square, Hughes had told Myers about the difficulties of daily life with Sylvia. Like many of Ted's friends, Myers believed that Hughes's marriage was harmful to him and that Sylvia was draining him.

After the long, harsh winter's siege of Devon in 1962, Ted and Sylvia decided 'to have several couples [they liked] down in the next month'. On Wednesday, 2 May they hosted writer Alan Sillitoe and his American wife, the poet Ruth Fainlight, for a long weekend at Court Green. The tension between Sylvia and Ted was palpable and Ruth noticed that they avoided looking at or addressing each other directly whenever they thought it was not too obvious.

On that occasion Sylvia showed Ruth her latest poem, 'Elm'. Written two weeks earlier, it explored a rift in a relationship. Love, Sylvia wrote in the poem, 'has gone off, like a horse'. In Professor Diane Wood Middlebrook's reading of the poem, 'Plath was detecting a shift in the emotional dynamics between herself and her husband.' Sylvia asked Ruth's permission to dedicate 'Elm' to her, and wondered if it should be to Ruth Sillitoe – i.e., as a mother and wife – or to Ruth Fainlight, as creative poet. Together they decided on the latter.

Apparently, Ted Hughes and Sylvia Plath did not have many close friends, for among their few guests that spring in Devon were their tenants from Chalcot Square in London. Assia was ecstatic about the visit and she shared her enthusiasm with her colleagues. 'Assia said in her rich deep voice, her green eyes challenging one to protest – I'm going to seduce Ted!' recalls her boss Angela Landels, who took it with a pinch of salt and simply muttered, 'I don't care what you do, as long as you come back on Monday in a better mood.'

For decades biographical literature on Plath and Hughes has portrayed Assia as a kind of Lilith tempting Ted, her Adam, out of his Eden. Assia is consistently blamed for initiating the affair that ensued and frequently the events of the Wevills' 48 hours in Devon are staged as a sinuous dance of calculated seduction on the part of Assia. In her every word and deed Assia seeks to ensnare her innocent Adam. With charm and attentiveness she plays up to the poet Hughes's considerable ego or, in a negligée, she stealthily descends the stairs and creeps up behind Ted while he's sitting alone at the kitchen table with his morning coffee. The story has Assia raising her nightgown up to her chin and then lowering it down over Hughes's face and torso until the two of them are straitjacketed in its fabric.

In fact, the events that weekend were not so sensational.

A day before the Wevills were due at Court Green, Sylvia planned the menu for the weekend – 'beef stew, corn chowder, ginger bread' – and also reminded herself to wash her hair. The entry on her calendar for the following day simply reads 'The Wevills'. When Sylvia anticipated a particularly exciting event, she would decorate the entry with a star, as she did for the Sillitoes. The Wevills, though, remained starless.

On Friday, 18 May at the end of their working day, Assia and David took the train from Waterloo to Exeter, where Ted was waiting to pick them up in his Morris Traveller. That evening they all dined in the big back room, at the round wooden table that the Wevills had loaned to Ted and Sylvia. David Wevill remembers: 'during dinner and after, we talked a lot, satirising people we knew. It was a lively conversation, and Assia told stories from Burma and other chapters in her life. Sylvia was a good listener, and she also told anecdotes of her life in the States. She and Ted gave the impression of a very close and devoted couple that had worked out a life for themselves.'

Though she enjoyed the company, Assia clearly did not like Court Green, which she found damp, 'with hideous grass gorging on the smooth brown stones. Grass almost grew in the house,' she later wrote in her diary. She liked even less Sylvia's whimsical decoration of the place – she seemed to have painted hearts and flowers everywhere – and Assia found the house to be 'very secret, red, childishly furnished. Naively furnished. The whole look of it improvised, amateurish.'

Decades later, some of Hughes's impressions of the Wevills' visit, and particularly of Assia, would appear in his *Birthday Letters* poems. Assia's silk orange dress, which she wore for dinner, emphasised her dark hair, and her carefully made-up eyes gave her 'the gaze of a demon'. Her hosts were captivated not only by her striking appearance but also by the elusive self inside her multiple European identities.

Among the four of them, Assia and Ted stood out in their alluring physical presence and captivating conversation; they charmed the opposite sex effort-lessly and they shared, too, an ability to draw out someone's inner self and make that person feel as if she or he stood at the centre of their universe. Assia, though, was unaware of her magnetism, as Edward Lucie-Smith, her colleague and confidant, notes:

> Unlike some stunning beauties, who know how to control the reactions they evoke, Assia, despite her striking beauty, was somewhat naïve about the way men reacted to her. Though sometimes she seemed to lead them on, it wasn't deliberate. She was often panic-stricken when men misinterpreted her warmth and friendliness, and started to pursue her. Perhaps this was why she created so many explosive situations around her.

In 'Dreamers', Hughes marked the moment of his falling in love with Assia: it was around the breakfast table, when she recounted a dream that she had that night of a huge pike. He seemed to believe that, unlike him, at that stage she was not yet aware of her feelings towards him. Rather, so he hinted, the two of them got caught up in an inevitability as he fell in love with this exotic woman who was sharing his innermost world, the world of his dreams. (Of course, the claim of fatal attraction also served to exonerate Hughes from any responsibility.) At this point in Hughes's life, pike – predatory fish that put up a fierce fight when hooked – figured significantly and recurrently in his dreams, and his best, most gratifying nights were filled with them. For the pike had become an integral part of his imaginative life, 'always an image of how I was feeling about life', as he would tell Thomas Pero of the American angling magazine, *Wild Steelhead & Salmon*. The night before his marriage to Plath, Hughes dreamt that he had hooked a pike and, when the fish began to surface, its head filled the entire lake. However weighty the dream's portent may have been, Hughes proceeded with his marriage plans. That Assia, like Hughes, should have dreamt of a pike, to judge by his account in 'Dreamers', left Plath overwhelmed and jealous, knowing, as she did, the significance of this particular fish for her husband. In reality, it did not seem to affect her behaviour, however, and even months later, she did not say or write anything about Assia's strangely sentient dream.

David Wevill does not remember that Assia recounted any dream at all during the visit. He and Assia commonly shared their dreams, but only with each other, not with strangers, he says, and anyway, 'that dream is not typical of her. It's loaded with mythic imagery, almost too much to go into.' Assia by nature did not have an exceptionally vivid dream life but, in any case, pike would seem to be an unlikely dream motif for an urban woman like her. Furthermore, judging by her surviving diaries and letters, Assia did not attach particular importance to her dreams, as she never bothered to write them down. Nor did she tell them to her friends.

If, however, Assia did discuss a dream, did she mischievously invent it to impress her host? A pike is the subject of one poem in Hughes's much acclaimed volume *Lupercal,* which had been published two years before the Wevills' visit and, in all likelihood, Assia had read it. But *Lupercal* considers numerous other creatures – birds, frogs, cats, dogs, horses – as well as a variety of fish and Assia could not have known the mythic, symbolic import – indeed, the fixation – that Ted attached to pike in particular. So did the scene in which Assia related a dream take place only in Hughes's fertile poetic imagination?

On Saturday, after breakfast, Ted brought out air rifles, and he and David shot at blackbirds perching on the roof. Sylvia and Assia meanwhile did some gardening and prepared lunch. Later the two men decided to drive to the moor with little Frieda but halfway there they ran out of petrol. They were walking back towards Court Green when an army truck stopped and offered them some petrol for the return home. After supper, they listened to a recording of the American poet Robert Lowell reading his poem 'The Quaker Graveyard in Nantucket'. David recalls: 'Sylvia spoke of my poems, we all spoke of one another's poems, and Assia took an active part in the conversation. Ted, I believe, liked my work, and I his, very much.' In the midst of the lively conversation, however, Sylvia abruptly arose and went upstairs. Ted did not follow her; evidently he preferred the company of his guests as he ignored Sylvia's repeated calls for him to come up to bed.

Five months later Hughes wrote (but never published) the poem 'Sunlight', which, according to Diane Wood Middlebrook, would appear to recreate the Wevills' visit and to suggest that by nightfall Assia already had Ted under her spell and 'all night, he ached with desire for her'.

The first day and a half of the visit passed smoothly enough. Sylvia and Ted found time to write a letter to Ted's brother, Gerald, in Australia about a fishing trip. Just a month earlier, in a letter to her mother, Sylvia had been vitriolic about weekend guests and their 'ghastly children', who 'had no inner life', and in another letter she had been complimentary about the Sillitoes, who had helped with the cooking and washing up. Apparently, though, Sylvia had nothing to write home about the Wevills.

'On Sunday morning we got up late and hung about until lunch,' David Wevill recalls. 'Assia was in the kitchen making a salad, and Ted was with her. Sylvia and I were sitting outside chatting. We could hear Assia and Ted's muffled voices, and suddenly Sylvia went very still. She touched me on the knee and said, "I'll be back." She jumped from her chair and ran into the kitchen as if she remembered that she had left some fire burning.'

David waited, but Sylvia did not return, and at lunch she was very quiet, 'as if a door had slammed down on her'. David supposed that their hostess had had enough of company or else she had had a quarrel with Ted. After lunch she drove the Wevills to the railway station, with Ted in the passenger seat next to her. 'She was very nervous, clashed the gears, and was on edge,' says David, but nonetheless, he is certain that he and Assia were not kicked out of Court Green, and did not leave any earlier than they had planned, as has been sometimes suggested; they were due to leave anyway that afternoon, to make the four-hour train journey to London, towards another busy working week ahead.

'We waved goodbye and as we were alone in the cabin, I said to Assia, "What happened to Sylvia? She changed completely, she was so friendly before." And Assia answered, "Ted kissed me in the kitchen, and Sylvia saw it."' David did not probe any further and Assia did not elaborate as to whether Ted had merely lightly brushed her lips with his or had proffered her a more sensuous kiss; nor did she indicate if she had reciprocated. 'It was the first time that something like that happened in our relationship, and it wasn't characteristic of her.' David had then put the fact of the kiss aside and minimised its significance. 'I wasn't terribly alarmed, and didn't want to make a scene. Mild flirtations can happen among friends, and I thought that Ted made the move since boys will be boys. I got the sense from Assia that the kiss surprised her, and that nothing would follow.'

David thought that Sylvia overreacted: 'I hadn't seen her nerves act up before. Had I known her past history, we would have come to the weekend more cautiously.' Assia was always remarkably outspoken with her friends about her love life; indeed, later in her affair with Hughes she would not spare them even the most intimate details of Ted's bedroom manners. Yet, when she reported back to her friends about the weekend in Devon, she did not mention a kiss or any other kind of intimacy. Was the kiss Assia's own invention, a provocative bit of drama created by her to rouse her husband, to kindle his desire and enliven their marriage?

Plath's emotional radar was extremely sensitive to the slightest perceived invasion of her conjugal space by other women. She had made a particularly nasty scene when, just a few years into the marriage, she suspected that Ted had been overly friendly with an attractive college student at Smith College. At the end of January 1961, too, Sylvia had blown up after answering a call from Ted's BBC assistant producer Moira Doolan, who had sounded entirely too cheerful to Plath's wary ear. Sylvia had also retaliated; she had shredded plays and poetry Ted was working on as well as his precious, red Oxford rice-paper edition of Shakespeare. On holiday with Ted in France some months later, Sylvia had exploded once again, this time because of her suspicion that their hostess, Dido Merwin, was being too intimate with Ted.

And just a month before the Wevills' visit, a suspicious and resentful Sylvia had confronted the daughter of the local National Provincial Bank manager. Nicola Tyrer was not yet sixteen, in fact, when she became a frequent guest at Court Green during her holidays from Headington School in Oxford. Sylvia, who 'saw women as competition, even teenagers', assumed an icy, rather intimidating attitude with the pretty, young girl, while Ted, warm and generous, introduced Nicola to his favourite books, music and films. The girl found him mesmerising, and 'he remained the focus of my teenage dreams,' Nicola recalls. Ted also used to go to the Tyrers for tea but he always went on his own and on those occasions he would engage Nicola in long conversation. One evening she accompanied him back to Court Green and, standing under the laburnum tree outside the house, they continued talking. Suddenly the door opened, and there stood Sylvia with baby Nicholas in her arms. 'Oh,' she said with blistering sarcasm. 'Are you seeing Ted home?' A frighteningly angry outburst from Sylvia ensued and Nicola, shocked and ashamed, fled home. The incident did not stop Ted from seeing Nicola again, however, and for her sixteenth birthday he presented her with a copy of his first book of poetry, *The Hawk in the Rain*, and his brand-new volume of children's verse, *Meet My Folks*. In one of them, he wrote a poem, and the other he inscribed, 'For Nicola, Who is not too young/Not too old/Just right, love from Ted.' A few days later the Tyrers left Devon for the southeast of England.

In 'Dreamers', Hughes ascribed his fascination with Assia to a stroke of fate that affected Sylvia as well. The critic Erica Wagner would appear to agree:

'Assia is a figure Plath has drawn from her subconscious, the dark fount of her work.' Wagner reads Assia as an embodiment of an idea in Plath's dream-self, with Sylvia assigning to Assia all the glamour that 'Plath, in her college-girl incarnation, had chased, the European sophistication she herself could never achieve,' and all the turbulence of the Jewish past with which both Sylvia and Ted identified. In Assia's Germanness, which appealed so strongly to Hughes, Plath also found an echo of her own German-born father and Austrian-American mother. Plath herself took great pains to learn her ancestral tongue by tuning in every Monday and Friday to the BBC's *Keep Up Your German*. Did the cosmopolitan Assia intrigue Sylvia enough to let down her conjugal guard, since nothing in her journals and correspondence that weekend indicates that Assia provoked her anger? Or perhaps Ted was able to convince Sylvia that nothing had happened between him and their captivating house-guest?

Whatever happened in the kitchen had no immediate effect on any member of the quartet. The kiss, if a kiss there was, did not mark for any of them a turning point, not even for Plath. She wrote to her mother, 'This is the richest and happiest time of my life,' and after the Wevills' visit, when Al Alvarez stopped at Court Green for a few hours on his way down to Cornwall, Sylvia seemed to him 'solid and complete, her own woman again' in a marriage that appeared to Alvarez to be strong and close. The poems that Plath worked on within hours of the visit do not in any way suggest her suspicion of a rival; they do not bear even a trace of the tremendous acrimony that informs the poetry written by Plath when the affair was full blown. Plath finished two poems by noon on Monday, 21 May, the day after the Wevills had departed and, while both of them – 'The Rabbit Catcher' and 'Event' – reflect a strained relationship, the origin of the injury precedes the entry of the Wevills into their lives in Devon by some while. Hughes's 'The Rabbit Catcher', published 46 years later, clarifies the background of Plath's poem of the same title. During a family picnic by the sea a few weeks earlier Sylvia had come across some rabbit snares. 'Murderers!' she had cried, and furious, she had torn them apart. Hughes, on the other hand, had spoken in defence of the poor peasants who had set the traps so that they would be able to put meat in the Sunday stew pot. It was an unfortunate incident and it served to heighten the diverse sympathies that had long been troubling the two poets' marriage.

The rabbit in Sylvia's poem may be related to the hare in Hughes's morality play, *Difficulties of a Bridegroom,* about which he wrote to his friends Bill and

Dido Merwin on 24 May, four days after the Wevills' return to London. The play tells the story of a groom, Sullivan by name, who is driving to London to meet his mistress when he quite deliberately runs over a hare. Sullivan then sells the carcass to poachers for five shillings, which he in turn gives to his mistress. Appalled by the deliberate killing, she refuses to accept what she calls 'blood money'. To make amends, Sullivan presents her with two red roses, which she reluctantly accepts. At the time, Hughes had been reading *The Chymical Wedding of Christian Rosenkreutz* by Johann Valentin Andreae, a seventeenth-century work that in the spring of 1962 influenced Hughes's play more than did his marital tension with Sylvia or his recent attraction to Assia. By the time *Bridegroom* was broadcast by the BBC in January 1963, however, the play had been revised considerably and Hughes's own personal drama was more clearly echoed in the text.

During the Wevills' visit Sylvia had told Assia that she would love to do tapestry and described a particular pattern that she had once seen in a newspaper but could not remember which or when. Upon returning to London, Assia did some research and discovered that the pattern – Rose Bouquet – had appeared in the *Sunday Times* two years earlier. She found it at Harrod's and, to save Sylvia the time and trouble of trying to find the materials in Exeter, she bought not only the pattern but also the thread in the whole range of colours required to complete the tapestry. In their monthly expenditure book, Assia put down the price of the gift: '£1.10.0.' In an adjoining letter to 'My dear Sylvia', she offered useful tips and warned of the danger of becoming 'seriously addicted'. The note was signed, 'Much love, Assia'. It was undoubtedly more a thank-you present from a thoughtful, courteous guest than it was a gift to at once assuage Assia's guilty conscience and further dupe her betrayed hostess. Assia's friends attest to her generosity; they might merely mention an especial item that they coveted and, be it a book or a fur hat, Assia would go out and buy it for them.

So it was that Sylvia added needlework to her daily routine. She often worked on the tapestry while she listened to French and German lessons on the radio, and her calendar shows that she reminded herself to set aside time for the tapestry on 29 May and 1 June and then again the following week. On 7 June she notified her mother that she found the needlework 'Wonderfully calming'. According to her calendar, she was still scheduling time for the tapestry on 1 July. Had she had any suspicions that Ted had been seriously attracted to, or been allured by, Assia, it is unlikely that Sylvia would ever have touched her rival's present.

In the letter to Sylvia that accompanied the tapestry, Assia did not send her regards to Ted or the children. She did not mention Ted at all, whether she was idly thinking of him or not. It would appear that if Assia was contemplating what might happen next with Ted, she was also leaving it entirely in his hands.

Sylvia made a habit of meticulously recording every aspect of the Plath-Hughes household on her calendar. '9.45 – Nancy', for instance, notes the expected arrival time of the cleaning lady Nancy Axworthy and the entry beneath it indicates which part of the house Nancy was to clean that day. Her calendar includes, too, menus she planned, chores she would attend to, doctors' appointments to be kept, radio programmes not to be missed ('10.25 – Bach'), language lessons that would be broadcast ('3.10 – Italian'). Although she and Ted rarely left the house as they took turns writing and minding the children, Sylvia also entered on her calendar Ted's every departure, such as his trips to the nearby town of Exeter. There is no entry for a trip to London until the end of June.

However captivated Hughes may have been by 'the seven treasures of Asia' and although he was a sexual stalker by nature, he was having difficulties in pursuing his prey. In the first week of June he was housebound as he was entertaining his parents and his Uncle Walt. The Hughes family enjoyed the visit and his mother Edith's letter to Sylvia's mother Aurelia makes no allusion to marital problems. In the second week Ted was suffering the effects of half a dozen slow-healing bee stings, which were still evident when his mother-in-law arrived from the United States on 21 June. Aurelia's babysitting services enabled Ted and Sylvia to travel to London. So, five weeks after meeting the Wevills at Court Green, Ted had his first opportunity to see Assia on her own.

Ten

An Illicit Affair

London, summer 1962

In her dark blue domestic-expenditures ledger, Assia entered the purchase of '3 Penguin books for Ted Hughes' on 17 June, for the price of £1.10s. It is unclear whether she bought the books as a gift or at his request but the entry does suggest that either by phone or by post there was some communication between Assia and Ted after the weekend in Devon.

Their first opportunity to meet came on Tuesday, 26 June, when Hughes and Plath drove into Exeter to catch the early express train to London. Ted had to be at the BBC by 9.30 for a rehearsal; he was narrating *Creatures of the Air*, a radio programme for schools that he had written. The programme's assistant producer was Moira Doolan. At 10.45, just as Ted was finishing his rehearsal, Plath stepped into a different studio to participate in a recording of *The World of Books*. The recording of Hughes's programme was scheduled for 1 p.m., so he had two free hours on his hands. He hurried to Berkeley Square, about ten minutes away by taxi, only to discover, when he arrived at the Colman, Prentice and Varley advertising agency, that Assia was not available. He scribbled a note and left it with the receptionist. Intimate though it was, Assia showed it to her friends. Suzette Macedo recalls that it read, 'I have come to see you, despite all marriages.'

Having always preferred rough waters to smooth sailing, Assia could not resist the thrill of responding. But she wanted to do it in striking, memorable fashion. From her office window she noticed that a gardener was mowing the lawn in the square below, and therein she found her inspiration. She went down, picked up a single blade of the freshly cut grass and sent it to Court Green. As Hughes recollects Assia's wordless message in the poem 'Chlorophyl' (from *Capriccio*), the blade of grass had been dipped in Dior perfume. Three days later an envelope arrived at Assia's office: in it, the blade of London grass lay beside one from Devon. Assia did not hesitate to share Ted's romantic gesture with her husband David. Indeed, not content with her husband's tenderness, she flaunted it, in the hope perhaps of intensifying David's desire or provoking his jealousy, or both. Assia would have revelled in being the cause of a duel between her devoted husband and her potential lover. David, however, remained his sweet, soft, loving and inert self.

Hughes and Plath revisited London on 3 July for a meeting and lunch at the BBC with George MacBeth and Douglas Cleverdon. Once again Hughes managed to slip away, only this time Assia was waiting for him. When she returned to the office after the rendezvous, their first, in amazement she told William Trevor, 'We met for tea!' Their next meeting was to take place on 19 July, the date of Ted's next trip to London.

On Monday, 9 July, Sylvia went shopping in Exeter with her mother. She bought a black cashmere sweater and a full black wool skirt for herself as well as two shirts for Ted. Sylvia and her mother had wine with their lunch at the Royal Clarence Hotel, and they returned to Court Green 'in high spirits'. Aurelia Plath was at the far end of the hall when the telephone rang. Sylvia picked up the receiver. The ensuing few seconds of silence prompted Aurelia to glance back at her daughter. Sylvia's face was 'ashen', and she called shrilly, 'Ted!' He almost fell down the stairs in his haste to get to the phone, while Sylvia dashed up the stairs. In the poem 'Words Heard, by Accident, Over the Phone', written two days later, Plath hints at Assia's name with the words 'Now the room is ahiss'. Four months later Plath returned to the incident, and in 'The Fearful' she identified the caller as a woman who 'says she's a man'. Hughes, too, would allude to the phone call in 'Do Not Pick Up the Telephone': in this poem the telephone becomes a deadly device for 'disguised voices' for heralding one's doom.

When a laconic Ted finished the conversation, Sylvia rushed back down the stairs and, in a fury, ripped the cord of the phone out of the wall and then raced back to the bedroom. Ted ran after her. The door to the bedroom slammed shut and, for several hours, Sylvia and Ted stayed in their room while Mrs Plath tried to calm her two grandchildren. She had no idea what had just transpired and 'thought that perhaps they had had bad news concerning some work sent out for publication'. When she later peeped into their room, Sylvia and Ted were in bed.

The following day they all drove to Exeter and, before Hughes boarded the train to London, with a strange little laugh he said to his mother-in-law, 'Well, I don't know just when I'll see you again, Aurelia, but have a good time.' He knew that Mrs Plath was planning to stay in Devon for another month, but his own future with her daughter was unclear. Only later that day did Aurelia Plath learn the reason for Sylvia's rage and Ted's abrupt departure: 'Ted had been having an affair for some time.'

Sylvia built a bonfire in the yard and to its flames she consigned Ted's letters and manuscripts. Strangely, she spared the tapestry and Assia's accompanying letter and although she stopped working on the tapestry from that day on, she did not dispose of Assia's gift. She was so shattered by the betrayal, however, that she ceased listening to the BBC German language course and also demanded that Ted remove the Wevills' table from Court Green. But the tapestry remained in the drawer of a desk in the sitting room. It was later found by Sylvia's friend Elizabeth Compton (later Sigmund), who completed the large grey and white roses 'as a kind of gesture of defiance against Assia, to say, this at least, will be completed'. Compton says that over the years the tapestry mildewed and finally crumbled to pieces.

It seems that Sylvia had detected an affair that had scarcely begun, the culprits having met only once. Ironically, it was Sylvia's rage over the telephone call that enabled the barely budding romance to quickly bloom. Upon his arrival in London, Ted set himself up temporarily in the spare room in Al Alvarez's studio, within walking distance of Chalcot Square. He told Alvarez that he was leaving Sylvia and that he was in love, but he offered no further details. He then went out and bought four bottles of champagne. He presented them to a very surprised David and Assia Wevill when he knocked on their door and asked them to join him in celebrating his birthday. In fact, his birthday was still five weeks away – on 17 August – so what he was celebrating was perhaps something more like a rebirth. He found his opportunity to speak in private with Assia when David went out to buy cigarettes. She was astounded to learn that Ted had left Sylvia. She also agreed with no hesitation to skip work and spend the next day with him.

Nathaniel Tarn, also known as Dr Michael Mendelson, the anthropologist and poet, was a member of the Group in London and had been a close friend of the Wevills in Burma. Without each other's knowledge, both David and Assia made Tarn their confidant and, mesmerised by the unfolding drama, he recorded its progress almost daily. Observant and sharp-witted, Tarn added to the Wevills' two separate accounts his own comments, analysis and opinion. After spending Wednesday, 11 July with Ted, Assia enthusiastically reported to Tarn that Ted was very virile and decisive: he did the kind of things that a man did and that David had stopped doing long ago. Assia, however, did make sure that she returned home at her usual time and told David nothing about her Wednesday escapade. Later that evening the two of them joined Hughes and Alvarez for a drink at a pub. One look at Hughes and Assia together was enough for Alvarez to realise that she was Ted's new flame.

Two days after, on Friday, 13 July, at lunchtime, Ted took Assia to a hotel, where he made love – as Tarn, in gentlemanly fashion hiding the principals behind their initials, wrote in his diary – 'so violent and animal, he ruptures her. A. turns against him, goes quite cold'. Assia did not confide solely in Tarn on this occasion. She also made no secret of Ted's ferocious lovemaking among her office friends. Equally repelled and fascinated, she told Edward Lucie-Smith, 'You know, in bed he smells like a butcher.' Hughes commemorated the occasion of their first lovemaking in 'Capriccios', the first of twenty poems about Assia that he published in 1990. The very same poem was published eight years later under the title 'Superstitions', at the end of *Howls and Whispers*, which focuses primarily on Sylvia. Famously drawn to the occult, Hughes joins Sylvia to Assia in the ill-omened date of Friday the 13th – the date on which he first went to bed with each of them – as he laments Plath, who 'Forgot death', and Assia, who 'Forgot life'. Hughes gets the day wrong in Sylvia's case, however: they first made love on a Friday but it was 23 March 1956. Hughes repeats the error in another poem, '18 Rugby Street' (*Birthday Letters*), this time adding to the symbolic import of Friday the 13th an Oedipal twist as he conflates the day that he and Sylvia first made love with her father's birthday. Otto Plath was indeed born on 13 April 1885 but 13 April that year fell not on a Friday but on a Monday.

At 8.30 p.m. on that ominous Friday in July Assia phoned David and told him she would be late because she had gone to see Ted off at Waterloo station. Armed with a knife, David hurried to the station but failed to find Ted. Overwrought, David returned to an empty house. His wrath battling with despair, he threw the manuscript of a new, not yet published, book of poems into the wastepaper basket and then swallowed twenty or thirty pink Seconal sleeping pills – afterwards he couldn't remember exactly how many. Finally, gripping a silver-handled Burmese knife with which he hoped to end his misery once he found the necessary courage, he lay down on the couch.

Assia arrived after midnight and found him 'lying so sweetly, so young (such contrast to fierce H). In bed'. He was barely conscious. She panicked. Shaking him desperately, she attempted to wake him. She called an ambulance. On the way to the hospital, while David lay in a semiconscious state, Assia was ruthless enough to announce that Hughes had raped her. David's stomach was pumped and all night Assia walked him around the hospital corridors to keep him awake. As he later wrote in a short story, 'Four Days', 'the details of his life and the reasons for his death had gone away . . . to wake among strangers was the greatest healing'. He was happy when, on Saturday afternoon, he had a visit from Assia, because she was 'the one too intimate, the one never far enough from himself, who later went the way he had almost gone, and was not found in time.' A taxi took them home on Sunday evening. David composed a short note to his rival: 'If you come near my wife again, I'll kill you.'

That weekend Hughes was called down to Devon urgently by a hysterical Plath: she'd had an accident and driven her car into a field. On hearing of David's suicide attempt, Hughes groaned that Wevill was the 'straightest man in the world'.

David recovered quickly enough, and the following weekend the Wevills travelled to Linsey, in Suffolk, where they were the guests of Royston and Celia Taylor. Royston headed the department in which David worked at Ogilvy's advertising agency, but his wife and Assia had never before met. Nonetheless, Assia was extremely candid with her hostess about even the most intimate matters: she confided to Celia that Ted had raped her the previous week. Throughout the visit David was tremendously upset – indeed, murderously so. Royston Taylor recalls how he and his wife and Assia, all three of them spellbound, stood at the gate of a meadow and watched David, in the middle of the field, pound a broken-winged crow to death with a rock. Taylor was horrified as 'David, pale and shaking a bit, said to me that he was putting the thing, which had been shot, out of his misery'.

The killing of a bird lies at the centre of Wevill's poem 'Body of a Rook'. This gregarious Old World bird is about the size and colour of its relative the American crow, but the verb 'to rook' also means 'to swindle' or 'to cheat'. Wevill's poem refers to the bird in the feminine and particularly emphasises her blue-black feathers – Assia's colours – as she is:

gnawing, clinging, flesh-stubbed
Teeth in me, my remembrance of her mouth.
It is a killing but who dies?

The first-person speaker of the poem, no doubt Wevill himself, kills the bird slowly with a lump of flint until he has made a pulp of her head, face, body and nerves: 'I know my own violence too,' he admits. And he recounts how he:

... watched
Those last sufferings leave her body too
Twitching black and rook-supple before
I kicked my damaged violence into the woods.

The poem was published a year after the incident that conjured it, in *Penguin Modern Poets 4,* and then in the first collection of Wevill's poetry, *Birth of a Shark*, which he dedicated to Assia. On the page facing the violent 'Body of a Rook' is the gentle, optimistic poem 'In Love', which begins with the words:

She touches me. Her fingers nibble gently,
The whole street leans closer

Echoing John Donne and the seventeenth-century Metaphysical Poets, with elaborate metaphor, 'In Love' celebrates the sublime and consuming love shared by the poet and his wife:

And this is my Sunday lesson she teaches me.
Her texts are pillows, strong wrists and liquid ankles.
I could paint her as I fell on her,
And did, with my tongue, lungs, and my whole heart,
Each breath exploding its hot ether
Lash through our wills to their blind core.
If this is love, I grieve for God's.

The poem holds no hint of any current or residual bitterness that David may have felt towards Assia, his tutor in love.

When Hughes returned from Court Green, Assia exulted in his declarations of hate for Plath: for four years he had been unable to write, he said, and then wrote *Lupercal* in ten days when Sylvia was away. Nevertheless, he returned to Sylvia on 26 July and together they travelled to Wales for three days, to see friends and attend a conference in Bangor. Indeed, almost weekly Ted returned to Devon and his wife and children. Resentful of the ties Ted maintained with his family, Assia confronted him, saying she didn't want 'a slinky affair', but she did not cut herself off from him. The future of his marriage to Sylvia was still unclear, and Ted did not establish a foothold in London, not just because renting a flat in the city was an expensive proposition but also because it made too drastic and unequivocal a statement. To all intents and purposes, Court Green continued to be his home and for his correspondence he used his North Tawton address. For the present, all he wanted was some time off from his marriage and a bit of breathing space so that he could more freely savour the London literary life and nourish his affair with Assia.

Because Ted was moving repeatedly from one friend to another and intentionally not leaving any forwarding addresses, Sylvia rarely knew his whereabouts in London. His friends were evasive and reluctant to help when she telephoned. 'Sylvia wanted to find out what I knew,' Al Alvarez wrote in his memoirs. 'Or maybe she wanted just to sniff around the lair where he had been. Anything to alleviate her terrible loneliness.' Well before Hughes entered her life, Assia sensed that Alvarez was attracted to her. Alvarez was recovering from a disastrous five-year marriage to Ursula, the daughter of Frieda von Richtofen, D H Lawrence's wife, and Assia told her friends that he courted her ardently. He pleaded with her, so she said, declaring that if she did not join him on his forthcoming trip to the United States, he would not go. Assia declined. According to Assia, Alvarez then dramatically upped the ante from a trip abroad to marriage, but Assia was too smitten with Ted to even consider the proposal. Decades later, in his autobiography *Where Did It All Go Right*, Alvarez did not mention any of that, and described Assia as a woman who 'made a pass at every man she met so automatically that it was hard to feel flattered'.

David's suicide attempt had no effect on Assia's affair with Ted. She usually met Ted during her much extended lunch breaks. Her colleagues covered for her by telling bosses and clients that she had just popped out to the toilet or was attending to urgent business. The love nest she shared with Ted was sometimes a 1950 white Ford van that one of Ted's friends loaned him. Once, preparing for a date with Ted, Assia took a large brandy goblet and, with a teenager's zest, placed inside it a stone, a feather and a seashell. Returning to the office some hours later, she recounted to Angela Landels how they had sat in the car, how Ted had held the glass in his hand and then flung it out of the window, how the glass had smashed against a wall. Landels was aghast, but Assia was ecstatic: 'Don't you see, it's the loveliest thing he could have done.' Frequently Assia and Ted went out to pubs and parties. On one occasion, at the Mendelsons' large house in Hampstead, Hannah Hobsbaum, Philip's attractive wife, was chatting with Ted when Assia, incensed, strode up to them and abruptly put an end to the conversation. Shocked by Assia's rudeness, Hannah whispered to her husband, 'If I didn't know better, I would say that Ted is having an affair with Assia.' The hostess, Patricia Mendelson — and Tarn's wife — remembers that she herself was shocked, on opening the door of a room, to discover Ted and Assia locked in a passionate kiss.

Ted visited Court Green on Friday, 3 August, to bid farewell to his mother-in-law, who was returning to the United States. On Sunday, 5 August, Al Alvarez took Ted, Sylvia, and the Wevills by surprise when he published three new poems – one by each of the three poets – in the *Observer*. Alvarez was then the paper's all-powerful poetry critic, and a great and early champion of Ted and Sylvia's work. Indeed, he did much to establish their reputations. Plath's 'Finisterre' was followed by Hughes's 'Mountain' and then David Wevill's 'Clean Break'. All three poems had been written and accepted for publication months earlier, so they bore no hints of the affair. That they appeared together on the same page barely three weeks after Ted had left Sylvia was in all likelihood seen as Alvarez's wink to the London literati, who had been buzzing with gossip about Hughes and the Wevills. Philip Hobsbaum finds in the poems by Hughes and Wevill both common and complementary characteristics: 'Both thought in sensuous images, both were romantics, and Wevill offers a more feminine, minor-key variant of Hughes's astonishingly thrasonic blast and bluster. Hughes was dramatic and thrusting, Wevill, lyrical and yielding.'

When Mrs Olive Higgins Prouty, Plath's benefactress and godmother, who had travelled to London from the United States, invited Sylvia and Ted to be her guests at the Connaught Hotel, her daughter remembers that her mother was not surprised to hear of the marital problems. She recalls her mother's words, ' "Sylvia is so intense! She can't be easy to live with, even for a husband whom she adores and who is himself a genius." ' Years later, Hughes told Prouty's daughter that her mother had tried to help but, regrettably, he and Sylvia disregarded her good advice.

Hughes celebrated his thirty-second birthday at Court Green and later in August, at the end of the month, he returned to Devon again, as Sylvia was bedridden with a severe case of influenza and a temperature of 103. During the latter visit he secretly opened a bank account in his name at Barclay's Bank in Exeter. For this account he did not use his Court Green address but rather that of his parents – The Beacon, Heptonstall, Hebden Bridge, Yorkshire.

The two couples were drifting with the events; neither was ready to take the rudder and steer in a definite direction. Shuttling between Devon and London and moving between Sylvia and Assia, Hughes refused, or was unable, to make a firm commitment to either one residence or one woman. Similarly, Sylvia was contemplating a life on her own while at the same time planning a holiday in Ireland with Ted. The Wevills, too, were restless. Though David found himself cast in the reversed role – that of the cuckolded husband – he remained tender and affectionate in his day-to-day relations with Assia, and hopeful that her infatuation with Hughes would fade. It was, he says, 'a part of Assia that I couldn't explain, her openness to experiences, and her trust in her own feelings, that had to be followed. I was hoping it would die out, and Assia gave me the sense it was not a lasting thing.' Tarn got the impression that David had 'a mythical view of his marriage' and needed to be told 'a few truths about keeping on top of one's woman'. As for Assia, she was torn between pity for her husband and infatuation with her lover. She told Tarn that she had decided to stay with David at least until he was able to get back on his feet properly. Although Tarn continued to be privy to – and to record – the juicy details of the affair, he was becoming sick to death of what he called the Wevills' world of half-secrets, half-lies and half-confessions. He suspected that both David and Assia had 'a compulsive need of gossip to keep them in the swim'.

On Thursday, 13 September 1962, Ted and Sylvia arrived by train in Galway. They rented a car from one of the garages and then drove the 57 miles to Cleggan, where the poet Richard Murphy was operating tour boats to the island of Inishbofin. They intended to stay with Murphy until the following Wednesday, as Sylvia wanted to investigate the possibilities of renting a cottage for herself and the children for the coming winter. In the visitors' book for Murphy's boat, *Ave Maria,* she gave as her address Court Green, North Tawton, Devon; Ted used his parents' address. Both of them confided in Murphy about their marital difficulties. Hughes told Murphy that 'the marriage had become destructive, and he thought the best thing to do was to give it a rest'. To that end, Hughes was planning to go to Spain for six months, which time Sylvia and the children would spend in Ireland. Murphy got the impression that Plath was still optimistic that ultimately nothing could destroy the union between her and Ted; she wanted a legal separation, not a divorce. Murphy advised her not to act hastily 'on account of an affair that might not last'.

On Sunday morning Murphy went to the harbour to prepare his boat for the eleven o'clock sailing. Hughes seized the opportunity to tell Plath that he was leaving. He discouraged her from joining him – he was going grouse shooting with a friend, he said – and promised to meet her on Wednesday so that they could return together to Devon. He kept his departure a secret from the recently divorced Murphy, who would vehemently have objected to the situation – scandalous in village dominated by the Catholic clergy – of being left alone with a married woman. Murphy would insist that he took Plath with him.

Packing just a few things, Hughes headed for County Clare. There, in a small house six miles from the village of Quin, lived the painter Barrie Cooke, who shared with Hughes a preoccupation with the behaviour of animals and 'a fascination with violence', in the opinion of John L Sweeney, the mutual friend who introduced them to each other. Cooke had no telephone in his house, so Hughes was unable to notify him in advance of his visit. Taking his chances, Hughes set out on a slow, three-hour drive over narrow, winding rural roads. He found Cooke at home and the following day the two of them drove north to the barren, windswept limestone plateau with its rocky terraces and huge megalithic tombs of the Burren. It was Hughes's first visit to the wild, spectacular, eerily lunar-like place and Cooke remembers that in the evening, 'we lay on our backs, hidden in slots of rocks, watching wild geese fly.'

Plath was meanwhile stranded in Cleggan, a tiny, remote village with no bus service or taxis. Eager to be free of Sylvia so as to avert any scandal, Murphy insisted that she join poet Thomas Kinsella, a weekend guest, on his return to Dublin. On Wednesday night, 19 September Plath waited in vain in Dublin harbour for Ted to arrive. At the last moment she boarded the mail boat to Holyhead. At home she found a telegram with an Irish postmark awaiting her. It was from Ted; he would be back within a week or two, he said. For the next fortnight Sylvia had no idea where her husband was. Not even her lawyer in London could trace him.

When Ted embarked on the Irish trip, he already knew that he and Sylvia would not be returning to England together. His visit to Barrie Cooke was little more than a subterfuge to get rid of her. Ted had a larger plan to pursue.

Eleven

Leaving Plath

London, autumn–winter 1962

The page for the second week of September is mysteriously missing from Plath's wall calendar. Although it is unclear when or by whose hand the page went missing, its disappearance could hardly have been accidental. Most likely it was torn out because of some offensive notation Plath had written on it after she had been ditched in Ireland.

In the last week of August, Assia Wevill flew to Canada to visit her mother, who was again struggling with breast cancer. She had not seen her family in three years, so she had much news, but none so dramatic as that of her affair. Her sister Celia recalls, 'She told us that she met this fabulous man who was married. She let me read her diary, and it was clear that she was madly in love with him. They did not plan to get a divorce and marry.' The bon vivant Dr Gutmann was not shocked by his daughter's adultery: 'As long as they don't have children, it's no big deal,' he said.

Two weeks later, without her husband's knowledge, Assia returned to London. Equally secretly Ted had by then left Ireland and he, too, was in London, where he was waiting for her. Together they travelled to Spain, the very place where Ted had honeymooned with Sylvia. Hughes's telegram to Sylvia was a ruse intended to lead her to believe that he was still in Ireland and to put her off his tracks. Before leaving for Spain, he had deposited a letter with a London friend, who in turn posted it to Sylvia a few days later. The envelope bore no return address and from the vague contents of the 'numb, utterly dumb letter' Plath could not figure out where he was, what he was doing, or when was he coming home. Deserted in the big house in North Tawton with two children and with her nerves increasingly on edge, Plath's apprehensions intensified. One stormy night she panicked. Certain that someone had broken in, she had soon convinced herself that it was Assia's husband, who had come down to Court Green to take revenge. She alerted the police. The only sign of any disturbance they found was a shattered window; the culprit was the storm.

For Ted and Assia, Spain was an oasis. At last they no longer had to make do with stolen hours; they could enjoy each other openly, comfortably, without fear of discovery, without restraints. They could, and they did. The trip delighted them both. It provided them, too, with a creative boost, and they began exchanging ideas for a film script they might write together. When they returned to London at the end of September, they took great care to remove every trace of their ten-day-long Spanish fiesta from their luggage. Indeed, it was three months before Plath found out about the trip and, when she did, she was outraged. David Wevill never suspected a thing; not until forty years later did he learn about it and even then he was incredulous 'of Assia and Hughes going to Spain in 1962, or how, or when, that could have happened'.

The abundant intimacy that Ted and Assia savoured in Spain did not translate into any determination to pursue a joint future. A few days after unpacking her suitcase Assia was repacking it for another preplanned trip, this one to Germany, with David. Eight years had passed since Assia had hitchhiked through Germany with Dick Lipsey, her second husband. With her third husband, just in time for the autumn wine festivals, she visited Heidelberg, Düsseldorf, Boppard, Bingen and Mainz. Assia continued to feel ambivalent about the country, although David Wevill remembers that she enjoyed the language. They bought some books of modern German poetry, which she and David then tried to translate together. And she spoke the language with vigour and style. She was not always favourably mistaken for a native, though. 'In a pub in Boppard we saw a sign for vacant rooms, and asked to stay the night,' Wevill recalls. 'The owner said, certainly, and called his wife. She came down, took one look as Assia, and said, no, we have no room, and disappeared. It cast a cloud over us, Assia felt her Jewishness had been detected. She was not frightened, but very disturbed.'

Before Hughes and Plath had taken the trip to Ireland, they had discussed vacating Court Green for the entire winter as one option by which they might resolve their marital crisis. For six months Sylvia would live in Ireland with the children, while Ted would take advantage of the notoriously cheap standard of living in Spain. The Wevills, on the other hand, had not broached the possibility of a trial separation. Even if they had, and subsequently had agreed to separate, it is doubtful that Assia would have then joined Ted in Spain, for she would have had to make too many significant changes in her life that she was not yet prepared to make. For one, she would have had to leave her well-paid job and thus, not only lose her hard-earned professional identity, but also find herself virtually totally dependent on Hughes and his meagre means. The situation would have been complicated even further, in fact, because David, who had won the Gregory Award – a literary prize that enabled writers to live abroad for a few months – was also planning an extended stay in Spain, so that he could pursue his interest in Spanish literature and indulge his fascination with the country's earthy charms.

With Assia away in Germany, Hughes had decided not to hang around London but, instead, to await her return at Court Green. Had he and Sylvia been able to declare a truce, they might have been able to resolve their differences enough to be able to save their marriage. Instead, they declared war. Housebound together for the first ten days of October, they wore increasingly on each other's nerves. The house became their battleground and their simplest interaction led them into an emotional minefield.

In a puzzling coincidence, the page for that first week of October, like that for the second week of September, is also missing from Plath's calendar (which Hughes later sold to the Lilly Library at Indiana University, in the United States). Although any notations that Plath may have jotted down in frustration or anger on that page are lost, her letters to her family and friends speak frankly of a 'ghastly week'. Hughes admitted to leading a secret love life in London and, adding insult to injury, said that he hated living with her as she bored and stifled him. For a long time, he told her, he had been looking for a chance to free himself from her. He said that he could get hordes of gorgeous women, and that she was 'a hag'. Sylvia thought that he and Assia wished her dead, knowing that she had already attempted suicide before; her death would be convenient to Ted, who could sell Court Green and live with the children elsewhere. In the midst of the commotion Hughes managed to find enough solitude and calm to compose 'Sunlight', a sentimental nostalgic poem for Assia, atypically for him: 'your absence is huge'.

In that ghastly week the tables had turned. For Plath, trial separation was now out of the question. Her union with Ted was not quite so indestructible after all. She wanted a clean break and evidently so did he: Sylvia stated that, like her, 'Ted is glad for a divorce.' The decision having been made, Hughes immediately phoned Assia to inform her that he was leaving home and that Sylvia intended to name her as the 'correspondent [*sic*] in a divorce suit'. On 11 October Plath drove Hughes along with all his belongings – clothes, books, papers – to the station. To judge by Plath's calendar, he did not return to Court Green or see his children for the next two months. Although he denied to Sylvia that he was planning a future with Assia and asserted that he wanted to live only for himself, Plath was certain he would soon marry his mistress: both of them, are cut for each other, being 'handsome and faithless', and he would join the parade of husbands that preceded him. In all her letters, Plath never mentioned Assia by name, and referred to her, for example, as 'the bitch' or the 'barren woman'. Sylvia's suspicions of her husband's former infidelities suddenly disappeared. She now averred that his affair with Assia was his first transgression; until he met her, he was a perfect husband, and Assia was the one who taught him that it is 'sophisticated to lie and deceive'.

Plath was convinced that much of Assia's appeal for Hughes was her childlessness – as a result of her many abortions. In Plath's view, Ted was intimidated by her writing and motherhood. Hughes, she concluded, wanted a woman who could neither challenge nor compete with him, a woman who was not creative and would admire his writing and be utterly devoted to him. Plath consoled herself with her evident superiority over Assia in motherhood and artistic endeavour: infertile in body and soul, Assia's only achievement – according to Sylvia – was her high salary. Plath welcomed and relished any gossip – the more vicious, the better – about her rival's behaviour, and she gleefully recorded that Assia had attacked her former husand with a knife, causing damage to his car.

Although Ted agreed to pay Sylvia yearly maintenance of £1,000 for the house and children's expenses, she feared that he would give in to his family's pressure and renege on his responsibilities. Thoughout their marriage Sylvia had tried to be on good terms with her in-laws, but now she turned against them, calling them 'inhuman Jewy working class bastards'. At the same time that she could declare 'I think I may well be a Jew' in her poem 'Daddy', in her letters she would use the word Jew derogatively. Her imagination ran riot with horrendous scenarios that her in-laws would force her to return to America as a ward of her family or that she would have to work as a waitress and put her children 'in an orphanage'. In a less virulent moment, she could also hope that Hughes's life with Assia might mellow him towards her and the children.

It was Dr Ruth Beuscher, Plath's therapist, who urged her to get a copy of Erich Fromm's *The Art of Loving*; 'as I think it very important for you to read this book at this time.' Plath kept this popular, now classic, psychological and philosophical work by her bedside and read it very carefully. She underlined and annotated passages that dealt with sex and love, symbiotic relationships, the nature of sadistic and masochistic personalities, and the fear of being alone, as well as the complex relationship between mother and child. On page 4, she marked a passage that may have described what had happened to her and Ted in the course of their own marriage: 'The two persons become well acquainted, their intimacy loses more and more its miraculous character, until their antagonism, their disappointments, their mutual boredom kill whatever is left of the initial excitement.'

Hughes, meanwhile, had abandoned his plan to move to Spain and had settled in a flat that Dido Merwin's mother had bequeathed to her at 17 Montague Square. In the coming year, however, he would continue to use his parents' address in Yorkshire for all official purposes. That autumn, after he had left Sylvia, Hughes confessed in a letter to his brother Gerald in Australia that he had finally found it impossible to stay married to Sylvia, especially because of her 'particular death-ray quality', and that he was pleased to have left her. Sylvia, who of course had her own version of the break-up, and did not hesitate to offer it, wrote to Gerald as well and in her letter described Ted as having a harem of women in London. Ted dismissed such tales as pure exaggeration prompted by Sylvia's jealousy of Assia. Again independent, happy with the flat in Montague Square, and relatively carefree, Hughes enjoyed his newfound freedom, and he put no pressure on Assia to come and live with him.

In matters of the heart Assia always took her time. She was not an initiator; she was a responder. She left it to her husbands to pull the chestnuts out of the fire and deal with the mess that got made of marital bliss. When John Steele could no longer bear her infidelities, he made the decision to divorce; so did Dick Lipsey, once it became intolerably apparent that Assia herself would end neither her tepid marriage to him nor her affair with David Wevill. Certainly, in that emotionally turbulent October, Assia was not prepared to force the issue of divorce from David or remarriage to Ted, not when she more than suspected that Ted was not keen on the idea of remarriage. And if she separated from David in order to live with Ted, she feared that Ted might eventually desert her and that she would then be left alone, with neither man. Alone was Assia's most dreaded scenario.

David was not forcing any issues, either. He continued to turn a blind eye to the affair as he strove ardently to please and appease Assia in his sincere attempt to save their marriage. 'We didn't want our marriage to end, and I didn't feel it was ending,' says Wevill. 'Assia told me that she didn't want the affair to happen, and regretted its happening. I was hoping it would die out.' Nathaniel Tarn, though, had the impression, as he wrote in his diary, that David was largely: 'in a pathetic state, doing some kind of manly acts: opening car doors for A; lighting her cigarettes, etc. She keeps looking dramatically at him, as if he were going to break. They are very lovey-dovey, arm in arm all the time.' David, like Steele and Lipsey before him, acquiesced in his rival's passion for Assia and to hers for him. Nor did Assia's romantic entanglement with Ted destroy the mutual appreciation that the two poets had for each other's work. David continued to admire Hughes's poetry, and Hughes, who said he would not have minded if he himself had written Wevill's 'Our Lady of Kovno', promised Assia that he would help David get his poems published in the *New Yorker*.

David's submissiveness in the face of the affair frustrated and outraged Plath, who expected the cuckolded husband to step into and rectify an untenable situation by reclaiming his wife. Sylvia's hope was that once he stood outside the influence of Assia's bewitching aura, Ted would come to his senses and return to Devon, to her and their children. On 27 October Sylvia celebrated her thirtieth birthday on her own and two days later travelled to London to record an interview with Peter Orr for the BBC. She met Al Alvarez and attended a PEN party, an occasion for which she braced herself against the curiosity of gossips and the possibility of meeting Ted and Assia. There is no record that Ted, Assia or David attended the party and, for her part, Sylvia had the floor to herself. She moved from one guest to another, and took every effort to impress all with a cool, dignified stance, reconciled to the pending divorce and eager to move beyond it – for the divorce, she declared, would liberate her from the strain that marriage had become and would allow her to write in peace. Nonetheless, Sylvia was distressed to discover that many of the PEN members and guests in fact approved of Ted's behaviour. At the same time that she feigned indifference to the affair, she fished for every titbit and scrap of information about it that she could. To that end she also asked Peter Porter to lunch. 'She knew I was a friend of Assia's,' Porter said, 'and she wanted to pump me about her rival. For the same reason, I prevaricated.'

At the beginning of November Plath went flat hunting in London with Hughes. They passed by their previous flat at 3 Chalcot Square, where Assia and David were now living and, on 23 Fitzroy Road, Plath found a flat. Indeed, she counted herself fortunate to have found the perfect place, not because it was barely a hundred yards away from Ted's mistress's window but because the house had once been occupied by the poet she idolised more than any other, William Butler Yeats. And there she would fantasise, just like Assia, of establishing a literary salon. Hughes always felt that Sylvia 'witched herself into that building.'

'Turn off gas'; 'trash bins down' – on her calendar Sylvia reminded herself of last-minute details to attend to before locking up Court Green on 10 December. When she arrived with the children at Fitzroy Road, she paid the rent for a year in advance. That same month the lease on the Chalcot Square flat expired, and Assia and David moved to a larger flat at 14 Highbury Place, in an old but completely modernised Georgian house owned by the author Sylvester Stein. In the nick of time, Hughes's wife and mistress were thus spared the embarrassment of bumping into each other in the local shops and pubs of Primrose Hill.

Every Thursday morning at ten Hughes visited his children at Sylvia's flat, though he would usually take them out to the zoo in nearby Regent's Park. Finances caused Sylvia bitterness, too. She envied Assia's high salary, which she believed to be £3,000 a year, a fortune from where Plath was sitting with two small children to feed and clothe.

Throughout their marriage Sylvia had resented Ted's contention that any values vested in clothes were superficial and even more she had resented his insistence that she buy her clothes at cut-price stores. She had complained that she had constantly had to cut her personal and household expenses so that he could afford to devote himself exclusively to his writing and not have to waste his energy or time on a drudge job. Plath channelled her fierce emotions into *Ariel*. In one of its poems, 'Amnesiac', which she read in a BBC interview, a man living on the banks of Lethe, the river of oblivion, forgets his wife and children. That December, too, she was writing – and by New Year hoped to finish – a semi-autobiographical novel, *Doubletake*, about a woman whose husband turns out to be a deserter and philanderer.

Sometime before Christmas Olwyn Hughes came from Paris to spend a couple of days with her brother. On that visit she met Assia for the first time, in a café on North Audley Street, and found her 'beautiful and very charming. Intelligent, humorous, likeable. She wore a very becoming black fur hat.' It was clear to Olwyn that her brother was in love, but neither he nor Assia even hinted to her of any plans for a future they might share together. For Christmas, which Ted celebrated in Yorkshire with his family, he invited his estranged wife but she declined and preferred to spend Christmas with 'someone else', he later wrote to Sylvia's mother.

Plath and her children in fact spent Christmas Day with her friends Suzette and Helder Macedo, who on the following day, Boxing Day, paid a visit to the Wevills. Assia and David had otherwise passed the holiday on their own. It was not generally Assia's favourite day of the year. 'Bloody Christmas, I do hate it, really,' Assia wrote to her sister Celia, to whom she'd also sent a cheque to buy their father a recording of the complete *Boris Godunov*; 'it's all like a school prize giving, when you know in advance that you are not going to get the worthwhile prize anyway, it's never really been Christmas since I left home.'

On 21 January and again on 9 February 1963, the BBC broadcast *Difficulties of a Bridegroom*. Hughes was familiar with the Cabbala, and the play owes much to the myth of Lilith, who seduces men in their sleep and then steals their semen; she also sometimes eats their flesh. Thus, in the broadcast version of Hughes's play, the voluptuous mistress is a 'man eater', who sets out to make the bridegroom forget his bride and have complete possession over him. An irresistible party animal, the mistress greedily demands a penthouse in Charlotte Street, a red Cadillac and an unlimited expense account. When the groom pleads that he wants to fulfil his poetic vocation, she pays him no heed and insists that he will simply have to get a proper job and begin dressing stylishly. Assia, who could not fail to see herself in the Lilithine mistress, detested the play. It was no less painful for Plath, who identified herself not with the play's bride but with the slaughtered hare.

On Thursday, 7 February Sylvia met Ted in his flat at 110 Cleveland Street and declared that she did not want a divorce at all: that 'the whole crazy divorce business was a bluff'. In his poem 'The Inscription' (*Birthday Letters*), Hughes alludes to the visit: Plath was imploring him that, by summer, they would be together in Court Green. He said they would, whether to mollify or calm or console her — he was also misleading her, because, in fact, by that February his relationship with Assia was positively blossoming. To his sister he wrote, 'the Assia saga is doing alright', and to the Merwins he added Assia's best wishes, an indication that she was the woman beside him. By then he and Assia were no longer making a secret of their affair. Heedless of what the gossips or anyone else thought, they went everywhere together, so much so that many people mistakenly thought that they were actually living together.

During the visit Sylvia made to Ted's flat she spotted a familiar-looking edition of Shakespeare's plays. Surprised at the apparent resurrection of the red Oxford volume she had slashed in jealous rage a year and a half earlier, she opened the book and read the inscription. Judging by her revulsion, it had been Assia's consoling gift to Ted, to replace the volume he had lost. For Sylvia, it was a fatal blow, like a bullet striking a running animal.

By then Assia was carrying Ted Hughes's child.

Twelve

The Shadow of Suicide

London, February–May 1963

It was close to eleven o'clock on Monday, 11 February, and Dr John Horder straightened up from the body that was lying in the middle of the sitting room. He estimated that his former patient had been dead for approximately six hours. Only when the ambulance doors had slammed shut behind the covered stretcher, did he turn to his car and drive the short distance to his clinic in Regent's Park Road.

The only close friends of Sylvia Plath's whose phone number he had were Gerry and Jillian Becker; he had already rung the Beckers three days earlier to check on Sylvia, who was their guest for the weekend, following his advice that she must not be left alone while taking anti-depressant medication. Dr Horder was now looking for Ted Hughes but Jillian Becker did not have his number. She called Suzette Macedo, who wavered between loyalty to Ted's wife and her friendship with his lover. Macedo too had no idea of Ted's whereabouts and phoned Assia. It was the mistress who had the grim task of notifying Hughes.

'Something terrible has happened: Sylvia has killed herself,' Assia announced, stepping into Art Director Julia Matcham's office. Assuming that Assia must be overwhelmed with guilt, Julia sympathised, 'Oh, you must feel awful.' Assia's eyes opened wide. 'Why should I? It was nothing to do with me.'

Hughes immediately moved into the flat where his wife had lived and died, to tend to Frieda and Nicholas. He notified his friends of the tragedy, and one by one they gathered in 23 Fitzroy Road. Among the first to arrive was Susan Alliston, an aspiring poetess with a shoulder-length mane of dark bronze hair; she had always reminded Hughes of an ancient Egyptian figure, and, in *Birthday Letters*, he named her — and not Assia — as the woman who was keeping him away from the telephone on the nights when Sylvia repeatedly called him and needed him most. 'I gave Susan a lift and as we entered the flat, Ted handed us the typed manuscript of what was to become *Ariel*. I read it and my hair stood on end,' recalls his friend David Ross.

Two days later, Lucas Myers, Ted's American friend, happened to pass through London and paid a condolence visit. Ted told him that he and Sylvia would probably have been 'reunited in two weeks' but Myers was not sure whether it was a real prospect, or the mind's way of dealing with shock and grief. Al Alvarez was sitting on a sheepskin rug by the fire, talking to Olwyn Hughes, who had hurried home from Paris. Ted's cousin Vicky and his aunt Hilda Farrar had come from Yorkshire to look after the children. Assia, feeling nausea, was resting in Sylvia's room upstairs; apparently, the wife's suicide did not make the illicit lovers dive underground. Myers went upstairs to keep Assia company and stayed in the flat for a few hours. 'Not much was said. Someone asked Ted to sing "Waltzing Matilda", and he did. It was like a wake without alcohol,' he recalls.

Sylvia's brother, Warren Plath, flew over from the United States with his newly wedded wife Margaret. They wished to take the children to be brought up in America and Ted asked for time to think it over. He let the young couple stay in Sylvia's flat to see how they got along with the children and moved back into his own flat. It is not clear if Hughes was stalling for time, or whether he was so shaken by grief that for a flickering moment he was actually considering the option of leaving his children. But he soon made it clear that he intended to raise them himself and Warren and Margaret left England empty handed, though not giving up on the idea entirely.

Since his own flat was too small and the rent had been paid a year in advance, Ted decided to live in Plath's flat. That same week David Wevill was called urgently to Ottawa, since his mother was terminally ill with cancer of the bowel. Being the eldest son and extremely attached to his mother, he planned to stay as long as it took. Assia continued to spend her nights in their Highbury flat, offering David long-distance support, while visiting Ted and his children after work. If there were any misgivings about her presence in Plath's flat, she and Ted paid no notice. The children did not ask for their mother and clung to any feminine figure, and Frieda expressed her delight that 'Daddy's back'.

Free to pry around, Assia was mesmerised by Plath's *Ariel* poems and, though they vilified and attacked her and Hughes, she admitted that they were 'most incredible'. She flattered herself that she was the tragic muse. Opening the maroon-backed ledger, she read Plath's last journal, ending three days before the suicide. Surprised to learn 'that the marriage was much dryer' than Ted had described it to her, she was shocked by the extent of Sylvia's hostility and hatred towards her. Reading the manuscript of Plath's second novel, Assia easily identified David and herself as the Goof-Hoppers, and was disgusted not only by her portrayal as an 'icy, barren woman', but also by David's character as 'detestable and contemptible'. Apart from Plath 'who is full of poems, kicks and kids, there are only saints and miserable sinners', she told Nathaniel Tarn. She hoped that Ted would destroy it all; whether he followed her wishes or not, the fact remains that the novel was never found. As for the journal, Hughes admitted that he destroyed it because he did not want his children ever to read it. Assia's account of Plath's diary and her unfinished novel is the only surviving testimony as to their content.

Guilt is the ever-smouldering ember plucked from the suicide pyre and hastily passed from hand to hand, its scorch too agonising to bear. Hurling it away from himself, Hughes blamed it on Sylvia's 'murderous self' and on her doctor's unfortunate choice of an anti-depressant. It was evident that Plath's friends would point the finger at the adulterer and his mistress. Assia's friends pressed her to show remorse but she would have none of it. She blamed Sylvia for killing herself deliberately to destroy her and Ted's happiness, complaining, 'It was very bad luck that the love affair was besmirched by this unfortunate event.'

Ruth Fainlight and Alan Sillitoe invited Ted over to pay their respects, and were astonished when he arrived accompanied by a 'strikingly beautiful woman – Assia Wevill'. Fainlight, loyal to Sylvia, hated Assia at first sight, but her rage was mixed with pity:

I saw two extraordinary handsome human beings in the prime of their lives – but the glamour was overshadowed by the cringing posture and bowed head. The appalled, averted gaze and devastated expression of Adam and Eve just expelled from Paradise. They might have been battling against a swirling sand storm, as if although only a few feet away, they were in another universe.

A few days later Ruth and Alan came to the flat in Fitzroy Road. With Frieda clinging to her father's legs and baby Nicholas moaning miserably from his cot,

'Ted and Assia seemed overwhelmed, even more accused and guilty than at our previous meeting. Now all I could feel was pity – for both of them.'

Hughes's first impulse was to make a clean break and get away from England, toying with every possible destination as far as China. But he soon realised that his children needed to be stabilised. His aunt Hilda found it difficult to cope with the children and, after nearly a month away from her Yorkshire friends and administrative job in a factory, she wanted to leave, complaining to the downstairs neighbour Dr Trevor Thomas that she 'didn't like London, the people, the shops or the situation upstairs'. She disapproved of Assia's presence and thought that the children would be better off in the United States, promising Sylvia's mother to bring them herself if Ted did not do it. Ted's mother could not help with the children since she was housebound in Yorkshire with arthritis and his sister, Olwyn, was not yet ready to give up her thrilling job in Paris.

Realising that a nanny cannot replace a mother, Hughes implored Assia to come and live with him. He assured her that she could rely on his true emotions and intentions. Assia consented but, as much as she yearned for his commitment, she made it clear that her move was temporary; her husband was at his mother's bedside and she wished to spare him a further blow. As she settled in her rival's flat, she established herself as the lady of the house by showing the door to Sylvia's friends, the gatekeepers who were constantly around. Lunching with Nathaniel Tarn, Assia looked unwell and did not touch the food. Though she raved about Ted having everything – charity, energy, love, genius – the list of his vices was as long as that of his virtues: she was alarmed by his voracious sexual appetite, his superstitions about marriage and his black moods. She felt that he was withdrawn and that he refrained from sharing his work with her, unlike David, who was not secretive about his writing, always let her in and made her feel that she was participating in it. But curiously, as much as her husband and her lover were worlds apart, she found them both irritating with their Puritanism. All in all, Tarn concluded, Assia was lost 'in a maze of reasons for NOT deciding'.

Not until 15 March 1963, did Hughes collect himself enough to write his account of the tragedy to Aurelia Plath, in order to counterbalance the letters Sylvia must have written to her. In Sylvia's last month, he said, they became friendly, and were closer than they had ever been in the last two years; he had intended to take Sylvia on a holiday by the sea that fatal Monday. Hughes portrayed himself as the one who tried to heal the marriage, persuading Sylvia to halt the divorce proceedings, and wrote that they were close to restoring their union. Aurelia Plath, who had the habit of scribbling her reactions on margins of letters that she received, noted down cynically, 'through adultery with Acia Weevil?'. The spelling mistake indicated that the otherwise pedantic Aurelia Plath never read Assia's name in her daughter's or in anybody else's letters. Hughes adhered to the reconciliation theory throughout his life and, in 1981, wrote to Dr Keith Sagar, his friend and critic that, by December 1962, Sylvia had 'almost completely repaired her relationship to me'.

Hughes suspected that Aurelia Plath has asked her daughter's friends in England to inform her of his whereabouts, collecting evidence against him, so that eventually she could take her grandchildren to the United States. But he had nothing to worry about: his family and Sylvia's friends sent Mrs Plath censored and favourable reports on life in Fitzroy Road: the house is spotless, Frieda is far happier and more at ease and has a hearty appetite, Ted 'looks so sad and so bent down', he and Nurse Jean 'are determined to bring those children up well and happy'. In the conspiracy of silence shared by all, Assia's presence in Sylvia's flat was kept a secret from Mrs Plath, who was led to believe that the only feminine presence there was the nanny.

There was another secret to be kept: Assia's pregnancy. There was no question about it being Ted's child, since for the past months there had been no sex between the Wevills. But Ted wanted no more children and, although Assia enjoyed the company of Frieda and Nicholas, she still abhorred the idea of pregnancy, birth and child rearing. Visiting her friend Celia Taylor in the maternity ward after the birth of her first son, Assia shuddered, 'How can you let that thing chew your breast?' And even if she and Ted wished to keep their love child, Plath's suicide made it morally unacceptable.

On Thursday, 21 March 1963, Elizabeth Compton, Sylvia's friend, took her daughter Meg to London for a treat after doing her 11+ exams, dropping in on Ted and the children. 'You know she's living here?' whispered the nanny. 'Who?' asked Elizabeth. 'Mrs Wevill. But they are out, she's having an operation.' 'What kind of operation?' inquired Elizabeth suspiciously. 'You know,' said the nanny evasively. As Elizabeth waited in the sitting room, the entrance door opened and she glimpsed Assia's stately figure swiftly disappearing up the stairs into the bedroom. 'I had to go and see a succession of Harley Street bastards,' Assia confided in her friend, Peter Porter's wife

Jannice, who was a nurse. She finally found an old Polish doctor in Maida Vale, who was kind and human. 'Could you come to visit me on Friday or Saturday in the ghost house? 23 Fitzroy Road,' she pleaded with Jannice, asking her to burn the note.

Recovering in Sylvia's bed, Assia was reading the just-published *The Nabobs*, a study of the social life of the English in eighteenth-century India, by Percival Spear. On a card that she left in the book, she inscribed a sentence that caught her fancy: 'The throats of our wrists brave lilies.' It was taken from 'Stings', Plath's poem that deals with the conflict between her domestic and poetic selves, as she aspired to get away from the beehive that had become a prison. Underneath the quote, Assia described her mood: 'so this is what's like. Time stretches on and on and on and on . . . it's like being four again by oneself . . . Tired. Not to bed, but tired, caged, slightly, upstairs.'

On another strip of paper, she phrased her basic queries to Ted, partly in Hebrew, partly in English: 'what do you want? What do you need? You're only in possession of what you don't want. Why are you relieved that I'm no longer pregnant? And when I'll go back home, will you be less sad?' The list ended with a statement in Hebrew: 'I'm just like Marilyn Monroe in the shape of a hot-water bottle.'

David Wevill did not know of the drama that was unfolding in London and was joyful about the sudden remission of his mother. He broke the good news to Assia and got ready to leave Canada by the end of the month. Not indifferent to competition, Ted wished to secure Assia for himself before her husband's return. He was fully aware that love had not died in the Wevill household and in his overwrought letter to Assia from 27 March, he was careful not to present his love for her as stronger than her husband's. He promised Assia that she had no reason to doubt his love: even his wife's suicide did not transform his feelings towards Assia: 'it's just shown me how final they are.' He tried to reason with her that divorcing David was unavoidable and that the sooner it happened the less misery for all involved. His main concern was the welfare of his children and his future with Assia. He argued that while David was waiting for the affair to exhaust itself, he believed it would last, and urged Assia to choose between them. Desperately, he wrote, 'if you stay with David I don't know what I shall do.' Assia was not convinced and they argued fervently about it. A few days later she returned to Highbury Place to wait for David.

On Saturday, 6 April, shortly after his return from Canada, the Wevills sailed on the night ferry to Dublin and rented a tiny Fiat. Assia brought with her the red exercise book she had already bought in October 1962, at a major crossroads in her life, when Ted Hughes left his family. But still, in the following turbulent months, the pages had remained blank. The first entry was made on 8 April 1963, in a Galway café, sitting at a table with an embossed white plastic cover and three daffodils in a vase, waiting for the dark-uniformed waitress with the starched apron to bring her order of bacon and tomatoes. Assia used a black fountain pen, her handwriting rapid and dense, with hardly any corrections, using only the right-hand pages. A hawk-eyed, critical observer, she noted, 'most Irish women are next to plain, most over 25 look ugly. They look to be without spirit, and suffer from piety. Piety makes plain women. The men, though, shine with something, sex maybe, or dissatisfaction, or good looks. The red, blue and black looks they have are masculine, women fade with it.' She got the impression that 'there are enough people who are poor and frightened enough to work as servants. But they look so infinitely more ambitious than the best-paid English.'

Less than two months had passed since her lover's wife had committed suicide and she herself was recuperating from a recent abortion and torn between a husband and a lover – yet none of these momentous events was even hinted at in Assia's diary. Furthermore, reading the ten-page account of the Irish journey, one could get the impression that Assia was travelling by herself. As if rehearsing to become a travel writer, she described Galway as 'dour-snug, Catholic, clean and bereft, utterly bereft of joy'. A shopping addict, she noted with disappointment that all the shops offered the same meagre choice of goods: 'Cadbury's Easter bunnies and Yardley's 4/9 talcum powder'. She also recorded that 'prices are high – "tea" for two will amount to 12/–.' Her language was extravagant, as if trying to impress her notebook with her choice of imagery – 'Ireland is wounded in a tea rose world of white flannels and well-connected curates' – but her tone was often ill tempered ('I sound as though I have toothache. Well, I have . . .'). Unlike Plath, who fell in love with the country and wanted to move there immediately, Assia disliked the experience. 'The Irish have no sense of taste whatsoever, the villages are ugly, there are no gardens, their clothes are ugly, their food is unspeakable. Only the country is beautiful.'

The Wevills drove to Cleggan and waited in the grey building of the Pier Bar for poet Richard Murphy. David went out to speak to the fishermen and

Assia drank ginger ale and stared at the fifty-odd cut-out sea birds, which were stuck on the wall. When Murphy arrived, he was astounded by Assia's 'Babylonian beauty' and 'voluptuous bosom'. He 'assumed they had come to find out what had happened at Cleggan to Ted and Sylvia'. Almost forty years later, David Wevill denies any knowledge of Plath and Hughes ever making the same journey: 'no footsteps were being followed. My mother's family was Irish, and with her failing health, I was curious to see the country. We both needed a break, following the turbulent events in London and in Ottawa.' Not wishing to impose on Murphy's hospitality, they returned later that day to their hotel in Galway.

Once again, Ireland failed to heal a marital discord and during the trip Assia and David 'attacked each other like cats'. They subsequently agreed to a six-month trial separation – which seemed a common panacea for couples in crisis at that time. David would use his Gregory grant to go to Spain while Assia could live with Ted and the children. To Tarn, she confessed that it was not a trial separation 'but it's really for good'. On 5 May Assia bade David farewell at the station; he was travelling to Paris on the way to Barcelona.

Locking up her flat and settling in Sylvia's, Assia rearranged it to her taste, throwing colourful fabrics on the furniture, replacing the pictures and scattering objects that she and David had brought from Burma. But although all parties to the ménage accepted the interim solution, Assia did not celebrate her freedom to love. On 15 May 1963 she turned 36, but felt a hundred years old. David was hardly gone and she was already gnawed with remorse. Flashbacks of him flooded her, as he was tying his shoelaces on the chair in the Chalcot Square kitchen – the sun behind him – 'the absolute grace of him, and his beautiful head in profile, straight, pale hair, massed across his forehead. The sun is in ashes.'

When Assia shuttled between the two men she was in control but with David absent, she felt lost in Ted's domination and under Sylvia's shadow. 'I'm immersed now in the Hughes's monumentality, hers and his,' she wrote in her diary. 'The weak mistress, forever in the burning shadows of their mysterious seven years.' She mourned: 'my third and sweetest marriage. David, my sweet husband, my most always favourite, my best and truest love. What insanity, what methodically crazy compulsion drove me to sentence him to being alone, and myself to this nightmare maze of miserable, censorious, middle-aged furies, and Sylvia, my predecessor, between our heads at night.'

Thirteen

Domesticity

London, summer 1963

During most of May, Assia was bedridden with an excruciating bout of chronic cystitis. 'There's a bruise on my left bosom. Ted inspects it with pleasure,' she wrote in her diary. She put on make-up but soon her face was teary and watery with mascara and she felt that her sickness made her 'a total loss'. When Theresa, the new au pair, implied that her ailments might be psychosomatic, Assia was appalled: 'How COULD it be? My God – what if it never went?' She was impatient to get well, afraid that Ted might find her repulsive: 'If we can't make love properly again, I'd just as soon not live.' Her illness removed whatever self-esteem she had, 'I have no will, no talent, a slight decorative intelligence and cystitis. Not <u>enough</u> vanity. No husband.' She shuddered at the possibility of rotting slowly on Sylvia's bed – 'not this one – the cost is too high' and consoled herself that until the end of the month she still had her Highbury flat. She would go there, lock herself in and swallow the 25 sleeping pills that she had accumulated, and end her misery. Nobody could rescue her, since only David had the other key and he was away in Spain. He, so she felt, was the only person who would truly grieve for her. Rather than an actual death wish, it was the sleepless, edgy and wretched state she was in that made her morose. As she recovered, she regained her spirits and set out to devour life.

For the previous sixteen years, since marrying at twenty, Assia had lived only as one of a pair, but she easily added the role of stepmother to that of spouse. 'I kissed Nick's neck over and over again. It kills me when he gurgles with it,' she wrote in her diary. She found Ted's children docile and touching and enjoyed the domestic scenes; she described Frieda leaning on Ted's knees, murmuring to herself and entertaining all with cute witticisms like 'the light hurts' or 'make the room brown'. When Nicholas waddled in, his sister would pile up all her possessions into a mound to keep them for herself. The three-year-old loved to take her blanket into what was now Ted and Assia's bedroom and adorn herself with Assia's jewellery and cosmetics. 'Fantastic, the way children (not even my own) have finally surrounded me. The children I like, very much. I shall like them even better, I think, when they are a little older.'

Dr Trevor Thomas was displeased with the change of tenants in 23 Fitzroy Road. He had not get along with Sylvia Plath and Assia and Ted irritated him even more. Living on the ground floor, by the main entrance, they treated him as a caretaker; there was no entrance phone, and they instructed their guests to buzz his bell, so that he would go and open the front door and save Assia or Ted the trouble of coming down the stairs to let the guests in. Once, when they returned from a weekend in the country, Thomas heard agitated voices and water being poured repeatedly on to his glass roof, as if someone was trying to wash something. The water soon dripped into his flat, and he shouted up for them to stop. The following morning, he discovered what the fuss was all about: 'It seems the people above had bought the fish before going away and had left it in a carrier bag in the sink. In the hot weather, the inevitable had happened, and they threw it out of the kitchen window': the rotten fish had crashed on to Thomas's glass roof. On another occasion, thinking that they were away again, he heard a door banging in their flat after midnight. He went into the entrance hall. The front door and the landing door were wide open and he could hear voices upstairs. Since the area had had a spate of burglaries in recent weeks, Thomas quickly dialled 999. Several patrol cars arrived within minutes and he directed the officers up. They banged on Hughes's door, Ted opened up and, after some angry exchange with the officers, shouted: 'It's only that silly old fool downstairs.'

Life eventually assumed quasi-normality in Ted and Assia's household. Assia's observations of him recorded in her diary offer a rare, first-hand account of Hughes at work: he would sit sideways, cross-legged, against Sylvia's black desk that was too small for him. Sipping tea from a mug, a sandwich in one hand and a pen in another, he was writing voraciously. 'His nostrils flared, his hair feathery, and leaping forward like a peacock's back train in reverse, swaying a little as he writes. Rather like a great beast, looking over an enormous feast, dazzled and confused by the variety.' Lifting her eyes and gazing at Ted's face intently, she was impressed by the massiveness of his square chin, which seemed to her to account for an eighth of his total weight.

Domesticity

She could watch him for hours on end and, with a painter's perception, noted that even physically Ted consisted of at least four different men; his high profile, discounting the deeply set eyes, was very similar to an etching they had of Holbein's Henry VIII. The left-hand side of his face seemed much younger and more handsome than the rest, and *en face*, with his eyes fully focused, 'one loses track and is either dazzled or dismayed. His mouth is grim – it's a sand ditch'. One night she was startled when in the half dark, Ted lay naked and the thick hair on his chest and stomach formed a diffused, moving and moustached face, like a tattooed snake. Assia experienced a panic and was overtaken by an image of the black killer-monster that used to frighten her in her Berlin childhood home.

She kept herself busy with *The Man Without Qualities* by Robert Musil, a monumental philosophical novel that portrayed the demise of the Austro–Hungarian Empire. With a schoolgirl's diligence she copied into her diary extracts that appealed to her, like 'the only ones that never succeed (to conform to the beauty standards of their time!) are born to strange triumphs, those in which the regal and exiled ideal beauty of another age is exposed without compromise.' Hughes worked with absolute concentration, in wild fever, like a man possessed, completely immune to all noises. 'He's almost incapable of performing one word wrong' she melted with adulation. He was genius, magnificent, ferocious with intelligence and magic, and she was afraid to occupy the space next to him. Awed by his presence and overwhelmed by her perceptions of his magnitude, Assia began – for the first time in her life – to doubt her own worth. 'I should be pleased that he appears to love me, and love him back – wholly. Make it whole. Please make me whole.'

When Hughes was angry his face turned black and the amorous impact of his eyes disappeared. His blackest, most demonic and destructive moods surfaced when he was suffering from writer's block. 'I hated him all night. Couldn't bear his arm under my head. Pretended it was a wooden bar.' Gradually, his preoccupation with his writing made her 'unsatisfied, untalked-out', alien and hostile. When she challenged him, he exempted himself with 'I'm dumb'. The expression infuriated her even further: she identified the phrase as coined by Sylvia: 'means unkind. He means blind, deaf. I am twice as deaf, blasphemously blind.' Reading Turgenev's *First Love*, she was intrigued by a description of a poet and underlined the words 'a rather cold man like nearly all writers'. In moments of frustration she defined Hughes in her derogatory private code: 'he IS Lipsey' – both men were reserved and aloof about their work. Assia could not escape knowing that Dick Lipsey, now a young, brilliant professor, was celebrating a huge success with his textbook *An Introduction to Positive Economics* that sold millions and made him not just world famous, but also a wealthy man. Another Mrs Lipsey was enjoying Assia's dreams of grandeur.

Assia and Ted were both busy with the literary work of their absent spouses. He was sending Plath's poems for publication and editing them into a book, as well as planning a reprint of *The Colossus*; Assia acted as David's literary agent and diligently sent his poems to six different publishers. Hughes was reluctant to speak to her about Sylvia but the air was filled with her desirable and greatly missed presence. 'Sylvia growing in him, enormous, magnificent. I shrinking daily, both nibble at me. They eat me.' Only in rare moments of intimacy did he allow himself to mention Sylvia openly and casually, and even voice some criticism. 'Surely by now he remembers nothing but the tenderest, the freshest, the most ever inaccessible again,' Assia tormented herself. She increasingly doubted the sincerity or permanence of Hughes's commitment to her. In her view, Sylvia would remain his precious wife, while she was cast for ever in the role of mistress. Her sense of inferiority was intensified by Plath's giant shadow and her own place at the bottom of Ted's priorities: 'at the forefront is Sylvia, and after that, the Grand Scheme, the Genius, the children, and the fixity of the sun, the millions of hawks and fishes and owls, and nightshade that I neither see nor hear.' A horrifying thought began to creep in: that she was inviting Sylvia's doom for herself. She confided in her diary:

with the enormous difference that she had a million times the talent, 1,000 times the will, 100 times the greed and passion that I have. I should never have looked into Pandora's box, and now that I have I am forced to wear her love-widow's sacking, without any of her compensations. What, in 5 years' time, will he reproach me for? What sort of woman am I? How much time have I been given? How much time has run out? What have I done with it? Have I used myself to the hilt already? Am I enough for him? AM I ENOUGH FOR HIM?

One morning the post brought John Malcolm Brinnin and Bill Read's *The Modern Poets – an American British Anthology*, Hughes leafed through the pages and came across a photograph of Sylvia, which he had never seen before. His mood went sour immediately. It was taken in the USA in 1958 and Sylvia was wearing a floral dress and a dark sweater, her hair in a bang, leaning against a wall. Assia thought that Sylvia looked tense, slightly reproachful, and very young. There was also a similar photo of Ted, laughing and very handsome. It was a cruel juxtaposition of them both: Sylvia, 'dour, paining, Puritanism bleaking her face . . . like a young girl after terrible strain, after an illness', and Ted, 'innocent of the Boulder in him. He's aged like weather'.

The following night, Ted dreamt that Sylvia's hair had turned white and that he shot a cat that they had in Boston but it refused to die. He woke into a wild hysteria lasting all morning, pouring the details all over Assia. His nightmares of that time infiltrated his poetry, describing within two months of her death three 'dream-meetings' with Sylvia. Only a few months earlier, when Ted was married to Sylvia, Assia was the one that hit his imagination in stealth, and it now dawned on her: 'we are in perfect reversal, it's Sylvia who's hit it again, and will remain there until he's middle aged, when she'll be relieved by a very young girl.' Hypnotised by both Ted and Sylvia, Assia remarked ironically, 'maybe I'll end up writing the biography of Plath.'

Both she and Ted were tied to their former lives in Gordian knots, reliving bonds that they had overlooked when the relationships were intact. The suicide awakened Ted's allegiance to his discarded marriage vows, and he sent Aurelia Plath lengthy demonstrations of his continuing love for Sylvia. He described his affair with Assia as 'madness' and declared that he would never marry another woman. Trapped under Ted's moody, domineering presence, Assia yearned desperately for David. She longed for the solitary early mornings in Chalcot Square, David lightly asleep, she drinking coffee and eating rolls with red-currant jam, reading, smoking. 'David. David. Where are you? Why can't I love you like I used to? My dearest – David. David, yellow boy, straight like cornstalk, smelling of talcum and chocolate, locked with unripe seed. But I did love you more than anyone, ever. I did once, I'll never forget.'

Her husband's despondent letters from Spain unsettled her further. She was heartbroken to read that he often went to Barcelona airport on the crazy notion that she might get off the plane. 'She sent me loving letters, telling me that she misses me terribly and wants me to come back,' Wevill recalls. Assia broke out in tears, telling her friend Patricia Mendelson that David was the only man she would ever love. 'I refuse to sink my teeth into T. If I'm not claimed, I can't claim. Only David can claim me morally,' she wrote in her diary. She envisaged a rescue plan: 'I'd move out, buy cigarettes, take a train to London, pack, ring Pickford's to cart the junk away, and take a train to Spain.' In an attempt to numb her infatuation with Ted, she persuaded herself: 'Reality is David, my own income. T is a long night of nightmares. Whatever the consequences for me, T is unconcerned.' She was quite certain that Ted would make no effort to retrieve her: 'after I leave him, he'll move from one woman to woman.' But as clear-eyed as she was about her prospects, she channelled her grim insights into sulking and not into action, once again entrusting her future to the hands of her men, waiting for either her husband or her lover to make a decisive move.

But David was still inert and resigned himself to composing forlorn love letters and Ted was unable to focus on a single scenario. He was paralysed; so many choices where to live, so many people meddling in his life, so many battles to wage. He and Assia often exploded into bickering quarrels and estrangement and their good days were rare. 'We've lived in peace for five days now, the longest (it seems) stretch since Sylvia died,' Assia noted on 12 June 1963. During a stay at his parents' home in Yorkshire, she was on one occasion not quick enough to bathe and dress in time to go shopping with Ted and the children. She sat by the window, livid with bitterness, waiting for his return. She felt that her existence was shrinking into that of a trophy and, at the age of 36, she doubted if she could fill that role. 'If only I could dress well and carefully <u>every</u> day. I mean, if my function in life is mainly decorative, (but <u>who's</u> cast me?), then I may as well fulfil it with some brio,' she sneered at herself. When Ted returned, Assia stormed outside. She saw him following her but continued walking without turning her head. He caught up with her and they walked for a while in a foul silence. The children were hungry and whining, so they returned home. Assia calmed down, and during supper, as she was leaning over the table to give Frieda her food, she and Ted collided in a kiss. 'I then flared up with enormous love. It's lasted all day.'

Assia rarely used Hebrew in her diary, and when she did, the right-to-left characters served as a secret code against peeping eyes. On 23 May, she wrote the biblical phrase *tohu va'vohu* (chaos) – to describe Ted's constant change of mind in just one day; would he live in London? Keep Court Green or sell it? Would he buy a house near his parents in Yorkshire, or settle in Wiltshire? Cumberland? Lancashire? Sutherland? A city girl and a career woman, she was not keen on moving to the country and being at Ted's mercy but kept her reservations to her diary: 'the North terrifies me. Big Boulder smashing me. I feel devoid of substance, of self.' She was envisioning a cold stone house: 'hands chapped and red, tired, children chattering like monkeys, Ted locked in a small icy room, coming out three times a day, foraging for food like a bear. Great monumental disregards. We all <u>look</u> unkempt, unkemptable. Patronising visitors come from London. I'm their <u>mother</u>. The thought of ever marrying him utterly repugnant. Let him continue to be her God.' Nevertheless, she was ready to give it a try and she joined Ted on his house-hunting trips.

Moving to London in 1954, Assia had left her parents and sister in Canada, and since two of her husbands were Canadian, she had neither direct family nor in-laws in England and was free from scrutiny. Like Sylvia, she found it difficult to adjust to the close-knit Yorkshire clan and their Puritan views: Ted's parents were dismayed by their son's scandalous relationship with a thrice-married woman; they feared that it had ruined his reputation, making him unsuitable to speak at schools, losing any chance of ever getting a knighthood; 'and will the Queen ever give me audience,' he wrote to the Comptons. Staying with his parents, she and Ted were put in separate bedrooms for the sake of decency: Ted, in 'the snow-flaked room', and Assia, in Olwyn's. Bringing coffee to Ted's bedroom in the morning, Assia could not stop thinking that '<u>they</u> probably slept in the room'. She felt unwanted, irritated with the 'endless idiotic conversations. Or rather rattles, not conversations, but retorts.' She was appalled by Ted's crudeness when he idly remarked over the breakfast table, in the presence of the entire family: 'Have you ever thought, what if you made one quid every time you make love, you'd be very rich by now.'

Hughes was alarmed when Mrs Plath informed him that she was coming to visit her daughter's grave in June and spend time with her grandchildren. He was worried that she might again try to get hold of Frieda and Nicholas. Since he failed to persuade Mrs Plath to postpone her visit, he tried to minimise the infringement on his privacy and instructed Elizabeth Compton, who was now living in Court Green, to hide photographs and albums and any of Sylvia's mementoes left behind and tell Mrs Plath that he had taken them. To prevent her visiting Sylvia's last address in London and bumping into Assia, Ted took the children to his aunt Hilda. He took care to clear off just before Mrs Plath's arrival in Yorkshire. Before setting off back to London he suddenly disappeared and Olwyn told Assia that he had gone to put flowers on Sylvia's grave. Assia immediately knew 'we shall have a properly gloomy journey back to London, with full honours.'

The Hughes family could not spare Aurelia Plath a room in Heptonstall and she had to stay with friends in Halifax, an hour's bus drive away. Unaware of Assia's place beside him, she assumed that Ted might give his children to be brought up by his aunt. Although very fond of Hilda, Mrs Plath was appalled by the little mill town so plagued by dampness that it formed acrid and thick smog that stung the eyes. Hilda's two-bedroom semi-detached stone house in a narrow street was too crowded with large furniture, leaving no room for a child to play.

After a week in Yorkshire, Mrs Plath came down to London and met Hughes. She restated her offer to take the children to the United States, to be raised in her son's spacious home, which had a large garden by a lake and a swimming beach, with schools that were among the very best in the country. Hughes flatly refused. In her diary, Assia cynically envisaged the dramatic meeting between Ted and Sylvia's mother – 'the chief plaintiff' – she imitated Ted's grovelling speech to his former mother-in-law: 'I was vaguely longing, you see, ma'am, loving her all the time, but my sperm was playing havoc with my loins, and my memories, and then it slipped, because I'm dumb, and your beautiful doll, earth-queen, fell and broke all by herself. Snapped in my hand. She did. My beauty and yours. And now we are mourners.'

If not in the United States, Aurelia Plath wished her grandchildren to grow up in her daughter's Devon nest, away from London's temptations, but Ted told her that he could not bring himself to live at the site of his 'crime against her', against himself. Endless deliberations resulted in a decision to buy Lumb Bank, a spacious manor house in Yorkshire, 'big enough for the tribe', the main disadvantage of which was its closeness to his parents' home. He found a prospective buyer for Court Green, due to move in on 15 August. In the meantime, they stayed with Ted's parents, and Assia felt 'caged with six macacos, wearing each other out, and with a noise enough to occupy a whole street'.

Just before the move, she and Ted drove to Court Green to pick up some items. It was her first visit since the fateful weekend that had ignited the affair a year earlier. 'Assia was stunningly beautiful, and my husband and I were overawed,' recalls Elizabeth Compton, who was watching over the house. The visit began on the wrong footing, when Elizabeth invited them to share the meal that she made for her four-year-old son James. Assia ate heartily but, with the airs of a white-gloved Kensington lady, blurted out, 'Oh my God, I haven't had a meal like that since I was in kindergarten.' Elizabeth was hurt by the bluntness and ingratitude and hostility increased when Assia turned to Ted and asked to see the house. Ted, silent and detached, made no move. Elizabeth felt that Assia did everything she could to step quickly into Sylvia's shoes but got up and led the way around a house that Assia already knew, stopping at the various rooms. Outside Sylvia's study, Assia turned to her and asked, 'Don't you feel like a traitor?' Elizabeth broke down in tears and rushed downstairs, to find Ted rolling a carpet, also weeping.

Left alone on the first floor, Assia delved into 'the Holy Study', as she ironically called it, and 'the God's bedroom' – and fetched out Sylvia's clothes and the drawers that were full of combs and ribbons and brushes and miscellaneous half-discarded things. She felt far from victorious: 'it was the funeral all over again. DAW [David Anthony Wevill] and mine funeral. And theirs,' she wrote in her diary. She went down, and, according to Compton, she asked, 'Do you think Ted and I can be happy together?' Elizabeth pointed at Ted, worn and shrunken, and said, 'Look at him. Sylvia's spirit will always stand between you.'

Fourteen

Torn Between Two Lovers

London, summer 1963–64

Assia's present for Ted's thirty-third birthday were the two volumes of the stories of Thomas Mann. Inside, she drew a red arrow above a single, almost white long hair and added the inscription 'Love is not love until love's vulnerable'. Those poignant words were a quote from 'The Dream', by the American poet Theodore Roethke, who was one of Assia and Ted's favourites; that same week Roethke made unfortunate headlines when he drowned in a friend's pool.

At the last moment, just when they were ready to move up north to Lumb Bank, Ted got cold feet and decided that Assia should remain in London until his family cooled off and resigned itself to her. Assia was to live in Sylvia's flat, which would be his home during his London visits, and join him for weekends in Yorkshire.

Then all of a sudden, the asking price for Lumb Bank was raised and Hughes failed to get his hoped-for price for Court Green. The financial gap forced him to give up Yorkshire and move back to Devon. It freed him from the scrutiny of his family but, for some reason, Assia did not follow him. It could not have been her aversion to the haunting presence of Plath; in fact, she stayed on in 23 Fitzroy Road, living on her own in the death flat, surrounded by Plath's belongings. Apparently, after six hard-pressed years with Plath and six tense months with Assia, Hughes wanted some time for himself. It looked like a temporary delay but two and a half turbulent years would pass before they would live again together under the same roof.

Assia had no choice but to comply. Alone in the maisonette, she picked up Erich Fromm's *The Art of Loving* and, beneath the inscription 'Sylvia Plath, Court Green, 9 November 1962' she added her own stamp of ownership and wrote 'Sept. 63'. She read the book, with Plath's many annotations, and added her own, especially underlining passages on page 97. The paragraph deals with the wish of an adult to be sucked back into the 'all-receiving – and all-destroying – womb' which Fromm diagnosed as a severe mental disturbance. Some mothers, Fromm wrote, 'want to keep the child, the adolescent, the man, with them; he should not be able to breathe, but through them; not able to love, except on a superficial sexual level – degrading all other women.' Was Assia thinking of Edith Hughes as the cause of Ted's sudden reluctance to include her in his life?

Attached to Assia's 1963 diary is an undated page, written when she settled back in London; unable to sleep, she got up and put Bach's Musical Offering on the gramophone, placing the needle on the Grand largo of the Trio Sonata. The serene sounds of the flute, cembalo and cello filled the living room. She stood by the window, staring at the flat opposite which was 'strewn, animated with legitimate domesticity'. A wife was leaning over her husband, her arm over his shoulder, while he was writing in concentration. The scene hit Assia. By now, she must have understood that she had no one to rely on but herself and she vowed to better herself; she strove to become not just the wife of a writer, but a writer herself: 'I shall will myself to write, to read with more concentration, less lasciviousness. Less promiscuity. I'll start by willing myself back – to the earliest, darkest, most fearful bedroom in my life.' It is unclear to what sort of childhood traumas she was referring, since no references of the kind have survived.

Assia found it difficult to face loneliness and the burden of the rent and introduced a lodger into Frieda and Nicholas's room while she slept in Sylvia's former bedroom. She tried to make peace with Dr Thomas, the ground-floor neighbour, but he was reluctant; he told Assia that he could not forget Sylvia's outcries against her as 'the evil who had come between them'. Assia exonerated herself by blaming Sylvia for giving Ted 'a very difficult time with her moods, tantrums and sentimentality'. Nevertheless, his sons enjoyed going upstairs, finding Assia 'a very nice lady'. Gradually Dr Thomas got over his initial dislike and complimented Assia on being 'charming, warm and outgoing.' She found a job for his rebellious seventeen-year-old son, but the young man soon left the office – and home – after falling in love with Assia's tenant, who by pure coincidence was the niece of Thomas's ex-wife.

At the end of September, Olwyn Hughes left her job in Paris to join Ted at Court Green, aunt Hilda came down to help them get settled and Elizabeth Compton popped in every day. For the past three months, Hughes had avoided writing to Mrs Plath and it was through Dr Horder, Sylvia's doctor, that Aurelia Plath learned that he had not moved to Yorkshire after all. Dr Horder regarded the stay in Devon favourably, since it should strengthen Ted's bond with his children, and it also meant that he was no longer 'living with that lady of his'. Once the lovers were living apart, the hush-up involving Assia was lifted; Winifred Davies, Sylvia's North Tawton nurse, was quick to inform Mr Plath that 'the lady-love has gone from the picture' and Jillian Becker wrote to her: 'Madame Asya [sic] has the flat, though I could be wrong. I hear that she's very unhappy, and my uncharitable soul is unable to shed a tear.' Aurelia Plath was grateful for the information but asked her correspondents to keep their communications a secret from Ted. He demanded that Elizabeth Compton cease writing to his former mother-in-law, but had no control over Dr Horder in London, who wrote to Mrs Plath on 17 October: 'there is at least a rumour that Ted will remarry.'

The reports were inaccurate; Assia and Ted did not break up but, at the same time, were not planning marriage. They overcame the geographical separation by an intensive exchange of letters and telegrams and frequently phoned each other knowing that there was no one to eavesdrop on them. Ted went to London as often and for as long as he wished, since his children were taken care of. He was concerned that the distance and tensions caused by his family's objections to her might erode her feelings for him: if they did, he told Assia, they would have no future 'but stupid friendship'.

When Ted Hughes's archive at Emory University in Atlanta, Georgia, was made available to the public in 2000, it was devoid of Assia's presence in his life: of the numerous letters that they exchanged, of all the notes, drawings and photos, none existed. Hughes admitted that he went over each piece of paper, and sorted them himself before packing and shipping the 86 crates to the United States, exercising self-concealment. In 2003, his widow sold to Emory six thousand volumes from his library and all of a sudden Assia surfaced. About eighty of the books either belonged to Assia, or were presents to Hughes from her.

Among them were five books that Ted and Assia exchanged in the month of October. The first was an English translation of Sergei Eisenstein's screenplay *Ivan the Terrible,* which Assia gave Ted on 20 October 1963, and inscribed with encouraging words, 'You'll "beat the lot, the lot/the lot!"/d'you hear?/My darling Ted'. On 20 October 1965, she gave him *Four Screenplays* by Ingmar

Bergman, 'to mark the departure of Opal/and with love and love and love.' Opal is October's birthstone, a symbol of trust and confidence.

The following year, Hughes gave Assia the just-published anthology of the *London Magazine Poems, 1961–1966*, selected by Hugo Williams, which included poems by him and by Plath.

In October 1967, Hughes gave Assia the first bound copy of the American edition of *Wodwo,* inscribed 'to sweetest Assiake, from Permanence'. And, in October 1968, Assia gave him *The Letters of William Blake.* The presentation inscription reads, 'For you, for you, for you, forever.'

There is no other instance in the entire collection that books were given repeatedly on the same month, year after year – except for May – which was Assia's birthday, and August, which was Ted's. The October gift-exchange therefore indicates some kind of intimate anniversary. Were they marking a new phase in their lives, when Ted left Court Green and Sylvia Plath in October 1962?

On 31 October 1963, Assia received a telegram from Madrid: ARRIVE SATURDAY EVENING WILL PHONE DAVID. It was obvious that Wevill regarded the separation as over, and Assia, still loving her husband, had no intention of slamming the door on him. Upon his return David moved in with her, not probing into her affairs and Assia continued her relationship with Hughes, only lowering the profile. It seems that the return of his rival aroused his jealousy and made his heart grow fonder: he told her that he loved her 'more now than any time yet'. Only too late, he expressed remorse for squandering the opportunity they had while David was away. Wishing to regain control over her life, he asked her to keep a journal and send it to him. In the many poetry readings that he was giving all over the country, he made a point of passing through London and stealing a few hours with Assia. She, however, did not make it easy for him, and tried to stick to her own agenda, making him change his schedule to fit hers.

Sylvia's suicide had plunged Assia and Ted into a commotion that left little time for intimacy and forced them to skip essential stages in the build-up to their relationship. Reverting to an affair rather than family life, they could pick up where they left off and restore their conjugality. He ached for her in his sleepless nights, and missed their long stimulating conversations. Their love life prospered in letters ('you onlyest', he called her). He sometimes made a doodle in the shape of a sun coming out from the letters of her name. But their correspondence was double-edged: mellow and romantic, laced with bickering possessiveness. They scrutinised each other's words with lynx eyes, reading in between the lines, analysing every sentence and checking each other's emotions. Invariably, their misinterpretations ignited a row, and he was quick to appease her. As far as Hughes was concerned, he was striving towards a joint future: working hard to earn money and cutting expenses. He urged Assia to do the same.

From the beginning of December 1963 to late March 1964, Lucas Myers stayed at Court Green. He recalls that Assia never came for a visit and that Ted saw her on his frequent trips to London. Myers joined him once, meeting Assia in The Lamb, a magnificent pub in the heart of Bloomsbury, made famous in the 1920s and 1930s by the Bloomsbury circle. The green-tiled interior of The Lamb had wood-panelled walls, decorated with a display of Hogarth's prints and sepia photographs of long-forgotten stars of the music hall and theatre. The horseshoe bar still had the original etched 'snob screens'; those rotating screens that shielded the pillars of Victorian society, when they were drinking in the company of women of dubious reputation.

Once again, Hughes had to rely on his friends' generosity to have a foothold in London. David Ross, who lived in Great Ormond Street, just by The Lamb, gave Ted the keys to his flat on the third floor, while he, Ross, stayed with his girlfriend in her first-floor flat. Ross used to go with Assia to the pub, to keep her company until Ted's arrival. 'It was always packed full with men, but when I entered with Assia, they all moved aside,' he recalls. 'She was stunningly beautiful, and had a strong likeness to Elizabeth Taylor. I felt very masculine in her presence, and it added a few feet to my height. She was great to be with, totally focused on her companion, until the moment that Ted appeared.' Ross had disliked Plath – he knew her from Cambridge – and thought that Ted was happier and more relaxed in Assia's company: 'I don't think Sylvia ever realised the importance of our gang for Ted, while Assia tried to make friends with us and fit into our group.' Ben Sonnenberg, Ted's friend and publisher of the literary journal *Grand Street,* was impressed by Assia's 'feral beauty, feral eyes, feral touch and feral movements. There was a feral purr in her voice and something feral in the arrangement of her hair. What a seductive animal,' he recalled.

Assia and Ted spent Christmas apart. Her husband's gift was the newly published *Ottoline – the Early Memoirs of Lady Ottoline Morrell*. This English socialite was a friend and patron of many artists, including Siegfried Sassoon, Aldous Huxley and D H Lawrence. Married to Liberal MP Philip Morrell, Ottoline was dallying with Bertrand Russell and other men and was portrayed – though grotesquely – in several novels, including *Women in Love*. Under the circumstances, it seemed a rather odd choice of a gift from a betrayed husband to his wife. Wevill declared his unconditional love against all odds, endorsing the book 'For Assia . . . in sickness & in health . . . /in bed or up, in a dressing gown – Christmas 1963'. Like Assia's previous husbands, David was still acquiescing in his wife's affair. 'She was very frank about this business of loving two men. And as much as it may sound strange, she was loyal to each one of us. We never had an argument of the *Who's Afraid of Virginia Woolf?* type.'

While Assia and David were celebrating Christmas in London, Ted had two female guests at Court Green: Susan Alliston who had been an early visitor to 23 Fitzroy Road on Plath's death, and Tasha Hollis. Hughes had first heard of Susan in the late 1950s, when he and Sylvia were living in the United States. A poem of hers was published in the *Nation* and he was told that she was a 'gorgeous English girl with extraordinary hair'. Two or three years later, visiting Faber and Faber, Hughes was sharing the lift with one of the secretaries at the publishing house. They stood in silence and he missed the opportunity to learn that she was Susan Alliston. He remembered her face when he saw her again in The Lamb a year later, after leaving Court Green. By then, she was divorced from American Clem Moore, and was sharing a flat with her friend Tasha, also a fresh divorcee. Rumours travelled as far as Court Green and, from Plath's letter to her mother on 22 November, it is clear that she knew that Ted was meeting Susan, who expressed a wish to meet her but Sylvia had no intention to comply. Ted and Susan kept in touch after Plath's death, and Lucas Myers recalls that 'their relationship was not essentially sexual, but one of intellectual and artistic sympathy and friendship, and Ted thought well of her poetry.'

Apparently, upon returning to London, Alliston bragged about the delightful Christmas she spent with Hughes. Now the rumours hit Assia; she was livid with jealousy, accusing Ted of entertaining the young poetess 'practically every weekend'. Ted was quick to blame Assia's women friends for distorting the nature of his acquaintance with Alliston, in order to set him and Assia apart: He vowed to Assia that as far as he was concerned, no other women existed: she was all he had got, all he wanted, and all his thoughts and plans were for her. Denying any improper relationship with Susan, Hughes repented that Christmas invitation. A year earlier, when Sylvia confronted him with details of his affair with Assia, Ted showed no remorse, nor did he promise to put an end to the affair. Now, in order to appease Assia, he assured her that it was the last he had seen of Susan and he would never speak to her again. He begged Assia to trust him, otherwise there was no future for them. His conclusion was rather radical: to get away from England and the Nosy Parkers, and live abroad.

But, in fact, and in spite of his promises to Assia, he did not severe his relationship with Alliston. Two years later she was diagnosed with Hodgkin's disease and Hughes admitted, 'our friendship took on new life, under that horrible cloud.' After her death, he collected Susan's manuscripts from her flat at 18 Rugby Street, with his sister Olwyn and friend Daniel Weissbort, hoping – in vain – to find a publisher for them. The unpublished poems, with a touchingly intimate introduction by Hughes, entitled 'a close friendship of six years', are kept in his archive at Emory University.

The Alliston affair ignited Assia's wrath, and on 22 January she wrote Hughes a letter, declaring that as much as it was hard on her, she had decided not to see him again:

> My future is blanked with you . . . I want to wind everything up, sell everything I possess, move, start from scratch . . . I'm convinced you have mayhemed my life. You've left me with a rubbishy life, with nothing to salvage. Absolutely nothing. The only revenge I can take on you is to go to bed with any attractive man who asks me. To hurt your sensations out of my body, if not out of my mind or blood.

Just as she was sealing the envelope, she heard the key turning in the front door. She quickly pushed the letter under the sofa but David caught the quickness of her move. There was a short, sad scene and she was furious that with her clumsiness, she caused anguish to her husband.

Later that evening, she re-opened the envelope and added a few more lines: 'Now I begin to think, superstitiously, that when I'm possessed with you, you magically have dispossessed me, and vice versa. When I feel free of you – then surely, you want me most – if only there was a way of testing it. It's Thursday,

8.30 p.m., and you are in total possession.' What began in defiance, ended in total surrender.

Hughes's letters were usually addressed with terms of endearment such as 'My sweet Assia, sweetest, sweetnessest, sweetnessest'. He constantly invented pet names for her like 'my fox', 'little pod', 'ovenfox', 'my lovely owl of halva', 'Chocolate Halva', 'honey pot' and the biblical fragrances of myrrh and cassia. While he was very flamboyant in his inscriptions, trying to woo her with his words, Assia was very sombre and straightforward. She addressed him as Ted, Teddy, or 'most darling Ted', and simply signed Assia or even AW.

Hughes encouraged Assia to keep herself occupied and resume painting, and send her work to him when she could not write a letter. At Ted's request, Assia taught him the Hebrew alphabet, and he used to transcribe English phrases in hesitantly drawn Hebrew letters and occasionally flawed grammar, for example 'to love in you and copulate for ever'. To disguise his Valentine's Day gift, Hughes suggested that she tell David that it was from her uncle Grisha Gutmann in Australia. When Ted fell ill, Assia sent him a 'get well' telegram but he was alarmed and warned her to be discreet next time, since the postmaster in North Tawton and his wife were opening his letters and reading her telegrams.

Lucas Myers remembers that there were times that Ted received communications at what must have been a post office box in the nearby town of Okehampton. Hughes was disturbed that Assia was saving his letters: he argued that he would have written much more openly and affectionately, but had reason to believe that she was showing his letters as well as her diary to her friends, who were meddling in their affairs. He urged her to burn them all. However, Assia kept Ted's letters. Most of her letters to him, though, have not survived.

He was at his desk twelve to fifteen hours a day, and reported his progress regularly to Assia. On 31 January 1964, he almost finished typing his play in verse *Gaudete*. The protagonist was Nicholas Lumb, an Anglican clergyman who was abducted to the underworld, the evil spirits replacing him with an exact duplicate, who brought chaos to the parish: fornicating with the married women, making them cheat on their husbands and eventually causing the death of those who loved him.

He shared with Assia the books he was reading – recommending Bashevis

Singer and advising her to give John Cowper Powys's *Wolf Solent* a miss. He recounted his dreams: they were walking together in the woods where he used to go shooting and he was selecting baby birch trees and beeches, which were only a few inches high, to plant in the garden. Giant pike continued to pop up in his dreams. Once he dreamt that he was the president of the English Literary Society at some grand university and managed to persuade Kafka to come and read to the students and staff. Kafka arrived and read for two hours. But Hughes woke up feeling inadequate for his presentation of Kafka to the plenum. Another time, waking up from a terrible dream about Assia, he was quick to phone her and breathed a sigh of relief when he heard her voice.

The odd writing jobs that Hughes undertook for the sake of money were distracting him from his true vocation. In mid-February he finished a film treatment of a farce about an American birdwatcher on a Hebridean island – admitting that it was banal. Together with Assia, he was writing another film script, which he referred to as 'our saga': it budded over a year earlier, during their Spanish escapade. The first scene takes place in a bar in a small mountain town in Spain. The protagonist is attracted to the local beauty and excited by her attention. She flirts with him for a while but leaves him for another man. The next scene takes place in Venice, when a clowning mob of prostitutes chases the protagonist out of the street. At the Acropolis in Athens, he chances upon an attractive Parisian art student, who sketches the ruins and asks him to pose for her, but ignores his attention. Hughes sent Assia the rough draft, and she developed some of the scenes. He praised her for the originality of her comments and suggested that they use the script as a pretext to travel abroad to the sites described, to check them out.

In addition to the film script she was working on with Hughes, Assia had her own project, developing Turgenev's *First Love* into a film script. The mid-nineteen-century novelette was a study of the adolescent love-at-first-sight of sixteen-year-old Vladimir, overwhelmed by the beauty of the capricious, shallow Zinaida. Obsessed with naïve infatuation, lost in love for the exquisite, domineering, flirtatious 21-year-old, Vladimir is added to Zinaida's herd of admirers, whom she keeps on strings at her feet. She amuses herself by raising their hopes one moment and their fears the next, twisting them round her little finger. Zinaida is looking for a man who can master and possess her and finds him in Vladimir's father, who is married to a woman he does not love. The destructive love affair leads to an inevitable separation and the lovers' early deaths. Scorned by his first love, Vladimir remains a bachelor.

The script has not survived but, on the opening page of Assia's copy of *Selected Tales of Ivan Turgenev*, she has scribbled some stage directions for a scene between Vladimir and his mother:

Very blindingly lit dining table. It's noon. Light behind seated woman. Move in on over-ringed, plump woman. She spoons soup into her mouth. Noise of starched napkin unfolding, of cutlery. Click. Clack. Move towards nested button of butter, and away. Now into tall portrait of sourly tempered woman and boy grinding their way through lunch.

Voice: my mother was ten years older than my father.

The camera remains on the boy's back, and relentlessly follows the woman, watches her like an enemy. In profile, it cruelly discovers her mountainous belly, the seam of her wig, the line of food-moistures above her lip. She eats greedily, and self-centredly. Wisps of her own hair show under her wig. She wears long pearl earrings.

Voice: she scarcely paid any attention to me although she had no other children. Other worries occupied her completely.

David Wevill applauded Assia on her project ('These scenes you imagined for *First Love* are beautiful – truly – and so clear and plain.'). He advised her to take writing seriously and write – paragraphs, tiny stories built around incidents. 'Work slowly, Trynchin, let your pulse be at normal pressure when you write: you don't have to lash yourself into energetic fury, like the cat on the stump.' The two men nurtured her and, when there was an opening for a job at the prestigious advertising agency, J Walter Thompson and Assia was full of apprehensions as to whether she was right for the job, both encouraged her. Ted reassured her that she was the best in her profession and David remarked, 'you are such a GOOD writer, and advertising wears good writers out.'

Assia was an integral part of her men's artistic work; she collected and typed reviews and articles, which Hughes needed in order to get a grant from Vienna, and assisted David in his efforts to find a publisher for *Birth of a Shark*. He dedicated the book 'for Assia', and his photograph, which she took on their trip to her beloved Pisa, appears on the inner jacket: standing in a crowd, Wevill looks withdrawn, his head tilted down, eyes half closed. One of the poems, 'Germinal', carries suppressed violence and scars of the drama which was overtaking their life: 'Wastes grow; you lean into the sun/As towards a good husband, hoping its fire/Will incinerate your trash and not you.'

On the publicity form that Wevill completed for the Macmillan publishing house, he remarked that his surname rhymed with 'devil'. The collection consisted of poems from the previous five years – covering his life with Assia and the various places of his domicile: England, Canada, Burma, Spain and even the brief trip that they made to Ireland. The background was an anchor for his poems: 'but events impose themselves: family relationships, love, breakages, hysteria, compromise, harmony and conflict, movement and fixity, cruelty and guilt . . . the poems are written around a contradiction: the desire to merge with things, and the need to break away.' He said that man dreams of action but is helpless to act; he dreams of peace of mind but acts to destroy it. The book was selling rather well, and Peter Orr, who interviewed Sylvia Plath, added David Wevill to his anthology *The Poet Speaks*, based on the radio interview. To Orr's question as to whether he had a specific audience in mind, Wevill replied, 'I prefer to have *one* person in mind all the time, because I find that personal, direct communication turns to unleash a lot more, than if you are thinking in terms of a mass of people.' When Hughes was asked by the *Sunday Times* to review some books, including *Penguin Modern Poets 4*, which included some of Wevill's poems, his sister Olwyn, acting as his agent, replied that he must decline since he was 'rather busy'.

In mid February, Assia was admitted to hospital. Returning home she was visited by Anne, then Alvarez's girlfriend and later his wife. Assia was lying in bed, wearing all white and lace. 'She was so beautiful, and kept on talking about Sylvia, and I thought that she has serious identity problems, and is breaking down.' Anne Alvarez, who is a psychologist, thought that Assia was totally obsessed by her predecessor: 'She had no chance, she was doomed from the start. Professionally I would say she had a counter-phobic reaction, and wanted to demonstrate that she was not afraid of Sylvia's demon. For her own good, she would have been much better off not to sleep in Sylvia's bed.' Having met Assia's two men, Anne Alvarez got the impression that Assia was more relaxed with David, and tense with Ted. When Ted and Assia visited the Alvarez home, there was a leaden silence between the lovers and, in their all-black clothes, they seemed like a pair of black panthers sitting across the fireplace, hissing at each other.

The past two years had been chaotic for David Wevill – he was plagued by

David Wevill, Burma, 1960
(courtesy of Patricia Mendelson)

Tea party in Mandalay, Burma, 1960. Nathaniel
Tarn is on the left (courtesy of Alton Becker)

A painting by Assia, Burma, 1960
(courtesy of David Wevill)

Tea Party, Mandalay, 1960
(courtesy of Alton Becker)

David and Assia Wevill,
England, early 1960s
(courtesy of Celia Chaikin)

Notleys advertisement, London,
Serpentine, June 1961. From left to
right: William Trevor, Marisa Martelli,
Assia, Sean Gallagher
(courtesy of Jane Donaldson)

We really *live* our work at Notleys

No, we don't have a champagne account at Notleys; we just happen to like
product testing. We came out here because things were 'not conducive to
creative thought' back at the office. And you can bet your elastic-sided boots
that *something* will come out of this session. **Ex Notleys semper aliquid novi.**

NOTLEY ADVERTISING LIMITED, 15 & 17 HILL STREET, BERKELEY SQUARE, LONDON W.1

David Wevill, drawn by Assia, early 1960s
(courtesy of Patricia Mendelson)

Ted Hughes, drawn by Assia, late 1960s
(courtesy of Emory University)

Sylvia Plath © Rex Features

May 22nd

My dear Sylvia,

Today I got the tapestry for you, or rather the materials for it. The pattern can only be had directly from the Sunday Times now. According to your descriptions of roses and ribbon, it looks as though the one you had in mind is called the Sunday Times Rose Bouquet, and was published about 2 years ago. I rang the Sunday Times, but the girl who deals with it was out. Harrods assure me that the pattern can still be had.

Tramming: that's when you stretch the thread across 5 or 6 inches of the canvas, and then work over it diagonally. I couldn't remember the word, d'you remember? but you'll see it clearly illustrated in the pattern. I bring it up again, because for tramming on this canvas use half the thread (quite easily divided) because otherwise you will overseed the stitches and everything will be too bulgy and fibrous.

Rather than encourage you to wander in the wastelands of trying to match the shading on the diagram with whatever you can find in the way of wool, I bought the whole shooting match, this will make things much easier for you, at least on your first tapestry. However, if you hate some of the colours (I thoughtactually that entirely white roses shaded with grey would be prettier) you could easily change them at Harrods, or send them to me, and I'll change them. On the little card you'll find certain substitutions in number. wool numbers, this is because Harrods had run out of one manufacturer's wools, and substituted with another manufacturers who uses a different numbering system. I hope that at least some th of this makes sense. I am writing in a tremendous hurry.

Let me warn you again that you can become seriously addicted to tapestry, and xxx you might find yourself staying up too late at night doing it, or stop eating, or mending and baking and working Please, please don't let it possess you . . .
But I hope you'll enjoy it.

Much love,

Assia

Assia's letter to Sylvia Plath, which accompanied the tapestry gift, 22 May 1962 (courtesy of Elizabeth (Compton) Sigmund)

Wednesday.

Darling Janice,

I tried to phone you today — but half-way through the 12th ring realized that you'd be out.

Tomorrow is the day. I found a very old Pole in Maida-Vale. It should be alright. At least he was kind and human. I had to go and see a succession of Harley St. bastards. Oh Janice. At least it'll be over by noon tomorrow.

Could you come to visit me on Friday, or Saturday in the ghost-house?

23 ## Fitzroy Rd. N.W.I. (It's just round the corner from Chalcot ?a.)

And please burn this note.

Love
Assia

Ted, Assia and Frieda, 1963 (courtesy of Celia Chaikin)

Shura, Ireland 1966
(courtesy of Celia Chaikin)

Shura, Ireland 1966
(courtesy of Celia Chaikin)

Shura's first birthday, with Frieda and
Nicholas Hughes, Ireland, March 1966
(courtesy of Celia Chaikin)

Frieda and Shura, Court Green, late 1966 (courtesy of Celia Chaikin)

his beloved wife's continuous adultery and the fatal illness of his mother. At the beginning of March, he flew to Ottawa urgently, to sit by her bed. In his love letters from Canada he urged Assia to look for a new flat: 'I'm weary of Fitzroy Road, the place's malice.' In April 1964, after his mother's death, he returned to England. By early summer he and Assia had moved into 25 Belsize Park Gardens. Ted rented out Sylvia's flat until the end of the year, and then took her furniture and curtains back to Court Green. He rented a room in London with his friend, psychiatrist Dr Nathaniel Minton and, in his tax statement for 1964, he declared that he made eighteen trips to London.

Fifty years earlier Belsize Park Gardens had been an affluent street: the writer Henry Brailsford had lived at number 37, the composer Frederick Delius at number 44. Its glory had faded by the time the Wevills moved into Flat b, on the ground floor facing the chestnut trees along the street. The living room had parquet floors and a large armoire and looked out into the garden. Assia decorated it tastefully with several framed miniatures of insects and flowers that she painted. At that time, David Wevill was making a poor living as a reader of uninspiring books and manuscripts for various publishers. Lucas Myers, who had meanwhile left Court Green, was offered a room with the Wevills. David was sleeping on the couch in the living room, while Assia slept in the bedroom. One day Myers noticed a book lying face down. He picked it up – it was *The Colossus*, Sylvia's first volume of poetry, open on the nine-line poem, 'Metaphors'. He stayed with the Wevills over two months and noted that, in the difficult and humiliating situation, David's demeanour was dignified and admirable, and that Assia had the tenderest feelings for him. She had several heart-to-heart talks with Myers and time and again she pondered, 'How is it possible to love two people at the same time?' David and Lucas also spoke about Ted, separately, occasionally and obliquely.

It seemed that all three protagonists were refraining from making a move that would rock the boat. David still hoped that his devotion would win Assia over; she and Ted became less adventurous in their affair, resigned to the incompleteness of their relationship, with no escapades abroad or inland. Assia could not fail to notice the unmistakable similarities between her life and the film script she was working on. Turgenev's heroine was surrounded by lovers: she had one who would readily have thrown himself into the fire for her, one who answered the poetic elements in her soul and one she could torment and into whose flesh she could stick a pin. Assia too was dependent on Hughes for the exhilarating challenge and on David for the safe haven. Her favourite literary heroine, Anna Karenina, dreamt that her husband cried and kissed her hands, while her lover was standing by. In her dream Karenina was joyful that both men seemed happy and content, which made everything simpler. But when she woke up, she was horrified. For Assia the duality was far from a nightmare: she loved them both and had the best of all worlds. She was careful not to torment David with details of her affair; and he felt that by remaining in London, she had made her choice, to live with him. But had Ted found room for her in his intricate life, she would have followed him instantly.

Tucked into Assia's copy of Edward Albee's play *Who's Afraid of Virginia Woolf?* was a coupon for a free booklet about the most popular and advanced methods of birth control, 'relieving anxiety about unwanted pregnancies and by ensuring that . . . children are wanted and welcome into a happy family'. Apparently, Assia did not fill in the form, or post it to the Family Planning. At the end of August 1964, she confided with Lucas Myers that she was pregnant. 'I knew it was Ted's child, but he did not know that with certainty.'

Fifteen

Birth

London, autumn 1964–winter 1966

When Assia had found herself pregnant in the winter of 1963, her relationship with Ted was not ripe for a baby and, before they could even weigh the possibility of parenthood, Sylvia's suicide tipped the scales. Now, the storm had abated, and the pregnancy did not create a scandal. Assia, at the age of 37, was past her dread of becoming a mother. At the time of the previous pregnancy and abortion, David had no knowledge of it but now he was a full partner and had reason enough to believe that the child might be his.

Assia and Ted invented a secret code for their correspondence and Ted was dispatching his daily letters to her home, addressed to 'F WALL, Esq.' This act of deception could not have been used at 23 Fitzroy Road, since there were only two tenants, the Wevills and Dr Thomas, and David would have caught on to the deceit. But it was easy at 25 Belsize Park Gardens, which was divided into six flats of changing tenants. 'F WALL, Esq.' was a private joke between Ted and Assia; he was the fly on the wall in the Wevills' home. Each morning, Assia would rush to pick up Ted's letter from the pile of post that had been pushed through the crack in the entrance door and was lying on the black-tiled floor. Hughes made a point of sending his letters first class, so they would arrive first thing in the morning, and not later in the day, when Assia was at work and David could have still been at home. It is unclear why they went to all this trouble, when they could easily have used Assia's office address, as they had before. Was it for the thrill, and the romantic intrigue?

Ted was careful not to sign his letters, although, if David had opened them, his rival's distinctive, flamboyant handwriting would have easily betrayed him; especially since Ted was naïve enough to address Assia by his usual terms of endearment, like Asseeke. He also mentioned Frieda and Nick by name, as well as other members of his family and friends and gave details of his literary activities and the titles and transmission times of his BBC radio plays. The heading of his letters of that period lacked the sender's address and even the date but the Royal Mail postmark from Devon would have exposed him outright. But David, although assuming that the affair was still going on, was not spying on Assia, preferring not to know. It worked all right until one day Assia found one of Ted's letters torn open. It was a bulky envelope with a manuscript that someone must have mistaken for a letter containing banknotes. Nothing was missing, but Ted was in panic; he reprimanded her for disclosing their code to her friends and insisted that she find the Nosy Parker.

Hughes reported to Assia at length, filling her in on his daily routine, as a kind of introduction to the life awaiting her in Court Green. For her part, she acted as his emissary in the big city, doing all sorts of errands on his behalf, like buying *The End of the Game* as a birthday present for Gerald. When Hughes heard that a drawing of him had been published in *The London Magazine*, he asked Assia to look for it and send him a copy.

Their meetings were not as frequent as Assia would have wished them to be, and it soured their relationship. They continued their petty squabbling. Hughes first referred to the baby in his letters to her only a month before the expected birth. He advised her to find the right balance between reasonable caution and over-anxiety and, as a seasoned parent, he advised her not to buy many clothes, only nappies and waterproof pants.

The pregnancy was much easier than Assia had expected and in its last weeks she was immersed in Pushkin's *Eugene Onegin*; she was enraptured with Tatiana, who had long been the Russian emblem of purity and fidelity and ideal womanhood. Tatiana was in love with Onegin but he refused to marry her, saying he would tire quickly of marriage. The most he could offer her was brotherly love. Three years later Onegin met the broken-hearted Tatiana again, now married to a prince she did not love. Onegin fell for her passionately but, although still loving him, Tatiana chose loyalty over love, and refused to betray her husband: long ago, she said, she and Onegin could have been happy but now he could bring her only sorrow. The analogies could not have escaped either Ted or Assia.

There was a snowstorm on 3 March 1965, when Assia was admitted to the delivery room of Charing Cross Hospital. She was in labour for nine hours, which were quite bearable except for the last 45 minutes. 'I emerged whole, ecstatic (in which condition I have been for ten days) and so did my daughter

Schura (to rhyme with Jura) whose full name is Alexandra Tatiana Elise,' she joyfully informed Lucas Myers. 'Miraculously unwrinkled, with black hair, very long, and North Sea blue eyes — skin fair as sweet friar, very equable, tactful, grave, very touching. Above all very touching.' Influenced by Hughes's fascination with astrology, she wrote down the hour of birth — 9.55 p.m. — and added that both moon and sun were in Pisces with Libra rising, though she had no idea what that meant.

Long aware of her mother's terminal cancer, Assia added her name to the baby's. Shortly after, on 18 March 1965, Elise Bertha Gutmann passed away in Canada, aged 76. On the birth certificate, Edward James Hughes, an author, from Court Green, North Tawton, Devon, is registered as the father of the newborn. However, it was David Wevill who gave the child his surname: thus, she was both men's daughter, and neither's. The given names, chosen by Assia and reflecting her sense of drama, pass on the mother's dreams of grandeur to the daughter: Alexandra, after the last tsarina, the German-born wife of Nicholas II and Tatiana, after Pushkin's romantic heroine. Doubly Russian, the name points up that Assia no longer wished to blur her foreign identity and asserts that, no matter which of the men, Ted or David, should rear the child, she belongs first and foremost to Assia.

That spring, the recently widowed Dr Leo Gutmann embarked on a three-month grand tour of Europe, and stopped in London to visit his new granddaughter. Assia did not reveal to him the identity of the father. Lonya brought with him the ancient family Bible and, on an inner page, Assia documented in German the birth and death dates of her mother and the birth date of her daughter. She also made an entry for herself (although not for her father or her sister), writing down her date of birth and enigmatically adding the word *gestorben* (passed away) — leaving a blank space for the date.

Gerald Hughes and his wife Joan knew of Assia, but Ted refrained from mentioning her in his letters. The first time he did was when asking Gerald not to inquire about Assia, because Olwyn was reading his post and he wanted to minimise friction with his family. The letter was written a day before Shura's birth but still there was not a word about the impending event. Only on 4 May, when Shura was two months old, did Ted tell Gerald in passing that Assia had a little girl, still not coming clean about his paternity. 'I suppose my parents accepted Shura. I suppose too they thought of her as Ted's,' recalls Olwyn. However, watching Shura asleep, Olwyn noticed her 'long eyelids and lashes

— like David'. Olwyn maintains that Ted was happy to take the child on, although Assia had told her that she did not know who the father was. Friends who visited the Wevills were impressed with David's loving paternal care of the baby and would not have suspected anything amiss had not Assia made a point of whispering that Ted was the father. 'Assia was very interested and absorbed in Shura, she was not unmaternal in her nature, but she was not Mother-Earth,' Wevill recalls.

Assia's female friends observed that a woman who had never demonstrated the slightest interest in children had been transformed overnight into a doting mother. 'She became soft, as if her whole hard edge had gone, she became vulnerable, and very protective of Shura,' remembers Patricia Mendelson. Assia apologised for the years that she was 'seriously flamed, bitch-woman', ignominiously indifferent to Andrea, Patricia's five-year-old daughter. She was grateful for the beautiful clothes that Patricia gave Shura, 'ever since she was born I wanted to buy her some really pretty things to wear, but the money never stretched that far. So I gave up. Women are utterly irrational about these things. Indeed, it is a sort of awful conspicuous consumption — in my case, quite fraudulent — but the pleasure they gave me today was quite out of proportion with my whining Puritan conscience's needle pricks,' she wrote to Patricia in December 1965. With the birth of Shura, Hughes wrote more freely about his children. He filled Assia in on his preparations for Frieda's party and the lunch of four trout that he made for him and Nick. Assia must have reported similarly about Shura, and Ted inquired, 'How are the two little ladies', asking Assia to give the baby two kisses for him.

Ben Sonnenberg recalls that Ted offered to cast the horoscope of his little daughter Susannah, trying to persuade him that 'sometimes it's a useful way of focusing one's attention on a person'. Sonnenberg declined but Ted went ahead and ordered one for Shura. The astrologer foresaw delicate health in childhood, but predicted that Shura would grow to be handsome, pretty, fair skinned, with abundant artistic talent, but too much emotion, too much acting out, laziness and willingness to manipulate others for services rather than just getting on with the job herself. In many ways, it seemed as if Assia's personality was imprinted in her daughter so deeply that they were inseparable. 'There'd be a lot of fantasy life, pretending, unreality and self deception, as well as willingness to be deceived by others,' the astrologer foretold Shura's character. 'It's possible that with the control that comes with age, this person will begin to produce and be more creative, but I think this is a hell of a chart to come in with – a real crucifixion . . . I really don't feel this chart is very promising.' Hughes viewed astrology not as a science, but as an instrument for a vivid expression of intuitive insight, explains Lucas Myers. Hughes informed his friend of Shura's horoscope, but did not comment on the ill omens in it, the astrologer having predicted: 'There would also be severe loss in this person's life – deaths, accidents, etc. in the family.'

In the spring of 1965, *Ariel* was launched and the sight of the daffodils bursting open in the yard of Court Green invoked memories of his last carefree spring with Sylvia.

His self-criticism was mercilessly harsh; he was over 34, but felt 'like the naïvest beginner', totally incompetent, distracted and wasted by humdrum jobs. He yearned for a steady income, since the struggle to make a living wore him out. Assia tried to ease his burden by typing the radio plays that he wrote for the BBC, *The Tiger's Bones* and *Beauty and the Beast*. On a J Walter Thompson/Creative Department letterhead, she typed a number of poems, titled 'Pear', 'Buttercup', 'Apple Blossom', 'Violet' and 'Primroses'. None of them was published.

Together they were working on another book that would illustrate his poems with Assia's drawings. The theme was 'A Full House': a pack of cards, in which the kings, queens and knaves were biblical, mythological and historical figures. The King of Spades was Solomon, who had 700 wives and 300 concubines. Caesar was the King of Clubs, Charlemagne was the King of Hearts, and there were also rhymes for Nebuchadnezzar, Alexander the Great, Victoria the Warrior, Cain and Don Juan. Hughes sent Assia the text to illustrate, suggesting the scenes, like three maidens dancing for Three of Hearts. Assia returned the drawings for Ted's inspection. He confessed that he hoped to solve his financial difficulties through this book, but some time later he decided that the poems were not good enough for publication and stored them away. The poems survived, but none of Assia's drawings has.

The poet and translator Michael Hamburger, Hughes's good friend, remembers another project of Assia's and Ted's: 'she showed me a book of her illustrations of poems by Ted, miniature paintings in brilliant colours with many animals and plants. This was never published, to my knowledge.' Equally continuing to help her husband in his poetical career, Assia sent five of David's poems to her former teacher and lover, Professor Earle Birney in

Vancouver, to be published in his magazine *Prism*. She was ecstatic when David won the Arts Council TriAnnual Book Prize, together with Philip Larkin.

In late June 1965, it was time for the Festival dei Due Mondi – Festival of the Two Worlds – in Spoleto, Italy, and Hughes was invited along with poets including Ezra Pound, Yevgeny Yevtushenko and Pablo Neruda. Assia would not have missed such a gathering of famous poets for the world and she left the three-and-a-half-month-old Shura in the care of David and the nanny. 'We lived like Americans. And got fat and brown,' she wrote to Lucas Myers.

Assia doted on her motherhood, rejoicing when the six-month-old Shura was 'no longer just human sea-weed, her small feet dangling between the seat and the first step, and she ate real bread and butter and egg for the first time. And immaculately. Like a real child.' To press on with her copywriting career at J Walter Thompson, she fired her nanny and hired a single mother from Barcelona named Mercedes, who moved in with her own child. Assia was bursting with ideas, and scribbled them everywhere; on the inside back page of *Who's Afraid of Virginia Woolf?* she wrote slogans for Lux soap – 'Cloud of gentleness', 'Lux the luxury detergent', 'rich, tight lather'. She was part of a team, headed by Jeremy Bullmore, that launched the campaign of Mr Kipling's bakery, under the slogan 'exceedingly good cakes', still in use some forty years later.

But she made a name for herself in another campaign, a ninety-second film commercial which she wrote for Elida Gibbs's Sea Witch hair colorants. Her script paid homage both to Greek mythology and to James Bond, who was becoming a cultural icon. Named *Lost Island*, the clip began with the brass fanfare from the last movement of Bartok's Concerto for Orchestra, showing seven men dressed in black standing on a speedboat, heading towards a tropical island. Thousands had tried before – the narrator dramatically said – but their scattered sculls, armoured visors and discarded military banners were a silent testimony to their defeat. Three women in white togas were sitting on the rocks with coiffed hair, black, auburn and fair. 'The Sea Witches. The Greeks knew about them, the faces of mortal women, but their hair . . . their hair is legend. Was this the real location of Eden? The banished descendants of Eve?' Assia wrote, invoking the legendary Lilith. While the three women were seductively letting their hair down, the soundtrack was taken over by Miles Davis's jazz beat. Attacked, the Amazons fought back with drawn fingernails, killing six men. Escaping by the skin of his teeth, the sole survivor stole a briefcase containing the twelve hair colours. The commercial ended on a humorous note – a man's hand emerging behind a chemist's counter and nonchalantly placing the desired package.

'It was an amazing mock-heroic epic, filmed at staggering expense in the Aegean, and made Bond films look a bit cheap,' Tom Rayfield recounted in his memoir *Fifty in 40*, about fifty years of J Walter Thompson's in 40 Berkeley Square. It was a breakthrough since, until then, most commercials of the sort were soft and romantic, with hardly any plot, usually showing women in exotic locations, waving their glossy hair. Assia's was full with suspense, danger, violence and death. The Sea Witch commercial was a huge success, and was applauded in cinemas. A shorter version was made for television. Assia got a standing ovation from her colleagues, as well as a nice salary rise and became known in the business as The Sea Witch Lady. Her friends recall that she was also involved in another unconventional hit, the advertisement for Yardley's cosmetics, portraying a leather bandolier holding a variety of lipsticks in place of bullets, playing on the visual similarity between the two, and the juxtaposition of Eros and Thanatos, sex and death.

Twice, a dramatic event changed the course of the affair between Assia and Ted and saved it from exhausting itself and withering away. Plath's suicide locked the two culprits together, and now, Shura's birth broke the deadlock and pointed towards the next chapter in their lives: living together and raising all three children. In September, Olwyn Hughes, who had lived with her brother in Court Green for the past two years and helped with his children and the household, decided to return to London. It was an opportunity for Hughes to bring Assia back into his life. His mother's arthritis was worsening and he planned to bring his parents down to Court Green for the winter and leave them with a housekeeper, while he, Assia and the children moved to Ireland.

Hughes wrote to Richard Murphy that he was looking for a house near the sea. Secretive about his plans, he did not mention that Assia and Shura were coming as well. Murphy found Doonreaghan House, a spacious house in the village of Cashel, on the west coast of Ireland, forty minutes' drive from his cottage. It belonged to Lt-Col. Browne-Clayton, who lived in a magnificent country house nearby and who rented out his smaller house to holidaymakers. The date was set for 1 November and the house was available until the end of March. Three years into the affair, she realised that this was the one chance that she could not afford to miss. As sorry as she was to cut her rising career short, apprehensive about Ted's full commitment, and still carrying unpleasant memories of their last attempt, Assia felt that their relationship was ripe for this long-overdue step.

They began preparing for the move; Hughes told Assia that he wished to start afresh with nothing whatsoever from their previous lives. Furnishing their nest, he allotted her a budget of £50 and she was instructed to purchase records of Bach, Handel and whatever else she liked, as well as art books — specifically pre-sixteenth-century art, anything that 'might enrich their life together in the womb'.

Only then, after a long silence, did Ted write to Aurelia Plath about his next move. It was a typed letter, with no date, and Aurelia added at the top, in huge black marker pen: 'Bomb number 1, December 1965'. He wrote to her that he was leaving for Ireland with the children and from there to Germany, at the invitation of the government that granted him three months' scholarship. He planned to prolong the stay until the autumn of 1966, and return to Ireland for at least five years. Since he reckoned that Irish education was of an inferior standard, he wished to place his children in a private school, which catered for the large German community in Ireland. As could be expected, he did not mention that Assia and Shura were coming with him. In his letters to his brother and friends as well, he only spoke of himself and his children, thereby not allowing his plans to be jeopardised.

But the deadline was constantly postponed: first Ted was waiting for his mother to leave hospital, then for his father to sell his newspaper and tobacco shop, and later for the end of his brother's visit. Hughes was so keen to leave, that for the next three months he kept paying the rent, to secure the house. Ted was looking for someone who could watch over Court Green and help his parents settle in. Elizabeth Compton knew the place well, and took care of the house after Sylvia's suicide, but now she was the last person on earth that he wanted there; he suspected that she was informing Aurelia Plath of his moves and did not want to give Compton access to his and Sylvia's papers, which were left in the house. He preferred the Heddens, whom he had known since 1964. Brenda was a young, slim, blonde, attractive social worker, and her husband Trevor was a drama teacher who believed in open marriage. They lived nearby, often came for dinner and poker games, and helped Ted take care of Frieda and Nicholas, when Olwyn wanted some time off. Brenda Hedden did not know that Ted had a girlfriend in London and Assia's name was never mentioned. 'The first time I saw her was when she came down to Court Green just before they all left for Ireland. I was struck by her beauty and her fragility,' Hedden recalls.

When the date was finally set for February, Assia broke the news to David. For the past three and a half years, David had been dreading that moment but was resigned to it, and when it arrived, he did not cling to Assia. 'We knew this was it.'

Sixteen

Bliss

Connemara, February 1966–Devon, April 1967

The night before leaving for Ireland Ted had a dream: he was walking by a river and big salmon were splashing their milt and spawn over him. From that night on, salmon replaced the pike in his fish dreams. Water was life, and fish, energy, and Hughes was excited about the long stay ahead.

It took them about five hours to reach the village of Cashel, and Doonreaghan House from Dublin. Thomas Hazell, a trader in kelp, had built the two-storey house in the late 1790s. It was erected on a slope, just fifty yards from the rocky beach, in order to monitor the boats carrying the brown seaweed. With time, Hazell became fabulously rich and fathered twelve children, so he moved into the newly built palatial Cashel House. When his 'whole tribe' or 'my herds' as Hughes called his newly united family, moved in there, Doonreaghan was rather run-down. Poorly insulated and draughty, the walls were black, the floorboards were rotten and the furniture was bric-à-brac.

Cashel had only one grocery shop, its choice of goods next to nothing: mainly bread, tea and bacon. Everything had to be bought in the district town of Clifden but the bus travelled there only once a week. With no driving licence, Assia was a willing prisoner, totally dependent on Ted. Taken aback by the high cost of living, they grew their own vegetables to ease the financial burden and vary the menu. Hughes's fishing skills proved useful, and he took the children with him as he drove to the lakes beyond the hill. There was no cinema in the area, and no other means of entertainment, and their only indulgence was to dine out in Clifden.

'The end of Europe and the real beginning of the American Atlantic coast,' was Assia's impression of the Connemara region. Though she had unpleasant memories of Ireland from her previous visit with David, the old cottage, remote and desolate, was now a palace to her, and she did not look back on the excitements and indulgences of London. After almost four tempestuous years, Assia finally found rest and refuge, away from it all: his parents, her husband, nosy friends and Sylvia's shadow. Walking on air, she practised a new signature: 'Assia Wevill-Hughes'. Only when it was a fait accompli did Ted find the courage to inform his brother Gerald: 'Assia is here with me, and a complete success.' A huge weight was lifted off his shoulders and he was happy that he got away from Court Green'.

A local girl named Teresa Manaion (now Reilly) came every day to help with the household chores. 'The house was known to be haunted, people said that there was a curse, and that no child had been born there for many decades,' she recalls. Soon after moving in, they celebrated Shura's birthday. Assia sent her family a photograph of the toddler in a white lace dress and a pink ribbon, sitting on a wooden bench at a table covered with a white tablecloth decorated with prints of Red Riding Hood. On the back of the photo it said, 'Shura Hughes 1st birthday'. The four-year-old Nick was sitting next to Shura, Frieda facing them and, on the table, laden with wrapped presents, a chocolate cake decorated with two candles for the birthday girl to grow up to. Other photos of the time show Shura and Nick together in the bath before bedtime; Shura wearing just a white undershirt, laughing joyfully; standing in a round playpen on the lawn; crawling on a blanket on the grass, her hair shimmering in the sun. Ted was delighted and relieved that his children had greatly taken to their half-sister.

In the corpus of his published poetry, Hughes never mentioned Shura by name, referring to her as 'your daughter' or 'her little girl'. But apparently, he did write a poem for his third and youngest child. It was 'Lines for Shura', and the title echoed, 'Lines to a Newborn Baby', an earlier poem that Hughes wrote for Frieda. The poem looks like a birthday benediction, full of good wishes for his daughter's future and the marvellous triumphs awaiting her. Hughes probably read it out aloud at the party but never published it.

The rugged and untouched landscape of Connemara attracted foreigners who were on the lookout for spiritual inspiration. It felt like the end of the world, a chance to leave civilisation behind, with its treasures and seductions. After so many vicissitudes and distractions, Hughes was finally free to be immersed in his true vocation. He was exploding with ideas that he believed would last him the next 25 years. Surrounded by all his dear ones, his sweetheart attending to all their needs, he found the strength to probe into the suicide of his wife and began writing *Crow*, 'which was, however improbably, the way he was finally able to write about his own experience of personal devastation,' writes Diane Wood Middlebrook. 'He is a scavenger poking his beak into a destroyed civilization. Wherever he finds a sign of life, Crow pounces on it with unselective appetite.' While Hughes was locked in his study, Assia wrote and painted by the window of her study or in the garden, which, just like Court Green, was overflowing with daffodils.

The lease ran out at the end of March and they took Teresa with them as they moved to Cleggan Farm, a mile and a half from Richard Murphy. The estate was built in the mid-nineteenth century and, next to the master house, there were two holiday cottages to let. Ted and Assia knew the area well: it was in Murphy's home in Cleggan that Ted dumped Sylvia in September 1962 and, seven months later, Assia and David visited the place. Their cottage was next to a stable and from the bedrooms on the first floor Ted and Assia could see Cleggan across the bay.

The small village of Cleggan had about ten houses in all, 'virgin, swept with no pretensions aside from the presence of Murphy and the expensive sailing boats,' was Assia's impression. Their cottage was isolated and inconvenient as was Doonreaghan House; five hours' drive from Dublin, and fifty years back in time, but Assia enjoyed every minute of it. They dined with Richard Murphy once a week, alternating between his place and theirs. They also enjoyed the occasional visits of painter Barrie Cooke and his wife Sonia. Cooke remembered his hosts 'seemed very happy together. Assia was not easy to get on with, but I liked her very much.'

Living in seclusion was an ultimate challenge of conjugality and family life, since they had to be self-reliant and self-contained, with no buffers and getaways. And they rose to the challenge. At the end of May they were due to go to Germany until the autumn and return to Ireland for a few more years. But life in paradise was cut short. Olwyn was exhausted from looking after their elderly parents and Ted, an ever-devoted son, overlooked his own interests and decided that they would all return to Court Green. He and Assia hoped it would be no more than an extended summer holiday: by October, they hoped with Edith recuperated, they would go back to Ireland.

Assia and Ted tried to recreate the Irish experience in Court Green: she put her green fingers to use and planted bulbs everywhere and made little gardens. She could not take her eyes off him toiling 'in sweet sweat' in the garden, which suddenly seemed to her like the primeval glossy jungle in the famous Rousseau painting. She melted at the sight of his 'superb legs and thighs –the beautiful Anatomical Man', as she wrote in her diary. From her study on the first floor she would gaze wistfully at the hut where Ted was working, expecting 'the hut to smoke with the temperature of his presence in it'. She felt reverence in the company of 'one of God's best creations' and wondered, 'Is God squandering him on me?'

She gave Ted a biography of Goethe, and inscribed it, 'The lady is speaking and/you can hear it yourself:/"Seamus!"' She transcribed the Irish name four times, the letters getting smaller and smaller, and added at the side, 'Darling, darling, darling.' Shortly afterwards Hughes presented her with a copy of the 1811 publication, leather-bound, *A General History of Quadrupeds*, by Thomas Bewick. This famous and rare book documented hundreds of species of animals, with elaborate woodcuts. Hughes inscribed it endearingly and appropriately to the Halva Taur and signed 'Cor Leonis Regulus'; it was the Lion's Heart, the brightest star of Leo, the king of the zodiacal animals, who was ambitious to rule over others. Hughes was indeed a Leo, Assia was a Taurus.

They entertained Alan Sillitoe and his wife Ruth – Ted and Sylvia's friends – who came from London for the weekend, as well as the Hungarian poet, Janos Csokits. They kept in touch with Teresa, their Irish help and, when she got pregnant, her boyfriend refusing to marry, Assia encouraged the girl to go on with the pregnancy, and invited her to come with the baby and work and live at Court Green. As Teresa approached childbirth, the pregnancy became so life-threatening that the priest summoned the reluctant father for the last rites. He married Teresa on her deathbed and she recovered miraculously. The young family remained in Cashel.

With her artistic flair, Assia went into business with one of Ted's local friends, an antique collector. Hughes was very proud of her taste and keen eye, finding a Georgian set of drawers, a much-coveted fifteenth-century lead gargoyle taken off a church and several paintings, one of them, they hoped, a Titian.

Bringing up Ted's children and living with his parents in Court Green were outward signs of domesticity and harmony. Winifred Davies aerogrammed Aurelia Plath: 'Ted's girlfriend, maybe wife I don't know, a baby, are also at Court Green,' and reported that Frieda and Nicholas adored the child. But the oppressive and demanding presence of Ted's parents marred their intimacy. 'We are here, in a nettle Emporium,' Assia cynically informed Patricia and Michael Mendelson in Hampstead. 'So are Mama and Papa. Also many "friends of the family". It is difficult, almost impossible, but not quite.' Edith Hughes was bedridden and needed extra care, and William Hughes was constantly bored, longing for his Yorkshire friends. Meanwhile, Assia's father sold his house and property in Canada and sailed again to England, hoping to settle near his beloved daughter and granddaughter. He tried to fit into Court Green but, unable to stand the squabbles, moved to a hotel in the village. A few months later he returned to Canada, his hopes frustrated, and Assia lost a vital ally. In September, Edith's health was declining rapidly and Ted and Assia were forced to postpone their return to Ireland. They were all waiting for Edith to improve enough to go back to Yorkshire with her husband. He and Assia kept separate accounts, with Ted paying for the household expenses. When she needed money for herself, he would give her a loan, noting it in his ledger, and marking her repayments.

In December 1966, Assia gave Ted *The Muses' Darling: The Life of Christopher Marlow,* by Charles Norman. She bought the book twelve years earlier, while married to Lipsey. Now she added a new inscription, punning on the title of the book: muse, Hughes and darling: 'for darling Mr Hughes, for whom feels full of sorrow'. William Blake was one of hers and Ted's most revered poets and they had several books by him or about him. That month, Assia bought the 1880 collectors' item *Life of William Blake,* by Alexander Gilchrist, as well as the impressive Oxford University Press edition of *Vala, or the Four Zoas.* In the long, epic poem, divided into nine nights, Blake attempted to write a history of the world. Assia's inscription echoed Blake's unique mythology, taken from Night the Third. The original line reads: 'Into the Caverns of the Grave & places of Human Seed'. Assia's inscription reads: 'to the lovely place and brain of Human Seed'.

In response to David Wevill's 'copious, devoted, interested pleas' Assia finally bought his second book of poetry, *A Christ of the Ice-Floes.* It included some poems that she had long thought highly of, like 'Our Lady of Kovno'. In other poems, written after their parting, she could identify traces of their predicament. 'Sense by sense we withdrew from each other,/Taste, first; then touch, smell, sound and sight/Now we need more than the rain to melt us together.' ('Infinity'.) There was no anger in the poems, only a poignant resignation; '. . . And the crime is single – no betrayal/only the mouths of each/for whom the same words have bone-different meanings.' ('Either/ Or'.) 'The Panther desired peace,/but by the mind's terms, peace was her killing.' ('Black Pantheress'.)

In Assia's current state of mind, her husband's poems left her cold and alienated: 'It is a ghost of a book. Where is the glossy abundance I remembered, the sense of solid, wrought, tough poems? where is the ice rapier?, the framed, dense things – what a paltry, melancholy dishevelled book it is,' she wrote in her diary. 'I hardly dare read the admired Surgeon's tale, just in case it too had withered in my absence.' It was not only the poetry; the man, over whose boyish good looks she was once ecstatic, now repulsed her. 'His eyes grew narrower in sorrow. He sits, troubled, grievous, disowning it in the cold . . . the thick veins on his elderly hands – sitting on the lowest part of his spinal cord, the hands helplessly falling on the armrests of the chair.' Her words echoed her reading of Anna Karenina, who, head over heels in love with Vronsky, suddenly saw her husband as repulsive and ludicrous, his ears sticking out.

Assia fell into self-loathing; the thoughts of her husband revived her guilt and the unpleasant memories of her clandestine affair with Hughes. She remembered the days without hope, the impatience for things to end, the touching faith that somehow, by sheer grace of time, things would fall into their right place. Her renewed cohesion with Ted had freed her of David's allure, and he 'has diminished to thinning symbols of my treachery, my selfishness . . . his anguish. His terrible bereaved anguish'. For the first time since she had fallen in love with Ted, she stopped acting like the biblical Lot's wife, who looked back and froze, unable to go forward. Assia finally freed herself from dependence on her husband's unwavering love and support, which had sustained her throughout the affair. At last she no longer regretted the step she had taken and stopped vacillating between her two loves. 'Assia and I have separated. She's well, living in the country,' David Wevill wrote laconically to Earle Birney in Canada. 'I'm trying to consolidate my coming life.' However, though they had been living apart for more than a year, with no prospect of reconciliation, David and Assia did not begin divorce proceedings. There was no urgency on her side, since she and Ted had not reached the point of talking about marriage: with his mother's fragile health, Ted was afraid that it might inflict a deadly blow on her.

For Valentine's Day of 1967, Assia made a card for Ted and drew a wide-boughed, leafless tree, planted in the grass, with three birds hovering in the distance. Its roots were suckling on a blood-red heart and in needle-thin letters she wrote, 'For the heart inside the heart of the dragon, for certain feathers in crow's wing, on the left there, my best heart, my valentine.' Overwhelmed by Hughes's attractiveness and 'so many perfections', she felt so lowly and fortunate, that she decided, 'I would in all truth not begrudge him an affair or two with other women – as long as [sic] remains loyal to me. I would suffer bitterly – but this in all truth is the only due thanks I could give him for all his grace.'

On the face of it, Assia had already resigned herself to the possibility of being betrayed and had decided to endure lovingly what her three husbands, Steele, Lipsey and Wevill, had gone through. But in reality, she was far from compliant. She was sensing some attraction between Ted and Brenda Hedden, who continued to be a frequent guest, often staying late with her husband for a loud game of poker with Ted's father. Assia was worn out from running the household, with three unruly children, ill-tempered in-laws and a reclusive Ted absorbed in his writing, and she had no patience for bawdy company. In any case, she despised card games and, in the Heddens' presence, she felt disowned in her own kingdom. A 'fiendish black secret battle' developed between the two women. 'The woman is my real enemy. An ex-social worker, ex-religious maniac, with the looks of an emaciated Marilyn Monroe. I beat her hollow in intelligence and experience, but she feels that I have usurped her place as the rightful soul of Court Green,' Assia wrote to her sister Celia. 'She hates me, has clearly hated me right away, but is either, or was, rather, too stupid or too cocksure to bother concealing it.' She often quarrelled with Ted over his open-door relationship with the Heddens and finally won. Brenda and Trevor hardly set foot in Court Green.

Once again, Assia was sleeping in Plath's bed, using her household utensils and linen. 'A strong sensation of her repugnant live presence,' she wrote in her diary. Plath's manuscripts and notebooks were lying everywhere, and Assia was browsing again in the diaries, stopping at Sylvia's pledge to 'work at femininity', followed by a list of resolutions and a shopping list which included a bathrobe, slippers and nightgown. Assia was engrossed in her predecessor's life to such an extent that Sylvia acquired gigantic, mythical dimensions. Were Sylvia's elbows 'really sharp? The hands enormous and knuckled? Or is this my imaginary shape-giving to the muscular brain, my envy of her splendid brilliance?' Assia pondered. The evocation of Sylvia stimulated her to do her own soul-searching: 'how spoilt I am. I'm spoilt to numbness . . . my best world, my best past lies before puberty. Buried. The rest is an accretion of sensation by reading, by what I have heard told, and deemed desirable. In the past two years I have scraped the barnacles of my social education off, but gained nothing new for myself. Only a naked talcumed self-love.'

Court Green was full of news from the United States that Plath had become an icon among students and Hughes was surprised by *Ariel*'s success. He was warding off attempts of journalists and researchers to pry into his life with Plath and into the cause of her death. Her memory was very much alive, not least because of Ted's parents who were still mourning her death; they had lived not far from Heptonstall cemetery and were the guardians of their dead daughter-in-law, putting a Christmas wreath on her grave and daffodils and lilies on Good Friday.

Winter incarcerated them and magnified the tension of opposites and Court Green turned into an inferno. Writing Ireland off proved a disaster; the four months in a paradisiacal cocoon were not enough to amalgamate Assia and Ted against the wedges that were being driven between them. His father could not bear the sight of Assia and never spoke to her. Hughes told Lucas Myers that Assia's accent was the cause of his father's enmity. Myers felt sorry that 'these two survivors of world wars did not see that they trod common ground', and the plainspoken Yorkshireman could not tolerate Assia's 'Versailles inflections and international elocution'. Engaged in a cold war, Ted's father demonstratively ignored Assia's presence and refused to sit with her at the same table. He averted his eyes when she put a plate of food in front of him. 'We used to lunch with his father (strain) now I lunch with Shura and he eats with his father alone,' Assia complained to her sister.

She lived practically like a pariah: after lunch, she would go alone to the bedroom upstairs, sleep and read for two hours, then come down for tea on her own, and then three hours of feeding the children, bathing them and putting them to sleep. She hardly saw Ted; he was locked for hours in his writing hut, struggling with *Crow*, which he thought was 'turning into a real epic', if he gave it three more years of hard labour. Leaving his desk, he would spend much time with his parents. 'The rest we spent desultorily in the library,' she wrote to her sister. The many portraits that she sketched of him disappeared, except one: Hughes looks withdrawn, grim, his shoulders sagging, his head bowed, his eyes deep set. Assia had difficulties in drawing his mouth, which she had once described as 'a sand ditch'. She made a few attempts and erased them. Frieda Hughes has a vague memory of her father and Assia sketching each other: one of Hughes's sketches portrayed Assia with accentuated eyebrows and introspective gaze, her hair parted down the middle, her lips voluptuous.

Ted often went fishing, twice a week he played snooker 'with his father and two nits', and some evenings he visited local friends, leaving Assia behind: in the small conformist, provincial village of North Tawton, her haughtiness and the trail of gossip worked against her. Elizabeth Compton saw Assia walking about in North Tawton, 'looking lost and miserable. She had aged and put on weight, and Ted told everyone she was dying her hair, as she was going quite grey by then.'

The doctors had nearly given up on her but Edith Hughes pulled through and was looking forward to receiving visitors from Yorkshire. Assia and Ted moved into a hotel in the village to avoid tension and have some privacy but were immediately called back from their sanctuary when Edith suffered a severe heart attack. The doctors predicted that it would take a year before she could return to Yorkshire. Ted juggled between his endless tasks: taking care of his three calves, tending to his garden, doing some writing jobs to pay for it all and polishing *Crow*. He was weighed down with the emotional demands of so many people in his household, and had an urge to lock the door behind him and run from it all. He tried to pacify both parties, looking for stolen moments with Assia, sneaking off to the nearby village of Chagford, their island of sanity, to indulge in luxurious, gigantic afternoon cream teas. But the atmosphere remained contentious and, in any disagreement between Assia and the Hugheses, Ted invariably sided with his parents. They were drifting apart, and Assia was again oscillating between reproach and adoration. 'I have these fits of huge love and admiration for him – but it is still two parts that, and one part memory of Ruthless. The Mouth.'

Assia found solace in her daughter and immersed herself in nurturing Shura. The child's talents intrigued her: still in nappies, she was singing to herself at night, dancing, 'her head tilted to one side in acute concentration. She dances most successfully to either Bach's Cantatas or pop.' A small card lists 'Shurik's' second birthday presents: a set of tin cooking utilities, a chocolate cake, a cheque for £5 from Grandpa Gutmann, and a lovely mackintosh and hat with little green flowers. The toddler was especially ecstatic to get a petticoat from her Canadian aunt: 'Frieda has one which was sent from America, which Shura has clearly secretly admired and coveted for months.' Now that Shura had one too, the two sisters were frolicking around the house in their flimsy petticoats. 'Shura is becoming a very beautiful precocious little girl – extremely intelligent,' Ted proudly wrote to Lucas Myers. The three children used to play with the Compton children and Elizabeth remembers Shura as 'a silent and sad child, and we never saw Ted give any indication that she was his daughter.'

Assia had no one to turn to and, although her relationship with her younger sister Celia had been strained from childhood, she sent her a very alarming letter on 11 March, a few days after Shura's second birthday. 'I'm clearly ill. The last four years have been a strain, simply too hard to bear.' She begged Celia to rush from Canada, 'I cannot tell you what pleasure and reassurance that would give me . . . please come, Cillik. Somehow arrange it, before either of us dies.'

Several times in the past, reaching impasses in her relationship with Ted, Assia channelled her frustration into telling him to vanish from her life. This time, she pointed her rage against herself. 'This summer I've been literally suicidal,' she wrote to Celia. She had made a few attempts on her life in the past but they seemed to be demonstrative, a plea for sympathy. It was done always within reach of help and she never took any risks or reached a point that required medical intervention. This time she felt a touch from death's door. Though she could go back to London with her daughter, Assia dismissed the idea. Just a year had passed since her triumphant Sea Witch campaign but she already felt over the hill professionally: 'I don't have the self confidence for advertising any more, things are very difficult in advertising now.' For her, it was living with Ted, or nothing.

She wrote a will and left the sealed envelope in her desk drawer, appointing her sister as Shura's legal guardian. 'I also hereby bequeath to you, or to you to bequeath to Shura when you see fit, all my worldly goods, manuscripts etc,' she wrote to Celia. She was well aware of the financial value of Hughes's and Plath's manuscripts – Ted boasted that he could sell every page of verse he wrote, even one with only ten lines all crossed out, for as much as £7 or £8. She selected about 25 to 30 pages of Plath's manuscripts and sent them to her sister, to help secure Shura's future. Celia Chaikin recalls that the manuscripts were not poetry but prose, part of a story or a novel, with Plath's handwritten corrections. Assia packed two trunks to be shipped to Canada and made out a cheque for $1,200 to pay for Shura's airfare and initial necessities when the time came. 'I couldn't bear some bloody woman looking after Shura. She is all I have. I adore her, as I only adored Mutti.'

Seventeen

Banished

Devon–London, spring 1967–winter 1967

Ted Hughes had not noticed the two packed trunks in Assia's study; and with Sylvia's papers chaotically scattered all over the place, he did not detect the disappearance of a few dozen sheets of manuscript. But first and foremost, he had no inkling of the emotional fluctuations that Assia was going through. On 27 April he wrote a six-page letter to his brother, sympathising with his mother's suffering and his father's depression; the letter lacks any mention of Assia's despair. Celia was apprehensive when she received her sister's letter but, being a housewife and mother of three small children, grounded in Montreal by her modest means and the needs of her family, she could not fly over to stand by her sister. She advised Assia to return to Canada. Assia declined: she refused to leave Ted even for a short while, fearing that in her absence another woman would soon take her place.

Apparently, writing a will and sending the SOS letter had a positive effect on Assia: having resolved to end her misery and attended to her daughter's future, she seemed to find her sense of control over her life restored. It also gave her energy to plod on. She persuaded herself that it was only a passing fit of depression, not admitting that the immanent failings in her relationship with Ted were sweeping her down into a miry pit.

All those months, Hughes was busy organising an International Festival of Spoken Poetry with Patrick Garland and he involved Assia in it as well. Already in 1966, with his close friend Daniel Weissbort, Hughes had launched *Modern Poetry in Translation*, featuring Polish poet Zbigniew Herbert, Czech Miroslav Holub, Yugoslav Vasco Popa and the Israeli Yehuda Amichai. Hughes called Amichai's poetry 'the under song of the people', and envied his ability to read the Bible like a newspaper, weaving biblical threads and elements from ancient Jewish history into a modern, secular imagination. In Weissbort's view, Amichai was 'a sort of guide, a Virgil for Ted in this ancient world'. In a conversation around the table of his friend and neighbour, the children's writer Michael Morpurgo, Hughes declared that 'he would have preferred to be Jewish, rather than question mark Anglican'. Horatio Morpurgo, Michael's son, sensed that Judaism fascinated Hughes and that he valued 'the spiritual tenacity and the receptiveness, that had, over the centuries, kept the Jews culturally confident in spite of everything, making them so fertile in religious ideas.' But Hughes's instant affinity with the Israeli poet also stemmed from more personal reasons. 'It came at a critical point in his own life, and helped him withstand the traumas of that period,' explains Weissbort. Amichai was his favourite poet, and he never travelled without a copy of one of his books. Amichai was his oxygen mask when he felt that his own writing was blocked.

It was his close friendship with Yehuda Amichai and Hughes's forthcoming journey to Israel, scheduled for March 1997, that made him give a rare personal interview to Eilat Negev. Hughes said, 'Every work of art stems from a wound in the soul of the artist. When a person is hurt, his immune system comes into operation, and a self-healing process takes place, mental and physical.' He called art 'a psychological component of the auto-immune system that gives expression to the healing process.' He said that the poems of Yehuda Amichai were full of evidence of pain and disruption but had a great ability to heal, unlike Plath, who 'tended to focus on the pain and to scratch at the wound. If she had been able to free herself from that one wound that wracked her, she might have changed, led a normal life, even perhaps have felt healthy enough to stop writing.'

Wishing to publish more poems of Amichai, Hughes suggested that Assia be the translator. 'Ted saw Yehuda as a life force that would do Assia good,' Weissbort recalls. Assia was eager to comply. Hughes was thinking of a full volume, and informed Amichai of his plan. He assured him: 'my wife grew up in Israel, and that they have already translated a number of Amichai's poems together; he promised to be there for her if she needed to consult him. Assia allotted an hour every morning and an hour in the afternoon for translating the poems, which were due to be published by Cape Goliard, with Olwyn Hughes as the literary agent for the project. Assia's selection of twenty poems from the large corpus of Amichai is intriguing. 'Dates are already in view/In which you no longer exist,/Already a wind blows clouds/Which will not rain on us both.' ('Like our Bodies' Imprint'.)

Since leaving Palestine in 1946, Assia had not read, written or spoken Hebrew and only in jest scattered a few words here and there in her correspondence with her sister or with Ted. She was out of touch with the changes in the resurrected language and its budding literature but, apparently, her childhood and adolescence in Tel Aviv, as well as her good ear for languages, furnished her with a firm enough base to produce very eloquent translations of poetry. Weissbort thinks that the fact that she was not a practising poet acted in her favour: 'it meant she won't try to do anything fancy with the poems.'

A few days before the gala opening of the International Festival of Spoken Poetry, Assia was delighted to get a postcard, addressed to 'Mrs Assia Hughes'. Ruth Fainlight invited her and Ted to stay over for the whole duration of the festival: 'it will be very convenient both for the Festival Hall and for Shura, (having children to amuse her, babysitter, etc).' The five days between 12 July and 16 July at the Queen Elizabeth Hall and the Purcell Room were beyond Assia's wildest dreams; she was taking part in the greatest literary party of the time, rubbing shoulders with W H Auden, Robert Graves, Pablo Neruda, Anne Sexton, Allen Ginsberg and Bella Akmadulina. She walked tall at Ted's side, reigning together as 'the royal couple' of the festival. Heads turned whenever she and Ted took their seats in the auditorium or attended a reception. At last she was an acclaimed society lady, attaining her dream of a grand literary salon.

Film-maker Mira Hamermesh attended one of those parties, and was standing at the rear of the hall next to Ruth Fainlight and Alan Sillitoe:

> . . . when the entrance door opened like a gate, and a couple emerged.
> I've never seen such beauty in my whole life. I asked Ruth, who are these
> gorgeous people, and she said, Ted Hughes and Assia Wevill. I thought
> to myself, could she be the Assia I lost contact with some twenty years
> ago? She and Ted walked towards us, and Alan introduced me. Assia
> reached out her hand majestically and muttered in her colonial voice,
> 'how do you do?' I teased her, 'Where is my choker?'

Assia's haughtiness melted away and the two women fell giggling into each other's arms; they were inseparable throughout the evening. 'What an insane week that was,' Assia later wrote to Amichai. 'I seem to remember us there in

P Grady's Seventh Salon, like the publicum in the Coliseum, watching ourselves being watched, the gladiators being our secret selves.'

Assia instantly fell for Yehuda Amichai and his Hannah who, like her and Ted, had experienced the joys and torments of an illicit affair; the 43-year-old poet had left his wife a few years earlier, after falling in love with Hannah, a young fellow teacher. They had been waiting impatiently for Amichai's much-delayed divorce to come through. 'You were the most agreeable guests we have ever had,' Assia wrote to her new Israeli friends after their overnight stay at Court Green. She found common ground with Amichai, who had fled Nazi Germany as a child with his parents, just like her.

With the ball over, Court Green received them with Edith Hughes's continuously failing health and her husband's constant irritability. Ted was so exhausted after the festival that he lapsed into lethargy, and was bedridden with excruciating back pains. It was the summer holidays and the children were unruly, and Assia complained to the Amichais: 'they blow soap bubbles in the yard, and Shura's profanities grow daily more amazing.' The deadline for the book approaching, she needed more time for herself and, together with Ted, compiled and introduced a set of rules for the children 'to annoy [them] less'.

For Ted's thirty-seventh birthday, Assia bought a green leather-bound edition of his first book, *The Hawk in the Rain,* which was republished after Plath's suicide and dedicated 'To Sylvia': on the first page of this expensive collector's item Assia wrote: 'for my most darling Ted' and added a card that she made herself. It was entitled, 'for sweet Ted on his birthday some apples', and she painted three stamp-sized scenes with apples: a tree with one red apple, a fruit bowl with a heart-shaped apple and Wilhelm Tell's son, an arrow cutting the air towards the apple that was placed on his feathered hat. On lifting each drawing, like a paper scroll, a short rhyme was revealed: 'Apple, apple/on the Tree,/I love Ted/Does he love/Me?' Underneath the bowl of fruit, it read: 'Apple, apple/ In the bowl,/Say I'm cold,/In my South/Pole!' Under the Wilhelm Tell scene Assia wrote, 'Apple, apple/On the hood/Tell how I'm,/Trying to be/good . . .' She was just past forty, but her love for Ted remained as fresh and naïve as a schoolgirl's.

The Amichai project was an opportunity for prolific collaboration, weighing words and seeking meanings together but it did not shield Assia and Ted from the sore points in their life. 'Things have reached a pitch of mild disaster,' Assia wrote to her friend Patricia Mendelson. 'Ted is exhausted with the war between parents and me, and I seem to be the most expendable factor.' Edith Hughes was moving from one bout of illness to another and it dawned on Ted that she would never get better as long as she and Assia lived under the same roof. To geth his and Assia's life back on track, he first had to get his mother strong enough to return to her home, and then look for a new house for him and Assia, far from both devon and Yorkshire. Until he could pull it off, Hughes initiated a disengagement plan: Assia and Shura would have to return to London. She would work there for four days a week and come to Court Green at weekends. 'All that remains are some photographs. Is this all there is to life? Just some photographs and passports?' she wrote to Patricia with exasperation. Hellish as it was, Court Green was still the only permanent dwelling that they had together, and being banished to London was 'terrible on the children, insufferable for Shura'.

The decision was taken in haste, culminating in Assia's feverish rush to London, to try to find a job within three days. She was dashing from one interview to another: 'at night I took a sleeping pill and just collapsed into bed.' When she spoke to Ted over the phone, he told her that Shura was weeping incessantly. Assia mobilised her advertising colleagues to help her find a job, not stopping at her husband, who made some inquiries on her behalf. She met Royston Taylor, who had been David Wevill's group head, and they discussed their love lives over lunch. 'She told me that things were not going well with Ted Hughes,' says Royston, whose marriage had broken up following an affair and whose wife was divorcing him. Royston secured her a job interview at Ogilvy & Mather, which she passed with flying colours and was offered a good contract. The following weekend, Royston took his two sons for a holiday in Cornwall and stayed the night at Court Green. 'When I arrived, Ted Hughes was out at the pub with his father. Assia told me she felt that his parents were blaming her for Sylvia's suicide. Ted hadn't come back when I went to bed – his car coming out backwards at a hell of a lick, nearly crashed into mine in the coach entrance.' Royston thought that Court Green was very gothic, rambling and badly lit. He shared a room with his sons, which Assia described as 'smelling of a dead cat'; it overlooked the graveyard, which seemed spooky in the moonlight. When they left the next morning Ted was not about and Frieda and Nicholas ran after Royston's car, begging his boys to stay.

Assia and Shura moved into flat Number 14 at 51 Marlborough Place, in affluent St John's Wood. From his perspective, she was on dry land while he was still battling the waves and when they had a vile phone conversation, he put the blame on the domestic strain, the children, his ailing mother and bored father, which were fouling his mood and hindering him from writing.

Hughes's friend, the Hungarian poet Janos Csokits, felt that the parting was meant to be kept a secret. Chatting with Assia at a bookshop in London, he was uncomfortable when the following day Olwyn Hughes happened to call him and inquired how Assia was. He answered laconically, 'Sad.' Olwyn asked whether Assia was still living in Devon, and he declined to answer. Csokits was quick to update Ted Hughes on the conversation and assured him: 'as long as Assia belongs to you, I would respect your wishes concerning her,' but declared that he would not criticise Assia 'only because Olwyn wants me to do so'. The network of informants was quick to pick up the news and spread it around. Ted's father phoned Hilda in Yorkshire, and she immediately wrote to Aurelia Plath to say how relieved and glad she was 'that Assia had returned to London along with her furniture'. The grandmother was told that the children did not appear to miss Shura and 'they were getting more attention now than they had had for some time'.

Assia feared that the separation might be irreversible and, when she met Richard Murphy, she asked him if he was sensing the same mood between her and Ted, as the one he had felt 'between him and Sylvia three months before Sylvia's suicide'. Murphy replied, to give her hope, that it was 'altogether different'. But unlike their previous cooling-off period in the autumn of 1963, when Devon was out of bounds for Assia, this time Court Green was her second home. She and Ted resumed their correspondence and he let her in on every bit of the daily routine in Court Green.

Hughes now had a foothold in London and brought with him his flower poems and playing-card poems for Assia to illustrate. He celebrated Christmas in her flat with his sister and the three children and Olwyn Hughes recalled that the dinner was 'a good feast' and that she dropped the turkey at one point. These were days of grace after a dreadful year, and the holiday season allowed the anticipation of a better 1968. Assia harnessed her artistic talent to make a New Year card. She painted two winged angels, and typed her prayer on a narrow scroll, which was the angels' gown:

Please God, send Ted a happy year – send him the Year he has waited for so long. And may he have more money than he absolutely needs, so that he won't ever again worry about ending up without any. And please God, make him feel truly well and in full control of his body – and make his spirit fiery and splendid as ever and, if you can spare it, God, more so than ever. And please heal all his bruises and his many wounds. Please make him utterly whole again, because he's one of your best creatures. And, please, make him forget our awful tribulations of the last year – and please restore him his heart wholly. And please ask him to forgive me my pride and its consequences. Look after him, God, because he's rare and marvelous and you spent so much love in creating him. And if it's the last thing I ever ask you, God, send him back to me loving and sweet as he was before our sorrows.

In those very days in Devon, Ted wrote a note of his own, pleading with Assia not to be so stubborn, to stop threatening to leave, to calm down and control her temper; if she endured just a little bit longer, by next year things would change for the better. Though different in style and intensity of emotion, both notes single Assia out as the guilty party, responsible for fouling up their relationship, while Ted remained irreproachable.

Eighteen

Love Me Back or Let Me Go

London, winter–spring 1968

But 1968 was ill-omened from the start. 'A feeling of last-ditch panic seems to fill the whole of England, and advertising always feels it most immediately, most acutely,' Assia wrote to Amichai on 11 January. She and her colleagues were made to work 'like slaves' until nine or ten o'clock at night: 'all in order to grab some £1,000,000 account from another agency – but the sensation is that if you don't do it, you're out.' In six weeks, 27 people were fired from Ogilvy: 'the survivors are treated to little cocktail parties in the evenings, where our brains are then further picked.' Assia counted herself lucky to be spared and harnessed all her skills for a TV commercial for Vesta Curry; Assia wrote the lyrics and Tom Boyd composed the music for one of the first ready-made TV-dinner commercials.

She apologised to Yehuda Amichai for the inevitable slowdown in her output; when she finally reached home each night she was totally exhausted and obviously she could no longer take her translation work to the office. Hughes helped her by reading her drafts and he 'combed them a little'. She consulted him when undecided about the choice of words; he agreed with her, for example, that between 'exercised' and 'trained', the former is more 'interesting, ambiguous in a desirable sense, whereas if one used "trained", one would have to qualify it, i.e. "trained" to do what?' Amichai had a good command of English and Assia relied on his taste and judgement, promising him: 'if you are unhappy about it, I should change it to "trained".'

Hughes was pleased with Assia's work and assured Amichai that he could not have found a better translator for his poems. Assia also put her artistic talents to use and designed the cover of the book, transcribing one of the poems in elaborate ancient Hebrew calligraphy. She was still married to David Wevill but, touching upon another facet of her identity, she thought it well to revert to her Jewish maiden name, which she had not used for the past twenty years. When Nathaniel Tarn edited a special poetry issue of *Afrasian*, the School of Oriental and African Studies student magazine, he selected four of Amichai's poems and introduced the translator as Anastassia Gutmann. It seems that at one point or another, Assia toyed with the idea of using the flamboyant Russian name; however, it does not appear in any of her official documents, and she is not known ever to have used this name before. Daniel Weissbort believes it was Ted's idea to put Assia's name in bold letters on the cover, an unusual credit for a translator: 'He really tried to promote her, to make her happy, though I don't think she had any ambition to become a full-time translator.' Weissbort did not get the impression that Amichai's poems drew Assia any closer to her Jewish roots; of the two, Ted showed the deeper interest in Judaism. It always struck Weissbort that in choosing his spouses, Ted went out of his natural element and was drawn first to the New World – Sylvia – and then to the ancient world, symbolised by Assia.

However, the renewed contact with Hebrew and the warm exchange of letters with Amichai made Assia, for the first time, nostalgic for the country she had left behind. 'Couldn't the Israeli government need Ted's presence in Israel next spring, say – it would be splendid to go there – and see you,' she wrote to Amichai. Watching a BBC documentary on Jerusalem after the June 1967 war, she tried to conjure up the smell of the buses and the dust: 'and nothing came, only the Indian food smell of the tenants below. How tantalisingly familiar and entirely out of reach Jerusalem looked.'

Assia's moods became increasingly dependent on Ted's temper and conduct. 'Dearest love, sweet Ted. Those were two of the best days for what now feels like years. Thank you,' she wrote to him on 2 February 1968. 'We've allowed so much scum to come between us. So much irrelevance, they now look like irrelevances. Most miraculous of all is that we have somehow survived – this week was excellent proof to me – I don't know what it looks like to you.' Two intimate days with him were enough to keep her going for a while. In the middle of the month, she was again admitted to the Middlesex Hospital in London, with a bout of cystitis. Ted came up from Devon to visit her, phoned several times and sent her letters; to cheer her up, he copied a school essay in the form of a poem that his eight-year-old Frieda wrote.

His adaptation of Seneca's *Oedipus* agonised him and invoked horrible dreams. It needed a lot of rewriting, and Assia's skiing friend and lawyer,

Martin Graham, who dealt with her divorce from Lipsey and later became a judge, recalls that she boasted that she assisted Ted. 'She was well read and had a good ear for words, but more than that, he wished to give her self-esteem.' Accompanying Ted to a rehearsal of the National Theatre at the Old Vic, Assia was far from enthusiastic; she thought that the production, directed by Peter Brook and featuring John Gielgud as Oedipus: 'looks like an exhibit in the Greek Pavilion of Expo '67. Golden cubes, revolving searchlights, the actors space-suited and a pink phallus 20 feet tall descends properly Deus ex Machina ready for an orgy in the last act. Ugh.' It was Hughes's first major work for the theatre and, capturing the excitement of the moment, he scribbled on Assia's playbill on the gala night, 19 March 1968, that she was 'the best sight'.

Assia felt trapped, enslaved by her devotion to him but she could endure living apart as long as Ted could promise her a joint future. At any moment she was prepared to follow him anywhere but there were no signs that Hughes was taking any concrete steps towards making her dream a reality. 'Ted's father is still there, Emperor of the Barn,' she complained to Amichai. Hughes was fighting on several fronts simultaneously: his writing, Plath's legacy and Assia's pressure, but primarily, his parents' health and presence.

Already while living together in Devon Assia had bought the book of manners *Galateo* by Giovanni della Casa. It was a Penguin edition of the famous Italian sixteenth-century book, which has been reprinted throughout the centuries. Based on the principle 'that no man should do anything to offend or displease another', it dealt with the foundations of good behaviour: the ills of scandalmongering, contradicting, giving advice, rebuking others and correcting their faults, and how perverseness can part friends: all of these were sources of annoyance. Only one page in the book was annotated and it is unclear by whom: that one should never boast, 'of his brains, neither should he make a fine tale of his talents and the great things he has done'. A year later Ted composed his own version of house manners, which were meant to help him and Assia reunite in bearable cohabitation. The Draft Constitution of house rules reads like conditions of acceptance rather than suggestions for improvement.

The first item in the two typed pages concerned the children: Assia was expected to play with them at least one hour per day, mend their clothes meticulously and supervise their washing, teeth cleaning and going to bed. She was to teach the children German two or three hours a week. The second batch of rules, innocently headed Cooking, echoes Ted's longings for Sylvia's high norms of good housekeeping and disappointment with Assia's. She'd have to vary her cooking and introduce a new recipe every week. The village bakery would be off-limits to her, and she would have to bake everything herself. She would have to prepare a cooked breakfast for the children, and teach Frieda some simple recipes. As for himself, he was to be totally exempt from doing any cooking and the daily help was to be reduced to one half-day. Every expense and bill was to be methodically registered in a logbook. Assia was ordered to be out of bed by 8 a.m., was forbidden to take a nap during the day, and had to be dressed up properly and not go around the house in a dressing gown. Hughes insisted that she improve her manners and tact, and would be always nice to his friends, including the ones that she despised.

Brenda Hedden, who was a frequent visitor to Court Green, remembers that Assia changed the furniture in the living room, put in exotic ornaments and hung heavy curtains to weigh the room down. Item seven on Hughes's list reflects his and Assia's endless arguments over her attempts to make Court Green more agreeable for herself: he thought that she was deliberately trying to erase any memory of Sylvia. She was required to stop pretending to be English, and stick to everything German and Israeli. She was not allowed to discuss him with anyone else. She'd have to promise to stay until the end of the year, and never threaten to leave.

Assia was invited to put forward comments and amendments. If she ever put her reservations in writing, or drafted her own version of the house rules, placing demands on Ted as well, these did not survive. Ted's edicts were beyond endurance and only increased Assia's anguish. She wrote to him at the end of March 1968:

This is the ancient steel nib with which I used to write you those broken nervous letters years ago. I wrote you a business letter this morning – through my throat. I'm writing this through my oesophagus, my throat a huge and growing wound. I'm writing to your big hands, to the lovely inside of your wrists, to your best-tempered eyes, to your brains not at all. And I'm not writing from my brain but from well bellow my oesophagus.

I want to know whether you want to mend us because you still love me, because you still feel the animal thing between us (the sight of me in that awful bed must have been pretty unappealing) or maybe you want me as your child keeper only.

I still have ABSOLUTE HOPES that we can build a happy, loving life together. I know that I can still love you fully with all my faculties and my body and my life – my darling Ted.

Open up – again – open out to me, as you used to – my love. And I could flourish under you, and care for you and give you everything I have . . .

So far, everybody but you and I have been dictating our lives – we need to be alone, to recover from our Intolerable. I feel so full of love to you at your sweet best, I admire you and I am frightened at the power you have over me. No man has ever had this power over me as a woman.

She ended her despondent loving appeal with an ultimatum: if by 8 April Ted did not reassure her of his intentions, she would leave for Canada within two months. 'Love me back – and if you can't, then say so, and let me go with whatever peace I can salvage.' She did not sign the letter but, at the bottom of the page she drew a dying bird, with outspread wings, looking like a woman who had jumped from a roof and was flattened on the ground.

But leaving for Canada was not a real option: Assia hated the four years she had almost been forced to spend there and thought it was a cultural desert. All that was waiting for her there was an ailing father and a sister tied down to her own family. Leaving England would have been a humiliating defeat, a public admission that she had lost the battle.

Hughes was not alarmed enough – or not caring enough – to respond. For years Assia was alternately pressing and begging, bestowing love and ultimatums and he always managed to slip away. Their love was running on parallel rails, sometimes in opposite directions, only occasionally converging. They differed in their perceptions of conjugality and of each other's attitude. Hughes deflected Assia's arrows of criticism back at her: she was the source of their troubles; she was the one who was kicking her heels, messing everything up, she was the one who did not make clear what she was willing to do in order to repair their relationship. He reproached her that she only wanted a home for Shura. They had exhausted all words. Only action could change the course of things but Hughes was reluctant to act.

When ultimatums failed to get results, Assia channelled her abysmal despair into writing more wills and testaments. 'In the event of my death, I wish all my furniture and furnishings to be sold by auction and the proceeds to go towards my estate, which I leave wholly to my only daughter, Alexandra Tatiana Elise Wevill. In the event of my daughter not surviving, I wish the proceeds as well as the rest of my savings at a deposit account at Lloyds Bank, Berkeley Square, W1, to go to my sister.' She nominated Celia as the beneficiary of 'any manuscripts of Ted Hughes in my possession, and inscribed books by him as well as all manuscripts and inscribed books by David Wevill.' She left Celia three oriental rugs, two oil paintings in gilt frames, a nineteenth-century watercolour of an archway, also in a gilt frame, and their precious family heritage of silver cutlery and the plated silver samovar. To her husband, David Wevill, she left her photo albums if 'he may care to have' them.

The detailed will indicates that Assia put a lot of thought into it, matching every item with its appropriate recipient, as if preparing birthday or holiday gifts. However, the short list of people proves how isolated and lonely she was: after fifteen years in England, she had no human safety net, no bosom friends, hardly anyone to turn to in her distress. She gave a Bulgarian rug embroidered with birds to Mira Hamermesh, with whom she had just resumed contact after twenty years of silence. The Mendelsons, whom she and David had befriended in Burma and kept in close contact with since, were invited to choose any ten objects or books from her apartment; to Peter Porter she left 'any records or books he may care to possess' and to his wife Jannice, who was the friend and nurse who supported her in her abortion in 1963, Assia left 'any pieces of jewellery she may care to have'. Fay Weldon, her friend from advertising, was invited to pick any piece or pieces of china and lawyer Martin Graham was offered any ten objects he chose.

Assia remembered each last one of her friends but made one person conspicuous by his absence; she took great pains that Ted Hughes would not own anything that belonged to her and would have nothing to do with her estate. She did not skip his children though: to six-year-old Nicholas, who was 'too young for possessions, I will all my most tender love', and 'to Frieda Rebecca Hughes I will also my love, and all the lace, ribbons and silks she can find, as well as a fine gold chain'.

To her father she left 'my regret and love'.

To Ted Hughes, 'I leave my no doubt welcome absence and my bitter contempt.'

She asked for her 'cadaver to be buried in any rural cemetery in England' and a tombstone to be erected with the epitaph, 'Here lies a lover of unreason and an exile.'

Assia was so distraught when writing this will that she made a typing error: she put the date as 'April 27th, 1967', while, from the contents of the will, the St John's Wood address and the reference to the royalties of her Amichai translations in the Cape Goliard edition which she bequeathed to her sister, it is clear that the year was in fact 1968. She left the will unfinished and unsigned. A year earlier, feeling at a dead end, she informed her sister that she had made out a will and nominated her as the executor. But this time, she did not update Celia about the new will. Celia was aware that her older sister was long inclined to depression and that 'she was fragile and fell apart when life didn't turn out the way she wanted it'. In her letter to Assia on 30 March 1968, Celia disclosed: 'We both suffer from insecurity, it's been ingrained in us.'

Assia and Ted seemed to have exhausted their relationship, drifting to extremes, creating a rift that could not be bridged. But in spite of the bitter strife, the threats, accusations and wills, their core of love was not crushed. That same month Assia bought a copy of Henri Troyat's newly published *Tolstoy* and dedicated it to 'My dear one, my dear one, to him.' She and Ted planned to celebrate her forty-first birthday together in London and Assia sent Ted a telegram in North Tawton to say she had managed to take the day off. She signed 'Esther', reverting to secrecy and to the Jewish name that she never used. Was she obeying Ted's command? Was he afraid of the village gossips, who knew that in her absence, other women had already entered his life?

Ted's birthday present to Assia in May 1968 was the two very thick volumes of Philipp Spitta's monumental biography of Johann Sebastian Bach, to which he added a laconic inscription. Two weeks later, when her translation of Yehuda Amichai was published, an immensely proud Assia handed Ted his copy, with the inscription, 'My dearest, my lovely lost Ted', and signed her own name in Hebrew. On the ochre-coloured opening page, in her calligraphic handwriting, she copied out a poem in both Hebrew and English: the first lines read, 'Open the gate love, rise and open the gate/ Terrified was my soul with a great rage.' Surprisingly, it was not one of Amichai's but her translation of the medieval Hebrew poet, Ibn Gabirol; Assia was already thinking ahead and planning her next project, which was a much greater and challenging undertaking.

Poet and critic Pat Kavanagh welcomed Amichai's book of poems with a rave review in the *Guardian*. 'The translations of his *Selected Poems* by Assia Gutmann are so stunning, such good poems in English, it seems absurd to treat them as translations at all.' In late June, Ted and Assia collaborated in a George MacBeth BBC Radio 3 programme, promoting the book. Just seven years earlier Hughes shared the same studio with Plath on the programme 'Two of a Kind', speaking of their poetry and symbiotic relationship. Now he read Assia's translations in his deep thundering voice, while her tone was icy and aloof as she introduced the poems and spoke about Amichai's poetic world. The choice of poems echoed dramatic chapters in Ted and Assia's lives: Amichai's 'My Father Fought Their War for Four Years', corresponded with Hughes's own experience, since his father, like Amichai's, was a First World War veteran. 'My Parents' Migration' paralleled Assia's own history, since her parents, just like Amichai's, made the same voyage from Germany to Palestine. Most revealing of all is the selection of love poems: 'Love appears as the most valuable element in life – but vulnerable, and doomed,' Assia read her narration, and Ted followed with Amichai's lines:

> A pity. We were such a good
> And loving invention.
> An aeroplane made from a man and wife.
> Wings and everything.
> We hovered a little above the earth.
> We even flew a little.

The image was a perfect reflection of Ted and Assia's ill-fated affair but no less of Hughes's marriage to Plath.

Assia was assembling more translations of Amichai for a Harper & Row edition but she still made time for her old passion, which at last was beginning to materialise: writing a television play. Hughes showed his support by furnishing her with two books on the subject by the legendary Sergei Eisenstein: *The Battleship Potemkin* and *The Film Sense*. She prepared an outline for Shelley Shelton, the creative director at Ogilvy, and managed to secure some £8,000 from the agency's budget; Shelton allowed her the use of the agency's Super 8 camera and lighting equipment. Assia rented the costumes from Berman's, a long frilly white dress and men's period suits. The actors were her office colleagues. 'I agreed to take part because I was extremely fond of Assia,' Chris Roos recalls. 'She was a lady of great integrity, great honesty and extremely good company. We had been spending days on end in the office, playing silly games with quotations, using the *Penguin Book of Literary Quotations* that was standing on the shelf.'

Assia chose art director Martin Baker to be in charge of photography. 'It wasn't a happy film; the mood was subdued and nostalgic,' Baker recalls. With the tradition of the romantic Russian novel in mind, Assia weaved the story of a love triangle that took place in 1914. Fay Maschler who, with her straight dark hair and oval face, bore a striking resemblance to Assia in her youth, played the heroine, who was wooed by her piano teacher (Jonny Gathorne-Hardy), but her heart belonged to her boyfriend (Chris Roos). When the boyfriend was killed in the First World War, the girl was devastated enough to marry the teacher that she did not love.

The shooting took place over two weekends and, though it was Assia's first experience as a director, Martin Baker was impressed by her professional conduct and infectious enthusiasm. About twenty minutes of rushes remain of the film, which was shot without sound. The outdoor scenes were shot on Hampstead Heath: again and again, the heroine runs up the hill towards her lover, but when they meet, affection soon dissolves into bitter arguments. When the shooting was over they all went to lunch and Baker took out the camera and panned on the jubilant faces around the table. Assia is seen lifting a plate to hide her face, her hair tied in a striped kerchief. 'She was very critical of her looks, edgy when people looked at her, and uptight when complimented on her beauty,' Baker comments.

Her sister Celia recalls that Assia was afraid of getting old and losing her beauty and wished to remain young for ever, like Lorca, her adored poet, who was shot to death in the Spanish Civil War, aged 38. 'She once said to me, "I'll kill myself at 42."' In her letter, written a day before their mother's birthday, Celia reminded Assia how Mutti, who was 76 at her death, disliked birthdays and how 'she put cream on her face even on the last day, and was always proud of her legs and unwrinkled face.' Assia equally abhorred a lined face and a baggy body and her concern for her for ever-young Aphrodite image was echoed in Hughes's poem, 'Fanaticism': ' "After forty I'll end it", you laughed.' Assia's friends took her threats lightly and put them down to her frivolity. But as ageing as Assia may have felt, young men in her office thought differently. She 'was one of the most beautiful human beings I have ever encountered, she wore her beauty innocently, even clumsily, as though she herself were unsure what to do with it,' in the 23-year-old Chris Wilkins's words.

Months went by, Assia was due to vacate her St John's Wood flat, and there was still no sign that Ted was any nearer to making room for her. 'How I want us to live together, the 5 of us, to make a family again, instead of running our separate nut-houses. These long absences feel so dangerous – they show me that I could live without you, but once I make contact with you again, the total independence seems worthless. Is this the nature of women, or only my own?' she asked Hughes on 9 July.

Teddy-sweet, go easy on the awful Truths – because knowing it only curdles oneself. I don't want to know the last-ditch condition of things or persons, I wish I could somehow regain meaningfully that glazed innocence I once had. Ridiculous. But I do like my friends – I want them as I think they possibly are. Knowing any more is more than I can take. I think all the pus should come out in writing – but in real life, I want the people with my glaze. Oh Teddy – I see things very clearly at the moment. Clearer than ever before even For us to continue living separately feels fundamentally wrong, the reasons for it are abstractions. We're meant to be together. And the children need both of us. And we need both of us, and it's worth the effort. Yes, the whole effort. No man's an island, which you're pretending you are, and I'm persuading myself that I am. I don't want to be. I want to be with you. Don't leave it long, dear love, otherwise there will be no means of return to you. I shall have turned into a salt pillar.

Later that day, Assia was summoned to the office of her boss, Dan Ellerington. He had sacked scores of employees at Ogilvy that year – and now he told Assia that he was not satisfied with her output. The campaign that she was working on did not result in enough sales and she was fired. It could not have come at a worse moment. In a profession that had become more aggressive and flashy, with most copywriters in their twenties, her experience and age were working against her. She had the rent to pay, a daughter to bring up – and she was well aware that Ted was not going to support them. The most she could expect from him – judging from the past – was an occasional small loan that he would write down in his ledger, which she would have to pay back without delay. Her good friend Ann Semple, who had been fired two months earlier and went back to Canada, tried to restore Assia's self-esteem: 'You were the only REAL LIVE writer left in that hell-hole,' Sample wrote from Montreal. She urged Assia to fight her terror and financial angst, and get another job quickly: 'Be calm. Ted will feel your panic otherwise.'

Throughout the winter, Aurelia Plath negotiated with Hughes over her grandchildren's summer visit. Ted was so reluctant to let them go that he used as an excuse the riots in Chicago following the assassination of Martin Luther King. Hughes had probably told Assia of his apprehension of the grandmother's influence on his children, or else Assia had read the correspondence; in any case, she decided to write to Mrs Plath and fill her in on Frieda and Nicholas. Aurelia Plath was taken aback but decided to forgo her reservations and the two embarked on an unlikely correspondence. Mrs Plath appreciated Assia's good will and concern and was willing to forgo her understandable hostility for the sake of having a channel of information about her grandchildren. Assia was the one who broke to Aurelia Plath the good news that Ted had finally booked the flight tickets for the children. Though grateful to Assia, Mrs Plath did not hide her resentment that she did not hear it from Ted. It was Olwyn Hughes who packed the kids off to America, with luggage so minimal that Mrs Plath had to purchase many items of clothing and personal hygiene.

In the mid 1980s, Richard Larschan, now a professor of English at the University of Massachusetts, did a televised interview with Aurelia Plath and became her confidant until her death in 1994. As he helped her sort the thousand letters or so that she kept, Larschan noticed some from Assia. 'I remember registering amazement, that Assia would write so familiarly to the mother of someone for whose death she, in some measure, could be considered at least partially responsible,' he says. The tone in Assia's letters was 'very much that of a daughter seeking parental support'. Assia complained to Aurelia Plath that Ted was brutalising her, with 'frequent mentions of emotional and physical abuse, some of it, I seem to recollect, sexual'. Larschan read in Sylvia's letters similar complaints about Ted's brutality and he was struck 'by the tremendous resemblance between the two women's anguished tone'. Aurelia Plath kept aside those of Assia's letters, together with Sylvia's, that had controversial contents; all of them were to be opened to the public after her death. Sylvia's letters were eventually given to Lilly Library, at Indiana University, but Assia's to Aurelia Plath are still kept back, and are possibly in Warren Plath's possession.

Nineteen

Despair

London, summer–autumn 1968

When Ted Hughes sold his archives to Emory University in Atlanta, Georgia, in 1997 it did not include any of his journals. The fact that he did keep a journal was hinted at in his 'Notes on Letters Home, Revised', written to Aurelia Plath on 12 January 1975; he said that the allegation that Plath willingly sacrificed herself to his ego will be refuted when 'her journals of the time, and mine' are presented to the public. But Plath's journal disappeared, and Hughes's were never made available. However, some journal-like entries are scattered in the notebooks that he was using to draft his poems and essays.

One of these rare entries was made on 6 August 1968. That day, Hughes escorted his children to Heathrow airport, seeing them off for the summer holiday with their grandmother. He pulled his notebook out and leafed through to find an empty space. He then jotted down some food-for-thought that eight-year-old Frieda had just left with him: that he 'ought to marry Ca and B, and then there'll be one mother each.' 'Ca' was doubtless Carol, the twenty-year-old daughter of his good friend and neighbour Jack Orchard from North Tawton. Carol had finished her training as a nurse and tended to Ted's mother. 'B' was Brenda Hedden, the attractive blonde social worker and mother of two small daughters whom he had known for a number of years.

If Hughes had worried about his children's reaction towards remarriage, he could rest assured; their yearning for a mother was so intense that they wanted not one, but two. And curiously, although Frieda had known Assia closely for five years and had lived with her and with her half-sister Shura, she did not suggest Assia as her father's future wife. Did the little girl dislike Assia, or did she grasp her father's reluctance to tie the knot with his mistress? Frieda's innovative notion, that he should marry both Carol and Brenda, indicated not only the two women's prominent presence at Court Green, but also that the eight-year-old sensed the mutual attraction between her father and each of the women. Hughes kept his thoughts to himself and did not comment on his daughter's idea in his notebook. After watching the plane to Boston take off he caught a bus to town and stopped to buy a few shirts; he was due to fly to Germany on a lecture tour with Assia and Shura. Exhausted, he fell asleep on the bus that drove him to Assia's new address in Clapham Common.

Royston Taylor, Assia's former colleague at Ogilvy who was getting divorced, suggested that she take over the lease of his flat in Okeover Manor. Built in 1935 on the north side of Clapham Common, the four-storey block of flats was made from dull brown brick, with a flat, projecting base linked by balconies, an art deco iron gate and a wooden entrance door. Two glass doors opened into a wide hall that led to an inner corridor serving two flats. Hughes accompanied Assia when she went to inspect flat Number 3 on the ground floor. The bare four-bedroom flat overlooked the back yard and a small garden. Number 5 was the London flat of MP Mr Goronwy Owen Roberts, who was Minister of State at the Foreign Office.

Hughes did not want Assia to rent Royston Taylor's flat 'because it was "tragic" – he spotted a child's shoe in a cupboard in the hall,' as Taylor recalls. Nevertheless, Assia decided to take up the lease, although she had to pay several hundred pounds extra for the new wall-to-wall carpet that Taylor had just put in. Shura occupied the first room on the right; the lounge was on the left side of that corridor, the German au pair Else Ludwig stayed in the next room, while Assia took the large bedroom at the end of the corridor. When Royston Taylor visited Assia some time later, he was struck by the stylish way in which she had furnished and decorated the flat – her utmost pride was the glass-fronted shelved cabinet, about shoulder-high, which displayed her cherished large collection of netsuke. Some dark green hessian in the living room transformed it into a nineteenth-century boudoir.

The trip to Germany was Assia's fourth, and she had made each one of them with a different male partner. On the first day, she and Ted visited Beethoven's house in Bonn and stayed the night at the nearby ancient town of Boppard. She retained bad memories from her visit there with David Wevill six years earlier, when her Jewishness was detected. She now wrote in her diary, 'In Boppard – evil, dangerous Boppard . . . The serious, unsmiling, unlovely people. I welcome being an outcast within them. I'm relieved that my only connection with them is historical. I'm about as German as I'm Israeli –

in reality, neither. For once, I'm pleased to be unrooted here.' This time, she decided not to visit her mother's relatives.

On an impulse, she and Ted decided to spend the next day in Würzburg, Yehuda Amichai's birthplace. It was a rainy day, and the round trip by train took them six hours. Glancing sideways to make sure that he was not being watched, Ted rapidly incised in the pink stucco façade of the thirteenth-century town hall, 'Yehuda Amichai born here'. One of the clerks looked down from his office with a flicker of suspicion but was not alarmed enough to call the guards. Hughes was so proud of his audacity that he bought a postcard and reported his feat to Amichai, adding 'many locals prospering on your absence. Although he signed the postcard 'Love from Ted and Assia', Assia felt the need to send her own account on another postcard. Twenty-three years after Germany's defeat, she was still spotting Nazis everywhere and wrote to Amichai: 'On the train here I spoke to a round robin of a man who was in the Waffen SS – yes, he knew Vilna backwards, my spine is still practically contracted.' And in Hebrew, her code language with her compatriot, she added, 'Me, half-German? No, no, no. Suddenly Germany disgusts me.' She was very defensive and throughout the visit distorted her perfect German and spoke with a heavy accent and scrambled grammar, hoping to be taken for a foreigner: 'to be taken for a German, would imply the whole treacherous structure of a German woman with an Englishman. The enemy,' she wrote in her diary on 8 August 1968.

Neither of Assia's homelands – Germany nor Israel – provided a safety net and she seemed to be letting go of them both. Hughes crystallised her state of mind perfectly in the poem 'Descent' that he wrote decades later: 'You had to strip off Germany' and to the list of abandoned identities he also added Russia and British Columbia. Assia was left with England, which in her eyes was epitomised by a life with Ted Hughes.

Hughes hardly spoke that day in Würzburg and Assia was gloomy as well, remembering the charge between them on their first holiday together, when they escaped to Spain in September 1962. Several times she tried to break the heavy silence in the train compartment, drawing Ted's attention to the swelling on the tip of her nose. A book had fallen on her from the glass vitrine just before leaving home and she thought it most significant that she was hit by their cherished and priceless *Book of Hours*, a medieval illuminated prayer book. 'T burst out in impatience – there was nothing remarkable in <u>that</u> book hitting my nose,' she wrote in her diary later that evening. His blunt reaction filled her eyes with tears: 'he uses the word <u>sentimental</u> frequently, whenever he refers to love between people. He condemns himself, us, whenever he says it. What he seems to say is that feelings, matters of the heart, matters of <u>my</u> heart, matters of his heart, that were, are unworthy of life. Unimportant.' Ted's cynicism distressed her and she fell back on her days with David, as she still did when she was left in the cold. She conjured up a bus trip that she and David had taken ten years earlier, when they were secret lovers. They were cuddling together on the seat, and a woman passenger remarked, to their excruciating embarrassment, 'Ah, young lovers.' It was not so much David that she missed, as the state of being wrapped in love.

During the entire German trip Ted's mood fluctuated, sweeping Assia along with him; she recorded how one moment was 'bleak with T's chemistry gone amok, an ugly impatient mood setting in', and the next, his good nature returned with magical abundance. He bought Shura two little wooden birds and played enchanting serious games with her. Shura called him Daddy and Assia noted that the three-and-a-half-year-old responded to him with complete, but slightly impertinent, adoration. It was a very rare opportunity for the three of them to be together on their own as a family. As the days went by, Ted became more relaxed, and Assia found him beguiling company. 'This morning T rowed us round the black lake . . . Shura's walking stick and the plastic whistle attached to it, her brave participation.'

That night, back in Court Green, Ted was overwhelmed by a dream; Sylvia had returned to life and met all her friends and spent a day and night with her children. Something could have been done to make her stay, but he didn't know what. At the end of the day she fell asleep and never woke up. This time he sadly acknowledged her death was final.

It was Ted's thirty-eighth birthday two days later, and Assia presented him with the recently published *Selected Poems* of Nelly Sachs. A year earlier, this Jewish poet, who had found refuge in Sweden, was awarded the Nobel Prize for Literature jointly with the Israeli novelist Agnon. Assia inscribed the book, 'To the master-Netsuke-master, with loving amazement.' Collecting netsuke was a long-standing passion of Assia's, which Hughes had recently taken an interest in. He admired Assia's exquisite taste and perception and complimented her when she returned from a sale of Japanese objets d'art with two extraordinary acquisitions, a mermaid and a couple. Netsuke was a booming market and Hughes instructed his brother Gerald in Australia to buy him some pieces for up to £300, which he hoped to sell for a high profit.

Since separating in the spring of 1959, and overcoming her post-divorce blues, Assia had been keeping in touch with Richard Lipsey, her second husband; by now he had become a distinguished world-renowned economist and immensely rich, due to his bestselling textbook *An Introduction to Positive Economics*. Three or four times a year, Assia would ring Lipsey and invite herself for lunch. Though increasingly reluctant to meet her, Lipsey found it hard to decline. 'Her troubles were always the main topic of conversation, and I tried to give her some emotional support,' he recalls. When they met in the summer of 1968, he still found her stunning; she never lost her fatal attraction and it seemed to him that her beauty would last many more years. She told him that she had broken up with Ted and was living in Clapham Common. 'All her life she used to say that the greatest disaster that could ever befall anybody is to live in a bedsitter in South London,' Lipsey says. 'For her, a garret in Hampstead was immensely better than a house across the river in the south. She threw herself on me, saying she was desperately broke and living in poverty.' By then, Assia was already working at Charles Hobson and Grey advertising agency, and there is no other evidence to the effect that she was hard pressed for money. Was she simply envious that she was not part of Lipsey's fortune? And why did she say that she was no longer with Ted? Was it to elicit his pity? Dick finally gave in and, before departing, handed Assia a hundred pounds, telling her, 'I don't want to see you again and don't want anything to do with you any more.'

She also kept in touch with David Wevill and, although it was two years since she had left him, she still remained possessive. Judge Martin Graham, Assia's friend, was an acquaintance of a young woman who had become David's girlfriend. 'His new companion was a very beautiful, leading model from South Africa who came to London to pursue her career. Assia would come around, screaming and banging on the door, making a scene. She had a very volatile temper, and was slightly neurotic, and she couldn't bear to see another woman living with David.'

But in the summer of 1968, Assia met David to discuss their divorce. 'For a long time, we knew it was coming. Nothing prevented it, except laziness and inattention,' Wevill recounts. 'She admitted that things were difficult with Ted, did not elaborate, but seemed anxious that the decree be made all the same.' As grounds for divorce Assia agreed to admit to the court that she had committed adultery with Ted Hughes. There was no property to divide, and it was clear that although Shura carried David's surname he had no claim for custody over the child. When David came to her flat in Clapham Common to sign some papers, Assia seemed withdrawn and was smoking heavily. 'I saw Shura – the little creature that I had raised as my own, and grown to like. She did not recognise me, and just accepted me as a visitor.' David felt a prick in his heart when Assia did not come forward to refresh Shura's memory. Before departing, she gave him a copy of Amichai's poems in her translation and inscribed it, 'If only it could have been different.' He was troubled by Assia's sombre mood, because 'the choice for her in this affair was always between devil or deep sea'. Still, he hoped that she was getting somewhere with her plans. He thought it was best to remove himself from her life, in spite of their mutual affection, 'so that she might plan more clearly in the direction of Ted, or just for herself and Shura alone . . . I hoped they could make some kind of life together,' he wrote to their good friends Patricia and Michael Mendelson. He was afraid for Assia, yet knew that 'she had this capacity to function and keep on living, she was a creature of life and not despair'.

By 9 October, when the marriage was dissolved by the Honourable Judge Dow, sitting at the Royal Court of Justice in the Strand, David Wevill was already in Austin, Texas. Assia hoped that by making herself legally free for Ted she would speed his decision to marry her.

But secretly, in Devon, Ted gave Brenda Hedden a golden bracelet with a pendant in the shape of a heart, inscribed 'Ted and Brenda'. It was identical to one that he had already given Assia, so he warned Brenda not to wear it when Assia came down to Court Green. He also secretly gave Brenda a copy of the deeply intimate 'Lovesong', creating the impression that she was the inspiration for the poem, which celebrated symbiotic conjugality; the lovers became one, exchanged limbs in their sleep, 'their brains took each other hostage'. Assia had her own copy of the poem, which was in fact intended for Sylvia.

By that time, Brenda Hedden was separated from her husband Trevor. She recalls:

We were nicely spaced out: Assia was in London, Carol in North

Tawton, and I, in Welcombe, 40 miles away from North Tawton, with my two daughters, aged four and one year old. Ted wished to diffuse the female power, and told me that after Sylvia, he no longer wanted to be dependent on one woman; he felt it was weakening and suffocating him. He kept us in the pecking order: we were the chickens in the coop competing over the rooster's favours. Assia was the chief hen, I was number two, and then there was Carol, and maybe others.

Brenda got the impression that it was Sylvia's death that left Ted glued to Assia but it was also their stumbling block. In her view, 'Assia fooled herself that she could have a life with Ted, but he had no intention of marrying her or anybody else, nor did he wish to break up with her.' A drawing that Hughes made at that time on a long strip of paper tells it all: two snakes, one blue, one pink, locked in an embrace which creates the shape of a heart; they hiss at each other, unable to break apart, each move of the one strangling the other.

But gossip travels fast and Assia was distraught to learn that Ted was conducting affairs with other women. On a torn-out diary page from 4 September, she spelt out the naked truth: 'It is only inevitable that the life I have led should end like this. That I should be subplanted (sub-planted!) by others.' Assia knew all about Brenda Hedden and Carol Orchard but she was discreet in her diary entry, not naming her rivals. Five years earlier, she had made a scene when Ted invited Susan Alliston for Christmas in Court Green; but this time, although having much greater grounds for alarm and fury, she did not confront him with his infidelity. In their surviving correspondence from that period, there is no reference to his unfaithfulness. Assia usually aired her difficulties with Ted in minute detail but none of her friends recalled that she spoke about his philandering. Did she belittle the threat that Brenda Hedden and Carol Orchard presented, thinking that neither woman was an obstacle to her own future with Ted? Or, on the contrary, was Assia so apprehensive and uncertain of her place and so desperate to be with him, that she was willing to turn a blind eye to his transgressions?

Peter Porter recalls reading a report that Ted Hughes submitted to the Arts Council, suggesting that it should set up a special rendezvous for poets in London, 'providing facilities for poets to meet and make love to a special corps of handmaidens assigned to the task of catering to the masculine muse. This

Ted with Assia and Shura, London 1967 (courtesy of Celia Chaikin)

Assia and Shura at Court Green
(courtesy of Patricia Mendelson)

Assia's Valentine card to Ted, 1967 (courtesy of Emory University)

Assia's birthday card to Ted, August 1967 (courtesy of Emory University)

Assia and Shura, London 1967
(courtesy of Celia Chaikin)

Assia at Court Green
(courtesy of Patricia
Mendelson)

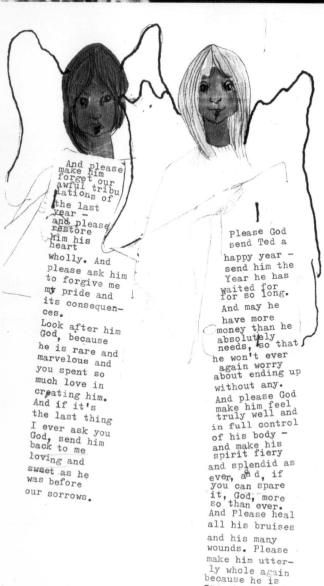

And please make him forget our awful tribulations of the last year – and please restore him his heart wholly. And please ask him to forgive me my pride and its consequences.
Look after him God, because he is rare and marvelous and you spent so much love in creating him. And if it's the last thing I ever ask you God, send him back to me loving and sweet as he was before our sorrows.

Please God send Ted a happy year – send him the Year he has waited for for so long. And may he have more money than he absolutely needs, so that he won't ever again worry about ending up without any. And please God make him feel truly well and in full control of his body – and make his spirit fiery and splendid as ever, and, if you can spare it, God, more so than ever. And Please heal all his bruises and his many wounds. Please make him utterly whole again because he is one of your best creatures.

Assia's New Year card to Ted,
January 1968
(courtesy of Celia Chaikin)

Assia and Shura, 3 Okeover Manor, Clapham Common,
London, December 1968 (photos by © Martin Baker)

Shura's last birthday at the Mendelson's, March 1969 (courtesy of Patricia Mendelson)

Assia and Shura, December 1968
(photos by © Martin Baker)

The British Council's poetry reading tour of Israel, 1971. Left to right: DJ Enright, Dannie Abse, the Israeli poet T Carmi, Peter Porter, Jeremy Robson, Ted Hughes, the Israeli poet Yehuda Amichai and Charles Osborne.

Ted Hughes, Dannie Abse and Yehuda Amichai at The Dome of the Rock, Jerusalem, 1971

Carol and Ted Hughes, Jerusalem 1971

Carol and Ted Hughes, Tel Aviv 1971

Ted Hughes and Eilat Negev, London, October 1996

was a joke, but much of Hughes's conduct supported a literal interpretation of the notion. The other parties to his affairs tended to feel that they were involved in the highest reaches of shamanism.' Conducting a number of parallel affairs was Ted Hughes's *modus operandi*. Invariably, he was not the one to terminate a relationship but, rather, he let his women do it; it was Plath who demanded that he leave home and, in later years, at the time of Hughes's second marriage to Carol Orchard, it was his mistresses who realised that he would never commit himself and broke off with him.

But he did not let Assia go, feeding their relationship with a constant drip of hope. There was no marked erosion in his outward treatment of her and he kept writing to her, 'I'm really missing you', and sending drafts of his *Crow* poems for her review and comment. When he was invited to a poetry reading at the Peacock Theatre in Dublin, it was Assia who was at his side. The Irish poet Eavan Boland, later a professor at Stanford University, recalls that at a party after the event, Ted introduced Assia to her: 'Standing in a smoky living-room in Dublin, with a fire sparkling behind us, her face oddly lighted, she was as polite as he was. We said a few words, that was that. Later, I would remember those two people, caught in the grind and ordeal of their moment, tied in a terrible Racine-like fashion to the events that were coming.'

In October, Ted's mother was driven in an ambulance to Yorkshire, followed by his father. The coast was clear but Assia was not invited to return. On the face of it, Ted acted as if he had agreed to live with her, but not in Court Green. They scouted estate agents' letting offers, glanced through brochures, and went house-hunting separately and together. But his quest lacked the energy and determination with which he set out for the country with Sylvia; then, he found the house in Devon in less than a week. Now, months passed and still nothing satisfied him. Time and again the deal was somehow aborted for no apparent reason.

One day, after years of silence, Assia surprised William Trevor, her advertising colleague from J Walter Thompson, asking him to meet her in the lounge of a bar near Waterloo station. She was chain-smoking, drank Coca-Cola and the time they spent together seemed to him 'like hours spent in a cinema'. Though he had known her well, it was the first time that Trevor heard Assia call herself 'a displaced person', complaining, 'she had created the woman she seemed to be'. She asked for his advice: would it be wise to enrol at the Heather Jenner Agency – an upmarket marriage bureau in New Bond

Street – and look for a widower somewhere in the countryside? She had had enough of poets, she said. 'With her eyes half-closed, against the stream of smoke from her cigarette, she even referred to a cottage garden, with lupins and fuchsia, and wisteria round the porch. She gave the impression that she meant every word of it.' She said that she wanted to do it for the sake of Shura, to give her conditions to thrive in, and – 'I think I might make a farmer happy.' She spoke with increased conviction about living in the country beside an elderly gentleman, having no doubt that she could make it happen, and 'nowhere in her features was there any sign that she felt sorry for herself. Her eyes were full of yet another *Alice in Wonderland* future.' However, when they bid farewell outside the pub and she turned up the collar of her smart tweed coat, for a single instant she seemed to him weary. ' "Actually I'm afraid," she murmured, before she smiled again and went away.'

Fay Weldon remembers that Assia did enrol at a marriage bureau and actually dated five or six men. 'Being a single mother in the late 1960s was difficult on all levels, and Assia found it hard to support Shura and herself. She felt that time was against her, she was getting older, and it was her last chance. For a woman as striking as she was, it was humiliating to revert to dating services, and it showed her degree of despair.'

Assia was lamenting her lost years and beauty but, at 42, men still found her attractive and craved her company; some of them were almost half her age. She used to bring her antique furniture for restoration at John Chambers's carpentry shop in St John's Wood: 'At that time, I did not know that she was fifteen years older than me. She mesmerised me, and I always felt uplifted in her presence. She complained that while in Devon, Ted used to disappear for long walks in the hills, while she'd rather be talking to him.' An unemployed musician, Guy Jenkin, gave Chambers a helping hand in his workshop and, when Assia learned that Jenkin had mastered the recorder, she was intrigued and asked if he could teach her to play. Jenkin was 23 years old, married with a young daughter, and he too found Assia strikingly beautiful; he was drawn to her aloofness, poise and a certain air of mystery about her. 'I fancied her, there was sexual tension on both sides,' but there was also a motherly, older-sister quality about her that stopped Jenkin from flirting with her.

Once a week, he drove from North London to Assia's flat in Clapham Common to give her music lessons. He never asked for a fee: 'I was not interested in money but in her, and wanted to find out more about her.' Assia would give the au pair the evening off, and Jenkin would come in the early hours of the evening and stay almost until midnight. Assia was a diligent student and showed considerable musical progress, playing on the cheap plastic recorder that she bought. Sometimes Jenkin brought his violin with him and they played together.

'It gives me such immense pleasure,' Assia wrote to her friend Patricia Mendelson, urging her to learn to play the recorder as well. 'The repertoire of music written for it is very large. We could play duets?'

After the music lesson, they would go to her kitchen for a light meal. On several occasions he brought his two-year-old daughter Sarah to play with Shura until falling asleep. They would return to the sitting room, which was full of Assia's drawings. Near the door Jenkin noticed a framed pencilled portrait of Ted Hughes, a vertical scar across his face. Jenkin did not dare inquire whether Assia slashed the drawing out of anger and pasted it together when she and Ted made up, or whether the slit was an integral part of her depiction of the 'dark and broody' Ted. Still, Jenkin could not feel Ted's presence in the flat. 'It was a woman and her daughter's flat and there were no signs of a man around,' he recalls. 'In the many evenings and the numerous hours that I spent there, the phone never rang, and no one dropped by.' Several times he went with Assia to concerts on the South Bank or to recitals at the Wigmore Hall.

I sensed her underlying unhappiness and isolation, filling her times with activities, going through the motions of normality such as learning to play the recorder. I felt there was something inside she needed to let go or get rid of, but it seemed she lacked the inner resources to find a means of exorcising her demons. I wanted to love her, to be her friend, to make it all OK for her, but was too aware of her darkness.

Assia remained obsessively loyal to Ted. None of her suitors could overcome her addiction to him and he remained her idol; the unrivalled Ultimate Man. Daily she waited in anticipation for a letter from him; the evenings stretched out as she waited for the phone to ring. Days passed as she awaited his occasional visits. She felt she was suffocating in the increasingly shadowy reality of him, yet she could not, and did not, wish to escape the spell that he seemed to have cast over her. Only she could not bear it much longer.

Twenty

The Die Is Cast

London, winter 1969

In a razor-sharp diary entry from September 1968, Assia dissected her life: 'I was endowed with too many minor qualities, but with neither the will or the huge intelligence to bring them a life of their own.' Her father expected from her nothing and too much, and so did she. Unsparing, she pronounced her own verdict: her past was a letdown, her present a mess and her future a cul-de-sac. In her defeat and helplessness she made Hughes her saviour or her doom.

About that time, Hughes invited the Hungarian poet Janos Csokits to have tea with them on the terrace of a tearoom near Paddington Station. Csokits happily complied. 'Then, we walked to the train station with little Shura. All of a sudden, Ted said a quick goodbye, and walked straight to the train, without looking back. Shura understood only too well what was happening, and flew into a tantrum, crying, shouting, Daddy! Daddy! She was stamping her feet, and Assia wept.' Csokits was bewildered, unable to soothe either mother or daughter. A long time passed before Assia finally composed herself, dried her tears and consoled the little girl. 'It was then that I understood why Ted had asked me to meet them that morning.'

Only two photos of Ted with Assia and Shura survived. In one of them, Assia holds Shura's hand, helping her to stand up; in the other she is pushing the pram. In both photos Ted stands reserved, uptight, his hands deep in his jacket pockets. They hardly look like a family, unlike a similar photo found in Assia's album, taken a few months after Sylvia's suicide: Assia and Ted are relaxed and smiling, standing close together, with the three-year-old Frieda between them, hugged in Ted's arms. In December 1968, her colleague from Ogilvy, Martin Baker, dropped in at Okeover Manor with his camera and took a whole sequence in black and white of the mother and daughter. Assia is detached, solemn and thoughtful, hardly smiling when hugging her daughter.

Shura is posing for the camera, inquisitively gazing at objects around her. She looks vulnerable in her small white dress; a bracelet hugs her thin arm, her hair is clasped behind. Baker recalls:

> Shura was hyperactive, running around and couldn't sit still. Assia did not restrain her; she let her express herself freely. I was writing a children's book about armour without a knight. My publisher said that children would never understand it, but Shura said, it's such a good idea. A funny, bright little girl, after a few minutes you forgot she was a child of four. She was very advanced for her age, and Assia treated her as an equal. They were inseparable.

Gerald and Joan Hughes came from Australia for the holiday season and Ted introduced Carol to them; Frieda Hughes remembers the wooden toy boxes that she got from Carol that Christmas. The Hughes family celebrated in Yorkshire, while Assia and Shura were left in London on their own. On Christmas Eve, she cooked a festive dinner and ate it with Shura in the living room by the decorated tree. Of all the games, toys and books that the child had received in her four years, only one survived; the large, illustrated Hans Christian Andersen's *Fairy Tales*, a Christmas present from her mother. It was Ruth Fainlight, Sylvia Plath's close friend, who tried to mitigate Assia's sense of desertion by inviting her and Shura to Christmas Day lunch. Assia spoke only of 'Shura. Money. Loneliness', Fainlight told Elaine Feinstein, Ted Hughes's biographer. The Sillitoes were renting a house from Mira Hamermesh, Assia's friend from Israel, and years afterwards Ruth heard from Mira that her Christmas invitation had stopped Assia 'from killing them both during the empty days of that endless, dead-of-winter northern festival'.

When Assia had left Court Green and moved to London a year earlier, Ted was constantly phoning her from Devon. Judge Martin Graham was present during one of those calls: 'Assia put the receiver down and said, "he's so possessive, he rings all the time when I'm away from him."' But now the telephone was dead and when she tried to phone him, more often than not he was unavailable.

Mira Hamermesh heard Assia talk several times about killing herself.

We had all been through the humiliation of waiting for a man to ring, so we didn't take it seriously, especially as Assia always said it with a smile, out of the blue, in the middle of dinner. We had all been in therapy, and were told that people who sound the alarm never commit suicide. We became so fed up with her theatrical threats, that once I silenced her and said, go ahead, do it. Had I the slightest suspicion that she was serious, I would never have dared even to joke about it.

Martin Baker, who frequently went with Assia to see the netsuke collection in the Japanese rooms of the British Museum, had a similar impression: 'in the 1960s, people in our circle either divorced or killed themselves. There was a general feeling of depression, and Assia was even less depressive than most of us.'

One day, Assia phoned Royston Taylor and asked to lunch with him. They met in a bright, busy, smart restaurant in Mayfair and talked about psychiatrists and injured parties in love. Assia told him about her discord with Ted Hughes, but said that they were trying to work something out. She described in detail house-hunting with Ted in Yorkshire, and Royston assumed 'that they hadn't quite crashed, if they were looking for somewhere to start afresh'. Well into the main course, the object of the lunch became clear: would he sell his service revolver together with ammunition? She offered one hundred pounds, which Royston thought was a very fair price. Assia knew about his revolver from their days at the agency, since he once brought it to work and fired accidentally through the floor of somebody's office. 'I said I didn't want her committing suicide, made a joke of it, and she was in quite high spirits. She laughed and said, no, she merely wanted a "terminal machine" for her bottom drawer.' Then they moved to other topics, laughing a lot, and before departing, Royston promised to think it over. He phoned her the next day, saying that if he thought she really needed it, he would not ask for money, but he had decided not to let it go. 'By that time, I speculated that she could do something bad with it, maybe shoot somebody. But suicide didn't really weigh on my mind,' he said.

Like many of Assia's friends, Edward Lucie-Smith had heard her threaten to end her life. 'I remember that she spoke about it in Bernard Stone's little book shop. She walked in, and declared that she was going to commit suicide. Her tone was like that of a person announcing that he's off to Paris or to Italy. It wasn't the tone of a depressed person.' However, when Guy Jenkin arrived once at Assia's flat for the scheduled music lesson, he was alarmed when she failed to answer the bell. He buzzed again and again and finally Assia came to the door, looking distraught. 'Oh, thank God, you've come,' she said. Stepping inside the flat, Jenkin had a sinister sensation. 'My arrival had interrupted a train of events. She didn't explain things, and I didn't ask her. I knew exactly what she meant and what she intended to do, and yet was dumb to help her.' There was no music lesson, and the evening was full of awkward silences. Little Shura was bouncing around in her pyjamas, as joyful as ever. Guy was suddenly alarmed by the countless jars of pills that he had always seen on Assia's bedside table. He left quite early but sat in his car outside her house, stunned, helpless. 'Should I go back and confront her? If so, then what? Who could I contact? I knew of no one other than Ted Hughes. What would I say even if I could find him? Would he be of any use?'

Assia's options narrowed to two: she scrutinised the newspapers for country houses to let, studied leaflets sent by estate agents, made phone calls, and every now and then travelled with Ted to inspect a house. Equally diligently, she was contemplating her demise. Already in the summer, she confided in Chris Wilkins, with whom she used to share an office at Ogilvy, that she was worried about her insecurity, and wanted to marry again and settle, but things were not going right with Ted. Chris and Assia went for a walk along the Embankment Gardens, and she told him 'that she couldn't stand the state of things as they were, and if it didn't change, she would kill herself'. Like all Assia's friends, Chris Wilkins thought it was just a passing depression. They were all dazzled by her lust for life and gushing vivacious demeanour, which she did not lose, and were misled by her tendency to hysteria and over-dramatisation.

Some months later, Assia phoned Wilkins again and asked to meet him: 'Assia asked me if I would mind being the executor of her will.' The 23-year-old Wilkins was startled. 'Partly because she seemed too young to be thinking about a will, and partly because I didn't feel myself a close enough friend to take on such a responsibility.' Assia did not look distressed, and retained 'her whole outward style and manner, lavishly colourful and seductive'. She led him to believe that making a will was a normal procedure for a responsible adult of her age, and explained, in a matter-of-fact way, that it was her solicitor who had instructed her to appoint someone younger than herself as executor.

She told Chris that in the event of her death, he would have first choice of any three objects in her flat, including her precious netsuke collection.

The change of executor from Assia's sister, who was just two years her junior, to Wilkins, who was almost half her age, could be interpreted as a rather positive sign: that Assia was not expecting her death to be imminent and therefore had picked an executor who would probably be around when her time came. But it was just the opposite: she felt it was unrealistic to appoint her sister, who was living in Canada and tied down with a husband and three small children. In her practical mind, she chose Wilkins because he was the only one of her friends who lived nearby; some ten minutes' walk from her flat. Following Wilkins's consent, she revised her will but, once again, as in all previous cases, left it unsigned. It seems that she could not yet sign her own death warrant.

In mid February, she got a letter from the court to the Principal Registry of the Family Division, that the decree of her divorce from David Anthony Wevill was made final and absolute and that the marriage was thereby dissolved. She wrote a postcard to Wevill in Austin, 'I wish you happiness – you deserve it so much.' She sent it without knowing that he was about to marry an American student named Sharon, whom he had just met at the university. Wevill did not reply; months later, he composed an imaginary monologue for a lifeless Assia: 'I'm so restless, so cold. I must see. Please give me eyes. Give me back my eyes. A woman can't live alone. She's only half herself, by herself.' Though they had not been living together for three years, Wevill felt that he could read Assia like an open book, and slip easily into her state of mind. The monologue continued:

By that time, I just wanted a little peace and quiet. I had my vanities. My wigs. My dresses. My faces. Certain opinions people held to be vanities, which were just my uncertainties, really, and a certain brightness of saying them. I had my small passions, netsuke, little ivory walnuts, children, animals, grace in welcoming strangers. If my grand manner was not working so well now, it was because I saw I could not hold on to things. People were my passion, and I could not change. It was amazing how suddenly my magic went, after you went, and you went, and no one else came, and when I cried for help the cracked hag voices of former confessors and friends were not on the phone, began to talk about me behind my back, and to my face as Anna Karenina or the demon mistress, whoever happened to suit their demonology of the moment, and salvage their straight selves, all striving to be good people and saints after lives that contradicted that.

For several months, the Mendelsons and their two children, Andrea and Mark, had been Assia and Shura's refuge. 'They used to come for Sunday lunch, and I can still see her, a cigarette in one hand, dancing in the kitchen with my little Andrea. Shura was jealous and ran to the door, sulking,' recalls Patricia. In a thank-you letter after one of those Sundays, Assia chastised herself for her choice of a partner, 'It's them bloody artists that bash up women's souls. I'm telling you.' It was self-evident that Shura's fourth birthday would be celebrated at the Mendelsons' spacious house in Hampstead. It was held on 2 March and Ted failed to attend. The hosts and guests tried to make up to the little girl, by showering her with presents and much attention, to distract her mind from the deeply felt absence of her father. A photograph depicts a sombre girl, surrounded by smiling children, as she holds her presents up to the camera.

Underneath, there was seething lava but, on the surface, it was still business as usual. Assia called Tom Boyd, with whom she had collaborated on the TV jingle for Vesta Curry, and invited him for lunch at her favourite Mayfair restaurant. She tried to rally him to a project she was contemplating: like many Britons in the past months, she was endlessly humming 'Those Were the Days, My Friend', an Apple Records release, produced by Paul McCartney and sung by Mary Hopkin. It stayed 21 weeks in the chart, six of them at number one. 'Assia told me that it was based on a Russian folk song, and that through her Russian and Jewish background, she knew many similar songs,' Boyd recalls. 'She proposed that we pick one and translate it into English, turning it into a hit.' Boyd said he would think it over, and discuss it with her the following week.

On Tuesday, 18 March 1969, Assia took several days off from work and travelled to Manchester, leaving Shura with the au pair. House-hunting was her 'oxygen mask' and, in high spirits, she waited for Ted in Manchester Central. But when he got off his train, he was angry and sullen. They travelled around Yorkshire and Northumberland. Assia fell in love with Green Farm, near Hexham, and the salmon in the nearby river added to the house's charm.

Even the rent was ridiculously low. The next address, Dower House, near Manchester, had magnificent gardens. A third house, in Manchester, included bed linen with no additional charge. Assia was ready to move right away into any of them, but Hughes found faults in them all, claiming that the houses were either too expensive or too remote from anywhere.

Assia lamented not so much the loss of the beautiful palatial houses as the missed opportunity to set up a family home: 'A pity about the three children. "They're just in average despair," he says. About F & N. Poor little Shoe isn't even mentioned,' she wrote in her diary. She was not pacified by Ted's promise that next time they would be looking for a house in Devon. When she voiced her disappointment, he reprimanded her: 'I can't bear any more show of temperament from anyone.' She interpreted his short temper as a clear proof of repulsion: 'He feels as though he has already buried me – that feels hideously accurate. That which allowed his previous graces was desire – and I know it's dead in him.' And still she continued to inquire about possible dwellings.

The actual reason for taking the trip was Ted's television reading in Manchester. However, Assia was left out of that too, not allowed even to watch it in the monitoring van and, when Ted was basking under the studio lights, she was pacing indignantly in the hall outside. During the meal afterwards, Ted got drunk, and in the lounge of the Elm Hotel, they had a 'terrible talk', and the truth came out. Later that evening Assia wrote in her diary: ' "It's Sylvia – it's because of her" – I can't answer that. No more than if it were a court sentence.' So it was not his parents who stood in their way, not even something that had to do with her own shortcomings. Assia could have handled that but she had no chance against the glowing presence of the dead wife. The lot was cast and the verdict was horrendous: 'It says die – die, soon. But execute yourself and your little self efficiently,' she wrote in her diary. 'I can't believe it – any more than I could believe hearing of my own death.'

The following two days, Assia was left on her own in the hotel, since Ted would not take her with him to visit his mother in hospital in Yorkshire. She walked into a surgery and talked the doctor into prescribing 35 Sonemyl sleeping pills and bought them in a nearby pharmacy. She felt criminal. 'My Shura. Feel totally bankrupt . . . I'm sinking – further and further inwards.' Alone in her room she tried to read Zbigniew Herbert's *Selected Poems*, but was left cold. The bedside light went out because of a fault and she switched on the radio, listening to a programme on the tragic life of Dorothy Wordsworth, the devoted sister of the well-known poet; 'she ended mad and old,' Assia wrote in her diary. 'The tenderness with which these terrible relationships are evoked once the players are dead. Their lives are so compost for the sentimental bouquets of "compilers" the future.' She fell asleep to Beethoven's String Quartet No 13, Op 130: 'I couldn't bear the dark with the quartet playing. It was sinister. It's thawing, slowly. Bricks of ice are heaped in the car park, twigs of oak lie spread over the yard . . . the house looms, genuine, terrorising, closed, as the tomb it is.'

On Saturday morning, 22 March she and Ted bid each other farewell on Manchester station. Assia boarded the train to London, and he travelled down to Court Green. She seemed to him in good spirits and he promised to call her the following day. However, her au pair had a different impression: when Assia walked into the flat that afternoon, she looked extremely depressed and told Else Ludwig that 'Mr Hughes didn't want her any more.'

In his poem 'Flame', that he published 21 years later, Hughes referred to a 'signed bit of paper' that awaited Assia upon her return. It is unclear whether it was an official document of some kind or a private letter with disturbing news or gossip. Olwyn Hughes believes that it concerned the final decree of Assia's divorce. Either way, it agitated Assia so much that she did not wait for Ted to call but phoned Court Green. It was noon, Sunday, 23 March. They had another intense, heated argument and Ted felt that she was questioning his commitment to her. There had been occasions in the past when she had threatened to kill herself but, this time, she made no mention of it.

Later that day, Else Ludwig asked permission to go to her friend Olga, who lived just a short walking distance away. She left at 7.30. An hour later, Mrs Margaret Jones, the elderly neighbour from flat Number 2, smelled gas. Mrs Jones, a shorthand tutor, hurried into her own kitchen and saw that all the taps were turned off. Then she checked her meter and it seemed all right. She sniffed around and noticed that the smell was stronger by the front door, so she opened it and stepped into the passage that connected her flat with flat Number 3. As she reached Assia's door, the smell got stronger. Mrs Jones rang the bell but there was no reply. She returned to her flat, went into her living room, where she could see into Assia's lounge. It was in darkness, so she presumed that all three were out. She decided to stay 'by the front door, awaiting their return, as I wanted to warn them of the gas leak'.

For about two hours, the old lady was standing in the hall, behind the glass front door. The first person to walk in, at about 10.45, was Mr Goronwy Owen Roberts, who had just returned to London from a weekend at his family home in Wales. She asked Mr Roberts if he could come with her and verify whether it was indeed gas that was coming out of flat Number 3. He put his face against the door, and pushed the letter opening inside, inhaling deeply. Since he was not sure that the smell came from within, there was no point in alerting the fire brigade, and he went up to his flat. Mrs Jones was still not pacified; she returned to stand guard in the cold, when some minutes later Assia's au pair turned up. 'I told her not to strike a match in the flat without turning off the gas and opening a window. Immediately I said that, she screamed and said, "something has happened." I said, "What do you mean, is there something wrong?" she said, "yes".'

The au pair opened the door warily with her key. She saw light at the end of the corridor and the fumes of gas hit her face. She became hysterical. Mrs Jones pulled the screaming, weeping Else out, and led her into her own flat. She then went up and banged on Mr Roberts's door and he immediately accompanied her down. As he entered Assia's flat, it became clear to him that the source of the smell was behind the shut kitchen door. Pushing it open, he turned the kitchen light on and saw the two bodies.

He quickly switched off the gas taps, pushed the window up as far as he could, and telephoned the police. Meanwhile, as they were all waiting for the inspectors to arrive, Mrs Jones suddenly remembered that a charge nurse lived in flat Number 6 and rushed upstairs to fetch her. 'Mrs Wevill was lying on some blankets on the floor on her left side, and her daughter was lying on her back, with her face inclined towards her mother,' the nurse, Mrs Jennifer Margaret Bangs later testified. She took their pulses but there weren't any. She looked at their pupils, discovering to her horror that they were fixed, dilated. 'The little girl was much colder than her mother.' Helped by Mr Goronwy Owen Roberts, the nurse did some cardiac massage on the mother and on the little girl but it was hopeless. The police doctor who had just arrived declared them both dead. The post-mortem examination report stated that the cause of the mother and daughter's death was carbon monoxide poisoning; there were no external marks of recent injury on Shura's body and, unlike with her mother, there were no signs of barbiturates and no evidence of alcohol. The pathologist, Professor Keith Simpson, remarked, 'The child bears every evidence of proper care and attention.'

To rule out the possibility of an accident, Mr F W Lucas, a service supervisor at the South Eastern Gas Board, was sent to the flat. He found no faults in the gas installation and appliances. His expert calculations showed that 'a normal healthy person would be expected to succumb to CO poisoning within one and a quarter hours'; so when Mrs Jones first smelled gas and frantically rang the bell at flat Number 3, Assia was most probably still alive. The police called Chris Wilkins: they found his name as executor of the will. 'They were investigating, rather than informing, and seemed interested in my interpretation of the facts,' Wilkins recalls. During that weekend, his telephone was continuously engaged, because his sister-in-law was staying in his flat, having advertised for accommodation for herself and her child. For all the years since he has never stopped tormenting himself that perhaps Assia had 'tried in desperation' to call him, but had been unable to get through. 'I could have reached her flat in five minutes.'

'I handled this one badly,' Hughes told his sister Olwyn when he put the receiver down after his last conversation with Assia. But he still did not grasp how close she was to death. The next morning, he was dumbfounded when policemen knocked on his door. He was summoned immediately to report to Southwark Mortuary in London. There, he identified 'the bodies of Assia Wevill and Alexandra Wevill', his daughter. Det. Sgt Loakman asked him to describe his relationship with the deceased woman; 'I first met Mrs Assia Wevill about seven years ago in London. I knew her husband, David Wevill, through the profession. Assia and I became very close friends, and eventually the friendship blossomed into love. We became intimate, and there was a girl born of this union.' Hughes told the detective that Mr Wevill knew of this association and that, eventually in February 1966, Assia left her husband and lived with him in Ireland, and then at his home in Court Green. 'She felt persecuted living at my home address, as we were living with my parents, and also because of gossip.' As things did not work out, he said, Assia left for London and he often visited her. Recently, they had been house-hunting, and she was hoping that one day they would 'find a place and live together'. Hughes later told Brenda Hedden that the police were unpleasant to him and very suspicious.

It was Assia who led the police to Hughes; Sgt Brian Lutley found two stamped envelopes on her bedside table, one typed and addressed to Dr L

Gutmann in Canada, and another, handwritten, to Mr Edward Hughes, North Tawton, Devon. But of the latter, the coroner's file contains only the envelope, complete with stamps. The letter itself has mysteriously disappeared.

The other letter, to 'My dearest Vatinka', had been written two months earlier, in January of that year. It began with: 'If you ever receive this letter, you will know that I have not taken this decision lightly'. Always sensitive to the meaning of words, Assia did not write 'when you receive', but, 'If you ever receive', indicating that despite her abysmal despair, she still nurtured some hope that somehow, she would stop before it was too late.

The prospect before me is so bleak, that to have lived my full life-span would have entailed more misery than I could possibly endure.

It is the life alone. Insecure, dependent on an au pair to look after my little Shuratchka properly – dependent on the sort of people for whom I work – a very bad, 3rd rate agency who would fire me in case of illness. No husband. No father for Shura.

I've often thought of this – but the pain it would give you, and the criminality perpetrated on my little Shuri – these thoughts often stopped me at the last sane moment, in the past.

I have lived on the dream of living with Ted – and this has gone kaput. The reasons are immaterial. There could never be another man. Never.

She expressed regret for not having the necessary resilience, to have recuperated from her disillusion.

Believe me, my dearest Vatinka, my friend, my colleague in exile and disaster, that what I have done was necessary – you wouldn't have wished another 30 years of hell for me – would you?

Life was very exciting at the beginning – but this living death was too much to pay for it.

Thank you for all your kindness to me throughout my life. I did so love you, my dearest father – and don't grieve for me. Believe me, I have done the right thing.

Please don't grieve for me, my darling Vatinka – life was infinitely worse – infinitely. I lived a full and comparatively long life. It is necessary to know when there's no more life to live.

Perhaps there is another world – and if there is, we shall meet – Mutti, and you, and I. You were excellent parents – and you both did everything you could for me. Please don't think that I'm insane, or that I have done this in a moment of insanity. It was simple accountacy. And I couldn't leave little Shura by herself. She's too old to be adopted.

Goodbye Lonya. Father. My past protector. I miss you very much. Goodbye my dearest.

And she signed 'Assia' on the bottom of the typed page, in her firm, dense, steady handwriting.

It is clear that by January, Assia had made up her mind to take her own life and not to leave her child behind. If she had wished, she could have used one of the au pair's days off or sent her away to town on some pretext. But the flicker of hope, the horror of taking Shura's life, and her father's grief, kept her going. Her mind was filled with the gas fumes and every friction with Ted could have ignited them. The deed was finally done on an impulse, using Else Ludwig's unexpected visit to her friend. Assia knew that she had no more than three hours in which to execute it all: to prepare the letters, clear the kitchen, lay the blankets, close the windows, swallow a package of pills gulping whisky, carry Shura from her bed, and turn on the gas taps. The use of multiple methods indicates that she was past the point of no return, and did not wish to be saved.

Twenty-one

Agony

March–July 1969

A Canadian police officer knocked at midnight on Dr Lonya Gutmann's door in Montreal, to notify him of the death of his daughter and granddaughter. He travelled to London on his own, Celia was anxious to attend her sister's funeral but they could not afford the expensive ticket. 'I knew she would one day, she has threatened for years, in her letters to me, but no one could stop her, it was just a matter of time,' she wrote to Patricia Mendelson.

In the British papers that week, John Lennon and Yoko Ono's week-long, anti-war protest in bed made headlines, as well as the Reverend Ian Paisley's imprisonment in Northern Ireland and the arrest of ten people following a nude play in New York about Che Guevara. The crime columns of the London newspapers ran items about the strangling of a wife in her home, a jail sentence for a man who killed a girl when he was thirteen, and the death of a girl who set fire to herself near the Arc de Triomphe. There was even an item about a dog that starved to death after being locked up in a flat for three weeks; the owner was fined £10 and was barred from keeping a dog for five years. But there was not a word about the ghastly deaths of Assia and Shura Wevill.

The local press in the Clapham Common area that week reported a baby girl's cot death, as well as two incidents of children who died in house fires: the four Pollock siblings who were trapped in their home when fire broke out in the first-floor flat, and a two-year-old baby whose bedding caught fire. Two suicides made headlines; a company manager who gassed himself in his kitchen after returning from hospital following an operation for removal of stomach ulcers and a 56-year-old woman who took an overdose of anti-depressant capsules. However, the double death at 3 Okeover Manor was kept away from the public.

It was the second time that the press refrained – for some mysterious reason – from reporting the death of the spouse of Ted Hughes; in February 1963, there was no word of Sylvia Plath's suicide and again in March 1969. Only one small, local newspaper, *The South London Press* violated what amounted to a total hush-up. But even there, the item was printed at the bottom of page 13 and squeezed under a much lengthier report entitled 'Luxury flat tenants object to rent rises'. The laconic heading read, 'Mother-girl inquiry opens', and the body of the item stated that 'poet and author Ted Hughes gave evidence of identification at Southwark on Tuesday, when the coroner opened the inquest'. It omitted any hint of an intimate connection between Hughes and the deceased or that he was the father of the child. The press continued to ignore the tragedy even when, in mid April, Hughes was summoned to the Coroner's Court and, in front of eight jurors, was questioned about his relationship with Assia Wevill and about her mental health. Hughes, already a well-known poet, was presented as a friend of the Wevills, and the fact that the dead girl was his daughter was not disclosed at all. To save Hughes further discomfiture, HM Coroner, Mr A Gordon Davies told the jury that he did not feel it necessary for them to read the private letters that were discovered in the death flat. 'I had been a friend of the family for about six years,' *The South London Press* reported Ted Hughes as saying. Assia was described as an attractive divorcee. 'As long as I have known her – about six years – she was subject to depressions,' quoted the *South London Advertiser and News*, hinting at the cause of death.

In her will, Assia expressed a distinct wish for her 'cadaver to be buried in any rural cemetery in England, the vicar of its parish not objecting to its burial'. She went into the smallest detail and asked that the parish church be paid £50 for the permission. In spite of her wish Hughes decided on cremation and instructed Ashton's Funeral Directors to organise the funeral for Friday, 28 March, giving Assia's father time to get to England for the service.

Leafing through Assia's address book, Hughes telephoned her friends. Eda Zoritte-Megged, the wife of the Israeli cultural attaché in London, remembered Ted's 'hoarse, grave voice, as if his shadow was speaking from inside him'. His first words were, ' "Assia is dead." After a pause he added, "And Shura as well".' Hughes was very laconic in his calls and no questions were asked. Like all the others, Zoritte-Megged tried to remember her last encounter with Assia and wondered if she could have done anything to stop her. That winter, Assia was translating from Hebrew Zoritte-Megged's play *Last Game*. The heroine, Bilha, was a lonely forty-year-old Israeli woman, deserted by her husband, and the play described her last day, a much-anticipated meeting with her estranged husband, in which her illusions were shattered one by one. In the last scene, the heroine is standing by the window, about to throw herself down. Assia complained that the play depressed her and Zoritte-Megged suggested that she put it aside for a while. Nevertheless, Assia staggered on and completed the translation just before going on her last house-hunting expedition with Ted. Keith Gems recalled that the week before, Assia had phoned his office and asked to see him but he told her that he was too busy. She wished to speak to his wife Pam but he forgot to pass on the message. Martin Baker remembered that he promised to phone Assia that very Sunday but failed to do so. And Patricia Mendelson could not forgive herself for not inviting Assia and Shura for the customary Sunday lunch.

Hughes notified some of his own friends as well. 'I asked him if there was anything I could do. "Nothing that anyone can do. Send flowers",' Richard Murphy recalled the answer. Murphy was reading Sir Thomas Browne at the time and copied in his notebook the following quotation: 'who can but pity the merciful intention of those hands that do destroy themselves?' Soon afterwards Murphy wrote three couplets for the dead child:

> *Lullaby*
> Before you'd given death a name
> Like Bear or Crocodile, death came
>
> To take your mother out one night.
> But when she'd said her last good night
>
> You cried, 'I don't want you to go',
> So in her arms she took you too.

Finishing the round of calls, Hughes sat down and wrote a note to Brenda Hedden, letting her know that he would be detained in London until the funeral. 'Ted told me that he was poisoned by his obsession with the words "black" and "death", which affected not just him but everybody around him. He vowed that if he survived the ordeal and found strength to go on writing, he would break away from these topics. As distraught as he was, he sent his love, and asked me to be strong and take it easy'.

Assia's unsigned will made it invalid so that the immediate beneficiary was her father. Her lawyer could have dealt with her estate, but he was not called upon to do so. Hughes, who had no legal standing, was the one who took over and decided what was to be done. When Dr Gutmann visited the flat, he read the will and collected as many personal items as he could push into his suitcase and set aside those that he wished Ted to ship to him later. Hughes phoned Chris Wilkins, who was named as the executor of the will. They met in Assia's flat. 'He was extremely distraught, his eyes red from weeping. He was bewildered by – and I think suspicious of – the fact that I had been named in the will,' remembers Wilkins. 'After he told me that the will was not signed, he had nothing further to do with me.' Wilkins left the flat and never picked out the mementoes that Assia bequeathed him.

Friday was a bleak and windy day and, wrapped in their coats, twenty people or so, most of them Assia's colleagues from work, assembled at 9.30 in the funeral parlour, which was just across the road from the death flat. Mrs Jones, the neighbour from flat number 2, shook Ted's hand and noticed that his sweater was worn-out at the elbows. She was remorseful for not being quick enough to smell the gas, and not insisting on having Assia's door broken open sooner. In the undertaker's car, which followed the flower-covered hearse, Ted looked completely crushed and disconsolate, remembers Peter Porter, who was there with his wife Jannice. It was Dr Gutmann, sitting next to Ted, who was whispering some words of comfort. The funeral procession stopped at Lambeth Cemetery, South London, and they all parked next to a red-brick one-storey building surrounded by wide, lush stretches of turf, a towering chimney at the back.

Inside the small, white-walled chapel, Hughes and Dr Gutmann sat in the front row, deadly silent. No one in the small gathering was able to stand up and eulogise Assia and Shura. It was left for the vicar to mutter a few words, which Edward Lucie-Smith found jarring and tactless. 'Ted was like a pillar of stone, tears streaming down his cheeks and nose,' he recalls. Nathaniel Tarn felt uneasy with the Christian ceremony, with no Kaddish, the Hebrew prayer for the dead. Soon after, he wrote a 'Requiem pro duabus filiis Israel' ('A Requiem for Two Daughters of Israel'), which he dedicated 'to A & S':

> Daughter of daughter in the founding line
> these daughters of the people gone   confused
> the alien language squatting on our tongues
> while from the coffin her clear cry for help
> participation   and a place to sleep
> in death's white syllables went misunderstood
> we gave her up now   to the lapping fire
> to Terezin   Auschwitz   and Buchenwald
> for laziness   for emptiness of spirit.

Silence prevailed, as all heads turned to the right. 'The memory of the two white coffins waiting before the fire curtain, the one, an adult coffin, and the other, a diminutive shape, will always haunt me,' says Peter Porter. Once the coffins disappeared behind the metal door, the participants were quick to disperse, not even stopping at the signpost outside the crematorium, which bore the note, 'Flowers to the memory of Assia and Alexandra Wevill'. 'It was terribly upsetting,' remembers Patricia Mendelson. 'Normally you wait outside for the ashes for an hour or so, shake hands and comfort one another, but we all left as quickly as we could.' Edward Lucie-Smith stopped the hasty withdrawal by inviting all to lunch. 'I felt that it mustn't end like this, and I led them to San Frediano, a fancy Italian restaurant in Fulham Road. We were about ten people, including Ted, and I picked up the bill for the enormous lunch.' After the meal, Ted went straight to Waterloo station and boarded the train to Devon. The following day, he took his car and drove to the nearby village of Bondleigh. There he met Brenda, who had come with her two daughters for a weekend with Trevor, her former husband. 'Ted was in deep shock, and he was relieved that Assia's death was not in the papers,' she recalls.

Upon returning to Montreal, Lonya Gutmann turned his flat into a shrine for Assia, surrounding himself with her mementoes, which were lying everywhere. 'I can't understand it,' he told Celia: 'People were killed in Bergen Belsen, and here's a woman who kills herself because of her love for a man.' Celia was given Assia's jewellery box and could not part with her sister's bracelets, wearing them all the time. 'I found two strands of her hair tangled in her necklace, it tore my heart.'

With his sister's help, Hughes started disposing of Assia's effects. Olwyn

Hughes remembers that Assia's furniture was taken to Harrod's sales rooms. The proceeds from the sale were sent to her father. Assia and Shura's clothes were given to the Oxfam shop opposite their flat to be sold for charity. It is not known what became of the valuable netsuke collection and Assia's paintings, including the portrait that she did of Hughes. Ted phoned Martin Baker, Assia's friend from Ogilvy, and told him that Assia had left him some of her records. 'He invited me to come and pick whatever I wanted, after he and Olwyn sorted the flat out,' remembers Baker. 'I called three weeks later to set the time, but the tone was so frosty, that I decided that I didn't want anything to do with the Hugheses any more.' Patricia Mendelson had a better experience. She was asked to come to the flat and help Ted and Olwyn go over the things; she was the only one of Assia's beneficiaries who actually got what Assia intended her to have: a white china candelabra with blue ornaments that Assia used at special dinner parties, a Victorian mirror and the still-life miniature painted by Assia, with a cockroach and a bee on either side of a bowl of fruit.

In a crate, Hughes packed Assia's photo albums, Persian carpets, the mementoes she received as a baby from her grandparents, her white baby dresses and shoes, and her share in the family heritage: silver cutlery and embroidered and initialised damask tablecloths and napkins. All were sent to Montreal. The ship caught fire and the cargo took months to arrive but, luckily, Assia's crate was among those that were not damaged. Hughes gathered Assia's papers, her diaries, her correspondence with him and with others, and dozens of books from her library: some that he gave her as presents but many books that she bought for herself, or owned in her previous marriages. The last addition to her library was just days before she died: *Selected Poems of Vasco Popa*. Hughes wrote the introduction to the book but, since there was no presentation inscription, only Assia's signature with the date, one can assume that she bought the book herself.

He loaded it all in his car and stopped at Ashton's Funeral Directors to pick up the two urns. For some reason, he did not have them buried in Lambeth Cemetery but took them with him to Devon. He had not decided what to do with them: a furtive burial or scattering the ashes. For the time being, he kept the urns in his bedroom at Court Green and, when he later moved to Yorkshire, he took them with him. In a statement he later made to the US Immigration Department he summed up the years after Plath's suicide, as 'a permanent emergency at sea in a slowly sinking ship'.

All through the funeral, Fay Weldon kept rehashing her last conversation with Assia, just a few months earlier. Assia had asked Fay if she would take Shura, should something happen to her. 'I thought she was afraid of some kind of terminal illness, and said, "Of course I would". I loved Shura, she was a delightful child, and I could easily have brought her up with my own three children. Killing your own child is inconceivable, but when I came home, my Irish cleaning lady said, "Of course, if you decide to go you must take your child with you." '

On 5 February 1963, just six days before her suicide, Plath had written the following disturbing lines in 'Edge'. The protagonist has taken her children and 'folded/Them back into her body . . .' Professor Richard Larschan thinks, 'Medea-like, Plath seriously contemplated destroying the life of her children.' Plath is generally perceived as a responsible adult and a loving mother, who before turning on the gas taps, took care to protect her children. 'In my mother's view,' writes Professor Anita Helle, Sylvia Plath's second cousin, 'the unpardonable crime Plath had committed in taking her life, was the *refusal to mother*, to uphold the maternal tradition, its sanctity and its essential righteousness. "What a selfish thing to do, leaving two children." '

Researchers Brian Barraclough and E Clare Harris found an average of sixty murder-suicide incidents in England and Wales each year between 1988 and 1992, a large proportion of which involved a mother who killed her child and herself. Often it was a disturbed form of love, and these mothers were found to have been extremely caring parents up to the killing. Dr Philip Resnick, a renowned American forensic psychiatrist and leading expert on filicide, defined five types of filicide: altruistic, acute psychotic, killing an unwanted or illegitimate child, death as a result of a fatal maltreatment and, the rarest of all, killing children out of revenge, most often for infidelity, in order to make the other parent suffer. The most common motive – 56 per cent – was 'altruistic'. 'Women have a much higher incidence of altruistic killing, because they view themselves as more inseparable from the child than the father. Through the depressed woman's skewed vision, the world can look utterly treacherous, and to take the child with them is to do the child a favour,' explains Dr Resnick, whose groundbreaking research on the subject was published in the year of Assia's death. 'The mother knows the nature and quality of her act, and that killing is legally wrong; however, the mother often believes she's doing what is morally right for her child.' These mothers see their children as an extension of themselves, do not want to leave them motherless in a cruel world and believe that the child will be better off in heaven with them. The mother sees 'a hell on earth. It's so miserable that she can no longer stand to live,' believes Dr Resnick. 'To leave that child in that world . . . and motherless, on top of it, will be more terrible than to murder.'

Shura was at the core of her mother's existence but almost non-existent in her father's life. In letters to family and friends, Hughes proudly detailed every accomplishment and witticism of Frieda and Nick but nothing of Shura. Only once in his extensive correspondence with his brother Gerald did he mention Shura, and even that was in passing, describing how much he needed a nanny for his children, like the one Assia has for 'her little girl'. 'Her', not 'our'. When describing their life in Ireland, Ted even bothered to mention the maid, Teresa, but no word about Shura. In the few posthumous poems that he wrote about Assia and mentioned Shura, he referred to her as Assia's daughter only; never once 'mine', or 'ours', or by her name. 'Her only daughter's/ Otherwise non-existent smile' ('Chlorophyl'). 'As your own hands, stronger than your choked outcry,/Took your daughter from you' ('Descent').

Fay Weldon recalls a visit with her husband to Assia's flat on Clapham Common; Ted gave Shura wine to drink and she danced and danced until she dropped into sleep. 'It was very sadistic on his part, and I'm sure he would not have dared to do the same to Frieda. But after all, Shura was the illegitimate child, the daughter of the mistress,' Weldon says. Assia complained to Martin Graham how upset she was that Ted was only interested in Plath's children and not in Shura. The burden of caring for the little girl, emotionally, physically and financially, always rested on her alone. She was quite certain that with her gone, Shura would be a second-class child in the Hughes's household. A few weeks after the suicide, Al Alvarez jotted down in his diary a conversation he had with Olwyn Hughes, who said, 'she [Assia] could hardly leave Ted with yet another motherless child.' Assia's murderous act was the outcome of distorted over-responsibility, a manifestation of altruistic filicide. At the decisive moment, she declined to send Shura overseas to an aunt who had never seen her and was weighed down with her own three children. She also feared that Shura was too old to be adopted and did not wish her to grow up alone as a foster child, an orphan. In her letter of condolence, Patricia Mendelson wrote to Assia's sister, 'Thank God Assia took her with her. Shura loved her Mummy so much and already suffered so much by the instability of

Ted's relationship. She would be heartbroken each time he went away again. Assia's loss would have dealt her a blow she could never have recovered from.'

Al Alvarez believes that, from the outset, Assia wanted Ted because he was Sylvia's husband; Sylvia was a woman to be reckoned with and Assia's 'only way of outdoing her dead rival was in the manner of her death'. 'Outdo', in Alvarez's perception, meant not just to kill herself in the same way as Plath but to kill her child as well, and create not just one tragedy, but a double one. Indeed, there are cases of copycat suicides – an imitation of the suicide of family members, peers, friends or cultural icons such as film stars – but many experts believe they are rare. A study in the *American Journal of Epidemiology* (15 June 2001) revealed that people were less prone to suicide if they had known someone who had killed himself. The head researcher, Dr James Mercy, argued that exposure to suicide is actually a deterrent.

Police records show that, in 1969, nearly two thousand women killed themselves in the UK, the largest group comprising the single, separated, divorced and widowed. The modal age was 42 years old: on all counts, Assia fell into the typical category. In 1963, when Plath killed herself, domestic gas was the main method of women's suicide in England. It began to change due to the detoxification of domestic gas and, by the late 1960s, barbiturate poisoning became the prevailing method. Assia started her quest of dying not with gas, but with the exploration of other options, such as pills and bullets. At the moment of her plunge into death, she intoxicated herself with large quantities of whisky, a drink she was not accustomed to, and an overdose of barbiturates. She switched on the gas, wishing to end Shura's life painlessly and decisively. 'Execute yourself and your little self efficiently,' she had written in her diary three days before the final deed.

In the weeks that followed, Hughes was in a daze. He kept asking himself how did he not perceive the depth of Assia's distress. Scores of times over the years they almost separated, but still he felt that they belonged together completely. 'Assia was my true wife and the best friend I ever had,' he wrote to Celia Chaikin. Meeting jeweller Pat Torney, he was enchanted by a ring that she had just made; if he had seen it a few weeks earlier, he would have bought it for Assia, 'because it is more like her than anything I ever bought her.' Now he felt that he must bury it with her ashes.

He told Aurelia Plath that he and Assia tried to atone for Sylvia's death but living in her house drew him and Assia 'into the utmost nightmare'. He was certain that Sylvia's suicide brought out all the demons inside him and had a destructive effect on others as well. He asked Aurelia to keep Assia and Shura's deaths a secret for a while, until he could find the right time to tell Frieda and Nicholas. He also kept it from his parents, fearing that his mother was too ill to withstand the shock.

With two suicides on his back, Hughes felt as though he was cursed. There was something in him, which was fatal for every woman who got involved with him. He infected them with his black moods, but they did not have the immunity that he had, and could not cope. 'I think this was very true of Assia', he wrote to his brother Gerald. In a letter to his close friend Lucas Myers, Hughes took full responsibility for the deaths of his two loved ones, confessing that with Sylvia, it was his 'insane decisions', while in Assia's case, it was his 'insane indecisions'. He was certain that on that doomed Sunday it was in his power to stop Assia from killing herself, had he 'only given her hope in slightly more emphastic words', as he wrote to her sister Celia. He and Assia had experienced similar clashes before, and always one of them sobered up before more damage was done, but their last conversation got out of control. He believed that if Assia had stuck to her plan to go to her friends in Dorset, she would not only have saved herself, but would have dragged him out of his exhaustion and passivity. But she was swept by one of her dark moods and was unstoppable. When interviewed in London in October 1996, Hughes compared the two tragedies in his life. 'My first wife's death was complicated and inevitable, she had been on that track most of her life. But Assia's was avoidable'.

His first impulse was to escape from the scene of his miseries and, once again, Ireland seemed an island of refuge. He went over to check the Newtown Quaker School in Waterford for his children, and then headed northwest to his friend Barrie Cooke, now living in Thomastown, County Kilkenny. Cooke was rushing around in his studio, packing the eight huge, heavy murals he had been painting for the past eighteen months, when suddenly, Ted appeared in the doorway. They did not exchange a word, and for the next two hours both men were sweating together, loading the panels on the lorry. When it drove away to Trinity College, Dublin, Cooke took out a bottle of whiskey and filled two glasses. 'I knew Ted as a man always in control, but now he looked choked, on the verge of tears. He said, "There's been a disaster, Assia killed herself." There was a long silence. Only later did he mention Shura. I have never seen him so shattered before or since.' Hughes stayed the night but was too numb to speak. He was envious of the simplicity and harmony that he saw in his friend's life, the way Cooke combined work and conjugality and seemed to find time for everything.

Hughes then drove to the town of Cashel, in Tipperary, and went to the Cashel Palace, built in 1730 and home to archbishops, earls and lords. This Palladian mansion had recently been converted into a luxurious hotel. He went two floors down to the sumptuous restaurant but found the meal distasteful. He crossed the corridor and stepped into the Derby Kitchen Bar, and ordered half a glass of brandy. From the windows he could see the illuminated Rock of Cashel, the cornerstone of Christianity in Ireland. It was the first day in many years that he was on his own. He took out his spiral notebook, which he had started in March 1968; it contained drafts of poems, alongside his monthly expenses, written in red ink: postage, phone calls, taxis, hotels, restaurants, cinemas and also a loan of £42 that he gave Assia.

On page 16 he wrote: 'Effect of A's [illegible word] – <u>Disastrous, yes,</u>' underlining the last words. He felt the pain spreading inside and overpowering him. Awake and asleep, he was seeing Assia's and Shura's faces everywhere. A few pages further, in an untitled poem, he lamented his women, 'with his long face/On their dead souls'. In another poem, on a loose blue sheet of paper, probably from the same period, he tormented himself why was he so destructive towards his nearest and dearest, 'who were my life'? He never published the poems. Was it because they contrasted the account that he wished to leave for posterity? In 1990 he published the twenty *Capriccio* poems, revolving around Assia. There is no mention of his own destructive forces and Assia is blamed for consciously burning herself on Sylvia's funeral pyre.

Meanwhile in Yorkshire, Edith Hughes appeared to be getting on well since the operation on her knee: her leg healed and she was due to leave hospital. It was nearly two months since she last saw her son, because following Assia and Shura's deaths, he had avoided his parents and did not visit, phone or write. When his father asked Olwyn what was going on with Ted, she told him of the tragedy but made him vow that he would keep it a secret. But Mr Hughes could not keep silent and broke the news to his wife. Edith was stricken with thrombosis and lapsed into a coma that lasted three days. She died on 13 May and was buried not far from Sylvia Plath. On the day of the funeral, Hughes finally made up his mind to buy Lumb Bank. Already in 1963, he had planned to buy the house and move there with Assia, 'the sort of place she would have made beautiful'.

Returning from his daughter and granddaughter's funeral, Dr Gutmann's blood pressure had soared up, and he too was stricken with thrombosis. He was hospitalised, to be operated on for the blockage of the veins in his legs, but his only kidney was severely damaged in the operation. He died in Montreal on 29 July. 'With all the medical terms they give it, I call it a broken heart,' Celia wrote to Assia's friend Patricia. Hughes shared the same sentiment and in his condolences to Celia, he admitted that it was Assia's suicide that gave the 'final blow' to both Dr Gutmann and his mother.

His wife's and mistress's suicides were 'giant steel doors shutting down over great parts' of himself, he wrote to Lucas Myers in 1984. At that time, while fencing away biographers and journalists who hounded him for details of his life, Hughes began to compose a new verse-version for posterity. He started with *Capriccio* and then *Birthday Letters*. In those later writings, he disassociated himself from the two suicides and used the same reasons for both women's decision to end their lives: a troubled background, a death wish and emotional instability. He linked the two suicides together, making each woman the cause of her rival's death. Poetically, he described Assia's suicide as a *fait accompli* from the outset; she was doomed already when they met. He argued that although Assia fled Nazi Germany, she could not escape the fate of her fellow Jews, and doomed herself to a terrible and untimely death: 'a long-cold oven/Locked with a swastika'. She was constantly challenging death, and her obsession with Sylvia, he argued in his poetry, and the guilt she felt after her rival's death, dealt the final blow: 'Why did you kneel down at the grave's edge/To be identified/Accused and convicted?'

Indeed, Assia lived in Plath's houses, slept in her beds, used her linen and cutlery, but she saw these places as Ted's homes, and used the household objects for practical reasons and not out of any obsession with her rival. She bowed to Plath's great talent, but knew better than to make her a role model by writing poetry, or become a domestic goddess like her. Sylvia was ambitious and fastidious but Assia remained shiftless and blasé, a bon vivant, and a rather sloppy housewife. For a life with Ted, she was willing to endure anything: gossip and accusations, Plath's radiant presence in Ted's life, and his absorption with her literary estate. But his wife's suicide while he was having an affair was an obstacle too large for

Hughes to overcome. In those circumstances, he could never marry the mistress.

'The times were against Assia, as against Sylvia,' Fay Weldon analyses the situation. 'Both talented women died of love, not depression, let alone suicidal tendencies. In those pre-Feminist days, women saw their lives in terms of being loved or not loved by a man. It was terrible to be abandoned, death was better than rejection.'

Twenty-two

Aftermath

In the summer of 1969 Hughes took Frieda and Nicholas with him to Brenda's house in Welcombe. The children enjoyed the company of Harriet and Judith, Brenda's two small daughters, and were thrilled when they took a holiday by the sea and Brenda taught them to surf. Now, with Assia no more at his side, Brenda Hedden climbed up the ladder: in September, all six of them moved to Lumb Bank. It was Hilda Farrar who disclosed the news of a new woman in Ted's life to Aurelia Plath, and added that the northern winter and the necessity of keeping house and taking care of four children was too heavy a burden on Brenda; she herself told Brenda to expect nothing from Ted and that she would do better to return to her husband, 'but some women will do anything to be close to a writer, and especially a poet'.

In no time Hughes understood that the hoped-for peace of mind and safe haven were not to be found in Yorkshire and that it was a mistake to live so close to his family: he felt that he should have followed his instincts and stopped being so considerate of others, at the risk of being labelled an egotist and 'a selfish bastard'. He became restless again and one morning Brenda woke up in an empty bed. There was no letter or note. He came back after several days. 'I've no idea where he was, and didn't want to know.' Hedden suspected that he was having romantic escapades in North Tawton with the twenty-year-old Carol Orchard. 'It happened again, many times. He did it not just to me, but to Assia as well, and to the others.'

One day Ted sat Brenda on his knee and declared that he had one final duty; to scatter Assia and Shura's ashes over a churchyard in Kent. He then asked her if she had happened to see the urns:

I had no idea what he was talking about. Our bedroom was full of his things, and he said that the urns were in a casket by our bed, but now he couldn't find it. I'm sure he did it on purpose, to scare me and leave me vulnerable. He had a way of undermining the women he loved. He could write love letters, and in the same breath, had a way of eroding your self-esteem, your self-assurance, and your confidence in the relationship. At that time, I was already disillusioned about him, in a way that poor Assia never was.

A few days later, Hughes disappeared again and the next that Brenda heard from him was via a postcard from Ashford, Kent: apparently, he had found the missing urns and completed the mission. In her will Assia clearly indicated that she wished to be buried. Did Hughes choose cremation in order to obliterate any trace of his daughter and of Assia? Was he apprehensive of the revealing epitaph, 'Lover of Unreason'? The fact remains that Assia, who was an unwilling wanderer on earth, and throughout her life yearned to strike roots, found no repose even in death.

Once again, the Hughes clan disapproved of Ted's living with a married woman and, after a turbulent Christmas with his relatives in Yorkshire, he took Brenda and the four children back to Devon. Now, he could save himself the journeys and be closer to his other love, Carol Orchard. In February 1970, he signed a contract with Faber and Faber, for the publication of *Crow*. It was a book that Assia was very much involved in writing and he used to send her draft after draft to read and comment on. His poetic attempt to confront death following Plath's suicide came to a halt when his life was plagued by another suicide; he did not write any more Crow poems after Assia's death. Hughes dedicated the book 'In Memory of Assia and Shura', and his initial plan was to have the dedication in Hebrew as well. When published, no public curiosity was aroused as to the identity of the deceased.

Once again, Hughes was vacillating between women, but Celia knew nothing of this. He presented himself as the ever-grieving lover of her dead sister, and told her that the memory of Assia was haunting him: 'the whole of England seems red-hot'. He was relieved when Celia sent back Sylvia's manuscripts, smuggled by Assia three years earlier, when she sought to finance Shura's future. When the time came to give Celia the proceedings of Assia's estate, he informed her that at Assia's death he had sublet the flat to a group of students, who painted the walls black and purple and ruined the flat. When he gave it back to Freshwater Flats, he had to pay £350 for redecorating, and subtracted it from the £2,156 of Assia's estate.

Court Green kept haunting Hughes and he and Brenda tried to get away from it, but their house-hunting was futile and they stayed on. In July, they entertained Seamus and Marie Heaney, who came for a weekend. 'Heaney was so impressed by our conjugality, that he wrote a poem, celebrating our harmonious relationship,' Brenda Hedden recalls. With Frieda and Nicky in the United States, Ted and Brenda planned to go to Ireland, to check the possibility of settling there, but in mid August, just after they celebrated Ted's fortieth birthday, he disappeared again. Brenda Hedden: 'A few days later, I received a postcard from London. Ted wrote that something terrible had happened, and that he needed my help. He arrived the following day. We were very passionate with each other, and after we made love, he told me that he had married Carol. He sent her to her family and spent his honeymoon with me.' In spite of his marriage, Ted and Brenda did not cancel their trip to Ireland but instead of house-hunting, they went camping in the mountains. Aurelia Plath learned of the marriage two months after the event and, even then, not from Ted but from the ever-faithful aunt Hilda. It took Hughes six months to tell even his close friend, Lucas Myers.

He continued to shuttle between the two women until Brenda broke off with him a few months later. She moved to Brighton and resumed her career as a social worker:

He was a real hunter. The moment I drew away from him and became independent, I was more attractive in his eyes, and he chased me and pleaded that I would come back. It was the same with Assia: when she tried to break away and was out of his reach, he became motivated. But when they were together, he did terrible things. I feared I would end up like her, and resisted his temptations. Her terrible suicide saved my life.

To a later lover, Emma Tennant, Hughes described the mating habits of the greylag goose, which remains faithful to its first mate: 'I may after all be a greylag goose,' he said.

For several years, Ted and Assia had been thinking of visiting Israel; 'I could have gone there, happily,' he wrote to Celia. In February 1971, he finally travelled to Israel as a guest of the British Council along with Peter Porter, Dannie Abse, D J Enright and Jeremy Robson. Before boarding the plane, Hughes had to spend several loud minutes persuading the police that the five-inch tiger's tooth he carried in his pocket was indeed a tiger's tooth, a present for his friend Yehuda Amichai. He was the only one who brought his wife along and they behaved as a honeymooning couple. In the basilica of Nazareth, a priest, noticing that Ted had put an arm round Carole's waist, reprimanded him: 'This is no no place for love!'

The group appeared throughout Israel, in *Poets Reading Their Work*. The playbill included the text of 'A Childish Prank' from *Crow*, which opens with 'Man's and woman's bodies lay without souls.' On stage, he read 'Full Moon and Little Frieda', and 'The Thought Fox'. Once again, he and Assia shared the same platform, since Yehuda Amichai was reading Assia's translation of two of his poems: 'God Has Pity on Kindergarten Children', ('But perhaps/He will have pity on those who love truly/And take care of them'). The second poem began with 'The end was quick and bitter'. One can only guess what was going inside Ted's head two years after the quick and bitter end and the death of the kindergarten child Shura.

On one of their free evenings, Peter Porter suggested that they attend the Israeli Philharmonic performance of Fauré's *Requiem*, while Ted proposed seeing Euripides' *Bacchai* in Hebrew at the Kameri Theatre. 'He had guaranteed that real blood (animal) would grace the staging,' commented Porter. Hughes was elated in Bethlehem and Massada, where he was awed by the collective suicide of almost a thousand Jews, besieged by the Romans. But Jerusalem was the most overwhelming place he had ever seen. He was mesmerised when the tour guide showed them the rock where Abraham went to sacrifice his only son Isaac: it 'must be the most electrical place on earth,' Hughes wrote to Peter Redgrove. He was taken by the Israelis' energy, vitality and cheerfulness, and expressed his wish to live there for a while. His Israeli hosts showed him a number of houses around Jerusalem. One of them in particular enchanted him: an Arab stone house on a mountain, overlooking the Judea Desert. The visit stayed with Hughes and, when interviewed in London in 1996, he spoke enthusiastically about it. Remembering the Dome of the Rock, he said, 'It's the most sacred and important place, where rites were probably performed, a place of shamans, of visionaries. In any culture, mountaintops are very sacred, and a cave on a mountaintop is more sacred than anything.'

Throughout his life, Hughes tried to ward off biographers and journalists from probing into his privacy. But already on 17 February 1963, Al Alvarez had hinted at the circumstances of Plath's death, publishing four poems in the *Observer*. A line in 'Edge' hints that the speaker took her own life – 'Her dead/ Body wears the smile of accomplishment'. Another poem, 'The Fearful', portrays a woman so frantic about her beauty that she abhors motherhood. Reading further into the poem, Plath's close friends remembered how she intercepted Assia's phone call, in which she disguised herself as a man, to Court Green. Plath left the poems in a black spring binder on her desk, and Alvarez collected it in one of his condolence visits to the flat.

Hughes asked his friends to refrain from mentioning him in interviews or in their memoirs. In March 1965, when Richard Murphy sent an elegy that he wrote about Sylvia for his approval, Hughes asked him to delete a reference to the circumstances of her death. His concern was that if the suicide was made public, his children may learn about it from their friends before he told them. But his arm could not cross the Atlantic and, in June 1966, *Time* magazine reviewed *Ariel*, stating that Plath 'was found in a London flat with her head in the oven and the gas jets wide open'. In 1970, Faber and Faber published *The Art of Sylvia Plath* edited by Charles Newman, which included an essay by Lois Ames, Plath's first appointed biographer. In her 'Notes Towards a Biography', Ames did not mention Hughes's adultery and, of course, gave no hint of Assia.

But like a Russian doll, the truth was revealed layer after layer. In his study of suicide, *The Savage God*, Al Alvarez described Plath's new drive to write as 'demonic possession', which could have been the reason why she and Ted 'temporarily parted'. However, he made no mention of the adultery, although he was a close witness to Ted's affair with Assia.

The full facts were whispered in literary circles and, in 1972, the American poet and feminist activist Robin Morgan published a book of poetry named *Monster*. In her poem 'Arraignment', she accused Hughes of the murder of Sylvia Plath. She also referred to the suicide of 'Assia Gutmann Wevill', the woman Hughes never formally married, who took her daughter Shura with her 'rather than letting Hughes raise the child'. The book was published only in the United States and although pirated editions were passed around in Canada, England and Australia, the information did not make any headlines.

In 1973, Yehuda Amichai's book of verse *Songs of Jerusalem and Myself* appeared in English. It included his eulogy of Assia, published in Hebrew two years earlier:

> I can't understand your death in London
> In the mist
> As I can't understand
> My life, here, in the bright light.

It was a lamentation for a dear friend who was untimely and inexplicably plucked away. The Hebrew title was 'The Death of Assia G.' while the English was the more obscure 'The Death of A.G.': Amichai's friendship with Ted Hughes made the change of title hardly coincidental. Over twenty years would pass before the full title was restored.

In 1975, Aurelia Plath published her daughter's *Letters Home*, with Hughes's reluctant consent. Though heavily edited, the letters made it clear that the separation was far from temporary and that Sylvia was seeking divorce on grounds of adultery. Plath did not call Assia by name, and referred to her as 'Ted's girl friend', or 'Ted's girl'. A year later, Professor Judith Kroll named Plath's rival, in her book *Chapters in a Mythology*. No biographical information was given and Kroll preferred to use Assia's maiden name, Gutmann, maybe out of consideration for the privacy of David Wevill, her colleague at the University of Texas in Austin. In May 1976, Elizabeth Compton published her memoir of Sylvia in the *New Review* monthly, published in London. She named Assia as the wife of a Canadian poet David Wevill and gave some biographical details, including her death with Shura. The information went unnoticed and when that year Edward Butscher published this same memoir in his *Sylvia Plath – Method and Madness,* it was censored. Assia was disguised as Olga – no surname, hinting at her Russian origins. Butscher gave an abundance of details – not always accurate – disclosing that she killed herself with her child, but did not say that she was Hughes's daughter. A year later, in a collection of essays and memoirs about Plath, *The Woman and the Work,* Butscher was still using 'Olga' and, only in 1979, in the British edition of the book, was Olga changed to Assia, but the surname was still withheld.

In 1984, Assia's friend Eda Zoritte-Megged published a detailed memoir in *Mosnayim,* the periodical of the Israeli Writers' Association. The revelations of

Hughes's neglect of Assia, his apathy towards Shura and the details of the suicide and funeral did not get much publicity, since it appeared only in Hebrew. In January 1987, Ted Hughes flew to the USA to attend a trial for libel in Court 11 at the Federal District Courthouse in Boston, brought by Dr Jane Anderson, an old friend of Sylvia Plath's, who accused him and a Hollywood film company of defaming her in the movie *The Bell Jar*, based on Plath's novel by that name. 'No one for instance – outside the immediate circle – knew who the other woman was,' wrote journalist Iain Walker in an Australian newspaper, *The Advertiser*. 'Today her identity can be disclosed. Her name was Assia Wevill. Hughes was asked about her at the Boston courtroom. He looked stunned and stared at the marble floor. "No comment," he said.' Walker interviewed friends of Assia and Sylvia and, in St Catherine's House in London, in the registry of births and deaths, found Shura's birth certificate, with Hughes's name recorded as the father. Walker brought it all out – the full name of the mistress, Ted's fatherhood and the horrible death. Later that year, Linda Wagner-Martin mentioned Assia Wevill in her *Sylvia Plath: A Biography*. In 1989 some more biographical information was published in Anne Stevenson's *Bitter Fame*, though nothing was said about Assia's suicide. It was Ronald Hayman, in *The Death and Life of Sylvia Plath* and Paul Alexander in *Rough Magic* who, in 1991, elaborated on Assia's suicide and on the fact that she had a daughter by Hughes, who died with her.

Hughes kept disregarding the publications about his relationship with Assia and was writing her out of his life story. In the few instances where he agreed to give some biographical details about himself, Assia was not mentioned. On 28 July 1989, in a letter to Leonard Scigaj, who was compiling a biographical essay, Hughes wrote that after Sylvia died, he lived for a while in her flat with their children, assisted only by his aunt. He was looking for a permanent feminine figure, but 'The right woman failed to materialise'. He then moved to Devon and his sister helped him look after the children. He tried to settle down in Ireland but had to return to Court Green and there he only had a local woman to help with with the daily chores. To Janet Malcolm, the author of *The Silent Woman*, Hughes wrote in 1992 that apart from the two years in which Olwyn lived with him and the children, he was constantly seeking a new home and 'a woman to replace their mother'. Assia was not mentioned, as the woman who was with him all that while in London, Ireland and Devon, and who mothered his children after their mother's death.

But throughout those years, Hughes was deeply occupied with Assia's life and death. Already in 1986, he was working with painter Leonard Baskin on *Capriccio*, which was published in 1990 in a limited edition of fifty extremely expensive copies. The cycle of twenty poems and paintings presents chunks of Assia's life and unmistakable details about her: Germany, Israel, Russia, British Columbia; 'After forty I'll end it', 'baby daughter', 'German au pair', 'Six full calendar years', 'Her grave'. Assia's features – her straight dark hair and green eyes – inspired some of Baskin's paintings. In his poetic version of the events, Hughes scattered all the clues for anyone to find, getting as close to the fire as playing on her name: 'he wanted the seven treasures of Asia.' Five years later Hughes published the more accessible edition of *New Selected Poems, 1957–1994*, with eight of the Assia poems from *Capriccio* and eight poems about Sylvia, which later appeared in *Birthday Letters*. He was relieved that readers and reviewers overlooked all sixteen autobiographical poems. 'I feel that my poems are obscure, I give the secret away without giving it. People are so dumb they do not know I've given the secret away,' he told Eilat Negev.

Hughes agreed to be interviewed then, because a bilingual edition of *The Thought Fox* had just been published in Israel and he was due to take part in an International Poets Festival in Jerusalem, scheduled for spring 1997. He hardly ever gave interviews, and avoided talking about his personal tragedies, but this time he did; maybe because the journalist came from Assia's country, maybe because he thought that an interview in Hebrew would remain obscure and be no risk to his privacy. He may also have wished to send up a trial-balloon: in those very days, he was going through his private archives, preparing them for shipment to Emory University in Atlanta, Georgia, and was completing *Birthday Letters*. He must have known that eventually the press would have a field day and may have wished to test the waters. 'I wrote many poems in which I referred to Sylvia, but there are many that I won't publish. I must think of my wife Carol, and how it would affect her,' he said. 'If I write love poems to my former love, showing how close we were, it's a kind of adultery. Sylvia has lived for two years in our Devon house, and Carol has been living in it for 25 years. I don't want her to feel as if she's living in a mausoleum, haunted by the spirit of her predecessor, like *Rebecca*.'

Hughes confirmed that he also wrote many poems about Assia but said that he was not sure that he 'wrote the ones [he] should have written'. When tragedy strikes, he said, people struggle with it and incorporate it into their lives.

But being a writer, these things are chewed all the time, because you write about them and they disturb you, and they keep appearing and disappearing. They keep hanging on your neck and you deal with the emotions again and again, as if it's a broken record, stuck in the same monumental groove. And instead of letting go of the past and living for the future, you find your past in front of you. A monument, sitting on your head.

When *Birthday Letters* was published in January 1998, Hughes had already been diagnosed with cancer. The book became an unprecedented poetry bestseller, all the attention naturally revolving around his relationship with Sylvia Plath. On 28 October 1998, Hughes died in London Bridge Hospital, a private clinic close to Guy's Hospital, where Assia and Shura's bodies were autopsied. He had requested cremation and his ashes were scattered over a forest in Dartmoor.

At his death Assia resurfaced, with Shura, regaining their rightful place beside him.

Notes

Frequently mentioned names, books and archive collections are abbreviated as follows: AP: Aurelia Plath; AW: Assia Wevill; CC: Celia Chaikin; DW: David Wevill; GH: Gerald Hughes; LM: Lucas Myers; RL: Richard Lipsey; SP: Sylvia Plath; TH: Ted Hughes. Emory: Ted Hughes Papers, Manuscript, Archives and Rare Book Library, Emory University, Atlanta, Georgia. Lilly: Sylvia Plath Collection, the Lilly Library, Indiana University, Bloomington, Indiana. Smith: Sylvia Plath Collection, Mortimer Rare Book Room, Smith College, Northampton, Massachusetts. The Tarn Papers: archive of Nathaniel Tarn, Department of Special Collections, Stanford University Libraries, Stanford, California. Yale: Yehuda Amichai Archives, Beinecke Rare Book and Manuscript Library, Yale University, New Haven, Connecticut.

Prologue

'Assia was reciting': TH–CC, in a letter, 14 April 1969. Emory.

Else had asked permission: statement of Else Ludwig to Det. Sgt J Loakman, Clapham Police Station, 23 March 1969.

Seven times: LM, *Crow Steered, Bergs Appeared*, Sewanee, USA, Proctor's Hall Press, 2001, p. 133.

One: Childhood

Information about the Gutmann and the Gaedeke families: interview with CC in Canada, May–June 2002, and subsequent emails, letters and telephone calls, July 2002–April 2006.

Documents and family photos, courtesy of Celia and Arnold Chaikin.

General background about Jewish life in Kagarlyk, Lutsk, Riga, Berlin, and life

under the Nazis: Beth Hatefutsoth, Museum of the Jewish Diaspora, Tel Aviv;
Yad Vashem, Holocaust Museum and Archives, Jerusalem.

physician to the Bolshoi Ballet': LM, *Crow Steered, Bergs Appeared*, p. 127.

'Her father/Doctor to the Bolshoi Ballet': TH, 'Dreamers' in *Birthday Letters,
Collected Poems*, Faber and Faber, 2003, p. 1145.

Lucas Myers recounts her stories: LM, email exchange, November
2001–December 2003.

displaced persons' camps: Philip Hobsbaum, email exchange, October 2001–May
2003.

'death-camp', 'ex-Nazi Youth Sabra', 'Hitler's mutilations': TH, 'Dreamers', in
Birthday Letters, Collected Poems, p. 1145.

'swastika': TH, 'The Locket', in *Capriccio, Collected Poems*, p. 784.

'hanged women choke': TH, 'Dreamers', in *Birthday Letters, Collected Poems*, p.
1145.

Two: A New Life
Information about the Gutmanns in Tel Aviv: interview with CC in Canada,
May–June 2002, and subsequent emails, letters and telephone calls, July
2002–April 2006.

Documents and family photos, courtesy of Celia and Arnold Chaikin.

General background about the German Jews' emigration to Palestine is based
on Tel Aviv Municipality archives; Gelber, Yoav, *A New Homeland – The
Immigration from Central Europe and its Absorption in Eretz Israel 1933–1948*,
Jerusalem Leo Baeck Institute and Yad Izhak Ben-Zvi, 1990 (in Hebrew);
Niederlander, Doron, 'The Influence of Immigrant Physicians from Germany
on the Development of Medicine in Palestine, 1933–1948', Jerusalem,
Hebrew University, 1982 (MA thesis, in Hebrew); Segev, Tom, *The Seventh
Million*, New York, Henry Holt, 2000.

'her parents made her go to the butcher's': RL, interview in Canada, June 2002,
and email exchange, July 2002–June 2003.

'last night, in the half dark': AW diary, 19 May 1963, in private hands.

Three: A Tabeetha Girl
Information about the Gutmanns in Tel Aviv: interview with CC in Canada,

May–June 2002, and subsequent emails, letters and telephone calls, July 2002–April 2006.

Documents and family photos, courtesy of Celia and Arnold Chaikin.

General background about Palestine during the Second World War, is based on the following sources: *The Hagana Book*, Maarachot, 1955–1972 (in Hebrew); Reich, Daniella, 'National Mission and Social Ostracism': the Liaisons between Jewish Women and British Servicemen, 1940–1948', Haifa University, 2003 (MA thesis in Hebrew); Segev, Tom, *The Seventh Million*, New York, Henry Holt, 2000; Tel Aviv Municipality archives.

'Me, half-German?': AW, postcard to Yehuda Amicai, August 1968, Yale.

Jane Walker-Arnott, who had left Glasgow: Isobel, Goodwin, *May You Live to Be 120! The Story of Tabeetha School, Jaffa, 1863–1983*. Saint Andrew Press, 2000, p. 18.

A column of smart chauffeured cars: Wedad and Leila Andreas, interview in Israel, November 2001.

Assia gave the credit: RL, interview in Canada, June 2002, and email exchange, July 2002–June 2003.

a stunning girl: Mira Hamermesh, interview in London, October 2001.

The son of a banker: John H Steele, letter exchange, July 2002–January 2004.

Four: A Teenager in Love

General information about British soldiers in Palestine: Hospitality Committee, 1940–7, Tel Aviv Municipality Archives; Hebrew newspapers in the 1940s: *Ha-aretz, Davar, Hazman, Iton Meyuhad, Laisha*; Reich, Daniella, 'National Mission and Social Ostracism: the Liaisons between Jewish Women and British Servicemen, 1940–1948', Haifa University, 2003 (MA thesis, in Hebrew); 'Sleeping with the Enemy'. BBC Radio 4, produced by Linda Pressly and Tanya Datta, July 2003.

The two airmen were a little nervous: Keith Gems, interview in London, December 2003, and letter exchange, August 2002–February 2004.

'Assia was but sixteen': John Steele's diary, April 1943, courtesy of John Steele.

Girls made Steele feel awkward: John Steele, letter exchange, July 2002–January 2004.

'May I kiss you': John Steele's diary.

'perfect gentlemen': Hannah Weinberg-Shalitt, interview in Israel, January 1999.

'I have imagined the worst': AW–Keith Gems, a letter, 18 November 1943, in private hands.

English culture: AW–Keith Gems, a letter, 30 January 1944, in private hands.

'a very conservative society': Hannah Weinberg-Shalitt, interview in Israel, January 1999.

Among Tabeetha graduates: Wedad and Leila Andreas, interview in Israel, November 2001.

'snuggles on benches': John Steele, letter exchange, July 2002–January 2004.

'at that moment I became something of a Zionist': John Steele, letter exchange, July 2002–January 2004.

he'd vowed to break it all: John Steele, letter exchange, July 2002–January 2004.

Assia took the courses in small arms: CC, interview in Canada, May–June 2002, and subsequent emails, letters and telephone calls, July 2002–April 2006.

'We feel like frightened heroes': AW–Keith Gems, a letter, 25 April 1946, in private hands.

'sheer suicide': AW–Keith Gems, a letter, 21 May 1946, in private hands.

On Monday, 22 July 1946: CC, interview in Canada, May–June 2002, and subsequent emails, letters and telephone calls, July 2002–April 2006.

Five: First Marriage

'She was like a goddess': Mira Hamermesh, interview in London, October 2001.

grumbled to Celia: CC, interview in Canada, May–June 2002, and subsequent emails, letters and telephone calls, July 2002–April 2006.

Steele was living at his parents' home: John Steele, letter exchange, July 2002–January 2004.

'In a family ruled by iron discipline': Keith Gems, interview in London, December 2003, and letter exchange, August 2002–February 2004.

'I saw myself losing all my money over an abortion': John Steele–Keith Gems, a letter, 19 January 1947, in private hands.

an art student: General Register Office, St Catherine's House, London.

the bride wore a severe black suit: John Steele, letter exchange, July 2002–January 2004.

'if this is paradise': AW–Keith Gems, a postcard, 29 May 1947, in private hands.

letting her room to a nurse: CC, interview in Canada, May–June 2002, and subsequent emails, letters and telephone calls, July 2002–April 2006.

'Assia was being difficult': John Steele, letter exchange, July 2002–January 2004.

'cold, unkind, and repulsive': Pam Gems, interview in London, December 2003, and letter exchange, August 2002–February 2004.

she swallowed fifty aspirins: Pam Gems, interview in London, December 2003, and letter exchange, August 2002–February 2004.

a hat-check girl in The Cave nightclub: John Steele, letter exchange, July 2002–January 2004.

his trunks full of typical African souvenirs: CC, interview in Canada, May–June 2002, and subsequent emails, letters and telephone calls, July 2002–April 2006.

'found some consolation': John Steele, letter exchange, July 2002–January 2004.

forcing her to marry: Edward Lucie-Smith, interview in London, October 2001, and email exchange, December 2002–August 2003.

His clinic was empty: CC, interview in Canada, May–June 2002, and subsequent emails, letters and telephone calls, July 2002–April 2006.

Assia was not academically inclined: John Bosher, telephone interview and email exchange, July–August 2002.

Assia was registered: University of British Columbia Yearbook, 1952.

It infuriated the Steele family: John Steele, letter exchange, July 2002–January 2004.

'She made an immediate impression': John Bosher, telephone interview and email exchange, July–August 2002.

'a passionate affair': RL, interview in Canada, June 2002, and email exchange, July 2002–June 2003.

Joan Fontaine's dresses: CC, interview in Canada, May–June 2002, and subsequent emails, letters and telephone calls, July 2002–April 2006.

'*Our eyes met, we smiled*': John Steele, letter exchange, July 2002–January 2004.

'*the cannery, with its erotic motif*': TH, 'Descent', in *Capriccio, Collected Poems*, p. 787.

'*I was only a boy*': John Bosher, telephone interview and email exchange, July–August 2002.

Her parents knew nothing of this: CC, interview in Canada, May–June 2002, and subsequent emails, letters and telephone calls, July 2002–April 2006.

'*Lilith of abortions*': TH, 'Dreamers', in *Birthday Letters, Collected Poems*, p. 1145.

'*He needed women*': Esther Bull Birney, telephone interview, December 2001, and letter January 2002.

'*He just wanted a fling*': Edward Lucie-Smith, interview in London, October 2001, and email exchange, December 2001–August 2003.

Six: A Second Husband

'*I often regret*': Professor Richard Lipsey, 'An Intellectual Autobiography', in *Macroeconomic Theory and Policy – the Selected Essays of Richard G Lipsey*.

One night in August: RL, interview in Canada, June 2002, and email exchange, July 2002–June 2003.

'*Assia's mother took care*': Thirell (Lipsey) Weiss, email exchange, August–December 2002.

'*To be with Assia*': Pam Gems, interview in London, December 2003, and letter exchange, August 2002–February 2004.

irritated by her concept of sharing: Jo (Reed) Price, email exchange, September–October 2002.

wheedle cigarettes: Thirell (Lipsey) Weiss, email exchange, August–December 2002.

'*rather slothful*': Ken Reed, letter to the authors, 24 November 2002.

go skiing: RL, interview in Canada, June 2002, and email exchange, July 2002–June 2003.

Lisa had severed her connections with her sister: CC, interview in Canada, May–June 2002, and subsequent emails, letters and telephone calls, July 2002–April 2006.

She and Dick travelled to Dachau: RL, interview in Canada, June 2002, and email exchange, July 2002–June 2003.

'*My diet this week*': AW–CC, a letter, 24 August 1955, in private hands.

'quietly in love with Assia': RL, interview in Canada, June 2002, and email exchange, July 2002–June 2003.

shopping sprees: Pam Gems, interview in London, December 2003, and letter exchange, August 2002–February 2004.

'absolutely exquisite': AW–CC, a letter, 24 August 1955, in private hands.

she tried to kill herself twice: RL, interview in Canada, June 2002, and email exchange, July 2002–June 2003.

Assia flew to Berlin: Pam Gems, interview in London, December 2003, and letter exchange, August 2002–February 2004.

'the English are inequipped': AW–CC, a letter, 24 August 1955, in private hands.

the very idea repulsed her: Pam Gems, interview in London, December 2003, and letter exchange, August 2002–February 2004.

Seven: Falling in Love

'some other middle-aged persons': RL, interview in Canada, June 2002, and email exchange, July 2002–June 2003.

'the young Gary Coooper': William Trevor, *Excursions in the Real World*, Hutchinson, 1993, p. 115.

sitting by the purser's office: DW, interview in Texas, November 2003, and email exchange, September 2002–December 2005.

'a certain restlessness': Peter Orr, ed. *The Poet Speaks*, Routledge & Kegan Paul, 1966, p. 272.

'Apples and Apples': DW, *Solo with Grazing Deer*, Toronto, Exile Editions, 2001, p. 62.

'It was more two lives than two ages': DW, interview in Texas, November 2003, and email exchange, September 2002–December 2005.

his wife's feelings: RL, interview in Canada, June 2002, and email exchange, July 2002–June 2003.

Pushkin's poems: Assia's copy of *The Poems, Prose and Plays of Alexander Pushkin* is in TH's library, Emory.

Just before Christmas, she informed Dick: RL, interview in Canada, June 2002, and email exchange, July 2002–June 2003.

taking David to her favourite jazz clubs: DW, interview in Texas, November 2003, and email exchange, September 2002–December 2005.

'uncomfortable tolerance of each other': Peter Porter, 'Ted Hughes and Sylvia

Plath: a Bystander's Recollections', *Australian Book Review*, August 2001, p. 23.

'I don't think she ever grew up fully': RL, interview in Canada, June 2002, and email exchange, July 2002–June 2003.

'Dick has a masochistic streak': Keith Gems, interview in London, December 2003, and letter exchange, August 2002–February 2004.

virtually separated: DW, interview in Texas, November 2003, and email exchange, September 2002–December 2005.

Assia teased Dick: RL, interview in Canada, June 2002, and email exchange, July 2002–June 2003.

they drew a fair amount together: DW, interview in Texas, November 2003, and email exchange, September 2002–December 2005.

only four have survived: Assia's paintings are all in private collections.

They wrote poems to each other: DW, interview in Texas, November 2003, and email exchange, September 2002–December 2005.

A Blot in the 'Scutcheon: the book is in TH's library, Emory.

'Those years, when Assia and I': DW, interview in Texas, November 2003, and email exchange, September 2002–December 2005.

'The thing that bound us together': Philip Hobsbaum, email exchange, October 2001–May 2003.

'a complete democracy': Edward Lucie-Smith, *The Burnt Child: An Autobiography*, Victor Gollancz, 1975, p. 165.

the slim, fair David: Philip Hobsbaum, email exchange, October 2001–May 2003.

'severely puritan teetotallers': Edward Lucie-Smith, *The Burnt Child*, p. 172.

'Poets came with manuscripts': Bruce Bennett, *Spirit in Exile: Peter Porter and his Poetry*, Melbourne, Oxford University Press, 1991.

'Ted once scandalised': Philip Hobsbaum, email exchange, October 2001–May 2003.

'some writers, when it came to the point': Edward Lucie-Smith, *A Group Anthology*, Oxford University Press, 1963, p. vii.

Hughes handed Hobsbaum: Philip Hobsbaum, email exchange, October 2001–May 2003.

'she could not accept criticism': Edward Lucie-Smith, interview in London, October 2001, and email exchange, December 2001–August 2003.

David and Assia never met Ted Hughes: DW, interview in Texas, November 2003, and email exchange, September 2002–December 2005.

Hughes kept in touch with the Group: Edward Lucie-Smith, *The Burnt Child*, p. 166.

'and I do praise the force': AW poem, 'Magnificat', unpublished.

'Winter End, Hertfordshire': AW poem, unpublished.

David and Assia walked a great deal: DW, interview in Texas, November 2003, and email exchange, September 2002–December 2005.

'a community of vision': Philip Hobsbaum, email exchange, October 2001–May 2003.

'There was a poetic spirit in Assia': DW, interview in Texas, November 2003, and email exchange, September 2002–December 2005.

lived like a hermit: RL, interview in Canada, June 2002, and email exchange, July 2002–June 2003.

'we thought that if I went east': DW, interview in Texas, November 2003, and email exchange, September 2002–December 2005.

some intimate moments: RL, interview in Canada, June 2002, and email exchange, July 2002–June 2003.

'My love, I'm so lonely': DW–AW, a letter, undated, in private hands.

'Wherever we walked together': DW, 'For Assia', unpublished poem.

Peter Porter spent an entire evening: Peter Porter, interview in London, September 2001, and letters, October–December 2001.

'All of a sudden, she confided': Thirell (Lipsey) Weiss, email exchange, August–December 2002.

'it still didn't get to the stage': RL, interview in Canada, June 2002, and email exchange, July 2002–June 2003.

Assia discovered that she was pregnant: RL, interview in Canada, June 2002, and email exchange, July 2002–June 2003.

the marriage was on the rocks: CC, interview in Canada, May–June 2002, and subsequent emails, letters and telephone calls, July 2002–April 2006.

'it came as a shock that I might get divorced': RL, interview in Canada, June 2002, and email exchange, July 2002–June 2003.

'The marriage was an empty shell': Martin Graham, interview in London, October 2001.

Dick drove her: RL, interview in Canada, June 2002, and email exchange, July 2002–June 2003.

Eight: Third Marriage

'*Monkeys are monogamous*': DW, interview in Texas, November 2003, and email exchange, September 2002–December 2005.

'*Assia stuck out*': Patricia Mendelson, interview in London, September 2001.

One of the party highlights: Alton Becker, email exchange, March–July 2002.

three seminar-sized classes: DW–Earle Birney, letter, 9 October 1959, Toronto.

A common practice: DW–Earle Birney, letter, 1 April 1960, Toronto.

whispers and frowns: Alton Becker, email exchange, March–July 2002.

British Council to Japan: DW–Earle Birney, letter, 8 February 1960, Toronto.

promoted herself: General Register Office, St Catherine's House, London.

the Burmese judge: DW, interview in Texas, November 2003, and email exchange, September 2002–December 2005.

found herself pregnant: Lisa Gutmann to AW, letter, 22 August 1960, in private hands.

began an affair: RL, interview in Canada, June 2002, and email exchange, July 2002–June 2003.

'*We never made plans*': DW, interview in Texas, November 2003, and email exchange, September 2002–December 2005.

'*was upset*': Fay Weldon, *Auto da Fay*, Flamingo, 2002, p. 350.

'*it was our duty*': ibid.

'*breed politics*': Peter Porter, 'Some People: Slogans for the Sixties', *Guardian*, 20 December 1988.

'*wonderfully mad place*': Douglas Chowns, email exchange, November 2001–June 2003.

published an ad: courtesy of Jane Donaldson.

'*Her figure*': Edward Lucie-Smith, interview in London, October 2001, and email exchange, December 2001–August 2003.

'*seldom met anyone*': Fay, Weldon, *Auto da Fay*, p. 326.

'*innocent toddler*': ibid, p. 322.

Peter Redgrove complained: Edward Lucie-Smith, interview in London, October 2001, and email exchange, December 2001–August 2003.

slightly swarthy face: Julia Matcham, interview in London, September 2001, and letter and email exchange, September 2001–December 2002.

'*What she related*': William Trevor, *Excursions*, p. 116.

'*very innovative*': Angela Landels, interview in London, October 2001.

'Burmese ceremonial dagger': RL, interview in Canada, June 2002, and email exchange, July 2002–June 2003.

'How dare he': Edward Lucie-Smith, interview in London, October 2001, and email exchange, December 2001–August 2003.

'original entertaining mind': Julia Matcham, interview in London, September 2001, and letter and email exchange, September 2001–December 2002.

'somebody's secretary': William Trevor, *Excursion*, p. 115.

'no note attached': RL, interview in Canada, June 2002, and email exchange, July 2002–June 2003.

decided to move: DW, interview in Texas, November 2003, and email exchange, September 2002–December 2005.

draw a map: TH Papers, Emory.

'too slow and polite': SP–AP, a letter, 13 August 1961, *Letters Home: Correspondence*, Faber and Faber, 1999.

'we got on with them': DW, interview in Texas, November 2003, and email exchange, September 2002–December 2005.

handcraft snake: Judith Kroll, email to the authors, 11 October 2004.

'indifferent to the occult': DW, interview in Texas, November 2003, and email exchange, September 2002–December 2005.

'very attractive, intelligent': SP–AP, letter, 14 May, 1962, *Letters Home*.

the couples corresponded: DW, interview in Texas, November 2003, and email exchange, September 2002–December 2005.

'recommended David Wevill': TH–Price Turner, a letter, 5 April 1962, Emory.

'many-blooded beauty' etc: TH. 'Dreamers', in *Birthday Letters, Collected Poems*, pp. 1145–1946.

Nine: A Fateful Meeting

Antonioni, Bergman and Fellini: DW, interview in Texas, November 2003, and email exchange, September 2002–December 2005.

wanted to die young: Angela Landels, interview in London, October 2001.

'a glorious poetic pair': Fay Weldon. *Auto da Fay*, p. 350.

'Sophia Lauren . . . Scott Fitzgerald people: William Trevor. *Excursions*, p. 115.

Among the guests: Philip Hobsbaum, email exchange, October 2001–May 2003.

'We were equals': DW, interview in Texas, November 2003, and email exchange, September 2002–December 2005.

'intolerable similarities': Al Alvarez, 'Sylvia Plath: A Memoir', in *Ariel Ascending*,

Paul Alexander, ed. New York, Harper & Row, 1985, p. 193.

prisoner: LM, *Crow Steered, Bergs Appeared*, p. 77.

'to have several couples': SP–AP, a letter, 16 April 1962, *Letters Home*.

avoided looking: Ruth Fainlight, 'Sylvia and Jane', *Times Literary Supplement*, 12 December 2003.

'has gone off': SP, 'Elm', *Ariel: The Restored Text*, Faber and Faber, 2005, p. 27.

'Plath was detecting': Diane Wood Middlebrook, *Her Husband: Hughes and Plath – A Marriage*. New York, Viking, pp. 161–2.

'I'm going to seduce Ted': Angela Landels, interview in London, October 2001.

in a negligée: Paul Alexander, *Rough Magic*, New York, Da Capo, 1999, p. 277.

'beef stew': SP calendar, Smith.

took the train: DW, interview in Texas, November 2003, and email exchange, September 2002–December 2005.

'hideous grass: AW's diary, 12 August 1963, in private hands.

'the gaze of a demon': TH, 'Dreamers', in *Birthday Letters, Collected Poems*, p. 1146.

unaware of her magnetism: Edward Lucie-Smith, interview in London, October 2001, and email exchange, December 2001–August 2003.

commonly shared their dreams: DW, interview in Texas, November 2003, and email exchange, September 2002–December 2005.

air rifles: DW, interview in Texas, November 2003, and email exchange, September 2002–December 2005.

'Sunlight': TH Papers, Emory.

appear to recreate: Diane Wood Middlebrook, *Her Husband*, p. 166.

a fishing trip: TH/SP–Gerald Hughes, letter, 19 May 1962, Lily.

'ghastly children': SP–AP, a letter, 16 April 1962, *Letters Home*.

'On Sunday morning: DW, interview in Texas, November 2003, and email exchange, September 2002–December 2005.

attractive college student: Elaine Feinstein, *Ted Hughes: The Life of a Poet*, Weidenfeld & Nicolson, 2001, p. 85.

Moira Doolan: ibid, p. 109

Dido Merwin: ibid, p. 101.

not yet sixteen: Nicola Tyrer, *Daily Mail*, 5 February 2004.

'Assia is a figure': Erica Wagner, *Ariel's Gift*, Faber and Faber, 2000, p. 163.

tuning in every Monday: SP calendar, Smith.

'the richest and happiest time': SP–AP, letter, 7 June 1962, *Letters Home*.

'solid and complete': Al Alvarez, *Ariel Ascending*, p. 192.

'Difficulties of a Bridegroom': TH Papers, Emory.

'My dear Sylvia': AW–SP, a letter, 22 May 1962, British Library.

attest to her generoisity: Mira Hamermesh, interview in London, October 2001.

'Wonderfully calming': SP–AP, a letter, 7 June 1962, *Letters Home*.

'the seven treasures of Asia': TH, 'Folktale', in *Capriccio, Collected Poems*, p. 788.

bee stings: Elaine Feinstein, *Ted Hughes: The Life of a Poet*, p. 125.

Ten: An Illicit Affair

to be at the BBC: TH Papers, Emory.

Suzette Macedo recalls: Elaine Feinstein, *Ted Hughes: The Life of a Poet*, p. 124.

freshly cut grass: William Trevor, *Excursions*, p. 117.

Hughes recollects: TH, 'Chlorophyl', in *Capriccio, Collected Poems*, p. 799.

Ted's romantic gesture: The Tarn Papers, Stanford.

revisted London: SP calendar, Smith.

'We met for tea!': William Trevor, *Excursions*, p. 118.

a black cashmere sweater: AP, *Letters Home*, draft notes, Lilly.

'Words Heard, by Accident, Over the Phone': SP, *Collected Poems*, Faber and Faber, 1981.

'The Fearful': ibid.

'Do Not Pick Up the Telephone': TH, *Collected Poems*, p. 585.

'thought that perhaps': AP, *Letters Home*, draft notes, Lilly.

'Well, I don't know': ibid.

'Ted had been having an affair': ibid.

bonfire: ibid.

the tapestry remained: Elizabeth (Compton) Sigmund, interview in England, August 2001, and subsequent email exchange, September–December 2001.

Ted set himself up: Al Alvarez, interview in London, September 2001.

he was in love: The Tarn Papers, Stanford.

four bottles of champagne: ibid.

Ted's ferocious lovemaking: Edward Lucie-Smith, interview in London, October 2001, and email exchange, December 2001–August 2003.

their first lovemaking: TH, 'Capriccios', in *Cappriccio, Collected Poems*, p. 783, and 'Superstitions', in *Howls and Whispers, Collected Poems*, p. 1183.

'18 Rugby Street': TH, *Birthday Letters, Collected Poems*, p. 1055.

At 8.30 p.m.: The Tarn Papers, Stanford.

Seconal sleeping pills: DW, interview in Texas, November 2003, and DW short story, 'Four Days' in *Casual Ties. Prose Sketches*, USA, Curbstone Press, 1986.
'lying so sweetly': The Tarn Papers, Stanford.
'If you come near my wife': ibid.
'straightest man in the world': ibid.
Ted had raped her: Royston Taylor, email exchange, November 2001–February 2002.
'Body of a Rook': DW, *Birth of a Shark*, Toronto, Macmillan, 1964, p. 7.
unable to write: The Tarn Papers, Stnaford.
'a slinky affair': ibid.
'Sylvia wanted to find out': Al Alvarez, *Where Did It All Go Right?* Richard Cohen Books, 1999, p. 206.
Alvarez was attracted to Assia: The Tarn Papers, Stanford.
'made a pass': Al Alvarez, *Where Did It All Go Right?*, p. 209.
Her colleagues covered for her: Edward Lucie-Smith, interview in London, October 2001, and email exchange, December 2001–August 2003.
preparing for a date: Angela Landels, interview in London, October 2001.
On one occasion: Philip Hobsbaum, email exchange, October 2001–May 2003.
locked in a passionate kiss: Patricia Mendelson, interview in London, September 2001.
'lyrical and yielding': Philip Hobsbaum, email exchange, October 2001–May 2003.
'Sylvia is so intense!': Prouty-Smith–TH, a letter, 14 June 1975, TH papers, Emory.
tried to help: TH–Prouty-Smith, a letter, 12 May 1975, TH papers, Emory.
opened a bank account: a letter from Barclays Bank, 20 High Street, Exeter, August 1962, TH papers, Emory.
'a part of Assia': DW, interview in Texas, November 2003, and email exchange, September 2002–December 2005.
Tarn got the impression: The Tarn Papers, Stanford.
In the visitors' book: Richard Murphy, *The Kick, A Memoir*, Granta Books, 2002, p. 222.
grouse shooting: SP–AP, 23 September 1962. Lilly. The paragraph was omitted from *Letters Home*.
'a fascination with violence: Barrie Cooke, 'With Ted Hughes', in *The Epic Poise, A*

Celebration of Ted Hughes, Nick Gammage, ed., Faber and Faber, 1999, p. 214.

Cooke had no telephone: Barrie Cooke, telephone interview in November 2002 and March 2004.

'We lay on our backs': Barrie Cooke, 'With Ted Hughes', in *The Epic Poise*, p. 214.

Murphy insisted: Richard Murphy, *The Kick*, p. 227.

she found a telegram: SP–AP, 23 September 1962. Lilly. The paragraph was omitted from *Letters Home*.

had no idea where her husband was: SP to Kathy Kane, letter, 29 September 1962. Lilly.

Eleven: Leaving Plath

'she met this fabulous man': CC, interview in Canada, May–June 2002, and subsequent emails, letters and telephone calls, July 2002–April 2006.

film script: The Tarn Papers, Stanford.

Wevill never suspected: DW, interview in Texas, November 2003, and email exchange, September 2002–December 2005.

'In a pub in Boppard': DW, interview in Texas, November 2003, and email exchange, September 2002–December 2005.

dependent on Hughes: The Tarn Papers, Stanford.

'a hag': ibid.

attempted suicide: SP–AP, letter, 16 October 1962, Lilly.

'Your absence is huge': TH, 'Sunlight', unpublished, Emory.

correspondent [sic] in a divorce suit: The Tarn Papers, Stanford.

marry his mistress: SP–Olive Prouty, letter, 18 October 1962, Lilly.

perfect husband: SP–Warren Plath, letter, 18 October 1962, Lilly. And also, SP–Mrs Prouty, a letter, 18 October 1962.

'writing and motherhood': SP–AP, letter, 21 October 1962, Lilly.

'not creative': ibid.

'high salary': SP–AP, letter, 7 November 1962, Lilly.

'causing damage to his car': SP–AP, letter, 24 September 1962, Lilly. Omitted from *Letters Home*.

'I think I may well be a Jew': SP, 'Daddy', *Ariel, The Restored Text*.

'in an orphanage': SP–Olive Prouty, letter, 18 October 1962, Lilly.

'to read this book': Dr Ruth Beuscher–SP, a letter, 26 September 1962, Smith.

'she underlined': Plath's copy of Fromm's *The Art of Loving* is in TH Papers, Emory.

'*death-ray quality*': TH–GH, letter, undated, Emory.

'*We didn't want our marriage to end*': DW, interview in Texas, November 2003, and email exchange, September 2002–December 2005.

'*Our Lady of Kovno*': LM, *Crow Steered, Bergs Appeared*, p. 129.

asked Peter Porter: Peter Porter, 'Ted Hughes and Sylvia Plath', *Australian Book Review*, August 2001, p. 25.

'*witched herself into that building*': Ben Sonnenberg, 'Ted's Spell', *Raritan* 21, no. 4, spring 2002.

14 Highbury Place: The Tarn Papers, Stanford.

cut-price stores: SP–Olive Prouty, letter, 15 December 1962, Lilly.

'*Amnesiac*': SP, *Ariel, The Restored Text*.

Doubletake: SP–Olive Prouty, letter 20 November 1962, Lilly.

she met Assia: Olwyn Hughes, letter exchange with the authors, August 2002–June 2003.

'*someone else*': TH–AP, letter, 12 January 1975, Emory.

'*Bloody Christmas*': AW–CC, letter, 18 December 1962, in private hands.

broadcast by the BBC: radio play text is at Emory.

'*The Inscription*': TH, *Birthday Letters, Collected Poems*, p. 1154.

'*The Assia saga is doing alright*': TH–Olwyn Hughes, letter, undated, Olwyn Hughes Papers, Emory.

Assia's best wishes: TH–the Merwins, letter, 21 January 1963, Emory.

Twelve: The Shadow of Suicide

She called Suzette Macedo: Macedo, telephone conversation with the authors, London, 5 October 2001.

'*Something terrible has happened*': Julia Matcham, interview in London, September 2001, and letter and email exchange, September 2001–December 2002.

Susan Alliston: David Ross, interview in London, March 2003.

keeping him away from the telephone: TH, '18 Rugby Street', in *Birthday Letters, Collected Poems*, pp. 1055–6.

'*reunited in two weeks*': LM, *Crow Steered, Bergs Appeared*, p. 80.

Assia, feeling nausea: LM, email exchange, November 2001–December 2003.

to be brought up in America: WP–AP, a letter, February 17, 1963. Lilly.

called urgently to Ottawa: DW, interview in Texas, November 2003, and email exchange, September 2002–December 2005.

The children did not ask for their mother: The Tarn Papers, Stanford.

'most incredible': ibid.

she read Plath's last journal: ibid.

Hughes admitted that he destroyed it: TH, interview in London, 8 October 1996.

Hughes blamed it on Sylvia's 'murderous self': ibid.

She blamed Sylvia for killing herself: Julia Matcham, interview in London, September 2001, and letter and email exchange, September 2001–December 2002.

'strikingly beautiful woman': Ruth Fainlight, 'Sylvia and Jane', *Times Literary Supplement*, 12 December 2003.

'didn't like London, the people': Trevor Thomas, unpublished memoir, 1989.

Hughes implored Assia: TH–AW, letter, 27 March 1963, Emory.

the list of his vices: The Tarn Papers, Stanford.

his account of the tragedy: TH–AP, letter, 15 March 1963, Lilly.

Hughes suspected: TH–Keith Sagar, letter, 23 May 1981, British Library.

'casting a sort of spy ring': TH–Elizabeth (Compton) Sigmund, letter, 26 May 1963, British Library.

'sad and so bent down': Elizabeth (Compton) Sigmund–AP, a letter, 26 March 1963, Lilly.

no sex between the Wevills: The Tarn Papers, Stanford.

'How can you let that thing chew your breast?': Royston Taylor, email exchange, November 2001–February 2002.

On Thursday, 21 March 1963: Elizabeth (Compton) Sigmund, interview in England, August 2001, and subsequent email exchange, September–December 2001.

an old Polish doctor in Maida Vale: AW–Jannice Porter, a postcard, courtesy of Peter Porter.

'what do you want?': AW, TH Papers, Emory.

he was careful not to present his love: TH–AW, letter, 27 March 1963, Emory.

the red exercise book: AW's Diary, in private hands.

'Babylonian beauty': Richard Murphy, *The Kick*, p. 229.

'no footsteps were being followed': DW, interview in Texas, November 2003, and email exchange, September 2002–December 2005.

'attacked each other like cats': The Tarn Papers, Stanford.

a hundred years old: AW's diary, 19 May 1963, in private hands.

Thirteen: Domesticity

'There's a bruise': AW's diary, 20 May 1963, in private hands.

Dr Trevor Thomas: Trevor Thomas, *Sylvia Plath: Last Encounters*, unpublished memoir, 1989, courtesy of Clarissa Roche.

he with sit sideways: AW's diary, 20 May 1963, in private hands.

three 'dream-meetings': 'The Offers', in *Howls and Whispers, Collected Poems*, pp. 1180–83.

'perfect reversal': AW's diary, 1 June 1963, in private hands.

'madness': TH–AP, letter, 13 May 1963. Lilly.

'David. David. Where are you?': AW's diary, in private hands.

'She sent me loving letters: DW, interview in Texas, November 2003, and email exchange, September 2002–December 2005.

'We've lived in peace for five days': AW's diary, 12 June 1963, in private hands.

'will the queen ever give me an audience': TH–Elizabeth and David Compton, letter, 31 July 1963, British Library.

Bringing coffee to Ted's bedroom: AW's diary, 1 June 1963, in private hands.

instructed Elizabeth Compton: TH–Elizabeth and David Compton, letter, June 1963, British Library.

put flowers on Sylvia's grave: AW's diary, 7 June 1963, in private hands.

Mrs Plath was appalled: AP–Dr John Horder, letter, 26 September 1963, Lilly.

'crime against her': TH–AP, letter, 13 May 1963, Lilly.

'big enough for the tribe': TH–Lm, letter, 28 August 1963, Emory.

'six macacos': AW's diary, 12 August 1963, in private hands.

'Assia was stunningly beautiful': Elizabeth (Compton) Sigmund, interview in England, August 2001, and subsequent email exchange, September–December 2001.

'the Holy Study': AW's diary, 12 August 1963, in private hands.

Fourteen: Torn Between Two Lovers

Thomas Mann: the inscribed books are in TH's library, Emory.

'The Art of Loving': Erich Fromm, G Allen & Unwin, 1960. The annotated copy is in TH's library, Emory.

unable to sleep: AW's diary, in private hands.

introduced a lodger: Anna (Owen) Bramble, interview in London, October 2001.

She tried to make peace: Trevor Thomas, *Sylvia Plath: Last Encounters*, unpublished memoir, 1989, courtesy of Clarissa Roche.

'the evil who had come betwen them': ibid.

'a very nice lady': ibid.

she found a job: Trevor Thomas–AP, letter, 27 April 1976, Lilly.

'living with that lady': Dr John Horder–AP, letter, 30 September 1963, Lilly.

'the lady-love': Winifred Davies–AP, letter, 19 November 19633, Lilly.

'Madame Asya': Jillian Becker–AP, letter, 11 November 1963, Lilly.

Elizabeth Compton cease writing: Winifred Davies–AP, letter, 19 November 1963, Lilly.

'there is at least a rumour': Dr John Horder–AP, letter, 17 October 1963, Lilly.

'stupid friendship': TH–AW, letter, 3 October 1963, Emory.

Ivan the Terrible: Sergei Eisenstein, Secker and Warburg, 1963. The inscribed book is in TH's library, Emory.

Four Screenplays: Ingmar Bergman, Simon and Schuster, 1960. The inscribed book is in TH's library, Emory.

London Magazine Poems, 1961–1966: selected by Hugo Williams, Alan Ross, 1966. The inscribed book is in Woodruff Special Collections, Emory.

Wodwo: TH, Harper & Row, 1967. The inscribed book is in TH's library, Emory.

The Letters of William Blake: Geoffrey Keynes, ed., Rupert Hart-Davis, 1968. The inscribed book is in TH's library, Emory.

Assia never came for a visit: LM, email exchange, November 2001–December 2003.

his friends' generosity: David Ross, interview in London, March 2003.

'feral beauty': Ben Sonnenberg, email exchange, August 2002.

Ottoline – the Early Memoirs of Lady Ottoline Morrell: Robert Gathorne-Hardy, ed, Faber and Faber, 1963. The inscribed book is in TH's library, Emory.

'She was very frank': DW, interview in Texas, November 2003, and email exchange, September 2002–December 2005.

'gorgeous English girl': Susan Alliston Project, typescript of introduction by TH, The Weissbort Papers, TH Papers, Emory.

it is clear that she knew: SP–AP, letter, 22 November 1963, Lilly.

'their relationship': LM, email exchange, November 2001–December 2003.

'our friendship took': Susan Alliston Project, typescript of introduction by TH,

The Weissbort Papers, TH Papers, Emory.

'my future is blanked with you': AW–TH, letter, 22 January 1964, Emory.

Hughes's letters: TH–AW, different dates, Emory.

'. . . ovenfox', 'my lovely owl of halva . . .: all these terms of endearment appear together in one letter, TH–AW, 18 February 1964, Emory.

post office box: LM, email exchange, November 2001–December 2003.

Gaudette: TH draft of the text is in Emory.

Kafka: TH–AW, letter, 19 February 1964, Emory.

a film treatment: TH–AW, letter, 11 February 1964, Emory.

'our sage': TH–AW, letter, 3 January 1964, Emory.

Selected Tales of Ivan Turgenev: Anchor Books, 1960. AW's copy of the book, in private hands.

Birth of a Shark: DW, *Birth of a Shark*.

his photograph: DW, interview in Texas, November 2003, and email exchange, September 2002–December 2005.

'I prefer to have one person': Peter Orr, *The Poet Speaks*.

'rather busy': Olwyn Hughes, *Sunday Times*, a letter, 21 May 1964, Emory.

'she has serious identity problems': Anne (Adams) Alvarez, interview in London, October 2001.

he flew to Ottawa: DW, interview in Texas, November 2003, and email exchange, September 2002–December 2005.

rented a room: TH expenditure report, 1 December 1964, TH Papers, Emory.

David was sleeping on the couch: LM, email exchange, November 2001–December 2003.

Myers noticed a book: LM, *Crow Steered, Bergs Appeared*, p. 128.

'I knew it was Ted's child': LM, email exchange, November 2001–December 2003.

Fifteen: Birth

F WALL esq.: TH Papers, Emory.

torn open: TH–AW, letter, undated, Emory.

'they never wear them': TH–AW, letter, 19 february 1965, Emory.

'I emerged whole': AW–LM, 13 March 1965, Emory.

Elise Bertha Gutmann: Assia's mother's full name varies from one document to another.

registered as the father: General Register Office, St Catherine's House, London.

'I suppose my parents': Olwyn Hughes, letter exchange with the authors, August 2002–June 2003.

'Assia was very interested': DW, interview in Texas, November 2003, and email exchange, September 2002–December 2005.

'She became soft': Patricia Mendelson, interview in London, September 2001.

'seriously flamed bitch-woman': AW–Patricia Mendelson, letter, December 1965, The Tarn Papers.

'two little ladies': TH–AW, letter, undated, Emory.

to cast the horoscope: Ben Sonnenberg, 'Ted's Spell', *Raritan* 21, no. 4, spring 2002.

ordered one for Shura: the two-page analysis of Shura's horoscope, in private hands.

'she showed me a book': Michael Hamburger, letters to the authors, June–July 2002.

'We lived like Americans': AW–LM, letter, 15 July 1965, Emory.

'no longer just human sea-weed': AW–Patricia Mendelson, letter, December 1964, The Tarn Papers.

'Cloud of gentleness': Edward Albee, *Who's Afraid of Virginia Woolf?*, Jonathan Cape, 1964. The book, with Assia's slogans for Lux soap, is in TH's library, Emory.

Elida Gibbs's Sea Witch: AW's commercial, in the archives of J Walter Thompson, London.

leather bandolier: Edward Lucie-Smith, interview in London, October 2001, and email exchange, December 2001–August 2003.

wrote to Richard Murphy: TH–Richard Murphy, letter, 3 September 1965, Richard Murphy Letters, University of Tulsa, Oklahoma.

'Very soon, you'll just come': TH–AW, letter, 14 September 1965, Emory.

Furnishing their nest: TH–AW, letter, November 1965, Emory.

'Bomb number 1': TH–AP, letter, December 1965, Lilly. AP wrote these words on the letter.

he preferred the Heddens: Brenda Hedden, interviews in England, September–October 2001.

'We knew this was it': DW, interview in Texas, November 2003, and email exchange, September 2002–December 2005.

Sixteen: Bliss

Ted had a dream: TH, 'Poet, Pike and a Pitiful Grouse', *Guardian*, 9 January 1999. This article contains excerpts from Hughes's interview with Thomas Pero, 'So Quickly It's Over', in *Wild Steelhead & Salmon* magazine, USA, 5, no. 2, winter 1999.

Thomas Hazell: information provided by the present owner of Doonreaghan House, Robert Jocelyn, Earl of Roden, interview in Ireland, March 2005.

'whole tribe': TH–LM, letter, undated, Emory.

'my herds': TH–Brenda and Trevor Hedden, spring 1966, in private hands.

Cashel had only one grocery shop: Ann Henning Jocelyn, interview in Ireland, March 2005.

'The end of Europe': AW's diary, in private hands.

'Assia Wevill-Hughes': AW, postcard to Patricia and Michael Mendelson (Tarn), The Tarn Papers, Stanford.

'Assia is here with me': TH–GH, letter from Cashel, April 1966, Emory.

'The house was known to be haunted': Teresa Reilly, telephone interview, April 2005.

greatly taken to their half-sister: TH–LM, letter from Cashel, undated, Emory.

'your daughter': TH, 'Descent', in *Capriccio, Collected Poems*, p. 787.

'her little girl': TH–GH, letter, 4 May 1965.

'Lines for Shura': TH, unpublished poem, Emory.

'the way he was finally able': Diane Wood Middlebrook, *Her Husband*, p. 230.

two holiday cottages: information provided by Hugh Musgrave, owner of Cleggan Farm, interview in Ireland, March 2005.

ten houses: AW's diary, in private hands.

would dine at Richard Murphy's place: Richard Murphy, *The Kick*, p. 251.

'seemed very happy together': Barrie Cooke, telephone interviews in November 2002 and in March 2004.

to go to Germany: TH–AP and Warren Plath, letter, March 1966, Lilly.

Olwyn was exhausted: TH–GH, letter, 11 June 1966, Emory.

'in sweet sweat': AW's diary, 31 November 1966, in private hands.

Goethe: Richard Friedenthal, *Goethe: His Life and Times*, Weidenfeld & Nicolson, 1965. The inscribed book is in TH's library, Emory.

A General History of Quadrupeds: Thomas Bewick, printed by Edward Walker, 1811. The inscribed book is in TH's library, Emory.

They entertained Allan Sillitoe: TH–GH, letter, undated, Emory.

she got pregnant: Teresa Reilly, telephone interview, April 2005.

Assia went into business: TH–Richard Murphy, letter, 21 July 1966, Richard Murphy Letters, McFarlin Library, Department of Special Collections, University of Tulsa, Oklahoma.

Winifred Davies: Winifred Davies–AP, letter, 12 December 1966, Lilly.

'nettle Emporium': AW–Patricia Mendelson, letter, undated, The Tarn Papers.

he returned to Canada: CC, interview in Canada, May–June 2002, and subsequent emails, letters and telephone calls, July 2002–April 2006.

he would give her a loan: i.e. 3 June 1966: loan cash, Assia, £100; 18 April 1968; £42, loan, Assia W. TH notes, Emory.

The Muses' Darling: Charles Norman, *The Muses' Darling: The Life of Christopher Marlowe*, Falcon Press, 1947. The inscribed book is in TH's library, Emory.

Assia's inscription: the inscribed book is in TH's library, Emory.

A Christ of the Ice-Floes: DW, Macmillan, 1966.

'it's a ghost of a book': AW's diary, 30 November 1966, in private hands.

'Assia and I have separated': DW–Earle Birney, letter, 19 April 1967, Earle Birney Papers, Tulsa.

Assia made a card: TH Papers, Emory.

'begrudge him an affair': AW's diary, 31 November 1966, in private hands.

'The woman is my real enemy': AW–CC, letter, 11 March 1967, in private hands.

Assia was browsing: AW's diary, 31 November 1966, in private hands.

'how spoilt I am': ibid.

His father could not bear the sight of Assia: TH–GH, letter, 25 April 1967, Emory.

Myers felt sorry: LM, email exchange, November 2001–December 2003.

refused to sit with her: AW–CC, letter, 11 March 1967, in private hands.

Hughes looks withdrawn: TH Papers, Emory.

Frieda Hughes has a vague memory: Frieda Hughes notes, TH Papers, Emory.

Elizabeth Compton saw: Elizabeth (Compton) Sigmund, interview in England, August 2001, and subsequent email exchange, September–Decembeer 2001.

'I have these fits of huge love': AW's diary, 31 November 1966, in private hands.

'head tilted': AW–CC, letter, 11 March 1967, in private hands.

'Shura is becoming': TH–LM, letter, undated, Emory.

'a silent and sad child': Elizabeth (Compton) Sigmund, interview in England, August 2001, and subsequent email exchange, September–December 2001.

'I don't have the self confidence': AW–CC, a letter, 11 March 1967, in private hands.

Celia recalls: CC, interviews in Canada, May–June 2002, and subsequent emails, letters and telephone calls, July 2002–April 2006.

Seventeen: Banished

International Festival of Spoken Poetry: TH Papers, Emory.

read the Bible: Daniel Weissbort, interview in London, May 2002, and letter exchange, April 2002–September 2005.

conversation around the table: Horatio Morpurgo, 'The Table Talk of Ted Hughes', *Arete*, issue 6, autumn 2001.

Judaism fascinated Hughes: Horatio Morpurgo, email exchange, April 2003.

most often took: TH, introduction in Amichai, Yehuda, *Selected Poems*, Faber and Faber, 2000.

a rare personal interview: TH, interview in London, 8 October 1996.

'My wife grew up in Israel': TH–Yehuda Amichai, letter, 7 May 1967, Yale.

invited her and Ted: Ruth Fainlight–AW, postcard, 7 July 1967, Emory.

film-maker: Mira Hamermesh, interview in London, October 2001.

'What an insane week': AW–Yehuda and Hannah Amichai, letter, 18 July 1967.

'they blow soap bubbles': AW–Yehuda and Hannah Amichai, 19 August 1967, Yale.

'to annoy [them] less': ibid.

The Hawk in the Rain: TH, Faber and Faber, 1964.

and added a card: TH Papers, Emory.

'a pitch of mild disaster': AW–Patricia Mendelson, letter, 12 September 1967, in private hands.

'All that remains': AW–Patricia Mendelson, 12 September 1967, in private hands.

rush to London: ibid.

'She told me': Royston Taylor, email exchange, November 2001–February 2002.

Chatting with Assia: Janos Csokits, interview in Budapest, March 2006, and letter exchange, December 2003–September 2005.

Assia had returned to London: Hilda Farrar–AP, letter, 23 October 1967, Lilly.

she asked him: Richard Murphy, *The Kick*, p. 260.

'a good feast': Olwyn Hughes, letter exchange, August 2002–June 2003.

'Please God': AW card, TH Papers, Emory.

Eighteen: Love Me Back or Let Me Go

'last-ditch panic': AW–Yehuda Amichai, letter, 11 January 1968, Yale.

Vesta Curry: Tom Boyd, telephone interview, September 2004.

'if you're unhappy': TH–Yehuda Amichai, 31 October 1967, Yale.

when Nathaniel Tarn edited: The Tarn Papers, Stanford.

'he really tried to promote her': Daniel Weissbort, interview in London, May 2002, and letter exchange, April 2002–September 2005.

'Couldn't the Israeli government': AW–Yehuda Amichai, December 1967, Yale.

Watching a BBC documentary: AW–Yehuda Amichai, letter, 6 March 1968, Yale.

'Dearest love, sweet Ted': AW–TH, letter, 2 February 1968, Emory.

she assisted Ted: Martin Graham, interview in London, October 2001.

'looks like an exhibit': AW–Yehuda Amichai, 11 January 1968, Yale.

Assia's playbill: TH's library, Emory.

'Emperor of the Barn': AW–Yehuda Amichai, 11 January 1968, Yale.

Galateo: Giovanni della Casa, Penguin Books, 1958. The book is in TH's library, Emory.

Draft Constitution: the two-page document is in TH Papers, Emory.

'This is the ancient steel nib': AW–TH, March 1968, Emory.

'a home for Shura': TH–AW, letter, undated, Emory.

'In the event of my death': AW's will, in private hands.

'she was fragile': CC, interviews in Canada, May–June 2002, and subsequent emails, letters and telephone calls, July 2002–April 2006.

'we both suffer': CC–AW, letter, in private hands.

Assia bought a copy: Henri Troyat, *Tolstoy*, WH Allen, 1968. The inscribed book is in TH's library, Emory.

Assia sent Ted: AW–TH, telegram, 14 May 1968, Emory.

monumental biography: Philipp Spitta, *Johann Sebastian Bach: His Work and Influence on the Music of Germany, 1685–1750*, Dover Publications, 1951. The two volumes are in TH's library, Emory.

Poet and critic Pat Kavanagh: 'An Awkward Shyness', *Guardian*, 12 July 1968.

BBC Radio 3 programme: a transcription of the programme is in TH Papers, Emory.

Potemkin: Sergei Eisenstein, *The Battleship Potemkin*, Lorrimer Pub. Co. 1968.

'I agreed to take part': Chris Roos, interview in London, October 2001.

'It wasn't a happy film': Martin Baker, interview in Oxfordshire, October 2001, and email exchange, November 2001–January 2004.

the outdoor scenes: Fay Maschler and Jonny Gathorne-Hardy, interview in London, October 2001.

Assia was afraid of getting old: CC, interviews in Canada, May–June 2002, and subsequent emails, letters and telephone calls, July 2002–April 2006.

'she put cream': CC–AW, letter, 30 March 1968, in private hands.

'Fanaticism': TH, in *Capriccio, Collected Poems*, p. 789.

'one of the most beautiful human beings': Chris Wilkins, email exchange, October 2001.

'How I want us to live together': AW–TH, letter, 9 July 1968, Emory.

did not result in enough sales: Dan Ellerington, telephone interview, January 2002.

'Ted will feel your panic': Anne Semple to AW, letter, 15 July 1968, in private hands.

she decided to write to Mrs Plath: AP–TH, letters 7 April 1968 and 14 June 1968, Lilly.

'I remember registering amazement': Richard Larschan, interview in Massachusetts, USA, June 2004, and email exchange, September 2001–December 2005.

Nineteen: Despair

'ought to marry': TH, diary note, Emory.

Hughes did not want Assia: Royston Taylor, email exchange, November 2001–February 2002.

'in Boppard': AW's diary, 7 August 1968, in private hands.

'many locals': TH–Yehuda and Hannah Amichai, postcard, 8 August 1968, Yale.

'On the train': AW–Yehuda Amichai, postcard, 8 August 1968, Yale.

'had to strip off': TH, 'Descent', in *Capriccio, Collected Poems*, p. 787.

overwhelmed by a dream: TH, diary note, 14–15 August 1968, Emory.

Nelly Sachs: Selected Poems, Jonathan Cape, 1968. The inscribed book is in TH's library, Emory.

complimented her: TH–GH, letter, 20 August 1968, Emory.

Assia would ring Lipsey: Richard Lipsey, interview in Canada, June 2002, and email exchange, July 2002–June 2003.

'His new companion': Martin Graham, interview in London, October 2001.

'For a long time': DW, interview in Texas, November 2003, and email

exchange, September 2002–December 2005.

to remove himself from her life: DW–Patricia and Michael Mendelson, letter, 1 April 1969, The Tarn Papers.

'she had this capacity': DW, interview in Texas, November 2003, and email exchange, September 2002–December 2005.

Ted gave Brenda: Brenda Hedden, interviews in England, September–October 2001.

'Lovesong': TH, 'Lovesong', in *Crow, Collected Poems*, p. 256.

two snakes: TH Papers, Emory.

'It is only inevitable': AW, a torn-out page from her diary, in private hands.

Ted Hughes submitted to the Arts Council: Peter Porter, 'Ted Hughes and Sylvia Plath', p. 24.

'I'm really missing you': TH–AW, letter, July 1968, Emory.

'Standing in a smoky living-room': Eavan Bowland, 'Ted Hughes Recollections', *PN Review*, Manchester 25, 5 May 1999.

'a displaced person': William Trevor, *Excursions in the Real World*, p. 119.

'Being a single mother': Fay Weldon, interview in London, September 2001.

'fifteen years older': John Chambers, interview in London, September 2001.

'I fancied her': Guy Jenkin, interview in London, October 2001.

'It gives me such immense pleasure': AW–Patricia Mendelson, letter, undated, in private hands.

Twenty: The Die Is Cast

razor-sharp diary entry: AW's diary, 4 September 1968, in private hands.

to have tea with them: Janos Csokits, interview in Budapest, March 2006, and letter exchange, December 2003–September 2005.

with his camera: Martin Baker, interview in Oxfordshire, October 2001, and email exchange, November 2001–January 2004.

Frieda Hughes remembers: notes of Frieda Hughes from 6 September 2004, accompanying a list of her father's letters to her, Emory.

invited her and Shura: Elaine Feinstein, *Ted Hughes: The Life of a Poet*, p. 169.

'from killing them both': Ruth Fainlight, 'Sylvia and Jane', *Times Literary Supplement*.

'Assia put the receiver down': Martin Graham, interview in London, October 2001.

killing herself: Mira Hamermesh, interview in London, October 2001.

'in the 1960s': Martin Baker, interview in Oxfordshire, October 2001, and email exchange November 2001–January 2004.

to lunch with him: Royston Taylor, email exchange, November 2001–February 2002.

threaten to end her life: Edward Lucie-Smith, interview in London, October 2001, email exchange, December 2001–August 2003

arrived once: Guy Jenkin, interview in London, October 2001.

she confided: Chris Wilkins, email exchange, October 2001.

'I wish you happiness': DW, interview in Texas, November 2003, and email exchange, September 2002–December 2005.

imaginary monologue: DW's 'Dead One', in Firebreaks, Macmillan, 1971.

'They used to come': Patricia Mendelson, interview in London, September 2001.

'bloody artists': AW–Patricia Mendelson, letter, undated, in private hands.

Shura's fourth birthday: Patricia Mendelson, interview in London, September 2001.

invited him for lunch: Tom Boyd, telephone interview, September 2004.

angry and sullen: AW's diary, 20 March 1969, in private hands.

they travelled around Yorkshire: TH's poetic description of this trip is in 'Flame', in Capriccio, Collected Poems, p. 798.

'A pity about the three children': AW's diary, 20 March 1969, in private hands.

felt criminal: AW's diary, 21 March 1969, in private hands.

she tried to read: Zbigniew Herbert, Selected Poems, Penguin, 1968. TH's library, Emory.

switched on the radio: AW's diary, 21 March 1969, in private hands.

'Mr Hughes didn't want her': statement of Else Ludwig to Det. Sgt J Loakman, Clapham Police Station, 23 March 1969.

smelled gas: statement of Margaret Jones to Det. Sgt J Loakman, Clapham Police Station, 27 March 1969.

He put his face against the door: statements of Goronwy Owen Roberts to Det. Sgt J Loakman, Clapham Police Station, 2 April 1969.

'Mrs Wevill was lying on some blankets': statement of Jennifer Margaret Bangs to Det. Sgt J Loakman, Clapham Police Station, 2 April 1969.

'They were investigating': Chris Wilkins, email exchange, October 2001.

'I handled this one badly': AL Alvarez, interview in London, September 2001.

the police were unpleasant: Brenda Hedden, interviews in England, September–October 2001.

Twenty-one: Agony

'I knew she would': CC–Patricia Mendelson, a letter, 31 March 1969, in private hands.

'hoarse, grave voice': Eda Zoritte-Megged, 'Intersections', *Mosnayim*, no. 9, September/October 1984 (in Hebrew).

'Send flowers': Richard Murphy, *The Kick*, p. 274.

'Lullaby': ibid, p. 275.

wrote a note: Brenda Hedden, interviews in England, September–October 2001.

Dr Gutmann visited the flat: CC, interviews in Canada, May–June 2002, and subsequent emails, letters and telephone calls, July 2002–April 2006.

'he was extremely distraught': Chris Wilkins, email exchange, October 2001.

his sweater was worn-out: John Wainwright, a later tenant in Assia's flat, interview in London, October 2001.

crushed and disconsolate: Peter Porter, interview in London, September 2001, and letters, October–December 2001.

eulogise Assia and Shura: Edward Lucie-Smith, interview in London, October 2001, email exchange, December 2001–August 2003.

'A Requiem for Two Daughters of Israel': in Nathaniel Tarn, *Selected Poems 1950–2002*, USA, Middletown, Wesleyan University Press, 2002.

'two white coffins': Peter Porter, interview in London, September 2001, and letters, October–December 2001.

inviting all to lunch: Edward Lucie-Smith, interview in London, October 2001, email exchange, December 2001–August 2003.

The following day: Brenda Hedden, interviews in England, September–October 2001.

taken to Harrod's: Olwyn Hughes, letter exchange, August 2002–June 2003.

'He invited me': Martin Baker, interview in Oxfordshire, October 2001, and email exchange, November 2001–January 2004.

go over the things: Patricia Mendelson, interview in London, September 2001.

In a crate: CC, interviews in Canada, May–June 2002, and subsequent emails, letters and telephone calls, July 2002–April 2006.

the last edition: Vasco Popa, *Selected Poems*, Penguin, 1969. Assia's copy is in TH's library, Emory.

he kept the urns in his bedroom: Brenda Hedden, interviews in England, September–October 2001.

'a permanent emergency': TH–Janet Malcolm, letter, 2 March 1992, Emory.

Assia had asked Fay: Fay Weldon, interview in London, September 2001.

'back into her body': SP, 'Edge', in *Ariel, The Restored Text*, Faber and Faber, 2005.

'Medea-like': Richard Larschan, interview in Massachusetts, USA, June 2004, and email exchange, September 2001–December 2005.

'the unpardonable crime Plath had committed': Anita Helle, 'Family Matters: An Afterword on the Biography of Sylvia Plath', *Northwest Review*, 26, no. 2, 1988.

60 murder-suicide incidents: Brian Barraclough and E Clare Harris, 'Suicide preceded by murder: the epidemiology of homicide-suicide in England and Wales, 1988–1992', *Psychological Medicine*, 2002, 32, 577–84. Cambridge University Press.

five types of filicide: Philip J Resnick, 'Child murder by parents: a psychiatric review of filicide', *American Journal of Psychiatry*, 1969; 126:325–34. Also in an email interview with Dr Resnick in April 2004.

'much higher incidence': Philip J Resnick, in Nancy Wride 'A Mother's Final Deadly Act', *Los Angeles Times*, 12 January 1992.

'The mother knows': Philip J Resnick, in Ken Hausman 'Classification Tries to Make Sense of Often Inexplicable Crime,' *Psychiatry News*, 20 December 2002, vol. 37, no. 24.

'another motherless child': Al Alvarez's diary, 2 May 1969, quoted in Elaine Feinstein, *Ted Hughes: The Life of a Poet*, p. 256.

'Thank God Assia took her': Patricia Mendelson–CC, letter, 13 April 1969, in private possession.

'only way of outdoing her': Al Alvarrez, *Where Did It All Go Right?*, p. 209.

'because it is more like her': TH–Pat Torney, letter, undated, Emory.

He told Aurelia Platt: TH–AP, letter, 14 April 1969, Lilly.

'very true of Assia': TH–GH, letter, May 1969, Lilly.

'insane decisions': TH–LM, letter, Emory.

'given her hope': TH–CC, letter, 14 April 1969, Emory.

When interviewed: Ted Hughes, interview with the authors in London, 8 October 1996.

Cooke was rushing around: Barrie Cooke, telephone interviews in November 2002 and in March 2004.

'*Effect of A's*': TH notebook, *c.* 1968–1969, Emory.

When his father asked Olwyn: TH–AP, letter, 10 July 1969, Lilly.

'*the sort of place*': TH–CC, letter, 11 March 1970, in private hands.

Dr Gutmann's blood pressure: CC, interviews in Canada, May–June 2002, and subsequent emails, letters and telephone calls, July 2002–April 2006.

'*longcold oven*': TH, 'The Locket', in *Capriccio, Collected Poems*, p. 784.

'*Why did you kneel*': TH, 'The Error', in *Capriccio, Collected Poems*, p. 795.

'*The times were against Assia*': Fay Weldon, interview in London, September 2001.

Twenty-two: Aftermath

In the summer of 1969: Brenda Hedden, interviews in England, September–October 2001.

'*but some women*': Hilda Farrar–AP, letter, 6 November 1969, Lilly.

'*It happened again*': Brenda Hedden, interviews in England, September–October 2001.

to have the dedication in Hebrew: TH Papers, Emory.

'*red hot*': TH–CC, letter, 11 March 1970, in private hands.

they entertained Seamus Heaney: Brenda Hedden, interviews in England, September–October 2001.

learned of the marriage: Hilda Farrar–AP, letter, 15 October 1970, Lilly.

'*Beat a woman with a hammer*': TH-LM, letter, February 1971, Emory.

'*He was a real hunter*': Brenda Hedden, interviews in England, September–October.

'*greylag goose*': Emma Tennant, *Burnt Diaries*. Canongate Books, 1999, p. 105.

'*she wasn't so sure*': TH–CC, letter, 11 March 1970, in private hands.

five-inch tiger's tooth: Jeremy Robson, 'Copy for Mr Feinstein', *London Magazine*, June–July 1971.

'*Don't cuddle your wife*': Peter Porter, 'Ted Hughes and Sylvia Plath', *Australian Book Review*, August 2001.

Poets Reading Their Work: playbill and publicity material in TH Papers, Emory.

'*The most electrical place*': TH–Peter Redgrove, undated, Emory.

'*live there*': TH–LM, February 1971, Emory.

showed him a number of houses: TH–GH, undated, Emory.

'*It's the most sacred*': TH, interview in London, 8 October 1996.

'*edge*': Sylvia Plath, *Ariel, The Restored Text*, 2005.

Murphy sent an elegy: Richard Murphy–TH, a letter, 5 March 1965, McFarlin Library, University of Tulsa.

asked him to delete: TH–Richard Murphy, a letter postmarked 8 April 1965, Tulsa.

'demonic possession': AL Alvarez, *The Savage God: A Study in Suicide*, Weidenfeld & Nicolson, 1971.

'Arraignment': Robin Morgan, *Monster: Poems*, New York, Random House, 1972, and also in *Upstairs in the Garden: Poems Selected and New*, New York, W W Norton, 1990.

'I can't understand': 'The Death of Assia G.' in *Songs of Jerusalem and Myself*, Harper & Row, New York, 1973.

'who the other woman was': Iain Walker, 'Poetic Justice? The Trials of Ted Hughes', Australia, *The Advertiser*, 7 May 1987.

'the right woman failed to materialise': TH–Leonard Scigaj, letter, 28 July 1989, Emory.

'a woman to replace their mother': TH–Janet Malcolm, letter, 2 March 1992, Emory.

Already in 1986: Leonard Baskin–TH, letter, 18 November 1986, Emory.

'After forty I'll end it': 'Fanaticism', in *Capriccio, Collected Poems*, p. 789.

'baby daughter', 'German au pair', 'Six full calendar years', 'Her grave', all in 'The Error', in *Capriccio, Collected Poems*, p. 796.

He was relieved: TH, interview in London, 8 October 1996.

'I wrote many poems': ibid.

Select Bibliography

Interviews

Immediate Circle

Celia (Gutman) Chaikin, telephone interview January 1999, email exchange January 1999–May 2002; interviews in Canada, May–June 2002, and subsequent emails, letters and telephone calls, July 2002–April 2006.

Arnold Chaikin, interviews in Canada, May–June 2002.

John Steele, letter exchange, July 2002–January 2004.

Richard (Dick) Lipsey, interview in Canada, June 2002, and email exchange July 2002–June 2003.

Thirell (Lipsey) Weiss, email exchange, August–December 2002.

David Wevill, interview in Texas, November 2003, and email exchange, September 2002–December 2005.

Ted Hughes, interview in London, 8 October 1996.

Olwyn Hughes, letter exchange, August 2002–June 2003.

Palestine–England–Canada, 1940–52

Leila Andreas, interview in Israel, November 2001.

Wedad Andreas, interview in Israel, November 2001.

Hannah Weinberg-Shalitt, interview in Israel, January 1999.

Mira Hamermesh, interview in London, October 2001.

Keith Gems, interview in London, December 2003, and letter exchange, August 2002–February 2004.

John Bosher, telephone interview and email exchange, July–August 2002.

Esther Birney, telephone interview, December 2001, and letter January 2002.

England–Burma, 1953–60

Lilian Archibald, interview in London, March 2003.

Alton Becker, email exchange, March–July 2002.

Marilyn Corry, email exchange, September 2002.

Pam Gems, interview in London, December 2003, and letter exchange, August 2002–February 2004.

Martin Graham, interview in London, October 2001.

Philip Hobsbaum, email exchange, October 2001–May 2003.

Edward Lucie-Smith, interview in London, October 2001, email exchange, December 2001–August 2003.

Patricia Mendelson, interview in London, September 2001.

Don Michel, email, September 2002.

Ian Montagnes, email exchange, September–October 2002.

Roger Philips, email exchange, November 2001.

Peter Porter, interview in London, September 2001, and letters, October–December 2001.

Jo (Reed) Price, email exchange, September–October 2002.

Kenneth Reed, letter November 2002.

England–Ireland, 1961–9

Al Alvarez, interview in London, September 2001.

Anne (Adams) Alvarez, interview in London, October 2001.

Martin Baker, interview in Oxfordshire, October 2001, and email exchange November 2001–January 2004.

Kathleen Becker, interview in London, September 2001.

Tom Boyd, telephone interview, September 2004.

Anna (Owen) Bramble, interview in London, October 2001.

Sue Byrne, email exchange, November 2001.

John Chambers, interview in London, September 2001.

Douglas Chowns, email exchange, November 2001–June 2003.

Barrie Cooke, telephone interviews in November 2002 and in March 2004.

Janos Csokits, interview in Budapest, March 2006, and letter exchange, December 2003–September 2005.

Jane Donaldson, email and letter exchange, November 2003–February 2004.

Dan Ellerington, telephone interview, January 2002.

Ruth Fainlight, email exchange, January–February 2004.

Jonny Gathorne-Hardy, interview in London, October 2001.

Michael Hamburger, letters June–July 2002.

Brenda Hedden, interviews in England, September–October 2001.

Guy Jenkin, interview in London, October 2001.

Ann Henning Jocelyn, interview in Ireland, March 2005.

Robert Jocelyn, Earl of Roden, interview in Ireland, March 2005.

Angela Landels interview in London, October 2001.

Richard Larschan, interview in Massachusetts, USA, June 2004, and email exchange, September 2001–December 2005.

Fay Maschler, interview in London, October 2001.

Julia Matcham, interview in London, September 2001, and letter and email exchange, September 2001–December 2002.

Horatio Morpurgo, email exchange, April 2003.

Lucas Myers, email exchange, November 2001–December 2003.

Hugh Musgrave, interview in Ireland, March 2005.

Keith Ravenscroft, email exchange, October 2001.

Teresa Reilly, telephone interview, April 2005.

Philip Resnick, email exchange, April 2004.

Clarissa Roche, interview in England, September 2001.

Chris Roos, interview in London, October 2001.

David Ross, interview in London, March 2003.

Ann Semple, telephone interview, January 2002.

Elizabeth (Compton) Sigmund, interview in England, August 2001, and subsequent email exchange, September–December 2001.

Ben Sonnenberg, email exchange, August 2002.

Royston Taylor, email exchange, November 2001–February 2002.

John Wainwright, interview in London, October 2001.

Daniel Weissbort, interview in London, May 2002, and letter exchange, April 2002–September 2005.

Fay Weldon, interview in London, September 2001.

Chris Wilkins, email exchange, October 2001.

Archives

The Department of Manuscripts, The British Library, London.

Ted Hughes Papers; Manuscript, Archives and Rare Book Library, Emory University, Atlanta, Georgia, USA.

Select Bibliography

Sylvia Plath Collection, the Lilly Library, Indiana University, Bloomington, Indiana, USA.

Sylvia Plath Collection, Mortimer Rare Book Room, Smith College, Northampton, Massachusetts, USA.

The Nathaniel Tarn Papers, Department of Special Collections, Stanford University Libraries, Stanford, California, USA.

Earle Birney Papers, Thomas Fisher Rare Book Library, University of Toronto, Canada.

Richard Murphy Letters, McFarlin Library, Department of Special Collections, University of Tulsa, Oklahoma, USA.

Yehuda Amichai Papers, Beinecke Rare Book and Manuscript Library, Yale University, New Haven, Connecticut, USA.

The Eric Walter White Papers, Miles Memorial Library, McMaster University, Hamilton, Ontario, Canada.

General Register Office, St Catherine's House, London.

Tel Aviv Municipality Archives; files of the Hospitality Committee and of the Religious Council, 1940–1947, Israel.

Poetry and Letters

Amichai, Yehuda. *Poems*. New York, Harper & Row, 1968.

— *Selected Poems*. Penguin, 1971.

— *Selected Poems*. Introduction, Ted Hughes, Faber and Faber, 2000.

— *Songs of Jerusalem and Myself*. New York, Harper & Row, 1973.

Hughes, Ted. *Collected Poems*. Keegan, Paul ed., London, Faber and Faber, 2003.

Plath, Sylvia. *Ariel, The Restored Text*. Faber and Faber, 2005.

— *Collected Poems*. Faber and Faber, 1981.

— *Journals of Sylvia Plath, 1950–1962. Kukil, Karen V ed.*, Faber and Faber, 2000.

— *Letters Home: Correspondence*. Faber and Faber, 1999.

Tarn, Nathaniel. *Selected Poems 1950–2000*. USA, Middletown, Wesleyan University Press, 2002.

Wevill, David. *Birth of a Shark*. Toronto, Macmillan, 1964.

— *Casual Ties. Prose Sketches*. USA, Curbstone Press, 1986.

— *A Christ of the Ice-Floes*. Macmillan, 1966.

— *Departures, Selected Poems*. Shearsman Books, 2003.

— *Firebreaks*. Macmillan, 1971.

— *Solo with Grazing Deer*. Toronto, Exile Editions, 2001.

Criticism and Memoirs

Books

Alexander, Paul ed., *Ariel Ascending: Writing about Sylvia Plath*. New York, Harper & Row, 1985.

— *Rough Magic,* 2nd ed. New York, Da Capo, 1969.

Alvarez, A. *The Savage God: A Study in Suicide*. Weidenfeld & Nicolson, 1971.

— *Where Did It All Go Right?* Richard Cohen Books, 1999.

— *Ariel Ascending* in 'Sylvia Plath: A Memoir', Alexander, Paul ed.

Becker, Jillian. *Giving Up: The Last Days of Sylvia Plath.* Ferrington, 2002.

Bennett, Bruce. *Spirit in Exile: Peter Porter and his Poetry*. Melbourne, Oxford University Press, 1991.

Blumenthal, Susan J ed., *Suicide Over the Life Cycle*. American Psychiatric Publishing Inc., 1990.

Brain, Tracy. *The Other Sylvia Plath*. New York, Longman, 2001.

Bundtzen, Lynda K. *The Other Ariel*. USA, University of Massachusetts Press, 2001.

Butscher, Edward. *Sylvia Plath: Method and Madness*. New York, Simon & Schuster, 1976.

—, ed., *Sylvia Plath: The Woman and the Work*. New York, Dodd, Mead, 1977.

Cameron, Elspeth, *Earle Birney – a Life*. New York, Viking, 1994.

Candell, Tim. *Sylvia Plath – a Critical Study*. Faber and Faber, 2001.

Efron, John. *Medicine and the German Jews*. USA, Yale University Press, 2001.

Farberow, Norman L and Shneidman Edwin. ed., *The Cry for Help*, New York, McGraw-Hill, 1965.

Feinstein, Elaine. *Ted Hughes: The Life of a Poet*. Weidenfeld & Nicolson, 2001.

Gammage, Nick ed., *The Epic Poise, A Celebration of Ted Hughes*. Faber and Faber, 1999.

Goodwin, Isobel. *May You Live to Be 120! The Story of Tabeetha School, Jaffa, 1863–1983*. Saint Andrew Press, 2000.

Hamermesh, Mira. *The River of Angry Dogs – A Memoir*. Pluto Press, 2004.

Hayman, Ronald. *The Death and Life of Sylvia Plath*. Sutton Publishing, 2003.

Kater, Michael. *Doctors Under Hitler*. USA, University of North Carolina Press, 1989.

Kroll, Judith. *Chapters in a Mythology: The Poetry of Sylvia Plath*. New York, Harper Colophon, 1976.

Lucie-Smith, Edward. *The Burnt Child: An Autobiography*. Victor Gollancz, 1975.

— ed., *A Group Anthology*. Oxford University Press, 1963.

Malcolm, Janet. *The Silent Woman*. Picador, 1994.

Middlebrook, Diane Wood. *Her Husband: Hughes and Plath — A Marriage*. New York, Viking, 2003.

Morgan, H G. *Death Wishes?* John Wiley, 1979.

Morgan, Robin. *Monster: Poems*, New York, Random House, 1972.

— *Upstairs in the Garden: Poems Selected and New*. New York, W W Norton, 1990.

Moses, Kate. *Wintering, a novel of Sylvia Plath*. New York, St Martin's, 2003.

Moulin, Joanny ed., *Alternative Horizons*. Routledge, 2004, includes: Bere, Carol. 'Complicated with Old Ghosts: The Assia Poems'; Robert, Neil J. 'Hughes and the Female Addressee'.

Murphy, Richard. *The Kick, A Memoir*. London, Granta Books, 2002.

Myers, Lucas. *Crow Steered, Bergs Appeared*. USA, Tennessee, Proctor's Hall Press, 2001.

Newman, Charles ed., *The Art of Sylvia Plath: A Symposium*. USA, Bloomington, Indiana University Press, 1970.

Ogilvy, David. *Confessions of an Advertising Man*. New York, Atheneum 1976.

Orr, Peter ed., *The Poet Speaks*. Routledge & Kegan Paul, 1966.

Rayfield, Tom. *Fifty in 40*. Rayfield Writers, 1996.

Rose, Jacqueline. *The Haunting of Sylvia Plath*. London, Virago Press, 1991.

Sagar, Keith. *The Laughter of Foxes*. Liverpool University Press, 2000.

Segev, Tom. *The Seventh Million*, New York, Henry Holt, 2000.

Skea, Ann. *Ted Hughes: The Poetic Quest*. Australia, University of New England Press, 1994.

Stevenson, Anne. *Bitter Fame: A Life of Sylvia Plath*. Penguin, 1990.

Tennant, Emma. *Burnt Diaries*. Canongate Books, 1999.

— *Sylvia and Ted, a novel*. New York, Henry Holt, 2001.

Trevor, William. *Excursions in the Real World*. Hutchinson, 1993.

Uroff, Margaret Dickie. *Sylvia Plath and Ted Hughes*. USA, Urbana, University of Illinois Press, 1979.

Van Dyne, Susan R. *Revising Life: Sylvia Plath's Ariel Poems*. USA, Chapel Hill, University of North Carolina Press, 1993.

Wagner, Erica. *Ariel's Gift*. Faber and Faber, 2000.

Wagner-Martin, Linda. *Sylvia Plath: A Biography*. New York, Simon & Schuster 1987.

— *Plath: a Literary Life*, 2nd ed. revised and extended, New York, Palgrave Macmillan, 2003.

Weldon, Fay. *Auto da Fay*. Flamingo, 2002.

— *Down Among the Women*. Penguin Books, 1973.

— *Mantrapped*. London, Harper Perennial, 2005.

Williams, Mark. *A Cry of Pain*, Penguin Books, 1997.

Articles

Barber, Jill. 'Ted Hughes, My Secret Lover'. *The Mail on Sunday*, 13 and 20 May 2001.

Barraclough, Brian and Harris, E Clare. 'Suicide preceded by murder: the epidemiology of homicide-suicide in England and Wales, 1988–1992'. *Psychological medicine*, 2002, 32, 577–584. Cambridge University Press.

Becker, Gerry. *'Plath–Hughes; One of Us Had to Die'*. Unpublished memoir, courtesy of Kathleen Becker.

Bowland, Eavan. 'Ted Hughes Recollections'. *PN Review*. Manchester, 25:5 May 1999.

Brown, Mick. 'Poetic Justice'. Interview with Frieda Hughes, *Telegraph Magazine*, 16 June 2001.

Churchwell, Sarah. 'Ted Hughes and the Corpus of Sylvia Plath'. *Criticism 40*, no. 1, winter 1998, pp. 99–132.

Cornwell, John. 'Bard of Prey'. *Sunday Times*, 3 October 1999.

Fainlight, Ruth. 'Sylvia and Jane'. *Times Literary Supplement*, 12 December 2003.

Feay, Suzi. 'The Ghost Winter'. Interview with Emma Tennant, *Independent on Sunday*, 20 May 2001.

Heinz, Drue. 'Ted Hughes: The Art of Poetry, LXXI'. Interview with Ted Hughes, *Paris Review* 134, spring 1995.

Helle, Anita. 'Family Matters: An Afterword on the Biography of Sylvia

Plath', *Northwest Review*, 26, no. 2, 1988.

Hobsbaum, Philip. 'Ted Hughes at Cambridge'. *The Dark Horse: The Scottish-American Poetry Magazine*, 8 Autumn 1999.

— 'In Conversation with Nicolas Tredell'. *PN Review* 119, January–February 1998.

Horder, John. 'Desk Poet'. *Guardian*, 23 March, 1965.

Hughes, Frieda. 'A Matter of Life and Death'. *The Times Magazine*, 30 September 2000.

— 'Daddy, I hardly read you'. *The Times*, 4 October 2003.

Hughes, Ted. 'Poet, Pike and a Pitiful Grouse'. *Guardian*, 9 January 1999.

Excerpts from Hughes's interview with Thomas Pero, 'So Quickly It's Over', in *Wild Steelhead & Salmon* magazine, USA, 5, no. 2, winter 1999.

Marzuk, P M, Tardiff K, Hirsch C S. 'The epidemiology of murder-suicide', *Journal of the American Medical Association*, 1992; 267:3179–3183.

Mercy, James *et al*. 'Is suicide contagious?' *American Journal of Epidemiology*, 15 July 2001, vol. 154, no. 2:120–127.

Meyer, Beate: 'The Mixed Marriage: a Guarantee of Survival, or a Reflection of German Society during the Nazi Regime', in Bankier, David. *Probing the Depth of German Antisemitism, German Society and the Persecution of the Jews, 1933–1941*, New York, Berghahn Books, 2000.

Morpurgo, Horatio. 'The Table Talk of Ted Hughes'. *Arete*, issue 6, autumn 2001.

Nikunen, Minna, 'Media, Myth and Mother-child Murder-suicide'. *Nikk Magasin*, The Nordic Institute for Women's Studies and Gender Research, no.3, 2005. Finland, Department of Women's Studies, University of Tampere.

Porter, Peter. 'Ted Hughes and Sylvia Plath: a Bystander's Recollections'. *Australian Book Review*, August 2001.

— 'Some People: Slogans for the Sixties'. *Guardian*, 20 December 1988.

Resnick, Philip J. 'Child murder by parents: a psychiatric review of filicide'. *American Journal of Psychiatry*, 1969; 126:325–334.

Robson, Jeremy. 'Copy for Mr Feinstein'. *London Magazine*, June–July 1971.

Sewards, Lisa. 'In the Name of My Father'. Interview with Frieda Hughes, *Daily Mail*, 3 November 2001.

Sigmund, Elizabeth. 'Sylvia 1962, a Memoir'. *The New Review*, vol. 3, no. 26, May 1976.

Sonnenberg, Ben. 'Ted's Spell'. *Raritan* 21, no. 4, spring 2002.

Stanton, A and Simpson, J. 'Maternal Filicide'. *Criminal Behaviour and Mental Health*, 2000, 10, 136–147.

Thomas, Trevor. *'Sylvia Plath: Last Encounters'*. Unpublished memoir, 1989, courtesy of Clarissa Roche.

Tyrer, Nicola. 'Secret Life of Sylvia Plath'. *Daily Mail*, 5 February 2004.

Walker, Iain, 'Poetic Justice? The Trials of Ted Hughes', Australia, *The Advertiser*, 7 May 1987.

Zoritte-Megged, Eda. 'Intersections'. *Mosnayim*, no. 9, September/October 1984 (in Hebrew).

Index

AW denotes Assia Wevill, TH denotes Ted Hughes.

Afrasian 173
Alliston, Susan 115, 116, 137–8, 190
Alvarez, Al 85–6, 92, 97, 98, 101, 102, 111, 116, 142, 213, 214, 223
Ames, Lois 223
Amichai, Hannah 168
Amichai, Yehuda 186
  AW translates 166–7, 168–9, 172, 173, 178, 179, 189
  AW, friendship with vi, 19, 167–8, 172, 174, 224
  'God Has Pity on Kindergarten Children' 222
  Songs of Jerusalem and Myself 223–4
  TH, relationship with vi, 165–6, 222
  'The Death of Assia G' vi, 224
Anderson, Dr Jane 225
Andreas, Leila 21
Andreas, Wedad 20, 21
Anna Karenina (Tolstoy) 144, 159, 199
'Arraignment' (Morgan) 223
Archibald, Chris 63, 72
Archibald, Liliana 62, 63, 69, 72
Art of Loving, The (Fromm) 110, 132–3
Art of Sylvia Plath, The (Newman) 223
Arts Council 190

B'nei Pinhas (Sons of Pinhas) 31–2

Baker, Martin 180, 194, 195, 196, 208, 211
Balfour Elementary School 16, 19, 20
Bangs, Jennifer Margaret 202
Barraclough, Brian 212
Baskin, Leonard 226
Battleship Potemkin, The (Eisenstein) 179
BBC 82, 95, 96, 111, 112, 113, 146, 149, 173, 179
Becker, Alton 74, 75
Becker, Gerry 115
Becker, Jillian 115, 134
Belsize Park Gardens, London 145
Beuscher, Dr Ruth 110
Birney, Earle 48, 74, 149–50, 159
Bitter Fame (Stevenson) 225
Boland, Eavan 191
Bosher, John 45, 46, 47, 48, 50, 76
Boyd, Tom 172, 199
British Council 70, 75, 222
Brook, Peter 174
Browne, Sir Thomas 208
Bull, Esther 48
Bullmore, Jeremy 150
Burma 70, 72, 73–4, 75, 82, 87, 97, 122

Canada 41–52, 59, 61, 71, 106, 120, 129, 143, 176
Cape Goliard 166, 178
Chaikin (née Gutmann), Celia (sister) 41
  AW, letters from 56, 106, 113, 160, 163, 165, 180

AW, relationship with 47, 56, 106, 160, 163, 164, 165, 180
AW's funeral, attends 206
AW's will, appearance and involvement in 177, 178, 198, 220
birth 4
childhood 5, 11, 12, 16, 18, 42
children 57, 113
father, relationship with 2, 13, 32, 40, 217
father's death, explains 217
Hebrew name 10
jobs 45
John Steele, relationship with 25, 31
military duty 42
mother, relationship with 37
parents enforce move to Canada 43
Plath manuscripts, possession of 163–4, 165
Plath's manuscripts, returns to TH 220–1
TH's letters to 214, 215, 220, 222
Chalcot Square, London 81–2, 86, 97, 112, 122, 127
Chapters in a Mythology (Kroll) 224
Charles Hobson and Grey 188
Chekov, Anton 13
Chowns, Douglas 77
Chymical Wedding of Christian Rosenkreutz, The (Andreae) 93
Cleverdon, Douglas 96
Colman, Prentice and Varley (CPV) 77–8, 95
Compton, Elizabeth 97, 119, 129, 130–1, 133, 152, 162, 163, 224
Compton, James 131
Compton, Meg 119
Cooke, Barrie 104, 105, 156, 215, 216
Cooke, Sonia 156
Cooper, Catherine 66
Cooper, Julian 66
Court Green, London 128, 129, 130, 132, 135, 136, 137, 146, 149, 151, 152, 153, 156, 157, 158, 160, 161–2, 168, 170, 175, 184, 187, 189, 190, 195, 201, 211, 221, 223, 225
Csokits, Janos 157, 170, 194

Daniels, Diana 76, 80
Davies, Winifred 134, 157
de Havilland, Walter 46
Death and Life of Sylvia Plath, The (Hayman) 225
Delta 67
Doctors Under Hitler (Kater) 6
Doolan, Moira 91, 95
Doonreagan House, Ireland 151–2, 154–6

Ellerington, Dan 181
Erikson, Arthur 51
Eugene Onegin 146

Faber and Faber 137, 220, 223
Fainlight, Ruth (wife of Alan Sillitoe) 86, 117–18, 157, 167, 195
Farrar, Hilda 116, 118, 129, 130, 133, 170, 219
Feinstein, Elaine 195
Festival dei Due Mondi 150
Film Sense, The (Eisenstein) 179
First Love (Turgenev) 125, 140–1, 143
First World War 3, 5, 6
Fitzroy Road, London 112, 115, 120, 124, 132, 137, 143, 145
Fontaine, Joan 46
Four Screenplays (Bergman) 134–5
Fraser, G S 67, 85

Gabirol, Ibn 179
Galateo (della Casa) 174
Gallagher, Sean 77
Garland, Patrick 165
Gems, Keith 23, 24, 25, 26, 27–8, 29, 33, 34, 37, 38, 39, 40, 41, 44, 52, 56,

64, 208

Gems, Pam 41, 52, 53, 54, 56–7, 58

General History of Quadrupeds, A (Bewick) 157

Germany 4–9, 14–15, 41, 55–6, 92, 107, 168, 185–7

Ghose, Zulfikhar 66

Gielgud, John 174

Graham, Martin 71, 72, 174, 177, 188, 195, 213

Grand Street 136

Great Arab Revolt 15–16

Greaves, Derek 65

Group, The 65–8, 69, 75, 81, 97

Gutmann, Celia *see* Chaikin, Celia (sister)

Gutmann, Elizabetha (Lisa) (mother)
  AW, gives birth to 3–4
  AW, relationship with 4–5, 13–14, 16, 19–20, 22, 24, 27, 29–30, 31, 32, 33–4, 37, 44, 47, 76
  Canada, life in 45, 47, 59, 71, 106
  cancer, diagnosed with 71
  character 4–5, 13–14, 22, 24, 25
  death 147
  dowry 9, 41
  finances 40, 41
  German family, breaks with 15, 55
  Germany, decides to leave 7
  Hebrew name 10
  housekeeper in England 42
  husband's family, relationship with 4
  John Steele's relationship with AW, encourages 24, 27, 29–30, 31, 33–4, 37, 44
  meets husband 1
  Palestine, life in 11, 12, 13–14, 18

Gutmann, Ephraim (grand-father) 1, 2, 3, 15

Gutmann, Grisha (uncle) 139

Gutmann, Dr Lonya (Leo) (father)
  appearance 25

AW's affair with Ted Hughes, reaction to 106

AW, relationship with 3, 4, 14, 16, 17, 19–20, 21, 22, 76, 106, 194

AW's suicide note, appearance in 204–5

AW's will, appearance in 209

Canada, moves to 44–5

character 2–3, 13, 16, 21, 22

England, visits 147, 158

death 217

death of daughter and granddaughter, reaction to 206

Dick Lipsey, relationship with 52

finances 40

flees Germany for Italy 7, 8–9

grand-daughter, relationship with 147, 163

Hebrew name 10

John Steele, relationship with 27, 29

Mozambique, leaves Palestine for 41, 42, 43

marries 3–4

Nazi Germany, life in 6, 7, 55

Palestine, decides to leave 34–5

Palestine, leaves Italy for 8–9

Palestine, life in 12, 18

reading 13, 52

youth 1–3

Gutmann, Nachman (great-grandfather) 1

Gutmann, Vanya (uncle) 2, 55

Haganah 32

Hamburger, Michael 149

Hamermesh, Mira 22, 23, 36–7, 167, 177, 195

Harper & Row 179

Harris, E Clare 212

Harrison Hot-Springs Resort 46

Hartz, Pat 66

Hazell, Thomas 154

Head, Thomas 68–9

Heaney, Marie 221

Heaney, Seamus 221
Heather Jenner Agency 191–2
Hedden, Brenda 152, 160, 175, 184,
    189–90, 208, 219–20, 221
Hedden, Harriet 219
Hedden, Judith 219
Hedden, Trevor 152, 153, 160, 189
Hefetz, Yasha 3
Helle, Professor Anita 212
Herbert, Zbigniew 165, 200
Hitler, Adolf 5, 6, 10, 18, 55, 74
Hobsbaum, Hannah 66, 102
Hobsbaum, Philip 8, 66, 67, 69, 85, 102
Hollis, Tasha 137
Holub, Miroslav 165
Horne, Lena 29
Hughes, Edith 94, 133, 158, 162, 168,
    169, 216
Hughes, Frieda 81, 82, 89, 115, 117–18,
    119, 123, 128, 129, 133, 145, 148,
    152, 155, 157, 162, 163, 169, 173,
    175, 177, 182, 184, 194, 195, 213,
    215, 219, 221
Hughes, Gerald 89, 110, 146, 147, 155,
    188, 195, 215
Hughes, Joan 147, 195
Hughes, Nicholas 85, 91, 115, 118–19,
    123–4, 129, 133, 145, 148, 152, 155,
    157, 169,   177, 182, 213, 215,
    219, 221
Hughes, Olwyn 113, 116, 118, 129, 130,
    133, 138, 142, 147–8, 151, 152, 166,
    170, 182, 201, 203, 211, 213, 216,
    225
Hughes, Rebecca 177
Hughes, Ted vi, 85, 227
  AW, RELATIONSHIP WITH:
  arguments with xvii, 125–6, 128,
    133–4, 175–8
  attempts to live with 15, 118, 119,
    121, 123–31, 135–7, 139, 151–2,
    154–63, 165, 168–9

attraction towards 83, 88
  begins affair with 90–3, 94, 95–105,
  106–14, 121
  child with 114, 119 *see also* Wevill,
  Shura
  deterioration in relationship xvii,
  159–64, 165, 168–70, 173–8,
  186–200
  exchanges books with 134–5, 136–7
  first kisses 90–1, 92
  first meets 81–3
inspires writing 3, 8, 47, 83, 87, 88,
  91–2, 113, 225–7
separates from 169–70
  sexual relationship with 98, 99, 102,
  123, 182–3
  similarities with 69
suicide, reaction to 203–4, 207–11,
  213, 214, 215–16, 219–27
taste, admires 157, 187
travels to Germany with 185–7
  travels to Ireland with 151–3, 154–6
  travels to Spain with 106, 107, 108,
  186
CHARACTER:
appearance 87–8, 124–5, 127, 156–7
  destructive moods 125–6, 127,
  173, 187, 215
dreams 127, 140, 154, 187
  occult, interest in 98, 148–9
self-criticism 149
  violence 98, 99, 102, 182–3
  working practices 124–6, 139
FAMILY:
children, relationship with vi, 115,
  117–18, 123, 134, 148, 155, 163,
  182, 184–5, 187, 199, 213, 214, 215,
  219–20
parents, relationship with 133, 156,
  158, 159, 161–2, 165, 169, 170, 174,
  191, 213, 215, 220
see also under individual name

FINANCES 107–8, 136, 140, 149, 152, 158, 163, 171, 182, 188

HOUSES 91, 94, 97, 101, 102, 103, 104, 107, 110, 112, 114, 128, 129, 130, 132, 135, 136, 137, 146, 149, 151, 152, 153, 156, 157, 158, 160, 161, 168, 170, 175, 184, 187, 189, 190, 195, 201, 211, 221, 223, 225

LOVE LIFE *see under individual name*

READING 89, 93, 134–5, 136–7, 139–40, 157, 158

SYLVIA PLATH, RELATIONSHIP WITH:

abandons in Ireland 104–5, 106, 156

breakdown of marriage 85–6, 89–94, 95–105, 106–15

love of 126–7

marriage to 50

sexual relationship with 98

suicide, reaction to 115–19, 122, 126, 127, 128, 130, 131, 135, 149, 151, 174, 175, 187, 190, 200, 214–15, 220, 226–7

WORKS, LETTERS AND JOURNALS:

'A Childish Prank' 222

'A Full House' 149

archive, Emory University, Atlanta 134, 138, 184, 226

Beauty and the Beast 149

Birthday Letters 87, 98, 114, 115–16, 217, 226, 227

'Buttercup' 149

Capriccio 95, 216, 217, 226

'Capriccios' 98

'Chlorophyl' 95–6, 213

Creatures of the Air 95

Crow 156, 161, 162, 191, 220

'Descent' 47, 213

Difficulties of a Bridegroom 92–3, 113

'Do Not Pick Up the Telephone' 96

'Dreamers' 3, 8, 88, 91–2

'18 Rugby Street' 98

'Fanaticism' 181

film scripts 107, 140

'Flame' 201

'Full Moon and Little Frieda' 220

journals 184

letters 118–19, 135–6, 139, 145–6, 152, 171

'Lines for Shura' 155

'Lines to a Newborn Baby' 155

'Lovesong' 189

Lupercal 89, 101

Meet My Folks 91

'Mountain' 102

'Notes on Letters Home, Revised' 184

New Selected Poems 226

Oedipus 173–4

'Pear' 149

'Primroses' 149

'Sunlight' 89, 108

'Superstitions' 98

The Hawk in the Rain 91, 168

'The Inscription' 114

'The Thought Fox' 220

The Thought Fox 226

Tiger's Bones 149

'Violet' 149

Wodwo 135

Hughes, William 158

International Festival of Spoken Poetry 165, 167

International Poets Festival, Jerusalem 1997 226

Ireland 103–5, 151–2, 153, 154–6, 215–16

Israel 166–7, 222

Italy 7–8, 9

Ivan the Terrible 134

IZL 34

J Walter Thompson 141, 150, 151, 191

Jenkin, Guy 192–3, 197

Jewish Agency 19, 32

Jones, Margaret 201

Kavanagh, Pat 179
Kinsella, Thomas 104–5
Klapholz, Kurt 63, 71
Kroll, Professor Judith 82, 224

Lamb, The 136, 137
Landels, Angela 79, 80, 84, 85, 86, 102
Larschan, Richard 182–3, 212
Levenson, Christopher 67
Life of William Blake (Gilchrist) 158
Lilly Library 183
Lipsey, Professor Richard (Dick) 12, 21, 76
    AW attempts to stab 79
    AW, divorce from 70–2, 75, 79, 80,
        110, 111, 174
    AW, first meets 46, 49–50
    AW, marriage to 49–59, 60–5, 69, 70,
        71, 107, 158
    AW seeks financial assistance from 188
    economist 126, 188
    second marriage, AW's jealousy over
        79–81
Lipsey, Thirell 51, 52, 53, 57, 59, 70
London Magazine Poems (Williams) 135
London Magazine, The 146
Lowell, Robert 89
Lucie-Smith, Edward 48, 65, 66, 67, 75,
    77, 78, 80, 88, 98, 196, 209
Ludwig, Else xvii, 185, 201, 202
Lumb Bank 132, 216–17, 219

MacBeth, George 96, 179
Macedo, Helder 113
Macedo, Suzette 95, 113, 115
Macmillan 142
Man Without Qualities, The (Musil) 125
Manaion, Teresa 155, 156
Mann, Thomas 132
Marlborough Place, London 170
Martelli, Marisa 77

Maschler, Fay 180
Matcham, Julia 80, 115
Medicine and the German Jews (Efron) 5–6
Mellor, Philip 63
Mendelson, Andrea 148, 199
Mendelson, Mark 199
Mendelson, Patricia 74, 102, 127, 148,
    158, 169, 177, 189, 193, 199, 206,
    208, 211, 213–14, 217
Menelson, Michael 158, 177, 189
Merwin, Bill 92, 110, 114
Merwin, Dido 91, 93, 114
Michel, Don 54
Middlebrook, Professor Diane 86, 89,
    156
Modern Poetry in Translation 165
Modern Poets – an American British Anthology,
    The (Brinnin & Read) 126–7
Moore, Clem 137
Morpurgo, Michael 166
Morpurgo, Horatio 166
Mosnayim 224–5
Mozambique 40, 41, 42
Murphy, Richard 103–4, 121, 122, 151,
    156, 170, 208, 223
Muses' Darling: The Life of Christopher
    Marlowe, The (Norman) 158
Myers, Lucas 2–3, 7–8, 86, 115, 136, 139,
    143, 144, 147, 149, 150, 161, 163,
    215, 217,   221

Nation 137
Nazi Party 5–6, 7, 8, 11, 14, 18, 19, 23,
    30, 48, 55, 168, 186, 217
Negev, Eilat 166, 226
New Review 224
North Tawton, Devon xvii, 82, 101, 104,
    106, 134, 139, 162, 171, 178, 184,
    190, 204, 219
Notley's 63, 65, 75, 76, 77

Observer 102, 223

Ogilvy, Benson & Mather 76–7, 99, 169, 172, 179–80, 181, 185, 194, 197, 211

Ogilvy, David 76

Okeover Manor, London 185, 188, 194, 206

Orchard, Carol 184, 189–90, 191, 195, 219, 220, 226

Orchard, Jack 184

Orr, Peter 111, 142

Ottoline – the Early Memoirs of Lady Ottoline Morrell 136–7

Palestine 8–9, 10–35, 37, 167

Parizeau, Jacques 56

Peacock Theatre, Dublin 191

PEN 111

Penguin Modern Poets 4 100, 142

Pintchuk, Menja Lipowa (great-grandmother) 1, 3

Plath, Aurelia
AW, letters from 182–3
daughters suicide, reaction to 118
Frieda and Nicholas Hughes, relationship with 129–30, 157, 170, 182, 184
Letters Home, publishes 224
TH, relationship with 118–19, 127, 129, 130, 134, 152, 157, 182, 214–15, 214–15, 219, 221
TH's affair with AW, learns of 96, 97
TH's family, relationship with 94, 130, 170, 219, 221
TH's letters to 118–19, 127, 152, 182, 214
TH's marriage to Carol Orchard, learns of 221

Plath, Margaret 116

Plath, Otto 98

Plath, Sylvia 15, 50, 85, 94, 106, 108
AW, RELATIONSHIP WITH:
AW's admiration for 116–17
jealousy of 88, 89, 90, 92, 96, 110

poetry inspired by 96
post-death influence upon 120, 123, 126, 127, 128, 130, 132–3, 135–6, 142, 145, 155, 160–1, 168, 182–3
receives gift from 93–4, 97
rivalry with 88, 89, 90, 92, 96, 97, 101, 106–7
similarities with vi, 91–2, 97, 182–3
thoughts on 8, 89, 96, 117
time spent together 89, 90
CHARACTER 67, 90–2, 103
criticism, reaction to 67
intensity 103
jealousy 90–2
DEATH
grave 129, 130
fame and 161, 223, 224, 225, 226
suicide 115–18, 184, 187, 190, 194, 200, 212
TED HUGHES, RELATIONSHIP WITH 85–7, 88, 89, 90, 91–2, 93–4, 96–7, 99, 101, 102–5, 106–7, 107, 108–10, 111–14, 120
WORKS, LETTERS AND JOURNALS:
'Amnesiac' 112
Ariel 112, 116–17, 149, 161, 223
Bell Jar 225
Colossus, The 126, 143
Doubletake 113
'Edge' 212
'Elm' 86
'Event' 92
'Finisterre' 102
journal 117
Letters Home 224
'Metaphors' 143
manuscripts, AW takes 163–4, 165
manuscripts returned to TH 220–1
second novel 117
'Stings' 120
'The Fearful' 96
'The Rabbit Catcher' 92–3

'Words Heard, by Accident, Over the Phone' 96
Plath, Warren 116, 183
Poet Speaks, The 142
Poetry from Cambridge 67
Poets Reading Their Work 222
Popa, Vasco 165
Porter, Jannice 120, 177
Porter, Peter 63, 66, 67, 70, 77, 112, 119–20, 177, 190, 209, 222
Prism 150
Prouty, Olive Higgins 102–3
Pushkin, Aleksandr 13, 62, 65, 146

Redgrove, Barbara 85
Redgrove, Peter 65, 66, 78, 81, 85, 222
Reed, Jo 53, 54
Reed, Ken 53–4
Regent Street Polytechnic School of Art 34, 37
Resnick, Dr Philip 212
Roberts, Owen 202
Roethke, Theodore 132
Roose, Chris 180
Ross, David 116, 136
Rough Magic (Alexander) 225

Sagar, Dr Keith 119
Savage God, The (Alvarez) 223
Scigaj, Leonard 225
Second World War 18–19, 23–4, 32
Selected Poems of Vasco Popa 211
Selected Tales of Ivan Turgenev 141
Semple, Ann 182
Shelton, Shelley 179–80
Silent Woman, The (Malcolm) 225
Sillitoe, Alan 86, 87, 89–90, 117–18, 157, 167, 195
Sillitoe, Ruth (*see* Fainlight, Ruth)
Sonnenberg, Ben 136, 148
South London Press 207
Spencer, Sarah 42–3

St Nicholas Church, Great Hormead 68–9
Steele, John 23, 24, 46
    AW, divorce from 43–4, 110, 111
    AW, engagement to 37–9
    AW, first meets in Palestine 25–6, 27, 28, 29–30, 31, 32–4, 36
    AW, marriage to 39–42, 43–4, 45, 46
    AW, reunited with in England 36
Steele, Pamela 45
Stein, Sylvester 112
Suez Canal 61–2
Sweeney, John L 104
Sylvia Plath – Method and Madness (Butscher) 224
Sylvia Plath: A Biography (Wagner-Martin) 225

Tabeetha High, Jaffa 19–22, 28
Tarn, Nathaniel 97–8, 102, 103, 111, 117, 118, 122, 173, 209
Taylor, Celia 99, 119
Taylor, Royston 99, 169, 185, 196
Tel Aviv Hospitality Committee 24
Tennant, Emma 221
Thomas, Dr Trevor 124, 133, 145
Tolstoy (Troyat) 178
Tolstoy, Leo 3, 31, 178
Torney, Pat 214
Trevor, William 60, 65, 77, 78, 79, 80, 85, 96, 191
Tyrer, Nicola 91

University of British Columbia 45
University of Mandalay 70, 73

Vala, or the Four Zoas (Blake) 158

Wagner, Erica 91–2
Weinberg-Shalitt, Hannah 27, 28
Weissbort, Daniel 138, 165–6, 167, 173
Weldon, Fay 76, 78, 85, 177, 192, 212, 213, 218

Index

Wevill, Assia
  ARTISTIC LIFE: 58, 157
    art 16, 22, 32–3, 34, 59, 65, 162
    art school 34, 37
    assists in partners' work 141–2, 149–50
    diary 54, 121, 122–3, 125, 130, 131, 133, 187, 190, 194, 200
    Eastern art, expertise in 73
    letters 33–4, 41, 42, 58, 75, 138, 169, 172, 173, 175–6, 182–3
    music lessons 192–3
    music, love of 84, 133, 178, 185, 192–3, 201
    netsuke, interest in 73, 187–8, 196
    poetry 16, 22, 48, 68–9
    reading 4–5, 28, 31, 61, 62, 65, 120, 125, 134, 144, 146, 157, 158, 159, 174, 178, 180, 200, 211
    writing 121, 133
  CAREER 32, 42–3, 46–7, 51, 54
    copywriter 22, 63, 76–9, 84, 141, 150–1, 163, 172, 181–2, 188, 191, 199
    film scripts 107, 140–1
    netsuke 73, 187–8, 196
    Reuters translator 61–2, 63
    television play, writes 179–80
    translates Amichai 166–7, 168–9, 172, 173, 178, 179, 189, 222
    translates Zoritte-Megged 208
  CHARACTER: vi–vii, 79
    age, attitude towards 84–5, 180–1
    alcohol, abstains from xviii, 28, 84
    anglophile 20–1, 22, 25–6, 28, 29, 37, 56
    artistic 57, 58, 65, 68
    beauty vii, 14, 16, 21, 22–3, 36–7, 45–6, 52, 53, 54, 57–8, 61, 66, 77, 78, 83, 84–5, 87–8, 113, 117, 130, 162, 180–1, 188, 192
    blunt 62, 96, 102, 131
    name changes 10, 45, 49, 52, 53–4

children, attitude towards 59, 123–4, 148, 155
Christmas, attitude towards 113
cruelty 64, 96, 131
dissatisfaction with life 194–200
diva 17, 21–2, 45, 46, 51–2, 79
dreams 88–9
exile viii, 8, 10, 12, 14, 16, 18, 19–20, 21, 31, 33–4, 35
filicide, reasons for 212–13, 214
flirtatious 38, 42, 47, 57–8, 94–5
fragility 54
free spirit 78–9
Germany, relationship with 4–9, 14–15, 19, 22, 55–6, 92, 107, 168, 185–7
hysteria 14, 197
Israel, attitude towards 33, 173
jealousy 64, 79, 80–1, 137–8, 160, 188
Jewishness vi, 1–4, 10, 12, 16, 22, 30, 31, 33, 35, 55, 56, 107, 185, 186
languages, talent for 9, 10, 12, 20–1, 22, 29, 46, 61–2, 63, 66, 73, 107, 167, 175
laziness 45, 46, 51–2, 54
Lilith character vi, 48, 86, 89, 113, 150
music, love of 84, 133, 178, 185, 201
reaction to sixties popular culture 84
rebelliousness 21–2, 28, 50
self-image viii, 125, 126, 174, 198, 204
self-doubt 125, 126, 174, 198–9, 200, 204
selfishness 17, 37, 45, 51, 52
sense of alienation vii, 8, 10, 12, 14, 16
shyness 54
smoking 53
style 22–3, 36–7, 52, 53, 73–4, 78
temper 14, 64, 79, 188
vanity 80–1, 123, 198
violence 14, 79
war, effect upon 8, 14, 18, 19, 24
wildness 47

EARLY LIFE:
  birth 3–4
  Canada, lives in 41–52, 59
  childhood 1–9
  England, moves to 34–5, 36–8
  Italy, time in 7–8, 9
  London, returns to 52–3
  Palestine 10–35
  school 7, 9, 16, 19–22, 28
EDUCATION:
  art school 34, 37
  reading 4–5, 28, 31, 61, 62, 65, 120,
    125,134, 144, 146, 157, 158, 159,
    174, 178, 180, 200, 211
  school 7, 9, 16, 19–22, 28
  university 45
FAMILY:
  birth of first child 146–7
  daughter, treatment of 148, 150,
    162–3,194–5
  parents, relationship with 12, 13–14,
    16–17, 21, 22, 24, 25, 28, 29–31,
    33, 34, 37, 41, 43, 44, 47, 71, 194
FINANCES:
  copywriter salary 76, 108, 113
  expenditures ledger 95
  first marriage 41, 42, 46
  parents 12, 20, 38, 45
  second marriage 52–4, 57, 58–9, 71
  shoplifting 46
  TH and 152, 182
  wills viii, 163, 164, 165, 177–8,
    197–8, 209, 220
  worries over 188, 192
HEALTH: 163
  cystitis 123, 173
  death vi, xvii–xviii, 200–5, 205, 206,
    208, 211, 212, 222, 223, 224, 225
  effect of Plath upon 142–3 see also Sylvia
    Plath, relationship with
  funeral 207, 209–12, 216–17, 220,
    225

hospitalised 142
suicide attempts 41, 57, 123
suicide letter 203–5
suicide xvii–xviii, 200–5, 212, 225
suicide, talks of 163, 181, 195–7, 200
LOVE LIFE:
  abortions 47–8, 71, 119–20, 121
  binds herself to men for identity vii, 47,
    48, 122, 133, 173, 194
  casual sex, attitude towards 58, 84
    David Wevill 61–72, 73–7, 79, 82,
    84, 85, 87, 88–9, 90–1, 92, 93, 94,
    96, 97–102, 107, 108, 120–2, 127–8,
    135–6, 137, 142–4, 148–9, 153,
    158–9
  divorce, first 43–4
  divorce, second 71–2
  Earle Birney 74
  fear of loneliness 111, 133, 195
  first forays into social scene 28–9
  John Bosher 45, 46, 47, 48, 50
  John Steele 25–31, 32, 33–4, 36,
    37–44, 46–7, 110, 111
  marriage, first 39–40
  marriage, second 50
  marriage, third 75
  marriage bureau, enrols at 191–2
  miscarriage 75–6
  Richard Lipsey 49–65, 69, 70–2, 75,
    79–81, 107, 110, 111, 126, 158, 174,
    188
  writing inspired by 61, 70, 100, 101,
    142
LOVE LIFE WITH TED HUGHES:
  accuses of rape 99, 100
  attraction towards 98, 102, 124–5,
    156–7, 160
  begins affair with 84–94, 95–105
  buys books for 95, 134–6, 158, 168,
    178
  deterioration in relationship 159–64,
    165, 168, 173–8, 186–91

effect of relationship upon TH's
marriage 86–94, 110–11
fear of 15, 125
film script ideas, exchanges with 107
financial interaction 158, 182
first meets 82–3
house hunting with/search for
permanent home vii, xvii, 128–9, 132
see also Belsize Park Gardens, Chalcot
Square, Court Green, Doonreagan
House, Fitzroy Road, Marlborough
Place, Lumb Bank and Okeover Manor
inspires TH's writing 3, 8, 47, 83, 87,
88, 91–2, 113, 225–7
Ireland, move to 151–3, 154–6
letters 135–6, 138–9, 146, 173
living with vi, 15, 19, 120, 123–31,
132, 156–8
joint projects 107, 150
loyalty towards 193–4
love of 106, 124–5, 135, 157, 158,
160, 168, 170, 171, 173, 175, 176,
177, 182, 183, 186, 187, 190, 193,
194, 200
Plath's effect upon 120, 123, 126, 127,
200
pregnancies 101, 114, 116–18, 119,
144, 145
reservations about affair 129
sacrifices career for 151
seduces, 86–7, 88–9
separates from 169–70
sexual relationship 98, 99, 102, 123,
175–6, 182–3
squabbles with xvii, 125–6, 128,
133–4, 175–8, 186, 187, 196, 200,
201
TH's other women, reactions to
137–9, 160, 190
TH's parents, relationship with 129,
132, 133, 157–8, 161–2, 165, 169,
174, 200

travels to Germany with 185–7
travels to Spain with 106, 107, 108,
186
written out of TH's life vi–vii, 206–7,
223–5
see also Hughes, Ted
SYLVIA PLATH, RELATIONSHIP
WITH:
admiration for 120
Plath's post-death influence upon 120,
123, 126, 127, 128, 130, 132–3,
135–6, 142, 145, 155, 160–1, 168,
182–3
similarities between vi, 91–2, 97,
182–3
steals manuscripts 163–4, 165
reaction to suicide of 116–18, 119, 126,
127, 128, 129–30, 131, 145, 194
relationship with vi, 8, 86, 89, 90, 91,
93–4, 101
rivalry with 101, 126, 142, 155, 161
Wevill, David 9, 84
appearance 85, 127
'Apples and Apples' 61
Arts Council TriAnnual Book Prize 150
AW, affair with 62, 63, 64–5, 66, 67–9,
70–1, 72, 73–5, 77
AW's affair with Ted Hughes, reaction to
90–1, 96, 98–100, 101–2, 103,
107–8, 111, 120–2, 142–3, 145–6,
148–9, 159
AW criticises poetry 158–9
AW, divorce from 188–9, 198, 201
AW, first meets 60–1
AW's involvement in creative output 61,
70, 126, 141–2, 158–9
AW's love of 122, 127–8
AW, marriage to 75–7, 85, 88–9, 135
AW, poems inspired by 61, 70
AW, separation from 107, 108, 122,
127–8, 135–6, 137, 142–4, 153,
158–9

AW, reaction to suicide of 198–9
Birth of a Shark 100, 141–2
'Body of a Rook' 99–100
career 69–70, 73, 74–5, 76, 77
Christ of the Ice-Floes, A 158
'Clean Break' 102
'Germinal' 141–2
Gregory Award 108, 122, 123
'In Love' 100
'Our Lady of Kovno' 111, 158–9
Shura Wevill, treatment of 148, 189, 194
Spain 122, 123, 127
suicide attempt 98–9, 101
Sylvia Plath, relationship with 67–8, 69, 82, 90
Ted Hughes, relationship with 67, 69, 82, 89
The Group, involvement in 66, 67
Wevill, Shura (daughter) 167, 170
ashes scattered 219, 227
AW and TH relationship, effect upon 151, 161, 176
AW, relationship with 148, 150, 162–3, 164, 192, 194–5, 200, 205, 213–14

character 162–3, 195, 197, 199
David Wevill, relationship with 189
death xvii, xviii, 205, 206, 208, 211, 222, 223, 224
Frieda and Nicholas Hughes, relationship with 155, 184
funeral 209
Ireland, visits with AW and TH 152
TH's family reaction to 147–8, 169
TH, relationship with 148, 155, 161, 163, 169, 187, 194, 199, 213, 214, 215–16, 225
West Germany, visits with AW and TH 19, 185
Where Did It All Go Right (Alvarez) 101
Who's Afraid of Virginia Woolf (Albee) 144, 150
Wilkins, Chris 181, 197, 198, 203, 209
Wordsworth, Dorothy 201
World of Books, The 95

Yeats, William Butler 112

Zermatt, Switzerland 54–5, 71
Zoritte-Megged, Eda 207–8, 224–5